An Introduction to Poetry

FIFTH EDITION

X. J. KENNEDY

LITTLE, BROWN AND COMPANY
Boston • Toronto

Library of Congress Catalog Card No. 81-82656

ISBN 0-316-489069

9 8 7 6 5 4 3 2

MU

Published simultaneously in Canada
by Little, Brown & Company (Canada) Limited

Printed in the United States of America

Acknowledgments

The paintings by Pieter Breughel on page 182 (*The Kermess,* collection of Kunsthistoriches Museum, Vienna) and page 289 (*Landscape with Fall of Icarus,* collection of Museum der Schone Kunste, Brussels) are reproduced courtesy of Marburg Art Reference Bureau.

James Agee. "Sunday: Outskirts of Knoxville, Tennessee" from *The Collected Poems of James Agee,* edited and with an Introduction by Robert Fitzgerald. Copyright © 1962, 1968 by the James Agee Trust. Reprinted by permission of Houghton Mifflin Company.

A. R. Ammons. "Spring Coming" is reprinted from *Collected Poems 1951-1971* by A. R. Ammons, with the permission of W. W. Norton & Company, Inc. Copyright © 1972 by A. R. Ammons.

John Ashbery. "City Afternoon" from *Self-Portrait in a Convex Mirror* by John Ashbery. Copyright © 1974 by John Ashbery. "The Cathedral Is" from *As We Know* by John Ashbery. Copyright © 1979 by John Ashbery. Reprinted by permission of Viking Penguin Inc.

Margaret Atwood. "You fit into me" from *Selected Poems* by Margaret Atwood. Copyright © 1976 by Margaret Atwood. Reprinted by permission of Simon & Schuster, a Division of Gulf & Western Corporation and the author.

W. H. Auden. "As I Walked Out One Evening," "Musée des Beaux Arts," and "The Unknown Citizen" reprinted from *W. H. Auden: Collected Poems* by W. H. Auden, edited by Edward Mendelson. Copyright 1940, renewed 1968 by W. H. Auden. Reprinted by permission of Random House, Inc., and Faber and Faber Ltd. "James Watt" from *Academic Graffiti* by W. H. Auden. Copyright © 1960 by W. H. Auden. Reprinted by permission of Random House, Inc. and Faber and Faber Ltd.

David B. Axelrod. "Once in a While a Protest Poem" from *A Dream of Feet* by David B. Axelrod. Reprinted by permission of the poet and Cross Cultural Communications.

Amiri Baraka. "Preface to a Twenty Volume Suicide Note" from *Selected Poetry of Amiri Baraka/LeRoi Jones* (1979). Copyright © 1961 by LeRoi Jones. Reprinted by permission of William Morrow & Company.

Ray Young Bear. "Grandmother" from *Winter of the Salamander* by Ray Young Bear. Copyright © 1980 by Ray Young Bear. Reprinted by permission of Harper & Row, Publishers, Inc.

Max Beerbohm. "On the imprint of the first English edition of *The Works of Max Beerbohm,* from *Max in Verse.* Reprinted by permission of Sir Geoffrey Keynes.

Hilaire Belloc. "The Hippopotamus" from *Cautionary Verses* by Hilaire Belloc. Published in 1940 by Gerald Duckworth & Co. Ltd., 1941 by Alfred A. Knopf, Inc. Reprinted by permission of the publishers.

Edmund Clerihew Bentley. "Sir Christopher Wren" from *Clerihews Complete* by E. C. Bentley. Reprinted by permission of Curtis Brown Limited.

Wendell Berry. "The Peace of Wild Things" from *Openings.* Copyright © 1968 by Wendell Berry. Reprinted from his volume *Openings* by permission of Harcourt Brace Jovanovich, Inc.

John Berryman. "Life, friends, is boring . . ." from *77 Dream Songs* by John Berryman. Copyright © 1959, 1962, 1963, 1964 by John Berryman. Reprinted by permission of Farrar, Straus & Giroux.

John Betjeman. "In Westminster Abbey" from *Collected Poems* by John Betjeman. (Houghton Mifflin Company, 1959). Reprinted by permission of John Murray Publishers Ltd.

Elizabeth Bishop. "The Fish," "The Filling Station," and lines from "Little Exercise" from *The Complete Poems* by Elizabeth Bishop. Copyright 1940, 1946, 1949, © 1955 by Elizabeth Bishop, renewed © 1973, 1976 by Elizabeth Bishop. "The Filling Station" appeared originally in *The New Yorker.* Reprinted by permission of Farrar, Straus & Giroux, Inc.

Robert Bly. "Driving to Town Late to Mail a Letter" from *Silence in the Snowy Field* by Robert Bly (Wesleyan University Press, 1962) and "Inward Conversation." Reprinted by permission of the poet.

David Bottoms. "Smoking in an Open Grave" from *Shooting Rats at the Bibb County Dump* by David Bottoms. Copyright © 1980 by David Bottoms. Reprinted by permission of William Morrow & Company.

Richard Brautigan. "Haiku Ambulance" excerpted from the book *The Pill Versus the Springhill Mine Disaster* by Richard Brautigan. Copyright © 1968 by Richard Brautigan. Reprinted by permission of Delacorte Press/Seymour Lawrence.

Van K. Brock. Quotation of three lines excerpted from "Driving at Dawn" from *The Hard Essential Landscape* by Van K. Brock, University Presses of Florida, 1979. Copyright © 1979 by Van K. Brock. Reprinted by permission.

Gwendolyn Brooks. "We Real Cool. The Poolplayers. Seven at the Golden Shovel," copyright © 1959 by Gwendolyn Brooks, and "The Rites for Cousin Vit," copyright 1949 by Gwendolyn Brooks Blakely, from *The World of Gwendolyn Brooks* by Gwendolyn Brooks. Reprinted by permission of Harper & Row, Publishers, Inc.

Sterling A. Brown. "Effie" from *The Collected Poems of Sterling A. Brown* selected by Michael S. Harper. Copyright © 1980 by Sterling A. Brown. Reprinted by permission of Harper & Row, Publishers, Inc.

Taniguchi Buson. "The Sudden Chilliness" from *An Introduction to Haiku* by Harold G. Henderson. Copyright © 1958 by Harold G. Henderson. Reprinted by permission of Doubleday & Company, Inc.

(continued on page 463)

PREFACE

What is poetry? Pressed for an answer, Robert Frost made a classic reply: "Poetry is the kind of thing poets write." In all likelihood, Frost was not trying merely to evade the question but to chide his questioner into thinking for himself. A trouble with definitions is that they may stop thought. If Frost had said, "Poetry is a rhythmical composition of words expressing an attitude, designed to surprise and delight, and to arouse an emotional response," the questioner might have settled back in his chair, content to have learned the truth about poetry. He would have learned nothing, or not so much as he might learn by continuing to wonder.

The nature of poetry eludes simple definitions. (In this respect it is rather like jazz. Asked after one of his concerts, "What is jazz?" Louis Armstrong replied, "Man, if you gotta ask, you'll never know.") Definitions will be of little help at first, if we are to know poetry and respond to it. We have to go to it willing to see and hear. For this reason, you are asked in reading this book not to be in any hurry to decide what poetry is, but instead to study poems and to let them grow in your mind. At the end of the book, the problem of definition will be taken up again (for those who may wish to pursue it).

Confronted with *An Introduction to Poetry*, you may be wondering "Who needs it?" and you may well be right. You hardly can have avoided meeting poetry before; and perhaps you already have a friendship, or at least a fair acquaintance, with some of the great English-speaking poets of all time. What this book provides is an introduction to the *study* of poetry. It tries to help you look at a poem closely, to offer you a wider and more accurate vocabulary with which to express what poems say to you. It will suggest ways to judge for yourself the poems you read. It may set forth some poems that are new to you.

A frequent objection to a book such as this is that poetry ought not to be studied at all. In this view, a poem is either a series of gorgeous noises to be funneled through one ear and out the other without being allowed to trouble the mind or an experience so holy that to analyze it in a classroom is as cruel and mechanical as dissecting a hummingbird. To the first view, it might be countered that a good poem has something to say that perhaps is worth listening to. To the second view, it might be argued that poems are much less perishable than hummingbirds, and luckily, we can study them in flight. The risk of killing a poem by observation is not nearly so great as the risk of not really seeing it at all. It is doubtful that any excellent poem has ever vanished from human memory because people have read it too closely. More likely, poems that vanish are poems that no one reads closely, for no one cares.

Good poetry is something to care about. In fact, an ancient persuasion of mankind is that the hearing of a poem, as well as the making of a poem, can be a religious act. Poetry, in speech and song, was part of classic Greek drama, which for playwright, actor, and spectator alike was a holy-day ceremony. The Greeks' belief that a poet writes a poem only by supernatural assistance is clear from the invocations to the Muse that begin the *Iliad* and the *Odyssey* and from the opinion of Socrates (in Plato's *Ion*) that a poet has no powers of invention until divinely inspired. Among the ancient Celts, poets were regarded as magicians and priests, and whoever insulted one of them might expect to receive a curse in rime potent enough to afflict him with boils and to curdle the milk of his cows. Such identifications between the poet and the magician are less common these days, although we know that poetry is involved in the primitive white-magic of children, who bring themselves good luck in a game with the charm "Roll, roll, Tootsie-roll!/ Roll the marble in the hole!" and who warn against a hex while jumping a sidewalk: "Step on a crack, / Break your mother's back." But in this age when men pride themselves that a computer may solve the riddle of all creation as soon as it is programmed, magic seems to some people of small importance and so does poetry. It is dangerous, however, to dismiss what we do not logically understand. To read a poem at all, we have to be willing to offer it responses *besides* a logical understanding. Whether we attribute the effect of a poem to a divine spirit or to the reactions of our glands and cortexes, we have to take the reading of poetry seriously (not solemnly), if only because—as some of the poems in this book may demonstrate—few other efforts can repay us so generously, both in wisdom and in joy.

If, as I hope you will do, you sometimes browse in the book for fun, you may be annoyed to see so many questions following the poems. Should you feel this way, try reading with a slip of paper to cover up the questions. You will then—if the Muse should inspire you—have paper in hand to write a poem.

The author cannot help having a few convictions. He thinks some of the poems in this book completely wonderful, and others, vile. He has done his best to step back and give you room to make up your own mind. But here and there, in the wording of a question, a conviction may stick out. If you see any, be assured that there is no one right interpretation of a poem, laid down by authority. Trust your own interpretation if in making it you have looked clearly and carefully at all the evidence.

A Word about Careers

Students tend to agree that to read poets such as Shakespeare, Keats, Emily Dickinson, and Robert Frost is probably good for the spirit, and most even take some pleasure in the experience. But many, if they aren't planning to teach English and are impatient to begin some other career, often wonder whether the study of poetry, however enjoyable, is not a waste of time or, at least, an annoying obstacle.

This objection may seem reasonable, but it rests on a shaky assumption. It can be argued that, on the contrary, success in a career is *not* mostly a matter of learning certain information and skills that belong exclusively to a certain profession. In most careers, according to a business executive, people often fail not because they don't understand their jobs, but because they don't understand the people they work with, or their clients or customers; and so they can't imagine another person's point of view. To leap outside the walls of your self, to see through another person's eyes—this is an experience that literature abundantly offers. Although, if you are lucky, you may never meet (or have to do business with) anyone *exactly* like the insanely jealous speaker of the poem "Soliloquy of the Spanish Cloister," you will probably learn much about the kind of person he is from Robert Browning's portrait of him. Who knows? Among your fellow students or co-workers may be a J. Alfred Prufrock (the central character of T. S. Eliot's poem), or someone like Randall Jarrell's "Woman in the Washington Zoo." What is it like to be black, a white may wonder? Perhaps Langston Hughes, Gwendolyn Brooks, Amiri Baraka, Etheridge Knight, Dudley Randall, James C. Kilgore, Sterling A. Brown, and others have something to tell. What is it like to be a woman? A man who would learn can read, for a start, Emily Dickinson, Sylvia Plath, Anne Sexton, Denise Levertov, Adrienne Rich, Ruth Pitter, Anne Bradstreet, May Swenson, and Tess Gallagher.

Racing single-mindedly toward careers, some students move like horses wearing blinders. For many, the goals seem fixed and sure: competent nurses, accountants, and dental technicians seem always needed. Still, many who confine their attention to a single kind of learning eventually come to feel a sense of dissatisfaction. Recently, a highly trained and highly paid tool and die maker, asked by his instructor at a college why he had enrolled in an evening literature course, replied, "I just decided there has to be more to life than work, a few beers, and the bowling alley." Other students find that in our society some careers, like waves in the sea, may rise or fall with a speed quite unexpected. Think how many professions we now take for granted didn't even exist a few years ago—for instance, jobs in computer programming, energy conservation, and disco management. Others that had once seemed a person's security for life have been cut back and nearly ruined: cobblery, commercial fishing, railroading. In a society always in change, perhaps the most risky course is to lock oneself into a certain career, unwilling to consider any other. In point of fact, the U.S. Department of Labor has shown that the average person changes careers three times in a working life. When for some unforeseen reason such a change has to be made, basic skills may be one's most valuable credentials, together with some knowledge (in depth) of the human heart.

Literature, as they know who teach it, has basic skills to provide. Being an art of words, it can help you become more sensitive to language – your own and other people's. Poetry especially helps you to see the difference between a word that is exactly right and a word that is merely good enough – what Mark Twain calls "the difference between the lightning and the lightning-bug." Read a fine writer alertly, with enjoyment, and some of the writer's ways with words may grow on you. Most jobs today (and even the task of making out a long-form tax return) still call for some close reading and comprehensible writing. (By the way, if a career you have in mind has anything to do with advertising – whether writing it or using it or resisting it – be sure to read Chapter Four, on suggestions inherent in words.)

That is why most colleges, however thorough the specialized career training they provide, see a need for generalized training as well, and insist on basic courses in the humanities. No one can promise, of course, that your study of literature will result in cash profit; but at least the kind of wealth that literature provides is immune to fluctuations of the Dow Jones average. Besides, should you discover in yourself a fondness for great reading, then it is likely that in no season of your life will you become incurably bored or feel totally alone – even after you make good in your career, even when there is nothing on television.

A Note on Texts and Dates

In this edition, poems are dated. To the right of each poem title is the date of its first known publication in book form. A date in parenthesis is a date of composition – given when it is known that a poem was composed much earlier than it was first printed (as in the case of the poems of Emily Dickinson). No attempt has been made to date traditional English and Scottish popular ballads such as "Bonny Barbara Allan," because such an attempt would be merely wild guesswork. Spelling has been modernized (*rose-lipped* for *ros-lip'd*) and made American, unless the sound of a word would be altered. But I have left the *y* in Blake's strange "Tyger" and let Walt Whitman keep his *bloom'd* on the conviction that *bloomed* would no more resemble Whitman than a portrait of him in a starched collar. Untitled poems are identified by their first lines, except for those given titles by custom ("The Twa Corbies," "Western Wind").

Changes in This Edition

Besides many alterations in content, wording, and emphasis suggested by more than fifty instructors familiar with the last edition, this book now has two large new features. In accord with the wishes of several instructors who use it in their creative writing courses, and many more who assign the writing of at least one poem, the book now offers an appendix, "Writing a Poem." Into the territory of advising anyone how to write poetry, angels fear to tread; but I have rushed in anyway, and also supply a list of experiments – not finger exercises but possibilities for poems a student might care to write.

Now there are *two* anthologies at the back of the book: the expected anthology of poems (expanded to 135 poems), and a new anthology of criticism for the instructor who lacks time to deal comprehensively with literary criticism, but who nevertheless would like students to have before them the texts of some of the more famous critical statements about poetry. *Anthology* is perhaps too grand a name for these twenty snippets. Included, by the way, are a few not-so-famous critical comments that I hope will prove fresh and discussable.

Poetry never stands still, and textbooks have to keep up with it. More than a hundred poems are new to this edition – some of them by poets of newly risen reputation, some by old masters not included before, whom many instructors have missed. More detailed information on changes in the book's organization and content will be found in the preface to the *Instructor's Manual to Accompany An Introduction to Poetry, Fifth Edition.*

Acknowledgments

Besides all the debts this book has contracted in the past, it now owes much to many who made fresh contributions. Among those who made suggestions and corrections, whether by mail or in person, are Grace Amigone, Canisius College; De Anne D. Adams, Montgomery College; Jonathan Aldrich, Portland School of Art; Mark Allen, University of Illinois, Urbana; R. E. Allen, Illinois State University, Normal; David Baker, University of Utah; Marilyn G. Barrette, University of Florida, Gainesville; Lindy Bonczek, Dean Junior College; Van K. Brock, Florida State University; Maurice F. Brown, Oakland University; E. J. Burde, State University of New York, Plattsburgh; Lawrence M. Clopper, Indiana University; Steve Cook, University of California, Santa Barbara; Michael R. Dressman, University of South Carolina at Spartanburg; Lois B. Fisher, Southwestern Oklahoma State University; D. R.

Fosso, Wake Forest University; Roberts W. French, University of Massachusetts, Amherst; Jerome Garger, Lane Community College; Richard L. Guertin, Normandale Community College, Bloomington, Minnesota; Daniel Hughes, Wayne State University; Jay Jacoby, University of North Carolina at Charlotte; Edward Jayne, University of Western Michigan; Ellwood Johnson, Western Washington University; Thomas Kaminski, Loyola University of Chicago; Judith J. Kollmann, University of Michigan, Flint; David Louie, University of Iowa; Richard Maxwell, Foothill College; Clark Mayo, California State College, San Bernardino; S. D. McFarland, University of Maryland; Nayan McNeill, Foothill College; Ellen Meyer, Dowling College; Walter S. Minot, Gannon University; Richard Moore, New England Conservatory of Music; Christopher Morris, Norwich University; Jeanne Nichols, Los Angeles Harbor College; Ellen J. O'Brien, Guilford College; Louis Oldani, S.J., Rockhurst College; Louis G. Pecek, John Carroll University; Charles Pennel, Northern Illinois University; Alan Powers, Bristol Community College; Jo Radner, American University; Willie Reader, University of South Florida; Morton D. Rich, Montclair State College; Nancy G. Schrier, Foothill College; Thomas H. Seiler, Western Michigan University; John N. Serio, Clarkson College; Dabney Stuart, Washington and Lee University; Thomas Swiss, Drake University; Tom Trusky, Boise State University; David Ned Tobin, Oxford College of Emory University; Roger Weaver, Oregon State University; Jayne A. Widmayer, Boise State University; and Karl Zender, University of California, Davis. Paul T. Hopper not only read and corrected this edition in manuscript; he corrected errors left over from two previous editions, and made incisive suggestions. Sylvan Barnet has continued to make valuable criticisms and to show me the way I should go. On the publisher's staff, Charles H. Christensen, Donna McCormick, Elizabeth N. Philipps, Elizabeth M. Schaaf, and Gail Stewart were some of those who made the book a mutual cause, not just a mutual product. I remain grateful to students at Tufts, Wellesley, Michigan, North Carolina (Greensboro), California (Irvine), and Leeds for helping me to see through some of the poems. Most of all I thank Dorothy M. Kennedy, who contributed some questions, some copyediting, and sensibility.

TOPICAL CONTENTS

CONTENTS

ANTHOLOGY: POETRY

TO THE MUSE

Give me leave, Muse, in plain view to array
Your shift and bodice by the light of day.
I would have brought an epic. Be not vexed
Instead to grace a niggling schoolroom text;
Let down your sanction, help me to oblige
Him who would lead fresh devots to your liege,
And at your altar, grant that in a flash
They, he and I know incense from dead ash.

X.J.K.

1 Entrances

How do you read a poem? The literal-minded might say, "Just let your eye light on it"; but there is more to poetry than meets the eye. What Shakespeare called "the mind's eye" also plays a part. Many a reader who has no trouble understanding and enjoying prose finds poetry difficult. This is to be expected. At first glance, a poem usually will make some sense and give some pleasure, but it may not yield everything at once. Sometimes it only hints at meaning still to come if we will keep after it. Poetry is not to be galloped over like the daily news: a poem differs from most prose in that it is to be read slowly, carefully, and attentively. Not all poems are difficult, of course, and some can be understood and enjoyed on first seeing. But good poems yield more if read twice; and the best poems—after ten, twenty, or a hundred readings—still go on yielding.

Approaching a thing written in lines and surrounded with white space, we need not expect it to be a poem just because it is **verse.** (Any composition in lines of more or less regular rhythm, usually ending in rimes, is verse.) Here, for instance, is a specimen of verse that few will call poetry:

Thirty days hath September,
April, June, and November;
All the rest have thirty-one
Excepting February alone,
To which we twenty-eight assign
Till leap year makes it twenty-nine.

To a higher degree than that classic memory-tickler, poetry appeals to the mind and arouses feelings. Poetry may state facts, but, more important, it makes imaginative statements that we may value even if its facts are incorrect. Coleridge's error in placing a star within the horns of the crescent moon in "The Rime of the Ancient Mariner" does not stop the passage from being good poetry, though it is faulty astronomy. According to one poet, Gerard Manley Hopkins, poetry is "to be heard for its own sake and interest even over and above its interest of meaning."

There are other elements in a poem besides plain prose sense: sounds, images, rhythms, figures of speech. These may strike us and please us even before we ask, "But what does it all mean?"

This is a truth not readily grasped by anyone who regards a poem as a kind of puzzle written in secret code with a message slyly concealed. The effect of a poem (one's whole mental and emotional response to it) consists in much more than simply a message. By its musical qualities, by its suggestions, it can work on the reader's unconscious. T. S. Eliot put it well when he said in *The Use of Poetry and the Use of Criticism* that the prose sense of a poem is chiefly useful in keeping the reader's mind "diverted and quiet, while the poem does its work upon him." Eliot went on to liken the meaning of a poem to the bit of meat a burglar brings along to throw to the family dog. What is the work of a poem? To touch us, to stir us, to make us glad, and possibly even to tell us something.

How to set about reading a poem? Here are a few suggestions.

To begin with, read the poem once straight through, with no particular expectations; read open-mindedly. Let yourself experience whatever you find, without worrying just yet about the large general and important ideas the poem contains (if indeed it contains any). Don't dwell on a troublesome word or difficult passage—just push on. Some of the difficulties may seem smaller when you read the poem for a second time; at least, they will have become parts of a whole for you.

On second reading, read for the exact sense of all the words; if there are words you don't understand, look them up in a dictionary. Dwell on any difficult parts as long as you need to.

If you read the poem silently to yourself, sound its words in your mind. (This is a technique that will get you nowhere in a speed-reading course, but it may help the poem to do its work on you.) Better still, read the poem aloud, or hear someone else read it. You may discover meanings you didn't perceive in it before. Even if you are no actor, to decide how to speak a poem can be an excellent method of getting to understand it. Some poems, like bells, seem heavy till heard. Listen while reading the following lines from Alexander Pope's *Dunciad.* Attacking the minor poet James Ralph, who had sung the praises of a mistress named Cynthia, Pope makes the goddess of Dullness exclaim:

> "Silence, ye wolves! while Ralph to Cynthia howls,
> And makes night hideous—answer him, ye owls!"

When *ye owls* slide together and become *yowls,* poor Ralph's serenade is turned into the nightly outcry of a cat.

Try to **paraphrase** the poem as a whole, or perhaps just the more difficult lines. In paraphrasing, we put into our own words what we understand the poem to say, restating ideas that seem essential, coming out and stating what the poem may only suggest. This may sound like a heartless thing to do to a poem, but good poems can stand it. In fact, to compare a poem to its paraphrase is a good way to see the distance between poetry and prose. In making a paraphrase, we generally work through a poem or a passage line by line. The statement that results may take as many words as the original, if not more. A paraphrase, then, is ampler than a **summary,** a brief condensation of gist, main idea, or story. (Summary of a horror film in *TV Guide:* "Demented biologist, coveting power over New York, swells sewer rats to hippopotamus-size.") Here is a poem worth considering line by line.

A. E. Housman (1859–1936)

Loveliest of Trees, the Cherry Now 1896

Loveliest of trees, the cherry now
Is hung with bloom along the bough,
And stands about the woodland ride
Wearing white for Eastertide.

Now, of my threescore years and ten,
Twenty will not come again,
And take from seventy springs a score,
It only leaves me fifty more.

And since to look at things in bloom
Fifty springs are little room,
About the woodlands I will go
To see the cherry hung with snow.

Though simple, Housman's poem is far from simple-minded, and it contains at least one possible problem: what, in this instance, is a *ride*? If we guess, we won't be far wrong; but a dictionary helps: "a road or path through the woods, especially for horseback riding." A paraphrase of the poem might say something like this (in language easier to forget than the original): "Now it is Easter time, and the cherry tree in the woods by the path is in blossom. I'm twenty, my life is passing. I expect to live the average life-span of seventy. That means I'm going to see only fifty more springs, so I had better go out into the woods and start looking." And the paraphrase might add, to catch the deeper implication, "Life is brief and fleeting: I must enjoy beauty while I may."

These dull remarks, roughly faithful to what Housman is saying, are clearly as far from being poetry as a cherry pit is far from being a cherry. Still, they can help whoever makes the paraphrase to see the main argument of Housman's poem: its **theme** or central thought. Theme isn't the same thing as **subject,** the central topic. In "Loveliest of trees," the subject is cherry blossoms, or the need to look at them, but the theme is "Time flies: enjoy beauty now!" Not all poems clearly assert a proposition, but many do; some even declare their themes in their very first lines: "Gather ye rose-buds while ye may" — enjoy love before it's too late. The theme stated in that famous opening line (from Robert Herrick's "To the Virgins, to Make Much of Time," page 761) is so familiar that it has a name: **carpe diem** (Latin for "seize the day"), a favorite argument of poets from Horace to Housman.

A paraphrase, of course, never tells *all* that a poem contains; nor will every reader agree that a particular paraphrase is accurate. We all make our own interpretations; and sometimes the total meaning of a poem evades even the poet who wrote it. Asked to explain his difficult *Sordello,* Robert Browning replied that when he had written the poem only God and he knew what it meant; but "Now, only God knows." Still, to analyze a poem *as if* we could be certain of its meaning is, in general, more fruitful than to proceed as if no certainty could ever be had. The latter approach is likely to end in complete subjectivity: the attitude of the reader who says, "Housman's 'Loveliest of trees' is really about a walk in the snow; it is, because I think it is. How can you prove me wrong?"

All of us bring to our readings of poems certain personal associations, as Housman's "Loveliest of trees" might convey a particular pleasure to a reader who had climbed cherry trees when he was small. To some extent, these associations are inevitable, even to be welcomed. But we need to distinguish between irrelevant, tangential responses and those the poem calls for. The reader who can't stand "Loveliest of trees" because cherries remind him of blood, is reading a poem of his own, not Housman's.

Housman's poem is a **lyric:** a short poem expressing the thoughts and feelings of a single speaker. (As its Greek name suggests, a lyric originally was sung to the music of a lyre.) Often a lyric is written in the first person ("About the woodlands *I* will go"), but not always. It may be, for instance, a description of an object or an experience in which the poet isn't even mentioned. Housman's first stanza, printed by itself as a complete poem, would still be a lyric. Though a lyric may relate an incident, we tend to think of it as a reflective poem in which little physical action takes place — unlike a **narrative poem,** one whose main concern is to tell a story.

At the moment, it is a safe bet that, in English and other Western languages, lyrics are more plentiful than other kinds of poetry (novels having virtually replaced the long narrative poems esteemed from the time of Homer's *Odyssey* to the time of Tennyson's *Idylls of the King*). **Didactic poetry,** to mention one other kind, is poetry apparently written to teach or to state a message. In a lyric, the speaker may express sadness; in a didactic poem, he may explain that sadness is inherent in life. Poems that impart a body of knowledge, like Ovid's *Art of Love* and Lucretius's *On the Nature of Things,* are didactic. Such instructive poetry was favored especially by classical Latin poets and by English poets of the eighteenth century. In *The Fleece* (1757), John Dyer celebrated the British woolen industry and included practical advice on raising sheep:

In cold stiff soils the bleaters oft complain
Of gouty ails, by shepherds termed the halt:
Those let the neighboring fold or ready crook
Detain, and pour into their cloven feet
Corrosive drugs, deep-searching arsenic,
Dry alum, verdegris, or vitriol keen.

One might agree with Dr. Johnson's comment on Dyer's effort: "The subject, Sir, cannot be made poetical." But it may be argued that didactic poetry (to quote a recent view) "is not intrinsically any less poetic because of its subject-matter than lines about a rose fluttering in the breeze are intrinsically more poetic because of their subject-matter."[1] John Milton also described sick sheep in "Lycidas," a poem few readers have thought unpoetic:

The hungry sheep look up, and are not fed,
But, swoll'n with wind and the rank mist they draw,
Rot inwardly, and foul contagion spread . . .

What makes Milton's lines better poetry than Dyer's is, among other things, a difference in attitude. Sick sheep to Dyer mean the loss of a few shillings and pence; to Milton, whose sheep stand for English Christendom, they mean a moral catastrophe.

Now and again we meet a poem—perhaps startling and memorable—into which the method of paraphrase won't take us far. Some portion of any deep poem resists explanation, but certain poems resist it almost entirely. Many poems of religious mystics seem closer to dream than waking. So do poems that record hallucinations or drug experiences, such as Coleridge's "Kubla Khan" (page 298), as well as poems that embody some private system of beliefs, such as Blake's "The Sick Rose" (page 292), or the same poet's lines from *Jerusalem,*

For a Tear is an Intellectual thing,
And a Sigh is the Sword of an Angel King.

So do nonsense poems, translations of primitive folk songs, and surreal poems.[2] Such poetry may move us and give pleasure (although not, perhaps, the pleasure of mental understanding). We do it no harm by trying to paraphrase it, though we may fail. Whether logically clear or

[1] Sylvan Barnet, Morton Berman, and William Burto, *A Dictionary of Literary, Dramatic, and Cinematic Terms,* 2nd ed. (Boston: Little, Brown, 1971).

[2] The French poet André Breton, founder of **surrealism,** a movement in art and writing, declared that a higher reality exists, which to mortal eyes looks absurd. To mirror that reality, surrealist poets are fond of bizarre and dreamlike objects such as soluble fish and white-haired revolvers.

strangely opaque, good poems appeal to the intelligence and do not shrink from it.

So far, we have taken it for granted that poetry differs from prose; yet all our strategies for reading poetry – plowing straight on through and then going back, isolating difficulties, trying to paraphrase, reading aloud, using a dictionary – are no different from those we might employ in unraveling a complicated piece of prose. Poetry, after all, is similar to prose in most respects; at the very least, it is written in the same language. And like prose, poetry imparts knowledge. It tells us, for instance, something about the season and habitat of cherry trees and how one can feel toward them. Maybe a poet knows no more of cherry trees than a writer of seed-catalog descriptions, if as much. And yet Housman's perception of cherry blossoms as snow, with the implication that they too will soon melt and disappear, indicates a kind of knowledge that seed catalogs do not ordinarily reveal.

Robert Francis (b. 1901)

Catch — 1950

Two boys uncoached are tossing a poem together,
Overhand, underhand, backhand, sleight of hand, every hand,
Teasing with attitudes, latitudes, interludes, altitudes,
High, make him fly off the ground for it, low, make him stoop,
Make him scoop it up, make him as-almost-as-possible miss it,
Fast, let him sting from it, now, now fool him slowly,
Anything, everything tricky, risky, nonchalant,
Anything under the sun to outwit the prosy,
Over the tree and the long sweet cadence down,
Over his head, make him scramble to pick up the meaning,
And now, like a posy, a pretty one plump in his hands.

Questions

1. Who are the two boys in this poem?
2. Point out a few of the most important similarities in this extended comparison.
3. Consider especially line 8: *Anything under the sun to outwit the prosy.* What, in your own words, does Robert Francis mean?

Linda Pastan (b. 1932)

Ethics — 1980

In ethics class so many years ago
our teacher asked this question every fall:
if there were a fire in a museum
which would you save, a Rembrandt painting
or an old woman who hadn't many

years left anyhow? Restless on hard chairs
caring little for pictures or old age
we'd opt one year for life, the next for art
and always half-heartedly. Sometimes
the woman borrowed my grandmother's face
leaving her usual kitchen to wander
some drafty, half imagined museum.
One year, feeling clever, I replied
why not let the woman decide herself?
Linda, the teacher would report, eschews
the burdens of responsibility.
This fall in a real museum I stand
before a real Rembrandt, old woman,
or nearly so, myself. The colors
within this frame are darker than autumn,
darker even than winter—the browns of earth,
though earth's most radiant elements burn
through the canvas. I know now that woman
and painting and season are almost one
and all beyond saving by children.

QUESTIONS

1. How has the passage of time influenced the speaker's attitude toward her teacher's question? Paraphrase her conclusion that "woman and painting and season are almost one and all beyond saving by children."
2. What is the subject of "Ethics"? What is its theme? Is the theme *carpe diem?* Is she saying, with Housman, "Life is fleeting; I'd better enjoy beauty while I may"?
3. Does the main impulse of the poem seem lyric, or narrative?
4. In what ways does "Ethics" differ from prose?

Donald Finkel (b. 1929)

HANDS

1966

The poem makes truth a little more disturbing,
like a good bra, lifts it and holds it out
in both hands. (In some of the flashier stores
there's a model with the hands stitched on, in red or black.)

Lately the world you wed, for want of such hands,
sags in the bed beside you like a tired wife.
For want of such hands, the face of the moon is bored,
the tree does not stretch and yearn, nor the groin tighten.

Devious or frank, in any case,
the poem is calculated to arouse.
Lean back and let its hands play freely on you:
there comes a moment, lifted and aroused,
when the two of you are equally beautiful.

Questions

1. At what moments in "Hands" do you sense that the poet is kidding?
2. Playful as this poem may be, what serious points does Finkel make about the nature of poetry? Explain how, in his view, "real life" relates to poetry (lines 1–3); how the world seems poorer without poetry (lines 5–9); how the reader can be *lifted and aroused* (line 12).

Andrew Marvell (1621–1678)

To His Coy Mistress 1681

Had we but world enough and time,
This coyness°, lady, were no crime. *modesty, reluctance*
We would sit down and think which way
To walk, and pass our long love's day.
Thou by the Indian Ganges' side
Should'st rubies find; I by the tide
Of Humber would complain°. I would *sing sad songs*
Love you ten years before the Flood,
And you should, if you please, refuse
Till the conversion of the Jews.
My vegetable° love should grow *vegetative, flourishing*
Vaster than empires, and more slow.
An hundred years should go to praise
Thine eyes, and on thy forehead gaze,
Two hundred to adore each breast,
But thirty thousand to the rest.
An age at least to every part,
And the last age should show your heart.
For, lady, you deserve this state°, *pomp, ceremony*
Nor would I love at lower rate.
   But at my back I always hear
Time's wingèd chariot hurrying near,
And yonder all before us lie
Deserts of vast eternity.
Thy beauty shall no more be found,
Nor in thy marble vault shall sound
My echoing song; then worms shall try
That long preserved virginity,
And your quaint honor turn to dust,
And into ashes all my lust.
The grave's a fine and private place,
But none, I think, do there embrace.
   Now therefore, while the youthful hue
Sits on thy skin like morning glew° *glow*
And while thy willing soul transpires
At every pore with instant° fires, *eager*
Now let us sport us while we may;

And now, like amorous birds of prey,
Rather at once our time devour
Than languish in his slow-chapped° power. *slow-jawed*
Let us roll all our strength and all
Our sweetness up into one ball
And tear our pleasures with rough strife
Thorough° the iron gates of life. *through*
Thus, though we cannot make our sun
Stand still, yet we will make him run.

TO HIS COY MISTRESS. 7. *Humber:* a river that flows by Marvell's town of Hull (on the side of the world opposite from the Ganges). 10. *conversion of the Jews:* an event that, according to St. John the Divine, is to take place just before the end of the world. 35. *transpires:* exudes, as a membrane lets fluid or vapor pass through it.

QUESTIONS

1. "All this poet does is feed some woman a big line. There's no time for romance, so he says, 'Quick, let's hit the bed before we hit the dirt.' " Discuss this summary. Then try making your own, more accurate one. (Suggestion: The poem is divided into three parts, each beginning with an indented line. Take these parts one at a time, putting the speaker's main thoughts into your own words.)
2. In part one, how much space would be "world enough" for the lovers? Exactly how much time would be enough time?
3. What is the main idea of part two? How is this theme similar to that of Housman's "Loveliest of Trees"?
4. Paraphrase with special care lines 37–44. Is Marvell urging violence?
5. Considering the poem as a whole, does the speaker seem playful, or serious?
6. "The poem makes truth a little more disturbing," says Donald Finkel in "Hands" (page 7). In what ways does Marvell's poem do this for us?

2 Listening to a Voice

TONE

In late-show Westerns, when one hombre taunts another, it is customary for the second to drawl, "Smile when you say that, pardner" or "Mister, I don't like your tone of voice." Sometimes in reading a poem, although we neither can see a face nor hear a voice, we can infer the poet's attitude from other evidence.

Like tone of voice, **tone** in literature often conveys an attitude toward the person addressed. Like the manner of a person, the manner of a poem may be friendly or belligerent toward its reader, condescending or respectful. Again like tone of voice, the tone of a poem may tell us how the speaker feels about himself or herself: cocksure or humble, for example. But most of the time when we ask, "What is the tone of a poem?" we mean, "What attitude does the poet take toward a theme or a subject?" Is the poet being affectionate, hostile, earnest, playful, sarcastic, or what? We may never be able to know, of course, the poet's personal feelings. All we need know is how to feel when we read a poem.

Strictly speaking, tone isn't an attitude; it is whatever in the poem makes an attitude clear to us: the choice of certain words instead of others, the picking out of certain details. In Housman's "Loveliest of trees," for example, the poet communicates his admiration for a cherry tree's beauty by singling out for attention its white blossoms; had he wanted to show his dislike for the tree, he might have concentrated on its broken branches, birdlime, or snails. Rightly to perceive the tone of a poem, we need to read the poem carefully, paying attention to whatever suggestions we find in it.

Theodore Roethke (1908–1963)

My Papa's Waltz 1948

The whiskey on your breath
Could make a small boy dizzy;
But I hung on like death:
Such waltzing was not easy.

We romped until the pans
Slid from the kitchen shelf;
My mother's countenance
Could not unfrown itself.

The hand that held my wrist
Was battered on one knuckle;
At every step you missed
My right ear scraped a buckle.

You beat time on my head
With a palm caked hard by dirt,
Then waltzed me off to bed
Still clinging to your shirt.

What is the tone of this poem? Most readers find the speaker's attitude toward his father affectionate, and take this recollection of childhood to be a happy one. But at least one reader, concentrating on certain details, once wrote: "Roethke expresses his resentment for his father, a drunken brute with dirty hands and a whiskey breath who carelessly hurt the child's ear and manhandled him." Although this reader accurately noticed some of the events in the poem and perceived that in the son's hanging on to the father "like death" there is something desperate, he missed the tone of the poem and so misunderstood it altogether. Among other things, this reader didn't notice the rollicking rhythms of the poem; the playfulness of a rime like *dizzy* and *easy;* the joyful suggestions of the words *waltz, waltzing,* and *romped.* Probably the reader didn't stop to visualize this scene in all its comedy, with kitchen pans falling and the father happily using his son's head for a drum. Nor did he stop to feel the suggestions in the last line, with the boy *still clinging* with persistent love.

Such a poem, though it includes lifelike details that aren't pretty, has a tone relatively easy to recognize. So does **satiric poetry,** a kind of comic poetry that generally conveys a message. Usually its tone is one of detached amusement, withering contempt, and implied superiority. In a satiric poem, the poet ridicules some person or persons (or perhaps some kind of human behavior), examining the victim by the light of certain principles and implying that the reader, too, ought to feel contempt for the victim.

Countee Cullen (1903–1946)

For a Lady I Know

1925

She even thinks that up in heaven
  Her class lies late and snores,
While poor black cherubs rise at seven
  To do celestial chores.

Questions

1. What is Cullen's message?
2. How would you characterize the tone of this poem? Wrathful? Amused?

In some poems the poet's attitude may be plain enough; while in other poems attitudes may be so mingled that it is hard to describe them tersely without doing injustice to the poem. Does Andrew Marvell in "To His Coy Mistress" (page 8) take a serious or playful attitude toward the fact that he and his lady are destined to be food for worms? No one-word answer will suffice. And what of T. S. Eliot's "Love Song of J. Alfred Prufrock" (page 310)? In his attitude toward his redemption-seeking hero who wades with trousers rolled, Eliot is seriously funny. Such a mingled tone may be seen in the following poem by the wife of a governor of the Massachusetts Bay Colony and the earliest American poet of note. Anne Bradstreet's first book, *The Tenth Muse Lately Sprung Up in America* (1650), had been published in England without her consent. She wrote these lines to preface a second edition:

Anne Bradstreet (1612?–1672)

The Author to Her Book — 1678

Thou ill-formed offspring of my feeble brain,
Who after birth did'st by my side remain,
Till snatched from thence by friends, less wise than true,
Who thee abroad exposed to public view;
Made thee in rags, halting, to the press to trudge,
Where errors were not lessened, all may judge.
At thy return my blushing was not small,
My rambling brat (in print) should mother call;
I cast thee by as one unfit for light,
Thy visage was so irksome in my sight;
Yet being mine own, at length affection would
Thy blemishes amend, if so I could:
I washed thy face, but more defects I saw,
And rubbing off a spot, still made a flaw.
I stretched thy joints to make thee even feet,
Yet still thou run'st more hobbling than is meet;
In better dress to trim thee was my mind,
But nought save homespun cloth in the house I find.
In this array, 'mongst vulgars may'st thou roam;
In critics' hands beware thou dost not come;
And take thy way where yet thou are not known.
If for thy Father asked, say thou had'st none;
And for thy Mother, she alas is poor,
Which caused her thus to send thee out of door.

In the author's comparison of her book to an illegitimate ragamuffin, we may be struck by the details of scrubbing and dressing a child: details that might well occur to a mother who had scrubbed and dressed many. As she might feel toward such a child, so she feels toward her book. She starts by deploring it but, as the poem goes on, cannot deny it her affection. Humor enters (as in the pun in line 15). She must dress the creature in *homespun cloth*, something both crude and serviceable. By the end of her poem, Mrs. Bradstreet seems to regard her book-child with tenderness, amusement, and a certain indulgent awareness of its faults. To read this poem is to sense its mingling of several attitudes. Simultaneously, a poet can be merry and in earnest.

Walt Whitman (1819–1892)

To a Locomotive in Winter 1881

Thee for my recitative,
Thee in the driving storm even as now, the snow, the winter-day declining,
Thee in thy panoply°, thy measur'd dual throbbing and thy beat convulsive, *° suit of armor*
Thy black cylindric body, golden brass and silvery steel,
Thy ponderous side-bars, parallel and connecting rods, gyrating, shuttling at thy sides,
Thy metrical, now swelling pant and roar, now tapering in the distance,
Thy great protruding head-light fix'd in front,
Thy long, pale, floating vapor-pennants, tinged with delicate purple,
The dense and murky clouds out-belching from thy smoke-stack,
Thy knitted frame, thy springs and valves, the tremulous twinkle of thy wheels,
Thy train of cars behind, obedient, merrily following,
Through gale or calm, now swift, now slack, yet steadily careering;
Type of the modern—emblem of motion and power—pulse of the continent,
For once come serve the Muse and merge in verse, even as here I see thee,
With storm and buffeting gusts of wind and falling snow,
By day thy warning ringing bell to sound its notes,
By night thy silent signal lamps to swing.

Fierce-throated beauty!
Roll through my chant with all thy lawless music, thy swinging lamps at night,
Thy madly-whistled laughter, echoing, rumbling like an earthquake, rousing all,
Law of thyself complete, thine own track firmly holding,
(No sweetness debonair of tearful harp or glib piano thine,)
Thy trills of shrieks by rocks and hills return'd,
Launch'd o'er the prairies wide, across the lakes,
To the free skies unpent and glad and strong.

Emily Dickinson (1830–1886)

I like to see it lap the Miles (about 1862)

I like to see it lap the Miles–
And lick the Valleys up–
And stop to feed itself at Tanks–
And then–prodigious step

Around a Pile of Mountains–
And supercilious peer
In Shanties–by the sides of Roads–
And then a Quarry pare

To fit its Ribs
And crawl between
Complaining all the while
In horrid–hooting stanza–
Then chase itself down Hill–

And neigh like Boanerges–
Then–punctual as a Star
Stop–docile and omnipotent
At its own stable door–

Questions

1. What differences in tone do you find between Whitman's and Emily Dickinson's poems? Point out in each poem whatever contributes to these differences.
2. *Boanerges* in Emily Dickinson's last stanza means "sons of thunder," a name given by Christ to the disciples John and James (see Mark 3:17). How far should the reader work out the particulars of this comparison? Does it make the tone of the poem serious?
3. In Whitman's opening line, what is a *recitative*? What other specialized terms from the vocabulary of music and poetry does each poem contain? How do they help underscore Whitman's theme?
4. Poets and song-writers probably have regarded the locomotive with more affection than they have shown most other machines. Why do you suppose this to be? Can you think of any other poems or songs for example?
5. What do these two poems tell you about locomotives that you would not be likely to find in a technical book on railroading?
6. Are the subjects of the two poems identical? Discuss.

John Milton (1608–1674)

On the Late Massacre in Piemont (1655)

Avenge, O Lord, thy slaughtered saints, whose bones
  Lie scattered on the Alpine mountains cold;
  Even them who kept thy truth so pure of old,
When all our fathers worshiped stocks and stones,

Forget not: in thy book record their groans
  Who were thy sheep, and in their ancient fold
  Slain by the bloody Piemontese, that rolled
Mother with infant down the rocks. Their moans
The vales redoubled to the hills, and they
  To heaven. Their martyred blood and ashes sow
O'er all the Italian fields, where still doth sway
  The triple Tyrant; that from these may grow
  A hundredfold, who, having learnt thy way,
  Early may fly the Babylonian woe.

On the Late Massacre in Piemont. Despite hostility between Catholics and Protestants, the Waldenses, members of a Puritan sect, had been living in the Piemont, that region in northwest Italy bounded by the crests of the Alps. In 1655, ignoring a promise to observe religious liberty, troops of the Roman Catholic ruler of the Piemont put to death several members of the sect. 4. *When . . . stones:* Englishmen had been Catholics, worshiping stone and wooden statues (so Milton charges) when the Waldensian sect was founded in the twelfth century. 12. *The triple Tyrant:* The Pope, to whom is attributed authority over earth, heaven, and hell. 14. *Babylonian woe:* Destruction expected to befall the city of Babylon at the world's end as punishment for its luxury and other wickedness (see Revelation 18:1–24). Protestants took Babylon to mean the Church of Rome.

Question

What is Milton's attitude toward the massacre? Does he express a single feeling, or a mingling of feelings?

THE PERSON IN THE POEM

The tone of a poem, we said, is like tone of voice in that both communicate feelings. Still, this comparison raises a question: when we read a poem, whose "voice" speaks to us?

"The poet's" is one possible answer; and in the case of many a poem, that answer may be right. Reading Anne Bradstreet's "The Author to Her Book," we can be reasonably sure that the poet speaks of her very own book, and of her own experiences. In order to read a poem, we seldom need to read a poet's biography; but in truth there are certain poems whose full effect depends upon our knowing at least a fact or two of the poet's life. In this poem, surely the poet refers to himself:

Trumbull Stickney (1874–1904)

Sir, say no more — 1905

Sir, say no more,
Within me 'tis as if
The green and climbing eyesight of a cat
Crawled near my mind's poor birds.

The subject of Stickney's poem is not some nightmare or hallucination. The poem may mean more to you if you know that Stickney, who wrote it shortly before his death, had been afflicted by cancer of the brain. But the poem is not a prosaic entry in the diary of a dying man, nor is it a good poem because a dying man wrote it. Not only does it tell truth from experience, it speaks in memorable words.

Most of us can tell the difference between a person we meet in life and a person we meet in a work of art—unlike the moviegoer in the Philippines who, watching a villain in an exciting film, pulled out a revolver and peppered the screen. And yet, in reading poems, we are liable to temptation. When the poet says "I," we may want to assume that he, like Trumbull Stickney, is making a personal statement. But reflect: do all poems have to be personal? Here is a brief poem inscribed on the tombstone of an infant in Burial Hill cemetery, Plymouth, Massachusetts:

Since I have been so quickly done for,
I wonder what I was begun for.

We do not know who wrote those lines, but it is clear that the poet was not a short-lived infant writing from personal experience. In other poems, the speaker is obviously a **persona** or fictitious character: not the poet, but the poet's creation. As a grown man, William Blake, a skilled professional engraver, wrote a poem in the voice of a boy, an illiterate chimney sweeper. (The poem appears on page 31.) No law decrees that the speaker in a poem even has to be human: good poems have been uttered by clouds, pebbles, and cats. A **dramatic monologue** is a poem written as a speech made at some decisive or revealing moment. It is usually addressed by the speaker to some other character (who remains silent). Robert Browning, who developed the form, liked to put words into the mouths of characters stupider, weaker, or nastier than he: for instance see "My Last Duchess" (page 294), in which the speaker is an arrogant Renaissance duke. Browning himself, from all reports, was neither domineering nor merciless.

Let's consider a poem spoken not by a poet but by a persona—in this case, a child. To understand the poem, you need to pay attention not only to what the child says, but also to how the poet seems to feel about it.

Randall Jarrell (1914–1965)

A Sick Child — 1951

The postman comes when I am still in bed.
"Postman, what do you have for me today?"
I say to him. (But really I'm in bed.)
Then he says—what shall I have him say?

"This letter says that you are president
Of—this word here; it's a republic."
Tell them I can't answer right away.
"It's your duty." No, I'd rather just be sick.

Then he tells me there are letters saying everything
That I can think of that I want for them to say.
I say, "Well, thank you very much. Good-bye."
He is ashamed, and turns and walks away.

If I can think of it, it isn't what I want.
I want . . . I want a ship from some near star
To land in the yard, and beings to come out
And think to me: "So this is where you are!

Come." Except that they won't do,
I thought of them. . . . And yet somewhere there must be
Something that's different from everything.
All that I've never thought of—think of me!

Questions

1. Would you call the speaker unfeeling or sensitive? Unimaginative or imaginative? How do you know?
2. Why is the postman *ashamed*?
3. Besides sickness, what is bothering the child? What does the child long for?
4. Do you think Jarrell sympathizes with the child's wishes and longings? By what means does he indicate his own attitude?

We tend to think of a poem as simply an expression of the feelings a poet had while writing it. And yet, as the following comic poem indicates, sometimes a poet in the process of writing a poem has feelings that the poem doesn't mention.

Alden Nowlan (b. 1933)

The Loneliness of the Long Distance Runner 1967

My wife bursts into the room
where I'm writing well
of my love for her

and because now
the poem is lost

I silently curse her.

Humorously, Nowlan suggests that loving his wife isn't the same as writing a poem about loving her. A good poem (if the poet can finish it) is a fixed and changeless thing; but evidently a living, changing poet with various emotions had to take a certain length of time in writing it.

In a famous definition, William Wordsworth calls poetry "the spontaneous overflow of powerful feelings . . . recollected in tranquillity."[1] But in the case of the following poem, Wordsworth's feelings weren't all his; they didn't just overflow spontaneously; and the process of tranquil recollection had to go on for years.

William Wordsworth (1770–1850)

I Wandered Lonely as a Cloud 1807

I wandered lonely as a cloud
  That floats on high o'er vales and hills,
When all at once I saw a crowd,
  A host, of golden daffodils,
Beside the lake, beneath the trees,
Fluttering and dancing in the breeze.

Continuous as the stars that shine
  And twinkle on the milky way,
They stretched in never-ending line
  Along the margin of a bay:
Ten thousand saw I at a glance,
Tossing their heads in sprightly dance.

The waves beside them danced; but they
  Out-did the sparkling waves in glee;
A poet could not but be gay,
  In such a jocund company;
I gazed—and gazed—but little thought
What wealth the show to me had brought:

For oft, when on my couch I lie
  In vacant or in pensive mood,
They flash upon that inward eye
  Which is the bliss of solitude;
And then my heart with pleasure fills,
And dances with the daffodils.

Between the first printing of the poem in 1807 and the version of 1815 given here, Wordsworth made several deliberate improvements. He changed *dancing* to *golden* in line 4, *Along* to *Beside* in line 5, *Ten thousand* to *Fluttering and* in line 6, *laughing* to *jocund* in line 16, and he added a whole stanza (the second). In fact, the writing of the poem was unspontaneous enough for Wordsworth, at a loss for lines 21–22, to take them from his wife Mary. It is likely that the experience of daffodil-watching was not entirely his to begin with but was derived in part

[1] For a fuller text of Wordsworth's statement, see page 404.

from the recollections his sister Dorothy Wordsworth had set down in her journal of April 15, 1802, two years before he first drafted his poem:

> When we were in the woods beyond Gowbarrow Park we saw a few daffodils close to the water-side. We fancied that the lake had floated the seeds ashore, and that the little colony had so sprung up. But as we went along there were more and yet more; and at last, under the boughs of the trees, we saw that there was a long belt of them along the shore, about the breadth of a country turnpike road. I never saw daffodils so beautiful. They grew among the mossy stones about and about them; some rested their heads upon these stones as on a pillow for weariness; and the rest tossed and reeled and danced, and seemed as if they verily laughed with the wind, that flew upon them over the Lake; they looked so gay, ever glancing, ever changing. This wind blew directly over the Lake to them. There was here and there a little knot, and a few stragglers a few yards higher up; but they were so few as not to disturb the simplicity, unity, and life of that one busy highway.

Notice that Wordsworth's poem echoes a few of his sister's observations. Weaving poetry out of their mutual memories, Wordsworth has offered the experience as if altogether his own, made himself lonely, and left Dorothy out. The point is not that Wordsworth is a liar or a plagiarist but that, like any other good poet, he has transformed ordinary life into art. A process of interpreting, shaping, and ordering had to intervene between the experience of looking at daffodils and the finished poem.

We need not deny that a poet's experience can contribute to a poem nor that the emotion in the poem can indeed be the poet's. Still, to write a good poem one has to do more than live and feel. It seems a pity that, as Randall Jarrell has said, a cardinal may write verses worse than his youngest choirboy's. But writing poetry takes skill and imagination—qualities that extensive travel and wide experience do not necessarily give. For much of her life, Emily Dickinson seldom strayed from her family's house and grounds in Amherst, Massachusetts; yet her rimed lifestudies of a snake, a bee, and a hummingbird contain more poetry than we find in any firsthand description (so far) of the surface of the moon.

Paul Zimmer (b. 1934)

THE DAY ZIMMER LOST RELIGION — 1976

The first Sunday I missed Mass on purpose
I waited all day for Christ to climb down
Like a wiry flyweight from the cross and
Club me on my irreverent teeth, to wade into
My blasphemous gut and drop me like a
Red hot thurible, the devil roaring in
Reserved seats until he got the hiccups.

It was a long cold way from the old days
When cassocked and surpliced I mumbled Latin
At the old priest and rang his obscure bell.
A long way from the dirty wind that blew
The soot like venial sins across the school yard
Where God reigned as a threatening,
One-eyed triangle high in the fleecy sky.

The first Sunday I missed Mass on purpose
I waited all day for Christ to climb down
Like the playground bully, the cuts and mice
Upon his face agleam, and pound me
Till my irreligious tongue hung out.
But of course He never came, knowing that
I was grown up and ready for Him now.

Questions

1. Who is the person in this poem? The mature poet? The poet as a child? Some fictitious character?
2. What do you understand to be the speaker's attitude toward religion at the present moment?

Richard Hugo (1923–1982)

In Your Young Dream

1977

You are traveling to play basketball. Your team's
a good one, boys you knew when you were young.
A game's in Wyoming, a small town, a gym
in a grammar school. You go in to practice.
No nets on the hoops. You say to the coach,
a small man, mean face, "We need nets on the rims."
He sneers as if you want luxury. You explain
how this way you can't see the shots go in.
You and another player, vaguely seen, go out
to buy nets. A neon sign on a local tavern
gives directions to the next town, a town
a woman you loved lives in. You go to your room
to phone her, to tell her you're here just
one town away to play ball. She's already
waiting in your room surrounded by children.
She says, "I'll come watch you play ball."
Though young in the dream you know you are old.
You are troubled. You know you need nets on the rims.

Question

Who is the *you* in this poem?

Experiment: *Reading with and without Biography*

Read the following poem and state what you understand from it. Then consider the circumstances in which it probably came to be written. (Some information is offered in a note at the end of this chapter.) Does the meaning of the poem change? To what extent does an appreciation of the poem need the support of biography?

William Carlos Williams (1883–1963)

The Red Wheelbarrow 1923

so much depends
upon

a red wheel
barrow

glazed with rain
water

beside the white
chickens.

IRONY

To see a distinction between the poet and the words of a fictitious character—between Randall Jarrell and "A Sick Child"—is to be aware of **irony:** a manner of speaking that implies a discrepancy. If the mask says one thing and we sense that the writer is in fact saying something else, the writer has adopted an **ironic point of view.** No finer illustration exists in English than Jonathan Swift's "A Modest Proposal," an essay in which Swift speaks as an earnest, humorless citizen who sets forth his reasonable plan to aid the Irish poor. The plan is so monstrous no sane reader can assent to it: the poor are to sell their children as meat for the tables of their landlords. From behind his falseface, Swift is actually recommending not cannibalism but love and Christian charity.

A poem is often made complicated and more interesting by another kind of irony. **Verbal irony** occurs whenever words say one thing but mean something else, usually the opposite. The word *love* means *hate* here: "I just *love* to stay home and do my hair on a Saturday night!" If the verbal irony is conspicuously bitter, heavy-handed, and mocking, it is **sarcasm:** "Oh, he's the biggest spender in the world, all right!" (The sarcasm, if that statement were spoken, would be underscored by the speaker's tone of voice.) A famous instance of sarcasm is Mark Antony's line in his oration over the body of slain Julius Caesar: "Brutus is an honorable man." Antony repeats this line until the enraged populace begins shouting exactly what he means to call Brutus and the other conspirators: traitors, villains, murderers. We had best be alert for irony on the printed page, for if we miss it, our interpretations of a poem may go wild.

Robert Creeley (b. 1926)

Oh No 1959

If you wander far enough
you will come to it
and when you get there
they will give you a place to sit

for yourself only, in a nice chair,
and all your friends will be there
with smiles on their faces
and they will likewise all have places.

This poem is rich in verbal irony. The title helps point out that between the speaker's words and attitude lie deep differences. In line 2, what is *it*? Old age? The wandering suggests a conventional metaphor: the journey of life. Is *it* literally a rest home for "senior citizens," or perhaps some naïve popular concept of heaven (such as we meet in comic strips: harps, angels with hoops for halos) in which the saved all sit around in a ring, smugly congratulating one another? We can't be sure, but the speaker's attitude toward this final sitting-place is definite. It is a place for the selfish, as we infer from the phrase *for yourself only*. And *smiles on their faces* may hint that the smiles are unchanging and forced. There is a difference between saying "They had smiles on their faces" and "They smiled": the latter suggests that the smiles came from within. The word *nice* is to be regarded with distrust. If we see through this speaker, as Creeley implies we can do, we realize that, while pretending to be sweet-talking us into a seat, actually he is revealing the horror of a little hell. And the title is the poet's reaction to it (or the speaker's unironic, straightforward one): "Oh no! Not *that!*"

Dramatic irony, like verbal irony, contains an element of contrast, but it usually refers to a situation in a play wherein a character, whose knowledge is limited, says, does, or encounters something of greater significance than he or she knows. We, the spectators, realize the meaning of this speech or action, for the playwright has afforded us superior knowledge. In Sophocles' *King Oedipus,* when Oedipus vows to punish whoever has brought down a plague upon the city of Thebes, we know—as he does not—that the man he would punish is himself. (Referring to such a situation that precedes the downfall of a hero in a tragedy, some critics speak of **tragic irony** instead of dramatic irony.) Superior knowledge can be enjoyed not only by spectators in a theater but by readers of poetry as well. In *Paradise Lost,* we know in advance that Adam will fall into temptation, and we recognize his overconfidence when he neglects a warning. The situation of Oedipus contains also **cosmic irony,** or **irony of fate:** some Fate with a grim sense of humor seems cruelly to trick a human being. Cosmic irony clearly exists in poems in which fate or the Fates are personified and seen as hostile, as in Thomas Hardy's "The Convergence of the Twain" (page 323); and it may be said to occur too in Robinson's "Richard Cory" (page 108). Evidently it is a twist of fate for the most envied man in town to kill himself.

To sum up: the effect of irony depends upon the reader's noticing some incongruity or discrepancy between two things. In *verbal irony,* there is a contrast between the speaker's words and meaning; in an *ironic point of view,* between the writer's attitude and what is spoken by a fictitious character; in *dramatic irony,* between the limited knowledge of a character and the fuller knowledge of the reader or spectator; in *cosmic irony,* between a character's aspiration and the treatment he or she receives at the hands of Fate. Although in the work of an inept poet irony can be crude and obvious sarcasm, it is invaluable to a poet of more complicated mind, who imagines more than one perspective.

W. H. Auden (1907–1973)

The Unknown Citizen — 1940

(To JS/07/M/378
This Marble Monument
Is Erected by the State)

He was found by the Bureau of Statistics to be
One against whom there was no official complaint,
And all the reports on his conduct agree
That, in the modern sense of an old-fashioned word, he was a saint,
For in everything he did he served the Greater Community.
Except for the War till the day he retired
He worked in a factory and never got fired,
But satisfied his employers, Fudge Motors Inc.
Yet he wasn't a scab or odd in his views,
For his Union reports that he paid his dues,
(Our report on his Union shows it was sound)
And our Social Psychology workers found
That he was popular with his mates and liked a drink.
The Press are convinced that he bought a paper every day
And that his reactions to advertisements were normal in every way.
Policies taken out in his name prove that he was fully insured,
And his Health-card shows he was once in hospital but left it cured.
Both Producers Research and High-Grade Living declare
He was fully sensible to the advantages of the Installment Plan
And had everything necessary to the Modern Man,
A phonograph, a radio, a car and a frigidaire.

Our researchers into Public Opinion are content
That he held the proper opinions for the time of year;
When there was peace, he was for peace; when there was war, he went.
He was married and added five children to the population,
Which our Eugenist says was the right number for a parent of his
 generation,
And our teachers report that he never interfered with their education.
Was he free? Was he happy? The question is absurd:
Had anything been wrong, we should certainly have heard.

QUESTIONS

1. Read the three-line epitaph at the beginning of the poem as carefully as you read what follows. How does the epitaph help establish the voice by which the rest of the poem is spoken?
2. Who is speaking?
3. What ironic discrepancies do you find between the speaker's attitude toward the subject and that of the poet himself? By what is the poet's attitude made clear?
4. In the phrase "The Unknown Soldier" (of which "The Unknown Citizen" reminds us), what does the word *unknown* mean? What does it mean in the title of Auden's poem?
5. What tendencies in our civilization does Auden satirize?
6. How would you expect the speaker to define a Modern Man, if a phonograph, a radio, a car, and a refrigerator are "everything" a Modern Man needs?

John Betjeman (b. 1906)

IN WESTMINSTER ABBEY 1940

Let me take this other glove off
 As the *vox humana* swells,
And the beauteous fields of Eden
 Bask beneath the Abbey bells.
Here, where England's statesmen lie,
Listen to a lady's cry.

Gracious Lord, oh bomb the Germans.
 Spare their women for Thy Sake,
And if that is not too easy
 We will pardon Thy Mistake.
But, gracious Lord, whate'er shall be,
Don't let anyone bomb me.

Keep our Empire undismembered,
 Guide our Forces by Thy Hand,
Gallant blacks from far Jamaica,
 Honduras and Togoland;
Protect them Lord in all their fights,
And, even more, protect the whites.

Think of what our Nation stands for:
  Books from Boots' and country lanes,
Free speech, free passes, class distinction,
  Democracy and proper drains.
Lord, put beneath Thy special care
One-eighty-nine Cadogan Square.

Although dear Lord I am a sinner,
  I have done no major crime;
Now I'll come to Evening Service
  Whensoever I have the time.
So, Lord, reserve for me a crown,
And do not let my shares° go down. *stocks*

I will labor for Thy Kingdom,
  Help our lads to win the war,
Send white feathers to the cowards,
  Join the Women's Army Corps,
Then wash the Steps around Thy Throne
In the Eternal Safety Zone.

Now I feel a little better,
  What a treat to hear Thy Word,
Where the bones of leading statesmen
  Have so often been interred.
And now, dear Lord, I cannot wait
Because I have a luncheon date.

IN WESTMINSTER ABBEY. First printed during World War II. 2. *vox humana:* an organ stop that makes tones similar to those of the human voice. 20. *Boots':* a cut-rate pharmacy.

QUESTIONS

1. Who is the speaker? What do we know about her life style? About her prejudices?
2. Point out some of the places in which she contradicts herself.
3. How would you describe the speaker's attitude toward religion?
4. Through the medium of irony, what positive points do you believe Betjeman makes?

Sarah N. Cleghorn (1876–1959)

THE GOLF LINKS

1917

The golf links lie so near the mill
  That almost every day
The laboring children can look out
  And see the men at play.

Questions

1. Is this brief poem satiric? Does it contain any verbal irony? Is the poet making a matter-of-fact statement in words that mean just what they say?
2. What other kind of irony is present in the poem?
3. Sarah N. Cleghorn's poem dates from before the enactment of legislation against child labor. Is it still a good poem, or is it hopelessly outdated?
4. How would you state its theme?

Constance Urdang (b. 1922)

The Miracle-Factory

1980

Papa's got a job in a miracle-factory
downtown someplace, one of those streets
west of the avenue, in an old
building taller than God. There's a marble lobby, two
elevators behind brass gates, a newsstand,
and a draft whenever anyone pushes through
the glass revolving doors. Upstairs
after the corridor, damp, windy, cold
RING BELL COME IN the loft
looks at an airshaft. Soot settles softly, like snow.

I went there once with Papa. Standing soldierly
put out my hand to the boss, said, How d'you do.
I didn't like it much. The boss said, Boy,
when you grow up I want you to remember
making miracles is just like any other line, profit and loss,
also supply and demand. You got to sell
the product, make them believe
in it! He shook my hand.
Papa said later, He's the boss, without
the boss, no factory. Remember that.

Questions

1. Who is the speaker?
2. Does this speaker seem aware that there is anything out-of-the-ordinary about a factory that produces miracles? What discrepancy do you suspect there to be between his view and the poet's view?
3. In the poet's making this factory an ordinary, run-down, back-street business (and not, say, the handsomely appointed studios of Miracle Productions), what does the poem gain?
4. Is the boss the Deity? (Don't be surprised if discussion should elicit more than one likely interpretation of this poem.)

Exercise: *Detecting Irony*

Point out the kinds of irony that occur in the following poem.

Thomas Hardy (1840–1928)

The Workbox

1914

"See, here's the workbox, little wife,
  That I made of polished oak."
He was a joiner°, of village life; *carpenter*
  She came of borough folk.

He holds the present up to her
  As with a smile she nears
And answers to the profferer,
  " 'Twill last all my sewing years!"

"I warrant it will. And longer too.
  'Tis a scantling that I got
Off poor John Wayward's coffin, who
  Died of they knew not what.

"The shingled pattern that seems to cease
  Against your box's rim
Continues right on in the piece
  That's underground with him.

"And while I worked it made me think
  Of timber's varied doom:
One inch where people eat and drink,
  The next inch in a tomb.

"But why do you look so white, my dear,
  And turn aside your face?
You knew not that good lad, I fear,
  Though he came from your native place?"

"How could I know that good young man,
  Though he came from my native town,
When he must have left far earlier than
  I was a woman grown?"

"Ah, no. I should have understood!
  It shocked you that I gave
To you one end of a piece of wood
  Whose other is in a grave?"

"Don't, dear, despise my intellect,
  Mere accidental things
Of that sort never have effect
  On my imaginings."

Yet still her lips were limp and wan,
  Her face still held aside,
As if she had known not only John,
  But known of what he died.

FOR REVIEW AND FURTHER STUDY

John Berryman (1914–1972)

LIFE, FRIENDS, IS BORING. WE MUST NOT SAY SO 1964

Life, friends, is boring. We must not say so.
After all, the sky flashes, the great sea yearns,
we ourselves flash and yearn,
and moreover my mother told me as a boy
(repeatingly) "Ever to confess you're bored
means you have no

Inner Resources." I conclude now I have no
inner resources, because I am heavy bored.
Peoples bore me,
literature bores me, especially great literature,
Henry bores me, with his plights & gripes
as bad as achilles,

who loves people and valiant art, which bores me.
And the tranquil hills, & gin, look like a drag
and somehow a dog
has taken itself & its tail considerably away
into mountains or sea or sky, leaving
behind: me, wag.

QUESTIONS

1. Henry (line 11) is the central figure of Berryman's *Dream Songs.* Achilles (line 12), Greek hero of the Trojan war, was portrayed by Shakespeare as a sulking malcontent. Is a comparison of Henry, a rather ordinary American citizen, to Achilles likely to result in a heightening of Henry's importance or in a sense of ironic discrepancy? Discuss.
2. What is confused or self-contradictory in the precept "Ever to confess you're bored means you have no Inner Resources"?
3. What could the poet be trying to indicate by capitalizing *Inner Resources* in line 7 but not in line 8? By writing *achilles* with a small letter?
4. In line 14, what discrepancy do you find between the phrases *the tranquil hills* and *a drag*?
5. In the last line, what double meaning is there in the word *wag*?
6. True or false? "In comparing 'ourselves' to the sky and to the 'great sea,' the speaker takes the attitude that he and his readers have dignity and grandeur, their emotions being as powerful as lightningbolts and tides." Do you find this paraphrase consistent or inconsistent with the tone of the poem? Why?

EXERCISE: *Telling Tone*

Here are two radically different poems on a similar subject. Try stating the theme of each poem in your own words. How is tone (the speaker's attitude) different in the two poems?

Richard Lovelace (1618–1658)

To Lucasta 1649

On Going to the Wars

Tell me not, Sweet, I am unkind
  That from the nunnery
Of thy chaste breast and quiet mind,
  To war and arms I fly.

True, a new mistress now I chase,
  The first foe in the field;
And with a stronger faith embrace
  A sword, a horse, a shield.

Yet this inconstancy is such
  As you too shall adore;
I could not love thee, Dear, so much,
  Loved I not Honor more.

Wilfred Owen (1893–1918)

Dulce et Decorum Est 1920

Bent double, like old beggars under sacks,
Knock-kneed, coughing like hags, we cursed through sludge,
Till on the haunting flares we turned our backs
And towards our distant rest began to trudge.
Men marched asleep. Many had lost their boots
But limped on, blood-shod. All went lame; all blind;
Drunk with fatigue; deaf even to the hoots
Of tired, outstripped Five-Nines° that dropped behind. *gas-shells*

Gas! Gas! Quick, boys!—An ecstasy of fumbling,
Fitting the clumsy helmets just in time;
But someone still was yelling out and stumbling
And flound'ring like a man in fire or lime . . .
Dim, through the misty panes and thick green light,
As under a green sea, I saw him drowning.
In all my dreams, before my helpless sight,
He plunges at me, guttering, choking, drowning.

If in some smothering dreams you too could pace
Behind the wagon that we flung him in,
And watch the white eyes writhing in his face,
His hanging face, like a devil's sick of sin;
If you could hear, at every jolt, the blood
Come gargling from the froth-corrupted lungs,
Obscene as cancer, bitter as the cud
Of vile, incurable sores on innocent tongues,—

My friend, you would not tell with such high zest
To children ardent for some desperate glory,
The old Lie: Dulce et decorum est
Pro patria mori.

DULCE ET DECORUM EST. A British infantry officer in World War I, Owen was killed in action. 17. *you too:* Some manuscript versions of this poem carry the dedication "To Jessie Pope" (a writer of patriotic verse) or "To a certain Poetess." 27–28. *Dulce et . . . mori:* a quotation from the Latin poet Horace, "It is sweet and fitting to die for one's country."

James Stephens (1882–1950)

A GLASS OF BEER 1918

The lanky hank of a she in the inn over there
Nearly killed me for asking the loan of a glass of beer;
May the devil grip the whey-faced slut by the hair,
And beat bad manners out of her skin for a year.

That parboiled ape, with the toughest jaw you will see
On virtue's path, and a voice that would rasp the dead,
Came roaring and raging the minute she looked at me,
And threw me out of the house on the back of my head!

If I asked her master he'd give me a cask a day;
But she, with the beer at hand, not a gill° would arrange! *quarter-pint*
May she marry a ghost and bear him a kitten, and may
The High King of Glory permit her to get the mange.

QUESTIONS

1. Who do you take to be the speaker? Is it the poet? The speaker may be angry, but what is the tone of this poem?
2. Would you agree with a commentator who said, "To berate anyone in truly memorable language is practically a lost art in America"? How well does the speaker (an Irishman) succeed? Which of his epithets and curses strike you as particularly imaginative?

Jonathan Swift (1667–1745)

ON STELLA'S BIRTHDAY (1718–1719)

Stella this day is thirty-four
(We shan't dispute a year or more)—
However, Stella, be not troubled,
Although thy size and years are doubled,
Since first I saw thee at sixteen,
The brightest virgin on the green,
So little is thy form declined,
Made up so largely in thy mind.

Oh, would it please the gods, to split
Thy beauty, size, and years, and wit,
No age could furnish out a pair
Of nymphs so graceful, wise, and fair,
With half the luster of your eyes,
With half your wit, your years, and size.
And then, before it grew too late,
How should I beg of gentle Fate
(That either nymph might have her swain)
To split my worship too in twain.

ON STELLA'S BIRTHDAY. For many years Swift made an annual birthday gift of a poem to his close friend Mrs. Esther Johnson, the degree of whose nearness to the proud and lonely Swift remains an enigma to biographers. 18. *my worship:* as Dean of St. Patrick's in Dublin, Swift was addressed as "Your Worship."

QUESTIONS

1. If you were Stella, would you be amused or insulted by the poet's references to your *size*?
2. According to Swift in lines 7–8, what has compensated Stella for what the years have taken away?
3. Comment on the last four lines. Does Swift exempt himself from growing old?
4. How would you describe the tone of this poem? Offensive (like the speaker's complaints in "A Glass of Beer")? Playfully tender? Sad over Stella's growing fat and old?

William Blake (1757–1827)

THE CHIMNEY SWEEPER

1789

When my mother died I was very young,
And my father sold me while yet my tongue
Could scarcely cry " 'weep! 'weep! 'weep! 'weep!"
So your chimneys I sweep, and in soot I sleep.

There's little Tom Dacre, who cried when his head,
That curled like a lamb's back, was shaved: so I said
"Hush, Tom! never mind it, for when your head's bare
You know that the soot cannot spoil your white hair."

And so he was quiet, and that very night,
As Tom was a-sleeping, he had such a sight!
That thousands of sweepers, Dick, Joe, Ned, and Jack,
Were all of them locked up in coffins of black.

And by came an Angel who had a bright key,
And he opened the coffins and set them all free;
Then down a green plain leaping, laughing, they run,
And wash in a river, and shine in the sun.

Then naked and white, all their bags left behind,
They rise upon clouds and sport in the wind;
And the Angel told Tom, if he'd be a good boy,
He'd have God for his father, and never want joy.

And so Tom awoke; and we rose in the dark,
And got with our bags and our brushes to work.
Though the morning was cold, Tom was happy and warm;
So if all do their duty they need not fear harm.

Questions

1. What does Blake's poem reveal about conditions of life in the London of his day?
2. What does this poem have in common with "The Golf Links" (page 25)?
3. How does "The Chimney Sweeper" resemble "A Sick Child" (page 16)? In what ways does Blake's poem seem much different?
4. Sum up your impressions of the speaker's character. What does he say and do that displays it to us?
5. What pun do you find in line 3? Is its effect comic or serious?
6. In Tom Dacre's dream (lines 11–20), what wishes come true? Do you understand them to be the wishes of the chimney sweepers, of the poet, or of both?
7. In the last line, what is ironic in the speaker's assurance that the dutiful *need not fear harm*? What irony is there in his urging all to *do their duty*? (Who have failed in their duty to *him*?)
8. What is the tone of Blake's poem? Angry? Hopeful? Sorrowful? Compassionate? (Don't feel obliged to sum it up in a single word.)

Information for Experiment: *Reading with and without Biography*

The Red Wheelbarrow (p. 21). Dr. Williams's poem reportedly contains a personal experience: he was gazing from the window of the house where one of his patients, a small girl, lay suspended between life and death. (This account, from the director of the public library in Williams's native Rutherford, N.J., is given by Geri M. Rhodes in "The Paterson Metaphor in William Carlos Williams' *Paterson*," master's essay, Tufts University, June 1965.)

3 Words

LITERAL MEANING: WHAT A POEM SAYS FIRST

Although successful as a painter, Edgar Degas struggled to produce sonnets, and found poetry discouragingly hard to write. To his friend, the poet Stéphane Mallarmé, he complained, "What a business! My whole day gone on a blasted sonnet, without getting an inch further . . . and it isn't ideas I'm short of . . . I'm full of them, I've got too many . . ."

"But Degas," said Mallarmé, "you can't make a poem with ideas—you make it with *words*!"[1]

Like the celebrated painter, some people assume that all it takes to make a poem is a bright idea. Poems state ideas, to be sure, and sometimes the ideas are invaluable; and yet the most impressive idea in the world will not make a poem unless its words are selected and arranged with loving art. Some poets take great pains to find the right word. Unable to fill a two-syllable gap in an unfinished line that went, "The seal's wide——gaze toward Paradise," Hart Crane paged through an unabridged dictionary. When he reached *S*, he found the object of his quest in *spindrift:* "spray skimmed from the sea by a strong wind." The word is exact and memorable. Any word can be the right word, however, if artfully chosen and placed. It may be a word as ordinary as *from*. Consider the difference between "The sedge is withered *on* the lake" (a misquotation of a line by Keats) and "The sedge is withered *from* the lake" (what Keats in fact wrote). Keats's original line suggests, as the altered line doesn't, that because the sedge (a growth of grasslike plants) has withered *from* the lake, it has withdrawn mysteriously.

In reading a poem, some people assume that its words can be skipped over rapidly, and they try to leap at once to the poem's general theme. It is as if they fear being thought clods unless they can find huge ideas in the poem (whether or not there are any). Such readers often ig-

[1] Paul Valéry, *Degas . . . Manet . . . Morisot*, translated by David Paul (New York: Pantheon, 1960), p. 62.

nore the literal meanings of words: the ordinary, matter-of-fact sense to be found in a dictionary. (As you will see in Chapter Four, "Saying and Suggesting," words possess not only dictionary meanings — **denotations** — but also many associations and suggestions — **connotations.**) Consider the following poem and see what you make of it.

William Carlos Williams (1883–1963)

This Is Just to Say

1934

I have eaten
the plums
that were in
the icebox
and which
you were probably
saving
for breakfast

Forgive me
they were delicious
so sweet
and so cold

Some readers distrust a poem so simple and candid. They think, "What's wrong with me? There has to be more to it than this!" But poems seldom are puzzles in need of solutions. We can begin by accepting the poet's statements, without suspecting him of trying to hoodwink us. On later reflection, of course, we might possibly decide that the poet is playfully teasing or being ironic; but Williams gives us no reason to think that. There seems no need to look beyond the literal sense of his words, no profit in speculating that the plums symbolize worldly joys and that the icebox stands for the universe. Clearly, a reader who held such a grand theory would have overlooked (in eagerness to find a significant idea) the plain truth that the poet makes clear to us: that ice-cold plums are a joy to taste, especially if one knows they'll be missed the next morning.

To be sure, Williams's small poem is simpler than most poems are; and yet in reading any poem, no matter how complicated, you will do well to reach slowly and reluctantly for generalizations. An adept reader of poetry reads with open mind — with (in Richard L. McGuire's phrase) "as much innocence as he can muster." For in order to experience a poem, you first have to pay attention to its words; and only if you see what the words are saying are you likely to come to the poem's true theme. Recall Housman's "Loveliest of trees" (page 399): a poem that contains a message (how rapidly life passes, how vital it is to make the most of every spring). Yet before you can realize that theme, you have to notice the color, the quantity, and the weight (*hung with bloom*) of Housman's imagined cherry blossoms.

Poets often strive for words that point to physical details and solid objects. They may do so even when speaking of an abstract idea:

Beauty is but a flower
Which wrinkles will devour;
Brightness falls from the air,
Queens have died young and fair,
Dust hath closed Helen's eye.
I am sick, I must die:
  Lord, have mercy on us!

In these lines by Thomas Nashe, the abstraction *beauty* has grown petals that shrivel. Brightness may be a general name for light, but Nashe succeeds in giving it the weight of a falling body.

If a poem reads *daffodils* instead of *vegetation, diaper years* instead of *infancy,* and *eighty-four* instead of *numerous,* we call its **diction**—its choice of words—**concrete,** or particular, rather than **abstract,** or general. In an apt criticism, William Butler Yeats once took to task the poems of W. E. Henley for being "abstract, as even an actor's movement can be when the thought of doing is plainer to his mind than the doing itself: the straight line from cup to lip, let us say, more plain than the hand's own sensation weighed down by that heavy spillable cup."[2] To convey the sense of that heavy spillable cup was to Yeats a goal, one that surely he attained in "Among School Children" by describing a woman's stark face: "Hollow of cheek as though it drank the wind / And took a mess of shadows for its meat." A more abstract-minded poet might have written "Her hollow cheek and wasted, hungry look." Ezra Pound gave a famous piece of advice to his fellow poets: "Go in fear of abstractions." This is not to say that a poet cannot employ abstract words, nor that all poems have to be about physical things. Much of T. S. Eliot's *Four Quartets* is concerned with time, eternity, history, language, reality, and other things that cannot be handled. But Eliot, however high he may soar for a general view, keeps returning to earth. He makes us aware of *things,* as Thomas Carlyle said a good writer has to do: "Wonderful it is with what cutting words, now and then, he severs asunder the confusion; shears it down, were it furlongs deep, into the true center of the matter; and there not only hits the nail on the head, but with crushing force smites it home, and buries it." Like other good

[2] *The Trembling of the Veil* (1922), reprinted in *The Autobiography of William Butler Yeats* (New York: Macmillan, 1953), p. 177.

writers, good poets remind us of that smitten nail and that spillable cup. 'Perhaps indeed," wrote Walt Whitman in *Specimen Days,* "the efforts of the true poets, founders, religions, literatures, all ages, have been, and ever will be, our time and times to come, essentially the same – to bring people back from their persistent strayings and sickly abstractions, to the costless, average, divine, original concrete."

Knute Skinner (b. 1929)

THE COLD IRISH EARTH 1968

I shudder thinking
of the cold Irish earth.
The firelighter flares
in the kitchen range,
but a cold rain falls
all around Liscannor.
It scours the Hag's face
on the Cliffs of Moher.
It runs through the bog
and seeps up into mounds
of abandoned turf.
My neighbor's fields are chopped
by the feet of cattle
sinking down to the roots
of winter grass.
That coat hangs drying now
by the kitchen range,
but down at Healy's cross
the Killaspuglonane graveyard
is wet to the bone.

QUESTIONS

1. To what familiar phrase does Skinner's poem lend fresh meaning? What is its usual meaning?
2. What details in the poem show us that, in using the old phrase, Skinner literally means what he says?

Henry Taylor (b. 1942)

RIDING A ONE-EYED HORSE 1975

One side of his world is always missing.
You may give it a casual wave of the hand
or rub it with your shoulder as you pass,
but nothing on his blind side ever happens.

Hundreds of trees slip past him into darkness,
drifting into a hollow hemisphere
whose sounds you will have to try to explain.
Your legs will tell him not to be afraid

if you learn never to lie. Do not forget
to turn his head and let what comes come seen:
he will jump the fences he has to if you swing
toward them from the side that he can see

and hold his good eye straight. The heavy dark
will stay beside you always; let him learn
to lean against it. It will steady him
and see you safely through diminished fields.

Question

Do you read this poem as a fable in which the horse stands for something, or as a set of instructions for riding a one-eyed horse?

Robert Graves (b. 1895)

Down, Wanton, Down!

1933

Down, wanton, down! Have you no shame
That at the whisper of Love's name,
Or Beauty's, presto! up you raise
Your angry head and stand at gaze?

Poor bombard-captain, sworn to reach
The ravelin and effect a breach—
Indifferent what you storm or why,
So be that in the breach you die!

Love may be blind, but Love at least
Knows what is man and what mere beast;
Or Beauty wayward, but requires
More delicacy from her squires.

Tell me, my witless, whose one boast
Could be your staunchness at the post,
When were you made a man of parts
To think fine and profess the arts?

Will many-gifted Beauty come
Bowing to your bald rule of thumb,
Or Love swear loyalty to your crown?
Be gone, have done! Down, wanton, down!

Down, Wanton, Down! 5. *bombard-captain:* officer in charge of a bombard, an early type of cannon that hurled stones. 6. *ravelin:* fortification with two faces that meet in a protruding angle. *effect a breach:* break an opening through (a fortification). 15. *man of parts:* man of talent or ability.

Questions

1. How do you define a wanton?
2. What wanton does the poet address?
3. Explain the comparison drawn in the second stanza.
4. In line 14, how many meanings do you find in *staunchness at the post*?
5. Explain any other puns you find in lines 15–19.
6. Do you take this to be a cynical poem making fun of Love and Beauty, or is Graves making fun of stupid, animal lust?

Peter Davison (b. 1928)

The Last Word 1970

When I saw your head bow, I knew I had beaten you.
You shed no tears—not near me—but held your neck
Bare for the blow I had been too frightened
Ever to deliver, even in words. And now,
In spite of me, plummeting it came.
Frozen we both waited for its fall.

Most of what you gave me I have forgotten
With my mind but taken into my body,
But this I remember well: the bones of your neck
And the strain in my shoulders as I heaved up that huge
Double blade and snapped my wrists to swing
The handle down and hear the axe's edge
Nick through your flesh and creak into the block.

Questions

1. "The Last Word" stands fourth in a series titled "Four Love Poems." Sum up what happens in this poem. Do you take this to be *merely* a literal account of an execution? Explain the comparison.
2. Which words embody concrete things and show us physical actions? Which words have sounds that especially contribute to the poem's effectiveness?

David B. Axelrod (b. 1943)

Once in a While a Protest Poem 1976

Over and over again the papers print
the dried-out tit of an African woman
holding her starving child. Over
and over, cropping it each time to one
prominent, withered tit, the feeble
infant face. Over and over to toughen
us, teach us to ignore the foam turned
dusty powder on the infant's lips,
the mother's sunken face (is cropped)
and filthy dress. The tit remains;

the tit held out for everyone to see,
reminding us only that we are not so hungry
ogling the tit, admiring it and in our
living rooms, making it a symbol of starving
millions; our sympathy as real as silicone.

Questions

1. Why is the last word in this poem especially meaningful?
2. What does the poet protest?

Miller Williams (b. 1930)

On the Symbolic Consideration of Hands and the Significance of Death

Watch people stop by bodies in funeral homes.
You know their eyes will fix on the hands and they do.
Because a hand that has no desire to make
a fist again or cut bread or lay stones
is among those things most difficult to believe.
It is believed for a fact by a very few
old nuns in France who carve beads out of knuckle bones.

Questions

1. Why, according to the poet, is it hard for us to believe in the literal fact of death? Why isn't such belief a problem for the nuns?
2. From just the title of the poem, would you expect the poem to be written in plain, simple language, or in very abstract, general language? In what kind of language *is* it written?
3. What possible reason could the poet have for choosing such a title? (Besides being a poet, Miller Williams is a critic and teacher of poetry. He probably knows many readers and students of poetry who expect poems *necessarily* to deal in symbolic considerations and large significances.)

John Donne (1572–1631)

Batter my heart, three-personed God, for You (about 1610)

Batter my heart, three-personed God, for You
As yet but knock, breathe, shine, and seek to mend.
That I may rise and stand, o'erthrow me, and bend
Your force to break, blow, burn, and make me new.
I, like an usurped town to another due,
Labor to admit You, but Oh! to no end.
Reason, Your viceroy in me, me should defend,
But is captived, and proves weak or untrue.

Yet dearly I love You, and would be lovèd fain,
But am betrothed unto Your enemy;
Divorce me, untie or break that knot again;
Take me to You, imprison me, for I,
Except You enthrall me, never shall be free,
Nor ever chaste, except You ravish me.

QUESTIONS

1. In the last line of this sonnet, to what does Donne compare the onslaught of God's love? Do you think the poem weakened by the poet's comparing a spiritual experience to something so grossly carnal? Discuss.
2. Explain the seeming contradiction in the last line: in what sense can a ravished person be *chaste*? Explain the seeming contradictions in lines 3–4 and 12–13: how can a person thrown down and destroyed be enabled to *rise and stand;* an imprisoned person be *free*?
3. In lines 5–6 the speaker compares himself to a *usurped town* trying to throw off its conqueror by admitting an army of liberation. Who is the "usurper" in this comparison?
4. Explain the comparison of *Reason* to a *viceroy* (lines 7–8).
5. Sum up in your own words the message of Donne's poem. In stating its theme, did you have to read the poem for literal meanings, figurative comparisons, or both?

THE VALUE OF A DICTIONARY

If a poet troubles to seek out the best words available, the least we can do is to find out what the words mean. The dictionary is a firm ally in reading poems; if the poems are more than a century old, it is indispensable. Meanings change. When the Elizabethan poet George Gascoigne wrote, "O Abraham's brats, O brood of blessed seed," the word *brats* implied neither irritation nor contempt. When in the seventeenth century Andrew Marvell imagined two lovers' "vegetable love," he referred to a vegetative or growing love, not one resembling a lettuce. And when King George III called a building an "awful artificial spectacle," he was not condemning it but praising it as an awe-inspiring work of art.

In reading poetry, there is nothing to be done about this inevitable tendency of language except to watch out for it. If you suspect that a word has shifted in meaning over the years, most standard desk dictionaries will be helpful, an unabridged dictionary more helpful yet, and most helpful of all the *Oxford English Dictionary (OED),* which gives, for each definition, successive examples of the word's written use down through the past thousand years. You need not feel a grim obligation to keep interrupting a poem in order to rummage the dictionary; but if the poem is worth reading very closely, you may wish any aid you can find.

One of the valuable services of poetry is to recall for us the concrete, physical sense that certain words once had, but since have lost. As the English critic H. Coombes has remarked in *Literature and Criticism,*

> We use a word like *powerful* without feeling that it is really "power-full." We do not seem today to taste the full flavor of words as we feel that Falstaff (and Shakespeare, and probably his audience) tasted them when he was applauding the virtues of "good sherris-sack," which makes the brain "apprehensive, quick, forgetive, full of nimble, fiery, and delectable shapes." And being less aware of the life and substantiality of words, we are probably less aware of the things . . . that these words stand for.

"Every word which is used to express a moral or intellectual fact," said Emerson in *The Conduct of Life,* "if traced to its root, is found to be borrowed from some material appearance. *Right* means straight; *wrong* means twisted. *Spirit* primarily means wind; *transgression,* the crossing of a line; *supercilious,* the raising of an eyebrow." Browse in a dictionary and you will discover such original concretenesses. These are revealed in your dictionary's etymologies, or brief notes on the derivation of words, given in most dictionaries near the beginning of an entry on a word; in some dictionaries, at the end of the entry. Look up *squirrel,* for instance, and you will find it comes from two Greek words meaning "shadow-tail." For another example of a common word that originally contained a poetic metaphor, look up the origin of the word *daisy.*

Experiment: *Seeing Words' Origins*

Much of the effect of the following poem depends upon our awareness of the precision with which the poet has selected his words. We can better see this by knowing their derivations. For instance, *potpourri* comes from French: *pot* plus *pourri.* What do these words mean? (If you do not know French, look up the etymology of the word in a dictionary.) Look up the definitions and etymologies of *revenance, circumstance, inspiration, conceptual, commotion, cordial,* and *azure;* and try to state the meanings these words have in Wilbur's poem.

Richard Wilbur (b. 1921)

In the Elegy Season

1950

Haze, char, and the weather of All Souls':
A giant absence mopes upon the trees:
Leaves cast in casual potpourris
Whisper their scents from pits and cellar-holes.

Or brewed in gulleys, steeped in wells, they spend
In chilly steam their last aromas, yield

From shallow hells a revenance of field
And orchard air. And now the envious mind

Which could not hold the summer in my head
While bounded by that blazing circumstance
Parades these barrens in a golden trance,
Remembering the wealthy season dead,

And by an autumn inspiration makes
A summer all its own. Green boughs arise
Through all the boundless backward of the eyes,
And the soul bathes in warm conceptual lakes.

Less proud than this, my body leans an ear
Past cold and colder weather after wings'
Soft commotion, the sudden race of springs,
The goddess' tread heard on the dayward stair,

Longs for the brush of the freighted air, for smells
Of grass and cordial lilac, for the sight
Of green leaves building into the light
And azure water hoisting out of wells.

An **allusion** is an indirect reference to any person, place, or thing —fictitious, historical, or actual. Sometimes, to understand an allusion in a poem, we have to find out something we didn't know before. But usually the poet asks of us only common knowledge. When Edgar Allan Poe refers to "the glory that was Greece / And the grandeur that was Rome," he assumes that we have heard of those places, and that we will understand his allusion to the cultural achievement of those nations (implicit in *glory* and *grandeur*).

Allusions not only enrich the meaning of a poem, they also save space. In "The Love Song of J. Alfred Prufrock" (page 310), T. S. Eliot, by giving a brief introductory quotation from the speech of a damned soul in Dante's *Inferno,* is able to suggest that his poem will be the confession of a soul in torment, who sees no chance of escape.

Often in reading a poem you will meet a name you don't recognize, on which the meaning of a line (or perhaps a whole poem) seems to depend. In this book, most such unfamiliar references and allusions are glossed or footnoted, but when you venture out on your own in reading poems, you may find yourself needlessly perplexed unless you look up such names, the way you look up any other words. Unless the name is one that the poet made up, you will probably find it in one of the larger desk dictionaries, such as *Webster's New Collegiate Dictionary, The American Heritage Dictionary,* or *The American College Dictionary.* If you don't solve your problem there, try an encyclopedia, a world atlas, or *The New Century Cyclopedia of Names.*

Some allusions are quotations from other poems. In L. E. Sissman's "In and Out: A Home Away from Home," the narrator, a male college student, describes his sleeping love,

> This Sally now does like a garment wear
> The beauty of the evening; silent, bare,
> Hips, shoulders, arms, tresses, and temples lie.

(For the source of these lines, see Wordsworth's "Composed upon Westminster Bridge," page 390.)

EXERCISE: *Catching Allusions*

From your knowledge, supplemented by a dictionary or other reference work if need be, explain the allusions in the following four poems.

Cid Corman (b. 1924)

THE TORTOISE 1964

Always to want to
go back, to correct
an error, ease a

guilt, see how a friend
is doing. And yet
one doesnt, except

in memory, in
dreams. The land remains
desolate. Always

the feeling is of
terrible slowness
overtaking haste.

J. V. Cunningham (b. 1911)

FRIEND, ON THIS SCAFFOLD THOMAS MORE LIES DEAD 1960

Friend, on this scaffold Thomas More lies dead
Who would not cut the Body from the Head.

Herman Melville (1819–1891)

THE PORTENT (1859)

Hanging from the beam,
  Slowly swaying (such the law),
Gaunt the shadow on your green,
  Shenandoah!

The cut is on the crown
  (Lo, John Brown),
And the stabs shall heal no more.

Hidden in the cap
  Is the anguish none can draw;
So your future veils its face,
  Shenandoah!

But the streaming beard is shown
  (Weird John Brown),
The meteor of the war.

John Dryden (1631–1700)

LINES PRINTED UNDER THE ENGRAVED PORTRAIT OF MILTON 1668

Three poets, in three distant ages born,
Greece, Italy, and England did adorn.
The first in loftiness of thought surpassed,
The next in majesty, in both the last:
The force of Nature could no farther go;
To make a third she joined the former two.

LINES PRINTED UNDER THE ENGRAVED PORTRAIT OF MILTON. These lines appeared in Tonson's folio edition of *Paradise Lost* (1668).

John Clare (1793–1864)

MOUSE'S NEST (about 1835)

I found a ball of grass among the hay
And progged it as I passed and went away;
And when I looked I fancied something stirred,
And turned again and hoped to catch the bird—
When out an old mouse bolted in the wheats
With all her young ones hanging at her teats;
She looked so odd and so grotesque to me,
I ran and wondered what the thing could be,
And pushed the knapweed bunches where I stood;
Then the mouse hurried from the craking° brood. *crying*
The young ones squeaked, and as I went away
She found her nest again among the hay.
The water o'er the pebbles scarce could run
And broad old cesspools glittered in the sun.

Questions

1. "To prog" (line 2) means "to poke about for food, to forage." In what ways does this word fit more exactly here than *prodded, touched,* or *searched*?
2. Is *craking* (line 10) better than *crying*? Which word better fits the poem? Why?
3. What connections do you find between the last two lines and the rest of the poem? To what are water that *scarce could run* and *broad old cesspools* (lines 13 and 14) likened?

Lewis Carroll
[Charles Lutwidge Dodgson] (1832–1898)

Jabberwocky 1871

'Twas brillig, and the slithy toves
 Did gyre and gimble in the wabe:
All mimsy were the borogoves,
 And the mome raths outgrabe.

"Beware the Jabberwock, my son!
 The jaws that bite, the claws that catch!
Beware the Jubjub bird, and shun
 The frumious Bandersnatch!"

He took his vorpal sword in hand;
 Long time the manxome foe he sought—
So rested he by the Tumtum tree
 And stood awhile in thought.

And, as in uffish thought he stood,
 The Jabberwock, with eyes of flame,
Came whiffling through the tulgey wood,
 And burbled as it came!

One, two! One, two! And through and through
 The vorpal blade went snicker-snack!
He left it dead, and with its head
 He went galumphing back.

"And hast thou slain the Jabberwock?
 Come to my arms, my beamish boy!
O frabjous day! Callooh, Callay!"
 He chortled in his joy.

'Twas brillig, and the slithy toves
 Did gyre and gimble in the wabe:
All mimsy were the borogoves,
 And the mome raths outgrabe.

Jabberwocky. Fussy about pronunciation, Carroll in his preface to *The Hunting of the Snark* declares: "The first 'o' in 'borogoves' is pronounced like the 'o' in 'borrow.' I have heard people try to give it the sound of the 'o' in 'worry.' Such is Human Perversity." *Toves,* he adds, rimes with *groves.*

Questions

1. Look up *chortled* (line 24) in your dictionary and find out its definition and origin.
2. In *Through the Looking-Glass,* Alice seeks the aid of Humpty Dumpty to decipher the meaning of this nonsense poem. "*Brillig,*" he explains, "means four o'clock in the afternoon—the time when you begin *broiling* things for dinner." Does *brillig* sound like any other familiar word?
3. "*Slithy,*" the explanation goes on, "means 'lithe and slimy.' 'Lithe' is the same as 'active.' You see it's like a portmanteau—there are two meanings packed up into one word." *Mimsy* is supposed to pack together both "flimsy" and "miserable." In the rest of the poem, what other portmanteau—or packed suitcase—words can you find?

Wallace Stevens (1879–1955)

Metamorphosis — 1942

Yillow, yillow, yillow,
Old worm, my pretty quirk,
How the wind spells out
Sep - tem - ber. . . .

Summer is in bones.
Cock-robin's at Caracas.
Make o, make o, make o,
Oto - otu - bre.

And the rude leaves fall.
The rain falls. The sky
Falls and lies with the worms.
The street lamps

Are those that have been hanged.
Dangling in an illogical
To and to and fro
Fro Niz - nil - imbo.

Questions

1. Explain the title. Of the several meanings of *metamorphosis* given in a dictionary, which best applies to the process that Stevens sees in the natural world?
2. What metamorphosis is also taking place in the *language* of the poem? How does it continue from line 4 to line 8 to line 16?
3. In the last line, which may recall the thickening drone of a speaker lapsing into sleep, *Niz - nil - imbo* seems not only a pun on the name of a month, but also a portmanteau word into which at least two familiar words are packed. Say it aloud. What are they?
4. What dictionary definitions of the word *quirk* seem relevant to line 2? How can a worm be a quirk? What else in this poem seems quirky?

J. V. Cunningham (b. 1911)

Motto for a Sun Dial 1947

I who by day am function of the light
Am constant and invariant by night.

Question

In mathematics, what do the words *function* and *constant* mean?

WORD CHOICE AND WORD ORDER

Even if Samuel Johnson's famous *Dictionary* of 1755 had been as thick as Webster's unabridged, an eighteenth-century poet searching through it for words to use would have had a narrower choice. For in English literature of the **neoclassical period** or **Augustan age**—that period from about 1660 into the late eighteenth century—many poets subscribed to a belief in **poetic diction:** "A system of words," said Dr. Johnson, "refined from the grossness of domestic use." The system admitted into a serious poem only certain words and subjects, excluding others as violations of **decorum** (propriety). Accordingly such common words as *rat, cheese, big, sneeze,* and *elbow,* although admissible to satire, were thought inconsistent with the loftiness of tragedy, epic, ode, and elegy. Dr. Johnson's biographer, James Boswell, tells how a poet writing an epic reconsidered the word "rats" and instead wrote "the whiskered vermin race." Johnson himself objected to Lady Macbeth's allusion to her "keen knife," saying that "we do not immediately conceive that any crime of importance is to be committed with a knife; or who does not, at last, from the long habit of connecting a knife with sordid offices, feel aversion rather than terror?" Probably Johnson was here the victim of his age, and Shakespeare was right, but Johnson in one of his assumptions was right too: there are inappropriate words as well as appropriate ones.

Neoclassical poets chose their classical models more often from Roman writers than from Greek, as their diction suggests by the frequency of Latin derivatives. For example, a *net,* according to Dr. Johnson's dictionary, is "any thing reticulated or decussated, at equal distances, with interstices between the intersections." In company with Latinate words often appeared fixed combinations of adjective and noun ("finny prey" for "fish"), poetic names (a song to a lady named Molly might rechristen her Parthenia), and allusions to classical mythology. Neoclassical poetic diction was evidently being abused when, instead of saying "uncork the bottle," a poet could write,

> Apply thine engine to the spongy door,
> Set *Bacchus* from his glassy prison free,

in some bad lines ridiculed by Alexander Pope in *Peri Bathous, or, Of the Art of Sinking in Poetry*.

Not all poetic diction is excess baggage. To a reader who knew at first hand both living sheep and the pastoral poems of Virgil—as most readers nowadays do not—such a fixed phrase as "the fleecy care," which seems stilted to us, conveyed pleasurable associations. But "fleecy care" was more than a highfalutin way of saying "sheep"; as one scholar has pointed out, "when they wished, our poets could say 'sheep' as clearly and as often as anybody else. In the first place, 'fleecy' drew attention to wool, and demanded the appropriate visual image of sheep; for aural imagery the poets would refer to 'the bleating kind'; it all depended upon what was happening in the poem."[3]

Other poets have found some special kind of poetic language valuable: Old English poets, with their standard figures of speech ("whale-road" for the sea, "ring-giver" for a ruler);[4] makers of folk ballads who, no less than neoclassicists, love fixed epithet-noun combinations ("milk-white steed," "blood-red wine," "steel-driving man"); and Edmund Spenser, whose example made popular the adjective ending in *-y* (*fleecy, grassy, milky*).

When Wordsworth, in his Preface to *Lyrical Ballads,* asserted that "the language really spoken by men," especially by humble rustics, is plainer, more emphatic, and conveys "elementary feelings . . . in a state of greater simplicity," he was, in effect, advocating a new poetic diction. Wordsworth's ideas invited freshness into English poetry and, by admitting words that neoclassical poets would have called "low" ("His poor old *ankles* swell"), helped rid poets of the fear of being thought foolish for mentioning a commonplace.

This theory of the superiority of rural diction was, as Coleridge pointed out, hard to adhere to, and, in practice, Wordsworth was occasionally to write a language as Latinate and citified as these lines on yew trees:

> Huge trunks!—and each particular trunk a growth
> Of intertwisted fibers serpentine
> Up-coiling, and inveterately convolved . . .

Language so Latinate sounds pedantic to us, especially the phrase *inveterately convolved.* In fact, some poets, notably Gerard Manley Hopkins, have subscribed to the view that English words derived from Anglo-Saxon (Old English) have more force and flavor than their Latin equivalents. *Kingly,* one may feel, has more power than *regal.* One argument for this view is that so many words of Old English origin—*man, wife,*

[3] Bonamy Dobrée, *English Literature in the Early Eighteenth Century, 1700–1740* (New York: Oxford University Press, 1959), p. 161.
[4] See Ezra Pound's version of an Old English poem, "The Seafarer," on page 352.

child, house, eat, drink, sleep — are basic to our living speech. It may be true that a language closer to Old English is particularly fit for rendering abstract notions concretely — as does the memorable title of a medieval work of piety, the *Ayenbite of Inwit* ("again-bite of inner wisdom" or "remorse of conscience"). And yet this view, if accepted at all, must be accepted with reservations. Some words of Latin origin carry meanings both precise and physical. In the King James Bible is the admonition, "See then that ye walk circumspectly, not as fools, but as wise" (Ephesians 5:15). To be *circumspect* (a word from two Latin roots meaning "to look" and "around") is to be watchful on all sides — a meaning altogether lost in a modernized wording of the passage once printed on a subway poster for a Bible society: "Be careful how you live, not thoughtlessly but thoughtfully."

When E. E. Cummings begins a poem, "mr youse needn't be so spry / concernin questions arty," we recognized another kind of diction available to poetry: **vulgate** (speech not much affected by schooling). Handbooks of grammar sometimes distinguish various **levels of usage.** A sort of ladder is imagined, on whose rungs words, phrases, and sentences may be ranked in an ascending order of formality, from the curses of an illiterate thug to the commencement-day address of a doctor of divinity. These levels range from vulgate through **colloquial** (the casual conversation or informal writing of literate people) and **general English** (most literate speech and writing, more studied than colloquial but not pretentious), up to **formal English** (the impersonal language of educated persons, usually only written, possibly spoken on dignified occasions). Recently, however, lexicographers have been shunning such labels. The designation *colloquial* has been expelled (*bounced* would be colloquial; *trun out,* vulgate) from *Webster's Third New International Dictionary* on the grounds that "it is impossible to know whether a word out of context is colloquial or not" and that the diction of Americans nowadays is more fluid than the labels suggest. Aware that we are being unscientific, we may find the labels useful. They may help roughly to describe what happens when, as in the following poem, a poet shifts from one level of usage to another. This poem employs, incidentally, a colloquial device throughout: omitting the subjects of sentences. In keeping the characters straight, it may be helpful to fill in the speaker for each *said* and for the verbs *saw* and *ducked* (lines 9 and 10).

Josephine Miles (b. 1911)

Reason — 1955

Said, Pull her up a bit will you, Mac, I want to unload there.
Said, Pull her up my rear end, first come first serve.
Said, Give her the gun, Bud, he needs a taste of his own bumper.

Then the usher came out and got into the act:
Said, Pull her up, pull her up a bit, we need this space, sir.
Said, For God's sake, is this still a free country or what?
You go back and take care of Gary Cooper's horse
And leave me handle my own car.

Saw them unloading the lame old lady,
Ducked out under the wheel and gave her an elbow,
Said, All you needed to do was just explain;
Reason, Reason is my middle name.

Language on more than one level enlivens this miniature comedy; the vulgate of the resentful driver ("Pull her up my rear end," "leave me handle my own car") and the colloquial of the bystander ("Give her the gun"). There is also a contrast in formality between the old lady's driver, who says "Mac," and the usher, who says "sir." These varied levels of language distinguish the speakers in the poem from one another.

The diction of "Reason" is that of speech; that of Coleridge's "Kubla Khan" (page 298) is more bookish. Coleridge is not at fault, however: the language of Josephine Miles's reasonable driver might not have contained Kubla Khan's stately pleasure dome. At present, most poetry in English appears to be shunning expressions such as "fleecy care" in favor of general English and the colloquial. In Scotland, there has been an interesting development: the formation of an active group of poets who write in Scots, a **dialect** (variety of language spoken by a social group or spoken in a certain locality). Perhaps, whether poets write in language close to speech or in language of greater formality, their poems will ring true if they choose appropriate words.

Experiment: *Wheeshts into Hushes*

Reword the following poem from Scots dialect into general English, using the closest possible equivalents. Then try to assess what the poem has gained or lost. (In line 4, a "ploy," as defined by *Webster's Third New International Dictionary*, is a pursuit or activity, "especially one that requires eagerness or finesse.")

Hugh MacDiarmid
[Christopher Murray Grieve] (1892–1978)

Wheesht, Wheesht

1926

Wheest°, wheesht, my foolish hert, *hush*
For weel ye ken° *know*
I widna ha'e ye stert
Auld ploys again.

It's guid to see her lie
Sae snod° an' cool, *smooth*
A' lust o' lovin' by—
Wheesht, wheesht, ye fule!

Not only the poet's choice of words makes a poem seem more formal, or less, but also the way the words are arranged into sentences. Compare these lines,

> Jack and Jill went up the hill
> To fetch a pail of water.
> Jack fell down and broke his crown
> And Jill came tumbling after.

with Milton's account of a more significant downfall:

> Earth trembled from her entrails, as again
> In pangs, and Nature gave a second groan;
> Sky loured, and, muttering thunder, some sad drops
> Wept at completing of the mortal sin
> Original; while Adam took no thought
> Eating his fill, nor Eve to iterate
> Her former trespass feared, the more to soothe
> Him with her loved society, that now
> As with new wine intoxicated both
> They swim in mirth, and fancy that they feel
> Divinity within them breeding wings
> Wherewith to scorn the Earth.

Not all the words in Milton's lines are bookish: indeed, many of them can be found in nursery rimes. What helps, besides diction, to distinguish this account of the Biblical fall from "Jack and Jill" is that Milton's nonstop sentence seems farther removed from usual speech in its length (83 words), in its complexity (subordinate clauses), and in its word order ("with new wine intoxicated both" rather than "both intoxicated with new wine"). Should we think less (or more highly) of Milton for choosing a style so elaborate and formal? No judgment need be passed: both Mother Goose and the author of *Paradise Lost* use language appropriate to their purposes.

Among languages, English is by no means the most flexible. English words must be used in fairly definite and inviolable patterns, and whoever departs too far from them will not be understood. In the sentence "Cain slew Abel," if you change the word order, you change the meaning: "Abel slew Cain." Such inflexibility was not true of Latin, in which a poet could lay down words in almost any sequence and, because their endings (inflections) showed what parts of speech they were, could trust that no reader would mistake a subject for an object or a noun for an adjective. (E. E. Cummings has striven, in certain of his poems, for the freedom of Latin. One such poem, "anyone lived in a pretty how town," appears on page 53.)

The rigidity of English word order invites the poet to defy it and to achieve unusual effects by inverting it. It is customary in English to place adjective in front of noun (*a blue mantle, new pastures*). But an unusual emphasis is achieved when Milton ends "Lycidas" by reversing the pattern:

> At last he rose, and twitched his mantle blue:
> Tomorrow to fresh woods, and pastures new.

Perhaps the inversion in *mantle blue* gives more prominence to the color associated with heaven (and in "Lycidas," heaven is of prime importance). Perhaps the inversion in *pastures new,* stressing the *new,* heightens the sense of a rebirth.

Coleridge offered two "homely definitions of prose and poetry; that is, *prose:* words in their best order; *poetry:* the best words in the best order." If all goes well, a poet may fasten the right word into the right place, and the result may be—as T. S. Eliot said in "Little Gidding"—a "complete consort dancing together."

Thomas Hardy (1840–1928)

The Ruined Maid

1901

"O 'Melia, my dear, this does everything crown!
Who could have supposed I should meet you in Town?
And whence such fair garments, such prosperi-ty?"—
"O didn't you know I'd been ruined?" said she.

—"You left us in tatters, without shoes or socks,
Tired of digging potatoes, and spudding up docks°; *spading up dockweed*
And now you've gay bracelets and bright feathers three!"—
"Yes: that's how we dress when we're ruined," said she.

—"At home in the barton° you said 'thee' and 'thou,' *farmyard*
And 'thik oon,' and 'theäs oon,' and 't'other'; but now
Your talking quite fits 'ee for high compa-ny!"—
"Some polish is gained with one's ruin," said she.

—"Your hands were like paws then, your face blue and bleak
But now I'm bewitched by your delicate cheek,
And your little gloves fit as on any la-dy!"—
"We never do work when we're ruined," said she.

—"You used to call home-life a hag-ridden dream,
And you'd sigh, and you'd sock°; but at present you seem *groan*
To know not of megrims° or melancho-ly!"— *blues*
"True. One's pretty lively when ruined," said she.

—"I wish I had feathers, a fine sweeping gown,
And a delicate face, and could strut about Town!"—
"My dear—a raw country girl, such as you be,
Cannot quite expect that. You ain't ruined," said she.

Questions

1. Where does this dialogue take place? Who are the two speakers?
2. Comment on Hardy's use of the word *ruined*. What is the conventional meaning of the word when applied to a girl? As 'Melia applies it to herself what is its meaning?
3. Sum up the attitude of each speaker toward the other. What details of the new 'Melia does the first speaker most dwell upon? Would you expect Hardy to be so impressed by all these details, or is there, between his view of the characters and their view of themselves, any hint of an ironic discrepancy?
4. In losing her country dialect (*thik oon* and *theäs oon* for *this one* and *that one*), 'Melia is presumed to have gained in sophistication. What does Hardy suggest by her *ain't* in the last line?

E. E. Cummings (1894–1962)

ANYONE LIVED IN A PRETTY HOW TOWN 1940

anyone lived in a pretty how town
(with up so floating many bells down)
spring summer autumn winter
he sang his didn't he danced his did.

Women and men(both little and small)
cared for anyone not at all
they sowed their isn't they reaped their same
sun moon stars rain

children guessed(but only a few
and down they forgot as up they grew
autumn winter spring summer)
that noone loved him more by more

when by now and tree by leaf
she laughed his joy she cried his grief
bird by snow and stir by still
anyone's any was all to her

someones married their everyones
laughed their cryings and did their dance
(sleep wake hope and then)they
said their nevers they slept their dream

stars rain sun moon
(and only the snow can begin to explain
how children are apt to forget to remember
with up so floating many bells down)

one day anyone died i guess
(and noone stooped to kiss his face)
busy folk buried them side by side
little by little and was by was

all by all and deep by deep
and more by more they dream their sleep
noone and anyone earth by april
wish by spirit and if by yes.

Women and men(both dong and ding)
summer autumn winter spring
reaped their sowing and went their came
sun moon stars rain

Questions

1. Summarize the story told in this poem. Who are the characters?
2. Rearrange the words in the two opening lines into the order you would expect them usually to follow. What effect does Cummings obtain by his unconventional word order?
3. Another of Cummings's strategies is to use one part of speech as if it were another; for instance, in line 4, *didn't* and *did* ordinarily are verbs, but here they are used as nouns. What other words in the poem perform functions other than their expected ones?

James Emanuel (b. 1921)

The Negro

1968

Never saw him.
Never can.
Hypothetical,
Haunting man.

Eyes a-saucer,
Yessir bossir,
Dice a-clicking,
Razor flicking.

The-ness froze him
In a dance.
A-ness never
had a chance.

Questions

1. How do you think the poet would define his coined words *the-ness* and *a-ness*?
2. In your own words, sum up the theme of this poem.

Richard Eberhart (b. 1904)

THE FURY OF AERIAL BOMBARDMENT 1947

You would think the fury of aerial bombardment
Would rouse God to relent; the infinite spaces
Are still silent. He looks on shock-pried faces.
History, even, does not know what is meant.

You would feel that after so many centuries
God would give man to repent; yet he can kill
As Cain could, but with multitudinous will,
No farther advanced than in his ancient furies.

Was man made stupid to see his own stupidity?
Is God by definition indifferent, beyond us all?
Is the eternal truth man's fighting soul
Wherein the Beast ravens in its own avidity?

Of Van Wettering I speak, and Averill,
Names on a list, whose faces I do not recall
But they are gone to early death, who late in school
Distinguished the belt feed lever from the belt holding pawl.

QUESTIONS

1. As a naval officer during World War II, Richard Eberhart was assigned for a time as an instructor in a gunnery school. How has this experience apparently contributed to the diction of his poem?
2. In his *Life of John Dryden*, complaining about a description of a sea fight Dryden had filled with nautical language, Samuel Johnson argued that technical terms should be excluded from poetry. Is this criticism applicable to Eberhart's last line? Can a word succeed for us in a poem, even though we may not be able to define it? (For more evidence, see also the technical terms in Henry Reed's "Naming of Parts," p. 356.)
3. Some readers have found a contrast in tone between the first three stanzas of this poem and the last stanza. How would you describe this contrast? What does diction contribute to it?

EXERCISE: *Different Kinds of English*

Read the following poems and see what kinds of diction and word order you find in them. Which poems are least formal in their language and which most formal? Is there any use of vulgate English? Any dialect? What does each poem achieve that its own kind of English makes possible?

Anonymous (American oral verse)

CARNATION MILK (about 1900?)

Carnation Milk is the best in the land;
Here I sit with a can in my hand—
No tits to pull, no hay to pitch,
You just punch a hole in the son of a bitch.

CARNATION MILK. "This quatrain is imagined as the caption under a picture of a rugged-looking cowboy seated upon a bale of hay," notes William Harmon in his *Oxford Book of American Light Verse* (New York: Oxford University Press, 1979). Possibly the first to print this work was David Ogilvy (b. 1911), who quotes it in his *Confessions of an Advertising Man* (New York: Atheneum, 1963).

A. R. Ammons (b. 1926)

SPRING COMING — 1970

The caryophyllaceae
like a scroungy
frost are
rising through the lawn:
many-fingered as leggy
   copepods:
a suggestive delicacy,
lacework, like
the scent of wild plum
   thickets:
also the grackles
with their incredible
vertical, horizontal,
reversible
tails have arrived:
such nice machines.

William Wordsworth (1770–1850)

MY HEART LEAPS UP WHEN I BEHOLD — 1807

My heart leaps up when I behold
   A rainbow in the sky:
So was it when my life began;
So is it now I am a man;
So be it when I shall grow old,
   Or let me die!
The Child is father of the Man;
And I could wish my days to be
Bound each to each by natural piety.

William Wordsworth (1770–1850)

MUTABILITY — 1822

From low to high doth dissolution climb,
And sink from high to low, along a scale
Of awful notes, whose concord shall not fail;
A musical but melancholy chime,

Which they can hear who meddle not with crime,
Nor avarice, nor over-anxious care.
Truth fails not; but her outward forms that bear
The longest date do melt like frosty rime°, *frozen dew*
That in the morning whitened hill and plain
And is no more; drop like the tower sublime
Of yesterday, which royally did wear
His crown of weeds, but could not even sustain
Some casual shout that broke the silent air,
Or the unimaginable touch of Time.

George Starbuck (b. 1931)

Verses to Exhaust My Stock of Four-Letter Words — 1978

From the ocean floors, where the necrovores
  Of the zoöoögenous mud
Fight for their share, to the Andes where
  Bullllamas thunder and thud,

And even thence to the heavens, whence
  Archchurchmen appear to receive
The shortwave stations of rival nations
  Of angels: "Believe! Believe!"

They battle, they battle—poor put-upon cattle,
  Each waging, reluctantly,
That punitive war on the disagreeor
  Which falls to the disagreeee.

Anonymous

Scottsboro — 1936

Paper come out—done strewed de news
Seven po' chillun moan deat' house blues,
Seven po' chillun moanin' deat' house blues.
Seven nappy° heads wit' big shiny eye *kinky*
All boun' in jail and framed to die,
All boun' in jail and framed to die.

Messin' white woman—snake lyin' tale
Hang and burn and jail wit' no bail.
Dat hang and burn and jail wit' no bail.
Worse ol' crime in white folks' lan'
Black skin coverin' po' workin' man,
Black skin coverin' po' workin' man.

Judge and jury—all in de stan'
Lawd, biggety name for same lynchin' ban',
Lawd, biggety name for same lynchin' ban'.
White folks and nigger in great co't house
Like cat down cellar wit' nohole mouse.
Like cat down cellar wit' nohole mouse.

SCOTTSBORO. This folk blues, collected by Lawrence Gellert in *Negro Songs of Protest* (New York: Carl Fischer, Inc., 1936), is a comment on the Scottsboro case. In 1931 nine black youths of Scottsboro, Alabama, were arrested and charged with the rape of two white women. Though eventually, after several trials, they were found not guilty, some of them at the time this song was composed had been convicted and sentenced to death.

4 Saying and Suggesting

To write so clearly that they might bring "all things as near the mathematical plainness" as possible—that was the goal of scientists according to Bishop Thomas Sprat, who lived in the seventeenth century. Such an effort would seem bound to fail, because words, unlike numbers, are ambiguous indicators. Although it may have troubled Bishop Sprat, the tendency of a word to have multiplicity of meaning rather than mathematical plainness opens broad avenues to poetry.

Every word has at least one **denotation:** a meaning as defined in a dictionary. But the English language has many a common word with so many denotations that a reader may need to think twice to see what it means in a specific context. The noun *field,* for instance, can denote a piece of ground, a sports arena, the scene of a battle, part of a flag, a profession, and a number system in mathematics. Further, the word can be used as a verb ("he fielded a grounder") or an adjective ("field trip," "field glasses").

A word also has **connotations:** overtones or suggestions of additional meaning that it gains from all the contexts in which we have met it in the past. The word *skeleton,* according to a dictionary, denotes "the bony framework of a human being or other vertebrate animal, which supports the flesh and protects the organs." But by its associations, the word can rouse thoughts of war, of disease and death, or (possibly) of one's plans to go to medical school. Think, too, of the difference between "Old Doc Jones" and "Abner P. Jones, M.D." In the mind's eye, the former appears in his shirtsleeves; the latter has a gold nameplate on his door. That some words denote the same thing but have sharply different connotations is pointed out in this anonymous Victorian jingle:

> Here's a little ditty that you really ought to know:
> Horses "sweat" and men "perspire," but ladies only "glow."

The terms *druggist, pharmacist,* and *apothecary* all denote the same occupation, but apothecaries lay claim to special distinction.

Poets aren't the only people who care about the connotations of language. Advertisers know that connotations make money. Recently a Boston automobile dealer advertised his secondhand cars not as "used" but as "pre-owned," as if fearing that "used car" would connote an old heap with soiled upholstery and mysterious engine troubles that somebody couldn't put up with. "Pre-owned," however, suggests that the previous owner has taken the trouble of breaking in the car for you. Not long ago prune-packers, alarmed by a slump in sales, sponsored a survey to determine the connotations of prunes in the public consciousness. Asked, "What do you think of when you hear the word *prunes*?" most people replied, "dried up," "wrinkled," or "constipated." Dismayed, the packers hired an advertising agency to create a new image for prunes, in hopes of inducing new connotations. Soon, advertisements began to show prunes in brightly colored settings, in the company of bikinied bathing beauties.[1]

In imaginative writing, connotations are as crucial as they are in advertising. Consider this sentence: "A new brand of journalism is being born, or spawned" (Dwight Macdonald writing in *The New York Review of Books*). The last word, by its associations with fish and crustaceans, suggests that this new journalism is scarcely the product of human beings. And what do we make of Romeo's assertion that Juliet "is the sun"? Surely even a lovesick boy cannot mean that his sweetheart is "the incandescent body of gases about which the earth and other planets revolve" (a dictionary definition). He means, of course, that he thrives in her sight, that he feels warm in her presence or even at the thought of her, that she illumines his world and is the center of his universe. Because in the mind of the hearer these and other suggestions are brought into play, Romeo's statement, literally absurd, makes excellent sense.

Here is a famous poem that groups together things with similar connotations: certain ships and their cargoes. (A *quinquireme*, by the way, was an ancient Assyrian vessel propelled by sails and oars.)

John Masefield (1878–1967)

CARGOES

1902

Quinquireme of Nineveh from distant Ophir,
Rowing home to haven in sunny Palestine,
With a cargo of ivory,
And apes and peacocks,
Sandalwood, cedarwood, and sweet white wine.

[1] For this and other instances of connotation-engineering, see Vance Packard's *The Hidden Persuaders* (New York: McKay, 1958), chap. 13.

Stately Spanish galleon coming from the Isthmus,
Dipping through the Tropics by the palm-green shores,
With a cargo of diamonds,
Emeralds, amethysts,
Topazes, and cinnamon, and gold moidores°. *Portuguese coins*

Dirty British coaster with a salt-caked smoke stack,
Butting through the Channel in the mad March days,
With a cargo of Tyne coal,
Road-rails, pig-lead,
Firewood, iron-ware, and cheap tin trays.

To us, as well as to the poet's original readers, the place-names in the first two stanzas suggest the exotic and faraway. Ophir, a vanished place, may have been in Arabia; according to the Bible, King Solomon sent there for its celebrated pure gold, also for ivory, apes, peacocks, and other luxury items. (See I Kings 9–10.) In his final stanza, Masefield groups commonplace things (mostly heavy and metallic), whose suggestions of crudeness, cheapness, and ugliness he deliberately contrasts with those of the precious stuffs he has listed earlier. For British readers, the Tyne is a stodgy and familiar river; the English Channel in March, choppy and likely to upset a stomach. The quinquireme is *rowing,* the galleon is *dipping,* but the dirty British freighter is *butting,* aggressively pushing. Conceivably, the poet could have described firewood and even coal as beautiful, but evidently he wants them to convey sharply different suggestions here, to go along with the rest of the coaster's cargo. In drawing such a sharp contrast between past and present, Masefield does more than merely draw up bills-of-lading. Perhaps he even implies a wry and unfavorable comment upon life in the present day. His meaning lies not so much in the dictionary definitions of his words ("*moidores:* Portuguese gold coins formerly worth approximately five pounds sterling") as in their rich and vivid connotations.

William Blake (1757–1827)

London 1794

I wander through each chartered street,
Near where the chartered Thames does flow,
And mark in every face I meet
Marks of weakness, marks of woe.

In every cry of every man,
In every infant's cry of fear,
In every voice, in every ban,
The mind-forged manacles I hear.

How the chimney-sweeper's cry
Every black'ning church appalls;
And the hapless soldier's sigh
Runs in blood down palace walls.

But most through midnight streets I hear
How the youthful harlot's curse
Blasts the new born infant's tear,
And blights with plagues the marriage hearse.

Here are only a few of the possible meanings of three of Blake's words:

chartered (lines 1, 2)

Denotations: Established by a charter (a written grant or a certificate of incorporation); leased or hired.

Connotations: Defined, limited, restricted, channeled, mapped, bound by law; bought and sold (like a slave or an inanimate object); Magna Charta; charters given crown colonies by the King.

Other Words in the Poem with Similar Connotations: *Ban,* which can denote (1) a legal prohibition; (2) a churchman's curse or malediction; (3) in medieval times, an order summoning a king's vassals to fight for him. *Manacles,* or shackles, restrain movement. *Chimney-sweeper, soldier,* and *harlot* are all hirelings.

Interpretation of the Lines: The street has had mapped out for it the direction in which it must go; the Thames has had laid down to it the course it must follow. Street and river are channeled, imprisoned, enslaved (like every inhabitant of London).

black'ning (line 10)

Denotation: Becoming black.

Connotations: The darkening of something once light, the defilement of something once clean, the deepening of guilt, the gathering of darkness at the approach of night.

Other Words in the Poem with Similar Connotations: Objects becoming marked or smudged (*marks of weakness, marks of woe* in the faces of passers-by; bloodied walls of a palace; marriage blighted with plagues); the word *appalls* (denoting not only "to overcome with horror" but "to make pale" and also "to cast a pall or shroud over"); *midnight streets.*

Interpretation of the Line: Literally, every London church grows black from soot and hires a chimney-sweeper (a small boy) to help clean it. But Blake suggests too that by profiting from the suffering of the child laborer, the church is soiling its original purity.

Blasts, blights (lines 15–16)

Denotations: Both *blast* and *blight* mean "to cause to wither" or "to ruin and destroy." Both are terms from horticulture. Frost *blasts* a bud and kills it; disease *blights* a growing plant.

Connotations: Sickness and death; gardens shriveled and dying; gusts of wind and the ravages of insects; things blown to pieces or rotted and warped.

Other Words in the Poem with Similar Connotations: Faces marked with weakness and woe; the child become a chimney-sweep; the soldier killed by war; blackening church and bloodied palace; young girl turned harlot; wedding carriage transformed into a hearse.

Interpretation of the Lines: Literally, the harlot spreads the plague of syphilis, which, carried into marriage, can cause a baby to be born blind. In a larger and more meaningful sense, Blake sees the prostitution of even one young girl corrupting the entire institution of matrimony and endangering every child.

Some of these connotations are more to the point than others; the reader of a poem nearly always has the problem of distinguishing relevant associations from irrelevant ones. We need to read a poem in its entirety and, when a word leaves us in doubt, look for other things in the poem to corroborate or refute what we think it means. Relatively simple and direct in its statement, Blake's account of his stroll through the city at night becomes an indictment of a whole social and religious order. The indictment could hardly be this effective if it were "mathematically plain," its every word restricted to one denotation clearly spelled out.

Wallace Stevens (1879–1955)

Disillusionment of Ten O'Clock 1923

The houses are haunted
By white night-gowns.
None are green,
Or purple with green rings,
Or green with yellow rings,
Or yellow with blue rings.
None of them are strange,
With socks of lace
And beaded ceintures.
People are not going
To dream of baboons and periwinkles.
Only, here and there, an old sailor,
Drunk and asleep in his boots,
Catches tigers
In red weather.

Questions

1. What are *beaded ceintures*? What does the phrase suggest?
2. What contrast does Stevens draw between the people who live in these houses and the old sailor? What do the connotations of *white-night gowns* and *sailor* add to this contrast?
3. What is lacking in these people who wear white night-gowns? Why should the poet's view of them be a "disillusionment"?

Guy Owen (1925–1982)

The White Stallion — 1969

The Runaway

A white horse came to our farm once
Leaping like dawn the backyard fence.
In dreams I heard his shadow fall
Across my bed. A miracle,
I woke beneath his mane's surprise;
I saw my face within his eyes,
The dew ran down his nose and fell
Upon the bleeding window quince. . . .

But long before I broke the spell
My father's curses sped him on,
Four flashing hooves that bruised the lawn.
And as I stumbled into dawn
I saw him scorn a final hedge,
I heard his pride upon the bridge,
Then through the wakened yard I went
To read the rage the stallion spent.

Questions

1. What do these words denote in Owen's poem: *scorn, pride, wakened, rage*? (What does the stallion do when he *scorns* the hedge? How can *pride* be heard? What has *wakened* in the yard? From what evidence can the stallion's *rage* be read?)
2. What words in the poem seem especially rich in connotations?
3. Here is one paraphrase of the poem: "A runaway horse wakes a boy up and does some damage." Make a better paraphrase, one that more accurately reflects the feelings you are left with after reading the poem.

Samuel Johnson (1709–1784)

A Short Song of Congratulation — (1780)

Long-expected one and twenty
  Ling'ring year at last is flown,

Pomp and pleasure, pride and plenty,
  Great Sir John, are all your own.

Loosened from the minor's tether;
  Free to mortgage or to sell,
Wild as wind, and light as feather
  Bid the slaves of thrift farewell.

Call the Bettys, Kates, and Jennys
  Every name that laughs at care,
Lavish of your grandsire's guineas,
  Show the spirit of an heir.

All that prey on vice and folly
  Joy to see their quarry fly:
Here the gamester light and jolly,
  There the lender grave and sly.

Wealth, Sir John, was made to wander,
  Let it wander as it will;
See the jockey, see the pander,
  Bid them come, and take their fill.

When the bonny blade carouses,
  Pockets full, and spirits high,
What are acres? What are houses?
  Only dirt, or° wet or dry. *either*

If the guardian or the mother
  Tell the woes of willful waste,
Scorn their counsel and their pother,
  You can hang or drown at last.

QUESTIONS

1. In line 5, what does *tether* denote? What does the word suggest?
2. Why are *Bettys, Kates,* and *Jennys* more meaningful names as Johnson uses them than Elizabeths, Katherines, and Genevieves would be?
3. Johnson states in line 24 the connotations that *acres* and *houses* have for the young heir. What connotations might these terms have for Johnson himself?

Timothy Steele (b. 1948)

EPITAPH 1979

Here lies Sir Tact, a diplomatic fellow
Whose silence was not golden, but just yellow.

QUESTIONS

1. To what famous saying does the poet allude?
2. What are the connotations of *golden?* Of *yellow?*

Richard Snyder (b. 1925)

A Mongoloid Child Handling Shells on the Beach 1971

She turns them over in her slow hands,
as did the sea sending them to her;
broken bits from the mazarine maze,
they are the calmest things on this sand.

The unbroken children splash and shout,
rough as surf, gay as their nesting towels.
But she plays soberly with the sea's
small change and hums back to it its slow vowels.

Questions

1. In what ways is the phrase *the mazarine maze* more valuable to this poem than if the poet had said "the deep blue sea"?
2. What is suggested by calling the other children *unbroken*? By saying that their towels are *nesting*?
3. How is the child like the sea? How are the other children like the surf? What do the differences between sea and surf contribute to Richard Snyder's poem?
4. What is the poet's attitude toward the child? How can you tell?
5. Since 1971, when this poem first appeared, the congenital condition once commonly named *mongolism* has come to be called *Down's syndrome,* after the physician who first identified its characteristics. The denotations of *mongolism* and *Down's syndrome* are identical. What connotations of the word *mongoloid* seem responsible for the word's fall from favor?

Geoffrey Hill (b. 1932)

Merlin 1959

I will consider the outnumbering dead:
For they are the husks of what was rich seed.
Now, should they come together to be fed,
They would outstrip the locusts' covering tide.

Arthur, Elaine, Mordred; they are all gone
Among the raftered galleries of bone.
By the long barrows of Logres they are made one,
And over their city stands the pinnacled corn.

Merlin. In medieval legend, Merlin was a powerful magician and a seer, an aide of King Arthur. 5. *Elaine:* in Arthurian romance, the beloved of Sir Launcelot. *Mordred:* Arthur's treacherous nephew by whose hand the king died. 7. *barrows:* earthworks for burial of the dead. *Logres:* name of an ancient British kingdom, according to the twelfth-century historian Geoffrey of Monmouth, who gathered legends of King Arthur.

Questions

1. What does the title "Merlin" contribute to this poem? Do you prefer to read the poem as though it is Merlin who speaks to us—or the poet?
2. Line 4 alludes to the plague of locusts that God sent upon Egypt (Exodus 10): "For they covered the face of the whole earth, so that the land was darkened . . ." With this allusion in mind, explain the comparison of the dead to locusts.
3. Why are the suggestions inherent in the names of *Arthur, Elaine,* and *Mordred* more valuable to this poem than those we might find in the names of other dead persons called, say, Gus, Tessie, and Butch?
4. Explain the phrase in line 6: *the raftered galleries of bone.*
5. In the last line, what *city* does the poet refer to? Does he mean some particular city, or is he making a comparison?
6. What is interesting in the adjective *pinnacled*? How can it be applied to corn?

Wallace Stevens (1879–1955)

The Emperor of Ice-Cream

1923

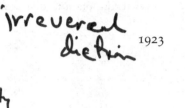

Call the roller of big cigars,
The muscular one, and bid him whip
In kitchen cups concupiscent curds.
Let the wenches dawdle in such dress
As they are used to wear, and let the boys
Bring flowers in last month's newspapers.
Let be be finale of seem.
The only emperor is the emperor of ice-cream.

Take from the dresser of deal,
Lacking the three glass knobs, that sheet
On which she embroidered fantails once
And spread it so as to cover her face.
If her horny feet protrude, they come
To show how cold she is, and dumb.
Let the lamp affix its beam.
The only emperor is the emperor of ice-cream.

The Emperor of Ice-Cream. 9. *deal:* fir or pine wood used to make cheap furniture.

Questions

1. What scene is taking place in the first stanza? Describe it in your own words. What are your feelings about it?
2. Who do you suppose to be the dead person in the second stanza? What can you infer about her? What do you know about her for sure?
3. Make a guess about this mysterious emperor. Who do you take him to be?
4. What does ice cream mean to you? In this poem, what do you think it means to Stevens?

Robert Frost (1874–1963)

Fire and Ice

1923

Some say the world will end in fire,
Some say in ice.
From what I've tasted of desire
I hold with those who favor fire.
But if it had to perish twice,
I think I know enough of hate
To say that for destruction ice
Is also great
And would suffice.

Questions

1. To whom does Frost refer in line 1? In line 2?
2. What connotations of *fire* and *ice* contribute to the richness of Frost's comparison?

5 Imagery

Ezra Pound (1885–1972)

In a Station of the Metro — 1916

The apparition of these faces in the crowd;
Petals on a wet, black bough.

Pound said he wrote this poem to convey an experience: emerging one day from a train in the Paris subway (*Métro*), he beheld "suddenly a beautiful face, and then another and another." Originally he had described his impression in a poem thirty lines long. In this final version, each line contains an **image,** which, like a picture, may take the place of a thousand words.

Though the term *image* suggests a thing seen, when speaking of images in poetry we generally mean *a word or sequence of words that refers to any sensory experience.* Often this experience is a sight (**visual imagery,** as in Pound's poem), but it may be a sound (**auditory imagery**) or a touch (**tactile imagery,** as a perception of roughness or smoothness). It may be an odor or a taste or perhaps a bodily sensation such as pain, the prickling of gooseflesh, the quenching of thirst, or—as in the following brief poem—the perception of something cold.

Taniguchi Buson (1715–1783)

The piercing chill I feel — (about 1760)

The piercing chill I feel:
 my dead wife's comb, in our bedroom,
  under my heel . . .

—Translated by Harold G. Henderson

As in this **haiku** (in Japanese, a poem of about seventeen syllables) an image can convey a flash of understanding. Had he wished, the poet might have spoken of the dead woman, of the contrast between her death and his memory of her, of his feelings toward death in general. But such a discussion would be quite different from the poem he actually wrote. Striking his bare foot against the comb, now cold and motionless but associated with the living wife (perhaps worn in her hair), the widower feels a shock as if he had touched the woman's corpse. A literal, physical sense of death is conveyed; the abstraction "death" is understood through the senses. To render the abstract in concrete terms is what poets often try to do; in this attempt, an image can be valuable.

An image may occur in a single word, a phrase, a sentence, or, as in this case, an entire short poem. To speak of the **imagery** of a poem—all its images taken together—is often more useful than to speak of separate images. To divide Buson's haiku into five images—*chill, wife, comb, bedroom, heel*—is possible, for any noun that refers to a visible object or a sensation is an image, but this is to draw distinctions that in themselves mean little and to disassemble a single experience.

Does an image cause a reader to experience a sense impression? Not quite. Reading the word *petals,* no one literally sees petals; but the occasion is given for imagining them. The image asks to be seen with the mind's eye. And although "In a Station of the Metro" records what Ezra Pound saw, it is of course not necessary for a poet actually to have lived through a sensory experience in order to write it. Keats may never have seen a newly discovered planet through a telescope, despite the image in his sonnet on Chapman's Homer (p. 336).

It is tempting to think of imagery as mere decoration, particularly when we read Keats, who fills his poems with an abundance of sights, sounds, odors, and tastes. But a successful image is not just a dab of paint or a flashy bauble. When Keats opens "The Eve of St. Agnes" with what have been called the coldest lines in literature, he evokes by a series of images a setting and a mood:

> St. Agnes' eve—Ah, bitter chill it was!
> The owl, for all his feathers, was a-cold;
> The hare limped trembling through the frozen grass,
> And silent was the flock in woolly fold:
> Numb were the Beadsman's fingers, while he told
> His rosary, and while his frosted breath,
> Like pious incense from a censer old,
> Seemed taking flight for heaven, without a death, . . .

Indeed, some literary critics look for much of the meaning of a poem in its imagery, wherein they expect to see the mind of the poet more truly revealed than in whatever the poet explicitly claims to believe. In his investigation of Wordsworth's "Ode: Intimations of Immortality," the critic Cleanth Brooks devotes his attention to the imagery of light and darkness, which he finds carries on and develops Wordsworth's thought.[1]

Though Shakespeare's Theseus (in *A Midsummer Night's Dream*) accuses poets of being concerned with "airy nothings," poets are usually very much concerned with what is in front of them. This concern is of use to us. Perhaps, as Alan Watts has remarked, Americans are not the materialists they are sometimes accused of being. How could anyone taking a look at an American city think that its inhabitants deeply cherish material things? Involved in our personal hopes and apprehensions, anticipating the future so hard that much of the time we see the present through a film of thought across our eyes, perhaps we need a poet occasionally to remind us that even the coffee we absentmindedly sip comes in (as Yeats put it) a "heavy spillable cup."

"The greatest poverty," wrote Wallace Stevens, "is not to live / In a physical world." In his own poems, Stevens makes us aware of our world's richness. He can take even a common object sold by the pound in supermarkets and, with precise imagery, recall to us what we had forgotten we ever knew about it.

Wallace Stevens (1879–1955)

Study of Two Pears

1942

I

Opusculum paedagogum°. *a little work that teaches*
The pears are not viols,
Nudes or bottles.
They resemble nothing else.

II

They are yellow forms
Composed of curves
Bulging toward the base.
They are touched red.

III

They are not flat surfaces
Having curved outlines.
They are round
Tapering toward the top.

IV

In the way they are modeled
There are bits of blue.

[1] "Wordsworth and the Paradox of the Imagination," in *The Well Wrought Urn* (New York: Harcourt Brace Jovanovich, 1956).

A hard dry leaf hangs
From the stem.

V

The yellow glistens.
It glistens with various yellows,
Citrons, oranges and greens
Flowering over the skin.

VI

The shadows of the pears
Are blobs on the green cloth.
The pears are not seen
As the observer wills.

Questions

1. What is Stevens's point in paying so much attention to what pears *don't* look like? Comment in particular on his poem's last two lines.
2. How hard is it to visualize the two pears? How clear are the poet's descriptions?

Experiment: *Illustrating a Poem*

Let an artist in the class sketch Stevens's two pears in color, following the poem as faithfully as possible, trying to add little that the poem doesn't call for. Then let the class compare poem and picture. A question for the artist: in rendering which details was it necessary to use your own imagination?

Theodore Roethke (1908–1963)

Root Cellar 1948

Nothing would sleep in that cellar, dank as a ditch,
Bulbs broke out of boxes hunting for chinks in the dark,
Shoots dangled and drooped,
Lolling obscenely from mildewed crates,
Hung down long yellow evil necks, like tropical snakes.
And what a congress of stinks!—
Roots ripe as old bait,
Pulpy stems, rank, silo-rich,
Leaf-mold, manure, lime, piled against slippery planks.
Nothing would give up life:
Even the dirt kept breathing a small breath.

Questions

1. As a boy growing up in Saginaw, Michigan, Theodore Roethke spent much of his time in a large commercial greenhouse run by his family. What details in his poem show more than a passing acquaintance with growing things?
2. What varieties of image does "Root Cellar" contain? Point out examples.

3. Which lines contain personifications, metaphors, or similes? How large a part of this poem is composed of these figures of speech?
4. What do you understand to be Roethke's attitude toward the root cellar? Does he view it as a disgusting chamber of horrors? Pay special attention to the last two lines.

Elizabeth Bishop (1911–1979)

THE FISH

1946

I caught a tremendous fish
and held him beside the boat
half out of water, with my hook
fast in a corner of his mouth.
He didn't fight.
He hadn't fought at all.
He hung a grunting weight,
battered and venerable
and homely. Here and there
his brown skin hung in strips
like ancient wall-paper,
and its pattern of darker brown
was like wall-paper:
shapes like full-blown roses
stained and lost through age.
He was speckled with barnacles,
fine rosettes of lime,
and infested
with tiny white sea-lice,
and underneath two or three
rags of green weed hung down.
While his gills were breathing in
the terrible oxygen
—the frightening gills,
fresh and crisp with blood,
that can cut so badly—
I thought of the coarse white flesh
packed in like feathers,
the big bones and the little bones,
the dramatic reds and blacks
of his shiny entrails,
and the pink swim-bladder
like a big peony.
I looked into his eyes
which were far larger than mine
but shallower, and yellowed,
the irises backed and packed
with tarnished tinfoil
seen through the lenses

of old scratched isinglass.
They shifted a little, but not
to return my stare.
—It was more like the tipping
of an object toward the light.
I admired his sullen face,
the mechanism of his jaw,
and then I saw
that from his lower lip
—if you could call it a lip—
grim, wet, and weapon-like,
hung five old pieces of fish-line,
or four and a wire leader
with the swivel still attached,
with all their five big hooks
grown firmly in his mouth.
A green line, frayed at the end
where he broke it, two heavier lines,
and a fine black thread
still crimped from the strain and snap
when it broke and he got away.
Like medals with their ribbons
frayed and wavering,
a five-haired beard of wisdom
trailing from his aching jaw.
I stared and stared
and victory filled up
the little rented boat,
from the pool of bilge
where oil had spread a rainbow
around the rusted engine
to the bailer rusted orange,
the sun-cracked thwarts,
the oarlocks on their strings,
the gunnels—until everything
was rainbow, rainbow, rainbow!
And I let the fish go.

Questions

1. How many abstract words does this poem contain? What proportion of the poem is imagery?
2. What is the speaker's attitude toward the fish? Comment in particular on lines 61–64.
3. What attitude do the images of the rainbow of oil (line 69), the orange bailer (bailing bucket, line 71), the *sun-cracked thwarts* (line 72) convey? Does the poet expect us to feel mournful because the boat is in such sorry condition?
4. What is meant by *rainbow, rainbow, rainbow*?
5. How do these images prepare us for the conclusion? Why does the speaker let the fish go?

Ray Young Bear (b. 1950)

GRANDMOTHER 1980

if i were to see
her shape from a mile away
i'd know so quickly
that it would be her.
the purple scarf
and the plastic
shopping bag.
if i felt
hands on my head
i'd know that those
were her hands
warm and damp
with the smell
of roots.
if i heard
a voice
coming from
a rock
i'd know
and her words
would flow inside me
like the light
of someone
stirring ashes
from a sleeping fire
at night.

QUESTIONS

1. What images do you find in this poem, by a member of the Sauk and Fox (Mesquaki) tribe? To what senses do these images appeal?
2. How does the speaker feel toward his grandmother? In what words or lines does he make his feelings clear?

ABOUT HAIKU

On the one-ton temple bell
a moonmoth, folded into sleep,
sits still.

—Taniguchi Buson

The name *haiku* means "beginning-verse"—perhaps because the form may have originated in a game. Players, given a haiku, were supposed to extend its three lines into a longer poem. Haiku (the word can also be plural) tend to consist mainly of imagery, but as we saw in

Buson's lines on the cold comb, their imagery is not always only pictorial.

> Heat-lightning streak—
> through darkness pierces
> the heron's shriek.
>
> —Matsuo Basho

In the poet's account of his experience, are sight and sound neatly distinguished from each other?

Note that a haiku has little room for abstract thoughts or general observations. The following attempt, though in seventeen syllables, is far from haiku in spirit:

> Now that our love is gone
> I feel within my soul
> a nagging distress.

Unlike the author of those lines, haiku poets look out upon a literal world, seldom looking inward to *discuss* their feelings. Japanese haiku tend to be seasonal in subject, but because they are so highly compressed, they usually just *imply* a season: a blossom indicates spring; a crow on a branch, autumn; snow, winter. Not just pretty little sketches of nature (as some Westerners think), haiku assume a view of the universe in which observer and nature are not separated.

A haiku in Japanese is rimeless, its seventeen syllables usually arranged in three lines, often following a pattern of five, seven, and five syllables. Haiku written in English frequently ignore such a pattern; they may be rimed or unrimed as the poet prefers.

If you care to try your hand at haiku-writing, here are a few suggestions. Make every word matter. Include few adjectives, shun needless conjunctions. Set your poem in the present—"Haiku," said Basho, "is simply what is happening in this place at this moment." Confine your poem to what can be seen, heard, smelled, tasted, or touched. Mere sensory reports, however, will be meaningless unless they make the reader feel something—as a contemporary American writer points out in this spoof.

Richard Brautigan (b. 1935)

HAIKU AMBULANCE 1968

A piece of green pepper
  fell
off the wooden salad bowl:
  so what?

Here, freely translated, are two more Japanese haiku to inspire you. Both are by Basho (1644–1694), the greatest master of the form. Classic haiku sometimes gain from our knowing when and where they were written: the first was composed on Basho's finding the site of a famous castle, which the hero Yoshitsune and his warriors had died trying to storm, reduced to wilderness.

Green weeds of summer
grow where swordsmen's dreams
once used to shimmer.

In the old stone pool
a frogjump:
splishhhhh.

Finally, here are eight more haiku written in English, of recent origin. (Don't expect them all to observe a strict arrangement of seventeen syllables. Does any observe such an arrangement?) As in Japanese, haiku is an art of few words, many suggestions. A haiku starts us thinking and feeling. "So the reader," says Raymond Roseliep, "keeps getting on where the poet got off."

A great freight truck
lit like a town
through the dark stony desert
—Gary Snyder

After weeks of watching the roof leak
I fixed it tonight
by moving a single board
—Gary Snyder

Sprayed with strong poison
my roses are crisp this year
in the crystal vase
—Paul Goodman

the old woman holds
lilac buds
to her good ear
—Raymond Roseliep

campfire extinguished,
the woman washing dishes
in a pan of stars
—Raymond Roseliep

Into the blinding sun . . .
the funeral procession's
glaring headlights.
—Nicholas Virgilio

The green cockleburs
Caught in the thick woolly hair
Of the black boy's head.
—Richard Wright

A dawn in a tree of birds.
Another.
And then another.
—Kenneth Rexroth

FOR REVIEW AND FURTHER STUDY

Jean Toomer (1894–1967)

Reapers — 1923

Black reapers with the sound of steel on stones
Are sharpening scythes. I see them place the hones
In their hip-pockets as a thing that's done,
And start their silent swinging, one by one.

Black horses drive a mower through the weeds,
And there, a field rat, startled, squealing bleeds,
His belly close to ground. I see the blade,
Blood-stained, continue cutting weeds and shade.

QUESTIONS

1. Imagine the scene Jean Toomer describes. Which particulars most vividly strike the mind's eye?
2. What kind of image is *silent swinging*?
3. Read the poem aloud. Notice especially the effect of the words *sound of steel on stones* and *field rat, startled, squealing bleeds.* What interesting sounds are present in the very words that contain these images?
4. What feelings do you get from this poem as a whole? Would you agree with someone who said, "This poem gives us a sense of happy, carefree life down on the farm, close to nature"? Exactly what in "Reapers" makes you feel the way you do? Besides appealing to our auditory and visual imagination, what do the images contribute?

Gerard Manley Hopkins (1844–1889)

Pied Beauty — (1877)

Glory be to God for dappled things—
  For skies of couple-color as a brinded° cow; *streaked*
    For rose-moles all in stipple upon trout that swim;
Fresh-firecoal chestnut-falls; finches' wings;
  Landscape plotted and pieced—fold, fallow, and plow;
    And áll trádes, their gear and tackle and trim°. *equipment*

All things counter, original, spare, strange;
  Whatever is fickle, freckled (who knows how?)
    With swift, slow; sweet, sour; adazzle, dim;
He fathers-forth whose beauty is past change:
                Praise him.

QUESTIONS

1. What does the word *pied* mean? (Hint: what does a Pied Piper look like?)
2. According to Hopkins, what do *skies, cow, trout, ripe chestnuts, finches' wings,* and *landscapes* all have in common? What landscapes can the poet have in

mind? (Have you ever seen any *dappled* landscape while looking down from an airplane, or from a mountain or high hill?)
3. What do you make of line 6: what can carpenters' saws and ditch-diggers' spades possibly have in common with the dappled things in lines 2–4?
4. Does Hopkins refer only to contrasts that meet the eye? What other kinds of variation interest him?
5. Try to state in your own words the theme of this poem. How essential to our understanding of this theme are Hopkins's images?

John Keats (1795–1821)

Bright star! would I were steadfast as thou art (1819)

Bright star! would I were steadfast as thou art—
  Not in lone splendor hung aloft the night,
And watching, with eternal lids apart,
  Like nature's patient, sleepless Eremite° *hermit*
The moving waters at their priest-like task
  Of pure ablution round earth's human shores,
Or gazing on the new soft-fallen mask
  Of snow upon the mountains and the moors—
No—yet still steadfast, still unchangeable,
  Pillowed upon my fair love's ripening breast,
To feel for ever its soft fall and swell,
  Awake for ever in a sweet unrest,
Still, still to hear her tender-taken breath,
And so live ever—or else swoon to death.

Questions

1. Stars are conventional symbols for love and a loved one. (Love, Shakespeare tells us in a sonnet, "is the star to every wandering bark.") In this sonnet, why is it not possible for the star to have this meaning? How does Keats use it?
2. What seems concrete and particular in the speaker's observations?
3. Suppose Keats had said *slow and easy* instead of *tender-taken* in line 13? What would have been lost?

Carl Sandburg (1878–1967)

Fog 1916

The fog comes
on little cat feet.
It sits looking
over harbor and city
on silent haunches
and then moves on.

Question

In lines 15–22 of "The Love Song of J. Alfred Prufrock" (page 310), T. S. Eliot also likens fog to a cat. Compare Sandburg's lines and Eliot's. Which passage tells us more about fogs and cats?

Experiment: *Writing with Images*

Taking the following poems as examples from which to start rather than as models to be slavishly copied, try to compose a brief poem that consists largely of imagery.

Walt Whitman (1819–1892)

The Runner — 1867

On a flat road runs the well-train'd runner;
He is lean and sinewy, with muscular legs;
He is thinly clothed—he leans forward as he runs,
With lightly closed fists, and arms partially rais'd.

T. E. Hulme (1883–1917)

Image — (about 1910)

Old houses were scaffolding once
and workmen whistling.

William Carlos Williams (1883–1963)

The Great Figure — 1921

Among the rain
and lights
I saw the figure 5
in gold
on a red
firetruck
moving
tense
unheeded
to gong clangs
siren howls
and wheels rumbling
through the dark city.

Robert Bly (b. 1926)

Driving to Town Late to Mail a Letter 1962

It is a cold and snowy night. The main street is deserted.
The only things moving are swirls of snow.
As I lift the mailbox door, I feel its cold iron.
There is a privacy I love in this snowy night.
Driving around, I will waste more time.

Gary Snyder (b. 1930)

Mid-August at Sourdough Mountain Lookout 1959

Down valley a smoke haze
Three days heat, after five days rain
Pitch glows on the fir-cones
Across rocks and meadows
Swarms of new flies.

I cannot remember things I once read
A few friends, but they are in cities.
Drinking cold snow-water from a tin cup
Looking down for miles
Through high still air.

Mid-August at Sourdough Mountain Lookout. *Sourdough Mountain:* in the state of Washington, where the poet's job at the time was to watch for forest fires.

H. D. [Hilda Doolittle] (1886–1961)

Heat 1916

O wind, rend open the heat,
cut apart the heat,
rend it to tatters.

Fruit cannot drop
through this thick air—
fruit cannot fall into heat
that presses up and blunts
the points of pears
and rounds the grapes.

Cut the heat—
plough through it,
turning it on either side
of your path.

Ted Kooser (b. 1939)

Beer Bottle 1969

In the burned-
out highway
ditch the throw-

away beer
bottle lands
standing up

unbroken,
like a cat
thrown off

of a roof
to kill it,
landing hard

and dazzled
in the sun,
right side up;

sort of a
miracle.

6 Figures of Speech

WHY SPEAK FIGURATIVELY?

"I will speak daggers to her, but use none," says Hamlet, preparing to confront his mother. His statement makes sense only because we realize that *daggers* is to be taken two ways: literally (denoting sharp, pointed weapons) and nonliterally (referring to something that can be used *like* weapons—namely, words). Reading poetry, we often meet comparisons between two things whose similarity we have never noticed before. When Marianne Moore observes that a fir tree has "an emerald turkey-foot at the top," the result is a pleasure that poetry richly affords: the sudden recognition of likenesses.

A treetop like a turkey-foot, words like daggers—such comparisons are called **figures of speech.** In its broadest definition, a figure of speech may be said to occur whenever a speaker or writer, for the sake of freshness or emphasis, departs from the usual denotations of words. Certainly, when Hamlet says he will speak daggers, no one expects him to release pointed weapons from his lips, for *daggers* is not to be read solely for its denotation. Its connotations—sharp, stabbing, piercing, wounding—also come to mind, and we see ways in which words and daggers work alike. (Words too can hurt: by striking through pretenses, possibly, or by wounding their hearer's self-esteem.) In the statement "A razor is sharper than an ax," there is no departure from the usual denotations of *razor* and *ax,* and no figure of speech results. Both objects are of the same class; the comparison is not offensive to logic. But in "How sharper than a serpent's tooth it is to have a thankless child," the objects—snake's tooth (fang) and ungrateful offspring—are so unlike that no reasonable comparison may be made between them. To find similarity, we attend to the connotations of *serpent's tooth*—biting, piercing, venom, pain—rather than to its denotations. If we are aware of the connotations of *red rose* (beauty, softness, freshness, and so forth), then the line "My love is like a red rose" need not call to mind a woman with a scarlet face and a thorny neck.

Figures of speech are not devices to state what is demonstrably untrue. Indeed they often state truths that more literal language cannot communicate; they call attention to such truths; they lend them emphasis.

Alfred, Lord Tennyson (1809–1892)

THE EAGLE 1851

He clasps the crag with crooked hands;
Close to the sun in lonely lands,
Ringed with the azure world, he stands.

The wrinkled sea beneath him crawls;
He watches from his mountain walls,
And like a thunderbolt he falls.

This brief poem is rich in figurative language. In the first line, the phrase *crooked hands* may surprise us. An eagle does not have hands, we might protest; but the objection would be a quibble, for evidently Tennyson is indicating exactly how an eagle clasps a crag, in the way that human fingers clasp a thing. By implication, too, the eagle is a person. *Close to the sun,* if taken literally, is an absurd exaggeration, the sun being a mean distance of 93,000,000 miles from the earth. For the eagle to be closer to it by the altitude of a mountain is an approach so small as to be insignificant. But figuratively, Tennyson conveys that the eagle stands above the clouds, perhaps silhouetted against the sun, and for the moment belongs to the heavens rather than to the land and sea. The word *ringed* makes a circle of the whole world's horizons and suggests that we see the world from the eagle's height; the sea becomes an aged, sluggish animal; *mountain walls,* possibly literal, also suggests a fort or castle; and finally the eagle itself is likened to a thunderbolt in speed and in power, perhaps also in that its beak is—like our abstract conception of a lightning bolt—pointed. How much of the poem can be taken literally? Only *he clasps the crag, he stands, he watches, he falls.* The rest is made of figures of speech. The result is that, reading Tennyson's poem, we gain a bird's-eye view of sun, sea, and land—and even of bird. Like imagery, figurative language refers us to the physical world.

William Shakespeare (1564–1616)

SHALL I COMPARE THEE TO A SUMMER'S DAY? 1609

Shall I compare thee to a summer's day?
Thou art more lovely and more temperate.
Rough winds do shake the darling buds of May,

Rough winds do shake the darling buds of May,
And summer's lease hath all too short a date.
Sometime too hot the eye of heaven shines,
And often is his gold complexion dimmed;
And every fair° from fair sometimes declines, *fair one*
By chance, or nature's changing course, untrimmed.
But thy eternal summer shall not fade,
Nor lose possession of that fair thou ow'st°; *ownest, have*
Nor shall death brag thou wand'rest in his shade,
When in eternal lines to time thou grow'st.
  So long as men can breathe or eyes can see,
  So long lives this, and this gives life to thee.

Howard Moss (b. 1922)

Shall I compare thee to a summer's day? 1976

Who says you're like one of the dog days?
You're nicer. And better.
Even in May, the weather can be gray,
And a summer sub-let doesn't last forever.
Sometimes the sun's too hot;
Sometimes it is not.
Who can stay young forever?
People break their necks or just drop dead!
But you? Never!
If there's just one condensed reader left
Who can figure out the abridged alphabet,
  After you're dead and gone,
  In this poem you'll live on!

Questions

1. In Howard Moss's streamlined version of Shakespeare, from a series called "Modified Sonnets (Dedicated to adapters, abridgers, digesters, and condensers everywhere)," to what extent does he use figurative language? In Shakespeare's original sonnet, how high a proportion of Shakespeare's language is figurative?
2. Compare some of Moss's lines to the corresponding lines in Shakespeare's sonnet. Why is *Even in May, the weather can be gray* less interesting than the original? In the lines on the sun (5–6 in both versions), what has Moss's modification deliberately left out? Why is Shakespeare's seeing death as a braggart memorable? Why aren't you greatly impressed by Moss's last two lines?
3. Can you explain Shakespeare's play on the word *untrimmed* (line 8)? Evidently the word can mean "divested of trimmings," but what other suggestions do you find in it?
4. How would you answer someone who argued, "Maybe Moss's language isn't as good as Shakespeare's, but the meaning is still there. What's wrong with putting Shakespeare into up-to-date words that can be understood by everybody?"

METAPHOR AND SIMILE

Life, like a dome of many-colored glass,
Stains the white radiance of Eternity.

The first of these lines (from Shelley's "Adonais") is a **simile:** a comparison of two things, indicated by some connective, usually *like, as, than,* or a verb such as *resembles.* A simile expresses a similarity. Still, for a simile to exist, the things compared have to be dissimilar in kind. It is no simile to say, "Your fingers are like mine," it is a literal observation. But to say, "Your fingers are like sausages" is to use a simile. Omit the connective—say, "Your fingers are sausages"—and the result is a **metaphor,** a statement that one thing *is* something else, which, in a literal sense, it is not. In the second of Shelley's lines, it is *assumed* that Eternity is light or radiance, and we have an **implied metaphor,** one that uses neither a connective not the verb *to be.* Here are examples:

Oh, my love is like a red, red rose.	*Simile*
Oh, my love resembles a red, red rose.	*Simile*
Oh, my love is redder than a rose.	*Simile*
Oh, my love is a red, red rose.	*Metaphor*
Oh, my love has red petals and sharp thorns.	*Implied metaphor*
Oh, I placed my love into a long-stem vase And I bandaged my bleeding thumb.	*Implied metaphor*

Often you can tell a metaphor from a simile by much more than just the presence or absence of a connective. In general, a simile refers to only one characteristic that two things have in common, while a metaphor is not plainly limited in the number of resemblances it may indicate. To use the simile "He eats like a pig" is to compare man and animal in one respect: eating habits. But to say "He's a pig" is to use a metaphor that might involve comparisons of appearance and morality as well.

In everyday speech, simile and metaphor occur frequently. We use metaphors ("She's a doll"), and similes ("The tickets are selling like hotcakes") without being fully conscious of them. If, however, we are aware that words possess literal meanings as well as figurative ones, we do not write *died in the wool* for *dyed in the wool* or *tow the line* for *toe the line,* nor do we use **mixed metaphors** as did the writer who advised, "Water the spark of knowledge and it will bear fruit," or the speaker who urged, "To get ahead, keep your nose to the grindstone, your shoulder to the wheel, your ear to the ground, and your eye on the ball." Perhaps the unintended humor of these statements comes from our seeing that the writer, busy stringing together stale metaphors, was not aware that they had any physical reference.

Unlike a writer who thoughtlessly mixes metaphors, a good poet can join together incongruous things and still keep the reader's respect.

In his ballad "Thirty Bob a Week," John Davidson has a British workingman tell how it feels to try to support a large family on small wages:

It's a naked child against a hungry wolf;
  It's playing bowls upon a splitting wreck;
It's walking on a string across a gulf
  With millstones fore-and-aft about your neck;
But the thing is daily done by many and many a one;
  And we fall, face forward, fighting, on the deck.

Like the man with his nose to the grindstone, Davidson's wage-earner is in an absurd fix; but his balancing act seems far from merely nonsensical. For every one of the poet's comparisons – of workingman to child, to bowler, to tight-rope walker, and to seaman – offer suggestions of a similar kind. All help us see (and imagine) the workingman's hard life: a brave and unyielding struggle against impossible odds.

A poem may make a series of comparisons, like Davidson's, or the whole poem may be one extended comparison:

Richard Wilbur (b. 1917)

A Simile for Her Smile — 1950

Your smiling, or the hope, the thought of it,
Makes in my mind such pause and abrupt ease
As when the highway bridgegates fall,
Balking the hasty traffic, which must sit
On each side massed and staring, while
Deliberately the drawbridge starts to rise:

Then horns are hushed, the oilsmoke rarifies,
Above the idling motors one can tell
The packet's smooth approach, the slip,
Slip of the silken river past the sides,
The ringing of clear bells, the dip
And slow cascading of the paddle wheel.

How much life metaphors bring to poetry may be seen by comparing two poems by Tennyson and Blake.

Alfred, Lord Tennyson (1809–1892)

Flower in the Crannied Wall — 1869

Flower in the crannied wall,
I pluck you out of the crannies,
I hold you here, root and all, in my hand,
Little flower – but *if* I could understand
What you are, root and all, and all in all,
I should know what God and man is.

How many metaphors does this poem contain? None. Compare it with a briefer poem on a similar theme: the quatrain that begins Blake's "Auguries of Innocence." (We follow here the opinion of W. B. Yeats who, in editing Blake's poems, thought the lines ought to be printed separately.)

William Blake (1757–1827)

To see a world in a grain of sand (about 1803)

To see a world in a grain of sand
And a heaven in a wild flower,
Hold infinity in the palm of your hand
And eternity in an hour.

Set beside Blake's poem, Tennyson's—short though it is—seems lengthy. What contributes to the richness of "To see a world in a grain of sand" is Blake's use of a metaphor in every line. And every metaphor is loaded with suggestion. Our world does indeed resemble a grain of sand: in being round, in being stony, in being one of a myriad (the suggestions go on and on). Like Blake's grain of sand, a metaphor holds much, within a small circumference.

Sylvia Plath (1932–1963)

Metaphors 1960

I'm a riddle in nine syllables,
An elephant, a ponderous house,
A melon strolling on two tendrils.
O red fruit, ivory, fine timbers!
This loaf's big with its yeasty rising.
Money's new-minted in this fat purse.
I'm a means, a stage, a cow in calf.
I've eaten a bag of green apples,
Boarded the train there's no getting off.

Questions

1. To what central fact do all the metaphors in this poem refer?
2. In the first line, what has the speaker in common with a riddle? Why does she say she has *nine* syllables?
3. How would you describe the tone of this poem? (Perhaps the poet expresses more than one attitude.) What attitude is conveyed in the metaphors of an elephant, "a ponderous house," "a melon strolling on two tendrils"? By the metaphors of red fruit, ivory, fine timbers, new-minted money? By the metaphor in the last line?

Jane Kenyon (b. 1947)

The Suitor 1978

We lie back to back. Curtains
lift and fall,
like the chest of someone sleeping.
Wind moves the leaves of the box elder;
they show their light undersides,
turning all at once
like a school of fish.
Suddenly I understand that I am happy.
For months this feeling
has been coming closer, stopping
for short visits, like a timid suitor.

Question

In each simile you find in this poem, exactly what is the similarity?

Emily Dickinson (1830–1886)

It dropped so low–in my Regard (about 1863)

It dropped so low–in my Regard–
I heard it hit the Ground–
And go to pieces on the Stones
At bottom of my Mind–

Yet blamed the Fate that flung it–*less*
Than I denounced Myself,
For entertaining Plated Wares
Upon My Silver Shelf–

Questions

1. What is *it*? What two things are compared?
2. How much of the poem develops and amplifies this comparison?

Ruth Whitman (b. 1922)

Castoff Skin 1973

She lay in her girlish sleep at ninety-six,
small as a twig.
Pretty good figure.

for an old lady, she said to me once.
Then she crawled away, leaving
a tiny stretched transparence

behind her. When I kissed her paper cheek
I thought of the snake,
of his quick motion.

QUESTIONS

1. Explain the central metaphor in "Castoff Skin."
2. What other figures of speech does the poem contain?

Denise Levertov (b. 1923)

LEAVING FOREVER

1964

He says the waves in the ship's wake
are like stones rolling away.
I don't see it that way.
But I see the mountain turning,
turning away its face as the ship
takes us away.

QUESTIONS

1. What do you understand to be the man's feelings about leaving forever? How does the speaker feel? With what two figures of speech does the poet express these conflicting views?
2. Suppose that this poem had ended in another simile (instead of its three last lines):

   I see the mountain as a suitcase
   left behind on the shore
   as the ship takes us away.

   How is Denise Levertov's choice of a figure of speech a much stronger one?

EXERCISE: *What Is Similar?*

Each of these quotations contains a simile or a metaphor. In each of these figures of speech, what two things is the poet comparing? Try to state exactly what you understand the two things to have in common: the most striking similarity or similarities that the poet sees.

1. Think of the storm roaming the sky uneasily
   like a dog looking for a place to sleep in,
   listen to it growling.
   —Elizabeth Bishop, "Little Exercise"
2. When the hounds of spring are on winter's traces . . .
   —Algernon Charles Swinburne, "Atalanta in Calydon"
3. The scarlet of the maples can shake me like a cry
   Of bugles going by.
   —Bliss Carman, "A Vagabond Song"

4. "Hope" is the thing with feathers–
That perches in the soul–
And sings the tune without the words–
And never stops–at all–
—Emily Dickinson, an untitled poem

5. Work without Hope draws nectar in a sieve . . .
—Samuel Taylor Coleridge, "Work Without Hope"

6. A new electric fence,
Its five barbed wires tight
As a steel-stringed banjo.
—Van K. Brock, "Driving at Dawn"

7. Spring stirs Gossamer Beynon schoolmistress like a spoon.
—Dylan Thomas, *Under Milk Wood*

OTHER FIGURES

When Shakespeare asks, in a sonnet,

O! how shall summer's honey breath hold out
Against the wrackful siege of batt'ring days,

it might seem at first that he mixes metaphors. How can a *breath* confront the battering ram of an invading army? But it is summer's breath and, by giving it to summer, Shakespeare makes the season a man or woman. It is as if the fragrance of summer were the breath within a person's body, and winter were the onslaught of old age.

Such is one instance of **personification:** a figure of speech in which a thing, an animal, or an abstract term (*truth, nature*) is made human. A personification extends throughout this whole short poem:

James Stephens (1882–1950)

THE WIND 1915

The wind stood up and gave a shout.
He whistled on his fingers and

Kicked the withered leaves about
And thumped the branches with his hand

And said he'd kill and kill and kill,
And so he will and so he will.

The wind is a wild man, and evidently it is not just any autumn breeze but a hurricane or at least a stiff gale. In poems that do not work as well as this one, personification may be employed mechanically. Hollow-eyed personifications walk the works of lesser English poets of the eighteenth century: Coleridge has quoted the beginning of one such neoclassical ode, "Inoculation! heavenly Maid, descend!" It is hard for the contemporary reader to be excited by William Collins's "The Passions, An Ode for Music" (1747), which personifies, stanza by stanza, Fear, Anger, Despair, Hope, Revenge, Pity, Jealousy, Love, Hate, Melancholy, and Cheerfulness, and has them listen to Music, until even "Brown Exercise rejoiced to hear, / And Sport leapt up, and seized his beechen spear." Still, the portraits of the Seven Deadly Sins in the fourteenth-century *Vision of Piers Plowman* remain memorable: "Thanne come Slothe al bislabered, with two slimy eiyen. . . ." In "Two Sonnets on Fame" John Keats makes an abstraction come alive in seeing Fame as "a wayward girl."

Hand in hand with personification often goes **apostrophe:** a way of addressing someone or something invisible or not ordinarily spoken to. In an apostrophe, a poet (in these examples Wordsworth) may address an inanimate object ("Spade! with which Wilkinson hath tilled his lands"), some dead or absent person ("Milton! thou shouldst be living at this hour"), an abstract thing ("Return, Delights!"), or a spirit ("Thou Soul that art the eternity of thought"). More often than not, the poet uses apostrophe to announce a lofty and serious tone. An "O" may even be put in front of it ("O moon!") since, according to W. D. Snodgrass, every poet has a right to do so at least once in a lifetime. But apostrophe doesn't have to be highfalutin. It is a means of giving life to the inanimate. It is a way of giving body to the intangible, a way of speaking to it person to person, as in the words of a moving American spiritual: "Death, ain't you got no shame?"

Most of us, from time to time, emphasize a point with a statement containing exaggeration: "Faster than greased lightning," "I've told him a thousand times." We speak, then, not literal truth but use a figure of speech called **overstatement** (or **hyperbole**). Poets too, being fond of emphasis, often exaggerate for effect. Instances are Marvell's profession of a love that should grow "Vaster than empires, and more slow" and Burgon's description of Petra: "A rose-red city, half as old as Time." Overstatement can be used also for humorous purposes, as in a fat woman's boast (from a blues song): "Every time I shake, some skinny gal loses her home."[1] The opposite is **understatement,** implying more than is said. Mark Twain in *Life on the Mississippi* recalls how, as an apprentice steamboat-pilot asleep when supposed to be on watch, he was roused by the pilot and sent clambering to the pilot house: "Mr. Bixby was close behind, commenting." Another example is Robert Frost's line "One could do worse than be a swinger of birches" – the conclusion of a poem that has suggested that to swing on a birch tree is one of the most deeply satisfying activities in the world.

In **metonymy,** the name of a thing is substituted for that of another closely associated with it. For instance, we say "The White House

[1] Quoted by Amiri Baraka [LeRoi Jones] in *Blues People* (New York: Wm. Morrow, 1963).

decided," and mean the president did. When John Dyer writes in "Grongar Hill,"

A little rule, a little sway,
A sun beam on a winter's day,
Is all the proud and mighty have
Between the cradle and the grave,

we recognize that *cradle* and *grave* signify birth and death. A kind of metonymy, **synecdoche** is the use of a part of a thing to stand for the whole of it or vice versa. We say "She lent a hand," and mean that she lent her entire presence. Similarly, Milton in "Lycidas" refers to greedy clergymen as "blind mouths." Another kind of metonymy is the **transferred epithet:** a device of emphasis in which the poet attributes some characteristic of a thing to another thing closely associated with it. When Thomas Gray observes that, in the evening pastures, "drowsy tinklings lull the distant folds," he well knows that sheep's bells do not drowse, but sheep do. When Hart Crane, describing the earth as seen from an airplane, speaks of "nimble blue plateaus," he attributes the airplane's motion to the earth.

Paradox occurs in a statement that at first strikes us as self-contradictory but that on reflection makes some sense. "The peasant," said G. K. Chesterton, "lives in a larger world than the globe-trotter." Here, two different meanings of *larger* are contrasted: "greater in spiritual values" versus "greater in miles." Some paradoxical statements, however, are much more than plays on words. In a moving sonnet, the blind John Milton tells how one night he dreamed he could see his dead wife. The poem ends in a paradox:

But oh, as to embrace me she inclined,
I waked, she fled, and day brought back my night.

EXERCISE: *Paradox*

What paradoxes do you find in the following poem? For each, explain the sense that underlies the statement.

Chidiock Tichborne (1558?–1586)

ELEGY, WRITTEN WITH HIS OWN HAND IN THE TOWER BEFORE HIS EXECUTION

1586

My prime of youth is but a frost of cares,
  My feast of joy is but a dish of pain,
My crop of corn is but a field of tares°, *weeds*
  And all my good is but vain hope of gain:
The day is past, and yet I saw no sun,
And now I live, and now my life is done.

My tale was heard, and yet it was not told,
  My fruit is fall'n, and yet my leaves are green,
My youth is spent, and yet I am not old,
  I saw the world, and yet I was not seen:
My thread is cut, and yet it is not spun,
And now I live, and now my life is done.

I sought my death, and found it in my womb,
  I looked for life, and saw it was a shade,
I trod the earth, and knew it was my tomb,
  And now I die, and now I was but made:
My glass is full, and now my glass is run,
And now I live, and now my life is done.

Asked to define the difference between men and women, Samuel Johnson replied, "I can't conceive, madam, can you?" The great dictionary-maker was using a figure of speech known to classical rhetoricians as *paranomasia*, better known to us as a **pun** or play on words. How does a pun operate? It reminds us of another word (or other words) of similar or identical sound but of very different denotation. Although puns at their worst can be mere piddling quibbles, at best they can sharply point to surprising but genuine resemblances. The name of a dentist's country estate, Tooth Acres, is accurate: aching teeth paid for the land. In poetry, a pun may be facetious, as in Thomas Hood's ballad of "Faithless Nelly Gray":

> Ben Battle was a soldier bold,
>   And used to war's alarms;
> But a cannon-ball took off his legs,
>   So he laid down his arms!

Or it may be serious, as in these lines on war by E. E. Cummings:

> the bigness of cannon
> is skilful,

(*is skilful* becoming *is kill-ful* when read aloud), or perhaps, as in Shakespeare's song in *Cymbeline*, "Fear no more the heat o' th' sun," both facetious and serious at once:

> Golden lads and girls all must,
> As chimney-sweepers, come to dust.

George Herbert (1593–1633)

The Pulley — 1633

  When God at first made man,
Having a glass of blessings standing by—
Let us (said he) pour on him all we can;

Let the world's riches, which dispersèd lie,
Contract into a span.

So strength first made a way,
Then beauty flowed, then wisdom, honor, pleasure:
When almost all was out, God made a stay,
Perceiving that, alone of all His treasure,
Rest in the bottom lay.

For if I should (said he)
Bestow this jewel also on My creature,
He would adore My gifts instead of Me,
And rest in Nature, not the God of Nature:
So both should losers be.

Yet let him keep the rest,
But keep them with repining restlessness;
Let him be rich and weary, that at least,
If goodness lead him not, yet weariness
May toss him to My breast.

QUESTIONS

1. What different senses of the word *rest* does Herbert bring into this poem?
2. How do God's words in line 16, *Yet let him keep the rest,* seem paradoxical?
3. What do you feel to be the tone of Herbert's poem? Does the punning make the poem seem comic?
4. Why is the poem called "The Pulley"? What is its implied metaphor?

To sum up: even though figures of speech are not to be taken *only* literally, they refer us to a tangible world. By *personifying* an eagle, Tennyson reminds us that the bird and humankind have certain characteristics in common. Through *metonymy,* a poet can focus our attention on a particular detail in a larger object; through *hyperbole* and *understatement,* make us see the physical actuality in back of words. *Pun* and *paradox* cause us to realize this actuality, too, and probably surprise us enjoyably at the same time. Through *apostrophe,* the poet animates the inanimate and asks it to listen – speaks directly to an immediate god or to the revivified dead. Put to such uses, figures of speech have power. They are more than just ways of playing with words.

Edmund Waller (1606–1687)

ON A GIRDLE

1645

That which her slender waist confined,
Shall now my joyful temples bind;
No monarch but would give his crown,
His arms might do what this has done.

It was my heaven's extremest sphere,
The pale° which held that lovely deer; *enclosure*
My joy, my grief, my hope, my love,
Did all within this circle move!

A narrow compass! and yet there
Dwelt all that's good, and all that's fair!
Give me but what this riband bound,
Take all the rest the sun goes round!

ON A GIRDLE. This girdle is a waistband or sash—not, of course, a modern "foundation garment." 1–2. *That which . . . temples bind:* A courtly lover might bind his brow with a lady's ribbon, to signify he was hers. 5. *extremest sphere:* In Ptolemaic astronomy, the outermost of the concentric spheres that surround the earth. In its wall the farthest stars are set.

QUESTIONS

1. To what things is the girdle compared?
2. Explain the pun in line 4. What effect does it have upon the tone of the poem?
3. Why is the effect of this pun different from that of Thomas Hood's play on the same word in "Faithless Nelly Gray" (quoted on p. 94)?
4. What does *compass* denote in line 9?
5. What paradox occurs in lines 9–10?
6. How many of the poem's statements are hyperbolic? Is the compliment the speaker pays his lady too grandiose to be believed? Explain.

Theodore Roethke (1908–1963)

I KNEW A WOMAN 1958

I knew a woman, lovely in her bones,
When small birds sighed, she would sigh back at them;
Ah, when she moved, she moved more ways than one:
The shapes a bright container can contain!
Of her choice virtues only gods should speak,
Or English poets who grew up on Greek
(I'd have them sing in chorus, cheek to cheek).

How well her wishes went! She stroked my chin,
She taught me Turn, and Counter-turn, and Stand;
She taught me Touch, that undulant white skin;
I nibbled meekly from her proffered hand;
She was the sickle; I, poor I, the rake,
Coming behind her for her pretty sake
(But what prodigious mowing we did make).

Love likes a gander, and adores a goose:
Her full lips pursed, the errant note to seize;
She played it quick, she played it light and loose;
My eyes, they dazzled at her flowing knees;

Her several parts could keep a pure repose,
Or one hip quiver with a mobile nose
(She moved in circles, and those circles moved).

Let seed be grass, and grass turn into hay:
I'm martyr to a motion not my own;
What's freedom for? To know eternity.
I swear she cast a shadow white as stone.
But who would count eternity in days?
These old bones live to learn her wanton ways:
(I measure time by how a body sways).

Questions

1. What outrageous puns do you find in Roethke's poem? Describe the effect of them.
2. What kind of figure of speech occurs in all three lines: *Of her choice virtues only gods should speak; My eyes, they dazzled at her flowing knees;* and *I swear she cast a shadow white as stone*?
3. What sort of figure is the poet's reference to himself as *old bones*?
4. Do you take *Let seed be grass, and grass turn into hay* as figurative language, or literal statement?
5. If you agree that the tone of this poem is witty and playful, do you think the poet is making fun of the woman? What is his attitude toward her? What part do figures of speech play in communicating it?

FOR REVIEW AND FURTHER STUDY

Robert Frost (1874–1963)

The Silken Tent 1942

She is as in a field a silken tent
At midday when a sunny summer breeze
Has dried the dew and all its ropes relent,
So that in guys° it gently sways at ease, *attachments that steady it*
And its supporting central cedar pole,
That is its pinnacle to heavenward
And signifies the sureness of the soul,
Seems to owe naught to any single cord,
But strictly held by none, is loosely bound
By countless silken ties of love and thought
To everything on earth the compass round,
And only by one's going slightly taut
In the capriciousness of summer air
Is of the slightest bondage made aware.

Questions

1. Is Frost's comparison of woman and tent a simile or a metaphor?

2. What are the ropes or cords?
3. Does the poet convey any sense of this woman's character? What sort of person do you believe her to be?
4. Paraphrase the poem, trying to state its implied meaning. (If you need to be refreshed about paraphrase, turn back to pages 398–399.) Be sure to include the implications of the last three lines.

James C. Kilgore (b. 1928)

The White Man Pressed the Locks 1970

Driving down the concrete artery,
Away from the smoky heart,
Through the darkening, blighted body,
Pausing at clotted varicose veins,
The white man pressed the locks
  on all the sedan's doors,
Sped toward the white corpuscles
  in the white arms
  hugging the black city.

Questions

1. Explain the two implied metaphors in this poem: what are the two bodies?
2. How do you take the word *hugging*? Is this a loving embrace or a stranglehold?
3. What, in your own words, is the poet's theme?

Ogden Nash (1902–1971)

Very Like a Whale 1934

One thing that literature would be greatly the better for
Would be a more restricted employment by authors of simile and metaphor.
Authors of all races, be they Greeks, Romans, Teutons or Celts,
Can't seem just to say that anything is the thing it is but have to go out of their way to say that it is like something else.
What does it mean when we are told
That the Assyrian came down like a wolf on the fold?
In the first place, George Gordon Byron had had enough experience
To know that it probably wasn't just one Assyrian, it was a lot of Assyrians.
However, as too many arguments are apt to induce apoplexy and thus hinder longevity,
We'll let it pass as one Assyrian for the sake of brevity.
Now then, this particular Assyrian, the one whose cohorts were gleaming in purple and gold,

Just what does the poet mean when he says he came down like a wolf on the fold?
In heaven and earth more than is dreamed of in our philosophy there are a great many things,
But I don't imagine that among them there is a wolf with purple and gold cohorts or purple and gold anythings.
No, no, Lord Byron, before I'll believe that this Assyrian was actually like a wolf I must have some kind of proof;
Did he run on all fours and did he have a hairy tail and a big red mouth and big white teeth and did he say Woof woof woof?
Frankly I think it very unlikely, and all you were entitled to say, at the very most,
Was that the Assyrian cohorts came down like a lot of Assyrian cohorts about to destroy the Hebrew host.
But that wasn't fancy enough for Lord Byron, oh dear me no, he had to invent a lot of figures of speech and then interpolate them,
With the result that whenever you mention Old Testament soldiers to people they say Oh yes, they're the ones that a lot of wolves dressed up in gold and purple ate them.
That's the kind of thing that's being done all the time by poets, from Homer to Tennyson;
They're always comparing ladies to lilies and veal to venison.
How about the man who wrote,
Her little feet stole in and out like mice beneath her petticoat?
Wouldn't anybody but a poet think twice
Before stating that his girl's feet were mice?
Then they always say things like that after a winter storm
The snow is a white blanket. Oh it is, is it, all right then, you sleep under a six-inch blanket of snow and I'll sleep under a half-inch blanket of unpoetical blanket material and we'll see which one keeps warm,
And after that maybe you'll begin to comprehend dimly
What I mean by too much metaphor and simile.

VERY LIKE A WHALE. The title is from *Hamlet* (Act III, scene 2): Feigning madness, Hamlet likens the shape of a cloud to a whale. "Very like a whale," says Polonius, who, to humor his prince, will agree to the accuracy of any figure at all. Nash's art has been described by Max Eastman in *Enjoyment of Laughter* (New York: Simon and Schuster, 1936):

> If you have ever tried to write rimed verse, you will recognize in Nash's writing every naïve crime you were ever tempted to commit—artificial inversions, pretended rimes, sentences wrenched and mutilated to bring the rime-word to the end of the line, words assaulted and battered into riming whether they wanted to or not, ideas and whole dissertations dragged in for the sake of a rime, the metrical beat delayed in order to get all the necessary words in, the metrical beat speeded up unconscionably because there were not enough words to put in.

QUESTIONS

1. Nash alludes to the opening lines of Byron's poem "The Destruction of Sennacherib" (see page 157):

   The Assyrian came down like the wolf on the fold,
   And his cohorts were gleaming in purple and gold;

and to Sir John Suckling's portrait of a bride in "A Ballad Upon a Wedding":

Her feet beneath her petticoat,
Like little mice stole in and out,
As if they feared the light: . . .

How can these metaphors be defended against Nash's quibbles?

2. What valuable functions of simile and metaphor in poetry is Nash pretending to ignore?

EXERCISE: *Figure Spotting*

In each of these poems, what figures of speech do you notice? For each metaphor or simile, try to state what is compared. In any use of metonymy, what is represented?

Richard Wilbur (b. 1921)

SLEEPLESS AT CROWN POINT

1976

All night, this headland
Lunges into the rumpling
Capework of the wind.

Anonymous (English)

THE FORTUNES OF WAR, I TELL YOU PLAIN

(1854–1856)

The fortunes of war, I tell you plain,
Are a wooden leg—or a golden chain.

Robert Frost (1874–1963)

THE SECRET SITS

1936

We dance round in a ring and suppose,
But the Secret sits in the middle and knows.

Margaret Atwood (b. 1939)

YOU FIT INTO ME

1971

you fit into me
like a hook into an eye

a fish hook
an open eye

Robert Graves (b. 1895)

Love Without Hope 1926

Love without hope, as when the young bird-catcher
Swept off his tall hat to the Squire's own daughter,
So let the imprisoned larks escape and fly
Singing about her head, as she rode by.

John Ashbery (b. 1927)

The Cathedral Is 1979

Slated for demolition.

Etheridge Knight (b. 1931)

For Black Poets Who Think of Suicide 1973

Black Poets should live—not leap
From steel bridges (like the white boys do).
Black Poets should live—not lay
Their necks on railroad tracks (like the white boys do).
Black Poets should seek—but not search too much
In sweet dark caves, nor hunt for snipe
Down psychic trails (like the white boys do).

For Black Poets belong to Black People. Are
The Flutes of Black Lovers. Are
The Organs of Black Sorrows. Are
The Trumpets of Black Warriors.
Let All Black Poets die as Trumpets,
And be buried in the dust of marching feet.

W. S. Merwin (b. 1927)

Song of Man Chipping an Arrowhead 1973

Little children you will all go
but the one you are hiding
will fly

Robert Burns (1759–1796)

Oh, my love is like a red, red rose (about 1788)

Oh, my love is like a red, red rose
  That's newly sprung in June;

My love is like the melody
  That's sweetly played in tune.

So fair art thou, my bonny lass,
  So deep in love am I;
And I will love thee still, my dear,
  Till a' the seas gang° dry. *go*

Till a' the seas gang dry, my dear,
  And the rocks melt wi' the sun;
And I will love thee still, my dear,
  While the sands o' life shall run.

And fare thee weel, my only love!
  And fare thee weel awhile!
And I will come again, my love
  Though it were ten thousand mile.

7 Song

SINGING AND SAYING

Most poems are more memorable than most ordinary speech, and when music is combined with poetry the result can be more memorable still. The differences between speech, poetry, and song may appear if we consider, first of all, this fragment of an imaginary conversation between two lovers:

> Let's not drink; let's just sit here and look at each other. Or put a kiss inside my goblet and I won't want anything to drink.

Forgettable language, we might think; but let's try to make it a little more interesting:

> Drink to me only with your eyes, and I'll pledge my love to you with my eyes;
> Or leave a kiss within the goblet, that's all I'll want to drink.

The passage is closer to poetry, but still has a distance to go. At least we now have a figure of speech – the metaphor that love is wine, implied in the statement that one lover may salute another by lifting an eye as well as by lifting a goblet. But the sound of the words is not yet especially interesting. Here is another try, by Ben Jonson:

> Drink to me only with thine eyes,
> And I will pledge with mine;
> Or leave a kiss but in the cup,
> And I'll not ask for wine.

In these opening lines from Jonson's poem "To Celia," the improvement is noticeable. These lines are poetry; their language has become special. For one thing, the lines rime (with an additional rime sound on *thine*). There is interest, too, in the proximity of the words *kiss* and *cup:* the repetition (or alliteration) of the *k* sound. The rhythm of the lines has become regular; generally every other word (or syllable) is stressed:

DRINK to me ON-ly WITH thine EYES,
  And I will PLEDGE with MINE;
OR LEAVE a KISS but IN the CUP,
  And I'LL not ASK for WINE.

All these devices of sound and rhythm, together with metaphor, produce a pleasing effect—more pleasing than the effect of "Let's not drink; let's look at each other." But the words became more pleasing still when later set to music:

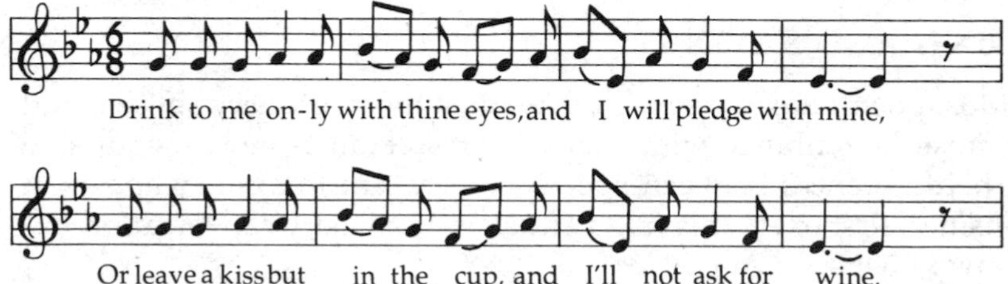

In this memorable form, the poem is still alive today.

Ben Jonson (1573?–1637)

To Celia

1616

Drink to me only with thine eyes,
  And I will pledge with mine;
Or leave a kiss but in the cup,
  And I'll not ask for wine.
The thirst that from the soul doth rise
  Doth ask a drink divine;
But might I of Jove's nectar sup,
  I would not change for thine.

I sent thee late a rosy wreath,
  Not so much honoring thee
As giving it a hope that there
  It could not withered be.
But thou thereon didst only breathe,
  And sent'st it back to me;
Since when it grows, and smells, I swear,
  Not of itself but thee.

A compliment to a lady has rarely been put in language more graceful, more wealthy with interesting sounds. Other figures of speech besides metaphor make them unforgettable: for example, the hyperbolic tributes to the power of the lady's sweet breath, which can start picked roses growing again, and her kisses, which even surpass the nectar of the gods.

This song falls into stanzas—as many poems that resemble songs also do. A **stanza** (Italian for "station," "stopping-place," or "room") is a group of lines whose pattern is repeated throughout the poem. Most songs have more than one stanza. When printed, the stanzas of songs and poems usually are set off from one another by space. When sung, stanzas of songs are indicated by a pause or by the introduction of a refrain, or chorus (a line or lines repeated). The word **verse,** which strictly refers to one line of a poem, is sometimes loosely used to mean a whole stanza: "All join in and sing the second verse!" In speaking of a stanza, whether sung or read, it is customary to indicate by a convenient algebra its **rime scheme,** the order in which rimed words recur. For instance, the rime scheme of this stanza by Herrick is *a b a b*; the first and third lines rime and so do the second and fourth:

> Round, round, the roof doth run;
>   And being ravished thus,
> Come, I will drink a tun
>   To my Propertius.

Refrains are words, phrases, or lines repeated at intervals in a song or songlike poem. A refrain usually follows immediately after a stanza, and when it does, it is called **terminal refrain.** A refrain whose words change slightly with each recurrence is called an **incremental refrain.** Sometimes we also hear an **internal refrain:** one that appears within a stanza, generally in a position that stays fixed throughout a poem. Both internal refrains and terminal refrains are used to great effect in the traditional song "The Cruel Mother":

Anonymous (traditional Scottish ballad)

The Cruel Mother

She sat down below a thorn,
  Fine flowers in the valley,
And there she has her sweet babe born
  And the green leaves they grow rarely.

"Smile na sae° sweet, my bonny babe," *so*
  Fine flowers in the valley,
"And° ye smile sae sweet, ye'll smile me dead." *if*
  And the green leaves they grow rarely.

She's taen out her little pen-knife,
  Fine flowers in the valley,

And twinned° the sweet babe o' its life, *severed*
And the green leaves they grow rarely.

She's howket° a grave by the light o' the moon, *dug*
Fine flowers in the valley,
And there she's buried her sweet babe in
And the green leaves they grow rarely.

As she was going to the church,
Fine flowers in the valley,
She saw a sweet babe in the porch
And the green leaves they grow rarely.

"O sweet babe, and thou were mine,"
Fine flowers in the valley,
"I wad cleed° thee in the silk so fine." *dress*
And the green leaves they grow rarely.

"O mother dear, when I was thine,"
Fine flowers in the valley,
"You did na prove to me sae kind."
And the green leaves they grow rarely.

Taken by themselves, the refrain lines might seem mere pretty nonsense. But interwoven with the story of the murdered child, they form a terrible counterpoint. What do they come to mean? Possibly that Nature keeps going about her chores, unmindful of sin and suffering. The effect is an ironic contrast. It is the repetitiveness of a refrain, besides, that helps to give it power.

Songs tend to be written in language simple enough to be understood on first hearing. Even the witty, trickful lyrics of Cole Porter, master songsmith for the Broadway stage, seem designed—for all their allusions—to be taken in at once. Here, for instance, is a stanza of "You're the Top," from the musical *Anything Goes* (1934):

You're the top! You're an an Arrow collar.
You're the top! You're a Coolidge dollar.
You're the nimble tread of the feet of Fred Astaire.
You're an O'Neill drama,
You're Whistler's mama,
You're Camembert.
You're a rose,
You're Inferno's Dante,
You're the nose
Of the great Durante.
I'm just in the way, as the French would say,
"De trop,"
But if, baby, I'm the bottom you're the top.

More recently, songwriters have assumed that their listeners would pay close attention to their words. Bob Dylan, Leonard Cohen, Don McLean, and others have written lyrics more complex and demanding than popular songs have featured before, requiring the listeners to play recordings many times, with trebles turned up all the way.

Many familiar poems began life as songs, but today, their tunes forgotten, they survive only in poetry anthologies. Shakespeare studded his plays with songs, and many of his contemporaries wrote verse to fit existing tunes. Some poets, themselves musicians (like Thomas Campion), composed both words and music. In Shakespeare's day, **madrigals,** short secular songs for three or more voice-parts arranged in counterpoint, enjoyed great favor. A madrigal by Chidiock Tichborne is given on page 93 and another by an anonymous poet, "The Silver Swan," on page 117.

Some poets who were not composers printed their work in madrigal books for others to set to music. In the seventeenth century, however, poetry and song seem to have fallen away from each other. By the end of the century, much new poetry, other than songs for plays, was written to be printed and to be silently read. Poets who wrote popular songs—like Thomas D'Urfey, compiler of the collection *Pills to Purge Melancholy*—were considered somewhat disreputable. With the notable exceptions of John Gay, who took existing popular tunes for *The Beggar's Opera,* and Robert Burns, who rewrote folk songs or made completely new words for them, few important English poets since Campion have been first-rate song-writers.

Occasionally, a poet has learned a thing or two from music. "But for the opera I could never have written *Leaves of Grass,*" said Walt Whitman, who loved the Italian art form for its expansiveness. Coleridge, Hardy, Auden, and many others have learned from folk ballads, and T. S. Eliot patterned his thematically repetitive *Four Quartets* after the structure of a quartet in classicial music. "Poetry," said Ezra Pound, "begins to atrophy when it gets too far from music." Still, even in the twentieth century, the poet has been more often a corrector of printer's proofs than a tunesmith or performer.

Some people think that to make a poem and to travel about singing it, as many rock singer-composers now do, is a return to the venerable tradition of the **troubadours,** minstrels of the late Middle Ages. But there are differences. No doubt the troubadours had to please their patrons, but for better or worse their songs were not affected by a stopwatch in a producer's hand or by the technical resources of a sound studio. Bob Dylan has denied that he is a poet, and Paul Simon once told an interviewer, "If you want poetry read Wallace Stevens." Nevertheless, much has been made lately of current song lyrics as poetry.[1] Are rock songs poems? Clearly some, but not all, are. That the lyrics of a song cannot stand the scrutiny of a reader does not necessarily invali-

[1] See the anthologies *The Poetry of Rock,* Richard Goldstein, ed. (New York: Bantam, 1969), and *Rock Is Beautiful,* Stephanie Spinner, ed. (New York: Dell, 1970).

date them, though; song-writers do not usually write in order to be read. Pete Seeger has quoted a saying of his father: "A printed folk song is like a photograph of a bird in flight." Still there is no reason not to photograph birds, or to read song lyrics. If the words seem rich and interesting, we may possibly increase our enjoyment of them and perhaps be able to sing them more accurately. Like most poems and songs of the past, most current songs may end in the trash can of time. And yet, certain memorable rimed and rhythmic lines may live on, especially if music has served them for a base and if singers have given them wide exposure.

EXERCISE: *Comparing Poem and Song*

Compare the following poem by Edwin Arlington Robinson and a popular song lyric based on it. Notice what Paul Simon had to do to Robinson's original in order to make it into a song, and how Simon altered Robinson's conception.

Edwin Arlington Robinson (1869–1935)

RICHARD CORY 1897

Whenever Richard Cory went down town,
We people on the pavement looked at him:
He was a gentleman from sole to crown,
Clean favored, and imperially slim.

And he was always quietly arrayed,
And he was always human when he talked;
But still he fluttered pulses when he said,
"Good-morning," and he glittered when he walked.

And he was rich—yes, richer than a king—
And admirably schooled in every grace:
In fine°, we thought that he was everything *in short*
To make us wish that we were in his place.

So on we worked, and waited for the light,
And went without the meat, and cursed the bread;
And Richard Cory, one calm summer night,
Went home and put a bullet through his head.

Paul Simon (b. 1942)

RICHARD CORY 1966

With Apologies to E. A. Robinson

RICHARD CORY, by Paul Simon. If possible, listen to the ballad sung by Simon and Garfunkel on *Sounds of Silence* (Columbia recording CL 2469, stereo CS 9269).

They say that Richard Cory owns
One half of this old town,
With elliptical connections
To spread his wealth around.
Born into Society,
A banker's only child,
He had everything a man could want:
Power, grace and style.

Refrain:

But I, I work in his factory
And I curse the life I'm livin'
And I curse my poverty
And I wish that I could be
Oh I wish that I could be
Oh I wish that I could be
Richard Cory.

The papers print his picture
Almost everywhere he goes:
Richard Cory at the opera,
Richard Cory at a show
And the rumor of his party
And the orgies on his yacht—
Oh he surely must be happy
With everything he's got. *(Refrain.)*

He really gave to charity,
He had the common touch,
And they were grateful for his patronage
And they thanked him very much,
So my mind was filled with wonder
When the evening headlines read:
"Richard Cory went home last night
And put a bullet through his head." *(Refrain.)*

BALLADS

Any narrative song, like Paul Simon's "Richard Cory," may be called a **ballad.** In English, some of the most famous ballads are **folk ballads,** loosely defined as anonymous story-songs transmitted orally before they were ever written down. Sir Walter Scott, a pioneer collector of Scottish folk ballads, drew the ire of an old woman whose songs he had transcribed: "They were made for singing and no' for reading, but ye ha'e broken the charm now and they'll never be sung mair." The old singer had a point. Print freezes songs and tends to hold them fast to a single version. However, if Scott and others had not written them down, many would have been lost.

In his monumental work *The English and Scottish Popular Ballads* (1882–1898), the American scholar Francis J. Child winnowed out 305 folk ballads he considered authentic—that is, creations of illiterate or semiliterate people who had preserved them orally. Child, who worked by insight as well as by learning, did such a good job of telling the difference between folk ballads and other kinds that later scholars have added only about a dozen ballads to his count. Often called **Child ballads,** his texts include "The Three Ravens," "Sir Patrick Spence," "The Twa Corbies," "Edward," "The Cruel Mother," and many others still on the lips of singers. Here is one of the best-known Child ballads.

Anonymous (traditional Scottish ballad)

Bonny Barbara Allan

It was in and about the Martinmas time,
  When the green leaves were afalling,
That Sir John Graeme, in the West Country,
  Fell in love with Barbara Allan.

He sent his men down through the town,
  To the place where she was dwelling:
"O haste and come to my master dear,
  Gin° ye be Barbara Allan." *if*

O hooly°, hooly rose she up, *slowly*
  To the place where he was lying,
And when she drew the curtain by:
  "Young man, I think you're dying."

"O it's I'm sick, and very, very sick,
  And 'tis a' for Barbara Allan."—
"O the better for me ye's never be,
  Tho your heart's blood were aspilling.

"O dinna ye mind°, young man," said she, *don't you remember*
  "When ye was in the tavern adrinking,
That ye made the health° gae round and round, *toasts*
  And slighted Barbara Allan?"

He turned his face unto the wall,
  And death was with him dealing:
"Adieu, adieu, my dear friends all,
  And be kind to Barbara Allan."

And slowly, slowly raise she up,
  And slowly, slowly left him,
And sighing said she could not stay,
  Since death of life had reft him.

She had not gane a mile but twa,
  When she heard the dead-bell ringing,
And every jow° that the dead-bell geid, *stroke*
  It cried, "Woe to Barbara Allan!"

"O mother, mother, make my bed!
  O make it saft and narrow!
Since my love died for me today,
  I'll die for him tomorrow."

BONNY BARBARA ALLAN. 1. *Martinmas:* Saint Martin's day, November 11.

QUESTIONS

1. In any line does the Scottish dialect cause difficulty? If so, try reading the line aloud.
2. Without ever coming out and explicitly calling Barbara hard-hearted, this ballad reveals that she is. In which stanza and by what means is her cruelty demonstrated?
3. At what point does Barbara evidently have a change of heart? Again, how does the poem dramatize this change without explicitly talking about it?
4. In many American versions of this ballad, noble knight John Graeme becomes an ordinary citizen. The gist of the story is the same, but at the end are these further stanzas, incorporated from a different ballad:

   They buried Willie in the old churchyard
     And Barbara in the choir;
   And out of his grave grew a red, red rose,
     And out of hers a briar.

   They grew and grew to the steeple top
     Till they could grow no higher;
   And there they locked in a true love's knot,
     The red rose round the briar.

   Do you think this appendage heightens or weakens the final impact of the story? Can the American ending be defended as an integral part of a new song? Explain.
5. Paraphrase lines 9, 15–16, 22, 25–28. By putting these lines into prose, what has been lost?

As you can see from "Bonny Barbara Allan," in a traditional English or Scottish folk ballad the storyteller speaks of the lives and feelings of others. Even if the pronoun "I" occurs, it rarely has much personality. Characters often exchange dialogue, but no one character speaks all the way through. Events move rapidly, perhaps because some of the dull transitional stanzas have been forgotten. The events themselves, as ballad scholar Albert B. Friedman has said, are frequently "the stuff of tabloid journalism—sensational tales of lust, revenge and domestic crime. Unwed mothers slay their newborn babes; lovers unwilling to marry their pregnant mistresses brutally murder the poor women, for which, without fail, they are justly punished."[2] There are also many ballads of the supernatural ("The Twa Corbies") and of gallant knights ("Sir Patrick Spence"), and there are a few humorous ballads, usually about unhappy marriages.

The ballad-spinner has at hand a fund of ready-made epithets: steeds are usually "milk-white" or "berry-brown," lips "rosy" or "ruby-red," corpses and graves "clay-cold," beds (like Barbara Allan's) "soft and narrow." At the least, these conventional phrases are terse and understandable. Sometimes they add meaning: the king who sends Sir Patrick Spence to his doom drinks "blood-red wine." The clothing, steeds, and palaces of ladies and lords are always luxurious: a queen may wear "grass-green silk" or "Spanish leather" and ride a horse with "fifty silver bells and nine." Such descriptions are naive, for as Friedman points out, ballad-singers were probably peasants imagining what they had seen only from afar: the life of the nobility. This may be why the skin of ladies in folk ballads is ordinarily "milk-white," "lily-white," or "snow-white." In an agrarian society, where most people worked in the fields, not to be suntanned was a sign of gentility.

A favorite pattern of ballad-makers is the so-called **ballad stanza,** four lines rimed *a b c b,* tending to fall into 8, 6, 8, and 6 syllables:

Clerk Saunders and Maid Margaret
  Walked owre yon garden green,
And deep and heavy was the love
  That fell thir twa between°. *between those two*

Though not the only possible stanza for a ballad, this easily singable quatrain has continued to attract poets since the Middle Ages. Close kin to the ballad stanza is **common meter,** a stanza found in hymns, such as "Amazing Grace," by the eighteenth-century English hymnist John Newton:

Amazing grace! how sweet the sound
  That saved a wretch like me!
I once was lost, but now am found,
  Was blind, but now I see.

Notice that its pattern is that of the ballad stanza except for its *two* pairs of rimes. That all its lines rime is probably a sign of more literate artistry than we usually hear in folk ballads. Another sign of schoolteachers' influence is that Newton's rimes are exact. (Rimes in folk ballads are often rough-and-ready, as if made by ear, rather than polished and exact, as if

[2] Introduction to *The Viking Book of Folk Ballads of the English-Speaking World,* edited by Albert B. Friedman (New York: Viking Press, 1956).

the riming words had been matched for their similar spellings. In "Barbara Allan," for instance, the hard-hearted lover's name rimes with *afalling, dwelling, aspilling, dealing,* and even with *ringing* and *adrinking.*) That so many hymns were written in common meter may have been due to convenience. If a congregation didn't know the tune to a hymn in common meter, they readily could sing its words to the tune of another such hymn they knew. Besides hymnists, many poets have favored common meter, among them A. E. Housman and Emily Dickinson. (For a well-known hymn to compare with some Dickinson poetry, see page 300.)

Related to traditional folk ballads but displaying characteristics of their own, **broadside ballads** (so called because they were printed on one sheet of paper) often were set to traditional tunes. Most broadside ballads were an early form of journalism made possible by the development of cheap printing and by the growth of audiences who could read, just barely. Sometimes merely humorous or tear-jerking, often they were rimed accounts of sensational news events. That they were widespread and often scorned in Shakespeare's day is attested by the character of Autolycus in *A Winter's Tale,* an itinerant hawker of ballads about sea monsters and strange pregnancies ("a usurer's wife was brought to bed of twenty money-bags"). Although many broadsides tend to be **doggerel** (verse full of irregularities due not to skill but to incompetence), many excellent poets had their work taken up and peddled in the streets —among them Marvell, Swift, and Byron.[3]

Because they stick in the mind and because they were inexpensive to publish and to purchase, broadsides in the nineteenth century often were used to convey social or political messages. Some of the best are **protest songs,** like "Song of the Lower Classes" (about 1848) by Ernest Jones. A stanza follows:

We're low—we're low—we're very very low,
  Yet from our fingers glide
The silken flow—and the robes that glow
  Round the limbs of the sons of pride.
And what we get—and what we give—
  We know, and we know our share;
We're not too low the cloth to weave,
  But too low the Cloth to wear!

Compare those lines with this modern protest ballad:

[3] A generous collection of broadsides has been assembled by Vivian de Sola Pinto and A. E. Rodway in *The Common Muse: An Anthology of Popular British Ballad Poetry, XVth-XXth Century* (St. Clair Shores, Mich.: Scholarly Press, 1957). See also *Irish Street Ballads,* edited by Colm O. Lochlainn (New York: Corinth Books, 1960), and Olive Woolley Burt, *American Murder Ballads and Their Stories* (New York: Oxford University Press, 1958).

Woody Guthrie (1912–1967)

Plane Wreck at Los Gatos (Deportee) 1961

The crops are all in and the peaches are rotting,
The oranges are piled in their creosote dumps;
You're flying them back to the Mexican border
To pay all their money to wade back again.

Refrain:

Goodbye to my Juan, Goodbye Rosalita;
Adiós mes amigos, Jesús and Marie,
You won't have a name when you ride the big airplane:
All they will call you will be deportee.

My father's own father he waded that river;
They took all the money he made in his life;
My brothers and sisters come working the fruit trees
And they rode the truck till they took down and died.

Some of us are illegal and some are not wanted,
Our work contract's out and we have to move on;
Six hundred miles to that Mexico border,
They chase us like outlaws, like rustlers, like thieves.

We died in your hills, we died in your deserts,
We died in your valleys and died on your plains;
We died neath your trees and we died in your bushes,
Both sides of this river we died just the same.

The sky plane caught fire over Los Gatos Canyon,
A fireball of lightning and shook all our hills.
Who are all these friends all scattered like dry leaves?
The radio says they are just deportees.

Is this the best way we can grow our big orchards?
Is this the best way we can grow our good fruit?
To fall like dry leaves to rot on my top soil
And be called by no name except deportees?

Plane Wreck at Los Gatos (Deportee), lyric by Woody Guthrie, music by Martin Hoffman, TRO. This song pays tribute to twenty-eight deported migrant workers killed when the airplane returning them to Mexico crashed on January 28, 1948, near Coalinga, California.

In making a song out of a news event, "Plane Wreck at Los Gatos" resembles a broadside ballad; but it is more like a folk ballad in that the singer, instead of sticking around to comment on the action, disappears and lets the characters speak for themselves. That is the way of most Child ballads: people in them may wail and mourn, but not the singer, who usually remains impersonal.

Literary ballads, not meant for singing, are written by sophisticated poets for book-educated readers who enjoy being reminded of folk ballads. Literary ballads imitate certain features of folk ballads: they may tell of tragic love affairs or of mortals who confront the supernatural; they may use conventional figures of speech, old-fangled diction, or ballad stanzas. Well-known poems of this kind include Keats's "La Belle Dame sans Merci" (page 223) and Coleridge's "Rime of the Ancient Mariner."

John Lennon (1940–1980)
Paul McCartney (b. 1942)

Eleanor Rigby — 1966

Ah, look at all the lonely people!
Ah, look at all the lonely people!

Eleanor Rigby
Picks up the rice in the church where a wedding has been,
Lives in a dream,
Waits at the window
Wearing the face that she keeps in a jar by the door.
Who is it for?

All the lonely people,
Where do they all come from?
All the lonely people,
Where do they all belong?

Father McKenzie,
Writing the words of a sermon that no one will hear,
No one comes near
Look at him working,
Darning his socks in the night when there's nobody there.
What does he care?

All the lonely people
Where do they all come from?
All the lonely people
Where do they all belong?

Eleanor Rigby
Died in the church and was buried along with her name.
Nobody came.
Father McKenzie,
Wiping the dirt from his hands as he walks from the grave,
No one was saved.

All the lonely people,
Where do they all come from?

All the lonely people,
Where do they all belong?

Ah, look at all the lonely people!
Ah, look at all the lonely people!

ELEANOR RIGBY, by John Lennon and Paul McCartney. This song first appeared in 1966 on the Beatles' album *Revolver* (Capital ST 2576).

QUESTION

Is there any reason to call this famous song lyric a ballad? Compare it with a traditional ballad, such as "Bonny Barbara Allan." Do you notice any similarity? What are the differences?

EXPERIMENT: *Seeing the Traits of Ballads*

In the anthology at the back of this book, read the Child ballads "Edward," "Sir Patrick Spence," "The Three Ravens," and "The Twa Corbies" (pages 280–283). With these ballads in mind, consider one or more of these modern poems:

W. H. Auden, "As I Walked Out One Evening" (page 287)
Bob Dylan, "Subterranean Homesick Blues" (page 307)
Dudley Randall, "Ballad of Birmingham" (page 354)
William Jay Smith, "American Primitive" (page 370)
William Butler Yeats, "Crazy Jane Talks with the Bishop" (page 393).

What characteristics of folk ballads do you find in them? In what ways do these modern poets depart from the traditions of folk ballads of the Middle Ages?

FOR REVIEW AND FURTHER STUDY

EXERCISE: *Songs or Poems or Both?*

Consider each of the following song lyrics. Which do you think can stand not only to be sung but to be read as poetry? Which probably should not be seen but only heard?

Augustus Montagu Toplady (1740–1778)

A PRAYER, LIVING AND DYING — 1776

Rock of ages, cleft for me,
Let me hide myself in Thee!
Let the Water and the Blood,
From Thy riven Side which flowed,
Be of sin the double cure;
Cleanse me from its guilt and pow'r.

Not the labors of my hands
Can fulfill Thy Law's demands:
Could my zeal no respite know,
Could my tears for ever flow,
All for sin could not atone:
Thou must save, and Thou alone.

Nothing in my hand I bring;
Simply to Thy Cross I cling;
Naked, come to Thee for dress;
Helpless, look to Thee for grace;
Foul, I to the Fountain fly:
Wash me, Savior, or I die!

While I draw this fleeting breath—
When my eye-strings break in death—
When I soar through tracts unknown—
See Thee on Thy Judgment throne—
Rock of Ages, cleft for me,
Let me hide myself in Thee!

A Prayer, Living and Dying. Universally known under the title "Rock of Ages," this hymn has often been altered to fit the theology of a denomination, or modernized. Lines 20–21, as sung today, usually go: "When my eyelids close in death— / When I soar to worlds unknown." This text is from the first edition of Toplady's *Psalms and Hymns* (1776). Compare William Cowper's hymn "Praise for the Fountain Opened," page 300.

Anonymous (English madrigal)

Fa, mi, fa, re, la, mi — 1609

Fa, mi, fa, re, la, mi,
Begin, my son, and follow me;
Sing flat, fa mi,
So shall we well agree.
Hey tro loly lo.
Hold fast, good son,
With hey tro lily lo.
O sing this once again, lustily.

Anonymous (English madrigal)

The silver swan, who living had no note — 1612

The silver swan, who living had no note,
When death approached unlocked her silent throat;
Leaning her breast against the reedy shore,
Thus sung her first and last, and sung no more.
Farewell, all joys; O death, come close mine eyes;
More geese than swans now live, more fools than wise.

Anonymous (Southern Appalachian song)

On Top of Old Smokey (before 1880)

On top of old Smokey, all covered with snow,
I lost my true lover for acourtin' too slow.
Now, courtin's a pleasure, but parting is grief,
And a false-hearted lover is worse than a thief;
For a thief will just rob you and take what you have,
But a false-hearted lover will lead you to the grave;
And the grave will decay you, and turn you to dust.
Not one boy in a hundred a poor girl can trust:
They'll hug you and kiss you, and tell you more lies
Than the crossties on a railroad, or stars in the skies.
So, come all you young maidens, and listen to me:
Never place your affections in a green willow tree;
For the leaves they will wither, and the roots they will die.
Your lover will forsake you, and you'll never know why.

Anonymous (American song)

Good Mornin', Blues 1959

I woke up this mornin' with the blues all round my bed,
Yes, I woke up this morning with the blues all round my bed,
Went to eat my breakfast, had the blues all in my bread.

"Good mornin', blues, blues, how do you do?" (2)
"I'm feelin' pretty well, but, pardner, how are you?"

Yes, I woke up this morning, 'bout an hour 'fore day, (2)
Reached and grabbed the pillow where my baby used to lay.

If you ever been down, you know just how I feel, (2)
Feel like an engine, ain't got no drivin' wheel.

If I feel tomorrow, like I feel today, (2)
I'll stand right here, look a thousand miles away.

If the blues was whisky, I'd stay drunk all the time, (2)
Stay drunk, baby, just to wear you off my mind.

I got the blues so bad, it hurts my feet to walk, (2)
I got the blues so bad, it hurts my tongue to talk.

The blues jumped a rabbit, run him a solid mile, (2)
When the blues overtaken him, he hollered like a newborn child.

Good Mornin', Blues. This folk song has been adapted by Alan Lomax from a version by singer Huddie Ledbetter (Leadbelly). The number (2) indicates a line to be sung twice.

Willie Nelson (b. 1933)

Heaven and Hell 1974

Well, sometimes its Heaven, and sometimes it's Hell,
And sometimes I don't even know;
And sometimes I take it as far as I can,
And sometimes I don't even go.

My front tracks are bound for a cold water well,
My back tracks are covered with snow;
And sometimes it's Heaven, and sometimes it's Hell,
And sometimes I don't even know.

Heaven ain't walking on a street paved with gold,
And Hell ain't a mountain of fire;
Heaven is laying in my sweet Baby's arms,
And Hell is when Baby's not there.

Well, my front tracks are bound for a cold water well
And my back tracks are covered with snow;
And sometimes it's Heaven, and sometimes it's Hell,
And sometimes I don't even know.

Well, sometimes it's Heaven, and sometimes it's Hell,
And sometimes I don't even know.

8 Sound

SOUND AS MEANING

Isak Dinesen, in a memoir of her life on a plantation in East Africa, tells how some Kikuyu tribesmen reacted to their first hearing of rimed verse:

> The Natives, who have a strong sense of rhythm, know nothing of verse, or at least did not know anything before the times of the schools, where they were taught hymns. One evening out in the maize-field, where we had been harvesting maize, breaking off the cobs and throwing them on to the ox-carts, to amuse myself, I spoke to the field laborers, who were mostly quite young, in Swahili verse. There was no sense in the verses, they were made for the sake of rime—"Ngumbe na-penda chumbe, Malaya mbaya. Wakamba na-kula mamba." The oxen like salt—whores are bad—The Wakamba eat snakes. It caught the interest of the boys, they formed a ring round me. They were quick to understand that meaning in poetry is of no consequence, and they did not question the thesis of the verse, but waited eagerly for the rime, and laughed at it when it came. I tried to make them themselves find the rime and finish the poem when I had begun it, but they could not, or would not, do that, and turned away their heads. As they had become used to the idea of poetry, they begged: "Speak again. Speak like rain." Why they should feel verse to be like rain I do not know. It must have been, however, an expression of applause, since in Africa rain is always longed for and welcomed.[1]

What the tribesmen had discovered is that poetry, like music, appeals to the ear. However limited it may be in comparison with the sound of an orchestra—or a tribal drummer—the sound of words in itself gives pleasure. However, we might doubt Isak Dinesen's assumption that "meaning in poetry is of no consequence." "Hey nonny-nonny" and such nonsense has a place in song lyrics and other poems, and we might take pleasure in hearing rimes in Swahili; but most good poetry has meaningful sound as well as musical sound. Certainly the words of a song have an effect different from that of wordless music: they go along

[1] Isak Dinesen, *Out of Africa* (New York: Random House, 1972).

with their music and, by making statements, add more meaning. The French poet Isidore Isou, founder of a literary movement called *lettrisme,* maintained that poems can be written not only in words but in letters (sample lines: *xyl, xyl, / prprali dryl / znglo trpylo pwi*). But the sound of letters alone, without denotation and connotation, has not been enough to make Letterist poems memorable. In the response of the Kikuyu tribesmen, there may have been not only the pleasure of hearing sounds but also the agreeable surprise of finding that things not usually associated had been brought together.

More powerful when in the company of meaning, not apart from it, the sounds of consonants and vowels can contribute greatly to a poem's effect. The sound of *s,* which can suggest the swishing of water, has rarely been used more accurately than in Surrey's line "Calm is the sea, the waves work less and less." When, in a poem, the sound of words working together with meaning pleases mind and ear, the effect is **euphony,** as in the following lines from Tennyson's "Come down, O maid":

> Myriads of rivulets hurrying through the lawn,
> The moan of doves in immemorial elms,
> And murmuring of innumerable bees.

Its opposite is **cacophony:** a harsh, discordant effect. It too is chosen for the sake of meaning. We hear it in Milton's scornful reference in "Lycidas" to corrupt clergymen whose songs "Grate on their scrannel pipes of wretched straw." (Read that line and one of Tennyson's aloud and see which requires lips, teeth, and tongue to do more work.) But note that although Milton's line is harsh in sound, the line (when we meet it in his poem) is pleasing because it is artful. In a famous passage from his *Essay on Criticism,* Pope has illustrated both euphony and cacophony. (Given here as Pope printed it, the passage relies heavily on italics and capital letters, for particular emphasis. If you will read these lines aloud, dwelling a little longer or harder on the words italicized, you will find that Pope has given you very good directions for a meaningful reading.)

Alexander Pope (1688–1744)

True Ease in Writing Comes from Art, Not Chance 1711

True Ease in Writing comes from Art, not Chance,
As those move easiest who have learned to dance.
'Tis not enough no Harshness gives Offence,
The *Sound* must seem an *Echo* to the *Sense.*
Soft is the strain when *Zephyr*° gently blows, *the west wind*
And the *smooth Stream* in *smoother Numbers*° flows; *metrical rhythm*
But when loud Surges lash the sounding Shore,

The *hoarse, rough Verse* should like the *Torrent* roar.
When *Ajax* strives, some Rock's vast Weight to throw,
The Line too *labors,* and the Words move *slow;*
Not so, when swift *Camilla* scours the Plain,
Flies o'er th' unbending Corn, and skims along the Main°. *expanse (of sea)*
Hear how *Timotheus'* varied Lays surprise,
And bid Alternate Passions fall and rise!
While, at each Change, the Son of *Lybian Jove*
Now *burns* with Glory, and then *melts* with Love;
Now his *fierce Eyes* with *sparkling Fury* glow;
Now *Sighs* steal out, and *Tears begin to flow:*
Persians and Greeks like *Turns of Nature* found,
And the *World's Victor* stood subdued by *Sound!*
The Pow'rs of Music all our Hearts allow;
And what *Timotheus* was, is *Dryden* now.

TRUE EASE IN WRITING COMES FROM ART, NOT CHANCE. (*An Essay on Criticism,* lines 362–383.) 9. *Ajax:* Greek hero, almost a superman, who in Homer's account of the siege of Troy hurls an enormous rock that momentarily flattens Hector, the Trojan prince (*Iliad* VII, 268–272). 11. *Camilla:* a kind of Amazon or warrior woman of the Volcians, whose speed and lightness of step are praised by the Roman poet Virgil: "She could have skimmed across an unmown grainfield / Without so much as bruising one tender blade; / She could have sped across an ocean's surge / Without so much as wetting her quicksilver soles" (*Aeneid* VII, 808–811). 13. *Timotheus:* favorite musician of Alexander the Great. In "Alexander's Feast, or The Power of Music," John Dryden imagines him: "Timotheus, placed on high / Amid the tuneful choir, / With flying fingers touched the lyre: / The trembling notes ascend the sky, / And heavenly joys inspire." 15. *Lybian Jove:* name for Alexander. A Libyan oracle had declared the king to be the son of the god Zeus Ammon.

Notice the pleasing effect of all the *s* sounds in the lines about the west wind and the stream, and in another meaningful place, the effect of the consonants in *Ajax strives,* a phrase that makes our lips work almost as hard as Ajax throwing the rock.

Is sound identical with meaning in lines such as these? Not quite. In the passage from Tennyson, for instance, the cooing of doves is not *exactly* a moan. As John Crowe Ransom pointed out, the sound would be almost the same but the meaning entirely different in "The murdering of innumerable beeves." While it is true that the consonant sound *sl-* will often begin a word that conveys ideas of wetness and smoothness—*slick, slimy, slippery, slush*—we are so used to hearing it in words that convey nothing of the kind—*slave, slow, sledgehammer*—that it is doubtful whether, all by itself, the sound communicates anything definite. The most beautiful phrase in the English language, according to Dorothy Parker, is *cellar door.* Another wit once nominated, as our most euphonious word, not *sunrise* or *silvery* but *syphilis.*

Relating sound more closely to meaning, the device called **onomatopoeia** is an attempt to represent a thing or action by a word that imitates the sound associated with it: *zoom, whiz, crash, bang, ding-dong, pitter-patter, yakety-yak.* Onomatopoeia is often effective in poetry, as in Emily Dickinson's line about the fly with its "uncertain stumbling

Buzz," in which the nasal sounds *n, m, ng* and the sibilants *c, s,* help make a droning buzz, and in Robert Lowell's transcription of a bird call, "yuck-a, yuck-a, yuck-a" (in "Falling Asleep over the Aeneid").

Like the Kikuyu tribesmen, others who care for poetry have discovered in the sound of words something of the refreshment of cool rain. Dylan Thomas, telling how he began to write poetry, said that from early childhood words were to him "as the notes of bells, the sounds of musical instruments, the noises of wind, sea, and rain, the rattle of milkcarts, the clopping of hooves on cobbles, the fingering of branches on the window pane, might be to someone, deaf from birth, who has miraculously found his hearing."[2] For readers, too, the sound of words can have a magical spell, most powerful when it points to meaning. James Weldon Johnson in *God's Trombones* has told of an old-time preacher who began his sermon, "Brothers and sisters, this morning I intend to explain the unexplainable—find out the indefinable—ponder over the imponderable—and unscrew the inscrutable!" The repetition of sound in *unscrew* and *inscrutable* has appeal, but the magic of the words is all the greater if they lead us to imagine the mystery of all Creation as an enormous screw that the preacher's mind, like a screw-driver, will loosen. Though the sound of a word or the meaning of a word may have value all by itself, both become more memorable when taken together.

William Butler Yeats (1865–1939)

WHO GOES WITH FERGUS? 1892

Who will go drive with Fergus now,
And pierce the deep wood's woven shade,
And dance upon the level shore?
Young man, lift up your russet brow,
And lift your tender eyelids, maid,
And brood on hopes and fear no more.

And no more turn aside and brood
Upon love's bitter mystery;
For Fergus rules the brazen cars°, *chariots*
And rules the shadows of the wood,
And the white breast of the dim sea
And all dishevelled wandering stars.

WHO GOES WITH FERGUS? *Fergus:* Irish king who gave up his throne to be a wandering poet.

[2] "Notes on the Art of Poetry," *The Texas Quarterly,* 1961; reprinted in *Modern Poetics,* James Scully, ed. (New York: McGraw-Hill, 1965).

Questions

1. In what lines do you find euphony?
2. In what line do you find cacophony?
3. How do the sounds of these lines stress what is said in them?

Exercise: *Listening to Meaning*

Read aloud the following brief poems. In the sounds of which particular words are meanings well captured? In which of the poems below do you find onomatopoeia?

John Updike (b. 1932)

Winter Ocean

1960

Many-maned scud-thumper, tub
of male whales, maker of worn wood, shrub-
ruster, sky-mocker, rave!
portly pusher of waves, wind-slave.

Frances Cornford (1886–1960)

The Watch

1923

I wakened on my hot, hard bed,
Upon the pillow lay my head;
Beneath the pillow I could hear
My little watch was ticking clear.
I thought the throbbing of it went
Like my continual discontent.
I thought it said in every tick:
I am so sick, so sick, so sick.
O death, come quick, come quick, come quick,
Come quick, come quick, come quick, come quick!

William Wordsworth (1770–1850)

A Slumber Did My Spirit Seal

1800

A slumber did my spirit seal;
I had no human fears—
She seemed a thing that could not feel
The touch of earthly years.

No motion has she now, no force;
She neither hears nor sees;
Rolled round in earth's diurnal course,
With rocks, and stones, and trees.

Emanuel diPasquale (b. 1943)

RAIN 1971

Like a drummer's brush,
the rain hushes the surface of tin porches.

ALLITERATION AND ASSONANCE

Listening to a symphony in which themes are repeated throughout each movement, we enjoy both their recurrence and their variation. We take similar pleasure in the repetition of a phrase or a single chord. Something like this pleasure is afforded us frequently in poetry.

Analogies between poetry and wordless music, it is true, tend to break down when carried far, since poetry—to mention a single difference—has denotation. But like musical compositions, poems have patterns of sounds. Among such patterns long popular in English poetry is **alliteration,** which has been defined as a succession of similar sounds. Alliteration occurs in the repetition of the same consonant sound at the beginning of successive words—"round and round the rugged rocks the ragged rascal ran"—or inside the words, as in Milton's description of the gates of Hell:

On a sudden open fly
With impetuous recoil and ja*rr*ing sound
The infe*r*nal doo*r*s, and on thei*r* hinges g*r*ate
Ha*r*sh thunde*r*, that the lowest bottom shook
Of E*r*ebus.

The former kind is called **initial alliteration,** the latter **internal alliteration** or **hidden alliteration.** We recognize alliteration by sound, not by spelling: *know* and *nail* alliterate, *know* and *key* do not. In a line by E. E. Cummings, "colossal hoax of clocks and calendars," the sound of *x* within *hoax* alliterates with the *cks* in clo*cks*. Incidentally, the letter *r* does not *always* lend itself to cacophony: elsewhere in *Paradise Lost* Milton said that

Heaven opened wide
He*r* eve*r*-du*r*ing gates, ha*r*monious sound
On golden hinges moving . . .

By itself, a letter-sound has no particular meaning. This is a truth forgotten by people who would attribute the effectiveness of Milton's lines on the Heavenly Gates to, say, "the mellow *o*'s and liquid *l* of *harmonious* and *golden*." Mellow *o*'s and liquid *l*'s occur also in the phrase *moldy cold oatmeal,* which may have a quite different effect. Meaning depends on larger units of language than letters of the alphabet.

Today good prose writers usually avoid alliteration; in the past, some cultivated it. "There is nothing more swifter than time, nothing more sweeter," wrote John Lyly in *Euphues* (1579), and he went on—playing especially with the sounds of *v, n, t, s, l,* and *b*—"we have not, as Seneca saith, little time to live, but we lose much; neither have we a short life by nature, but we make it shorter by naughtiness." Poetry, too, formerly contained more alliteration than it usually contains today. In Old English verse, each line was held together by alliteration, a basic pattern still evident in the fourteenth century, as in the following description of the world as a "fair field" in *Piers Plowman:*

> A *f*eir *f*eld *f*ul of *f*olk *f*ond I ther bi-twene,
> Of alle *m*aner of *m*en, the *m*ene and the riche . . .

(For a modern imitation of Old English verse, see Ezra Pound's "The Seafarer," page 352.) Most poets nowadays save alliteration for special occasions. They may use it to give emphasis, as Edward Lear does: "*F*ar and *f*ew, *f*ar and *f*ew, / Are the *l*ands where the Jumblies *l*ive." With its aid they can point out the relationship between two things placed side by side, as in Pope's line on things of little worth: "The courtier's *p*romises, and sick man's *p*rayers." Alliteration, too, can be a powerful aid to memory. It is hard to forget such tongue twisters as "Peter Piper picked a peck of pickled peppers," or common expressions like "green as grass," "tried and true," and "from stem to stern." In fact, because alliteration directs our attention to something, it had best be used neither thoughtlessly nor merely for decoration, lest it call attention to emptiness. A case in point may be a line by Philip James Bailey, a reaction to a lady's weeping: "I saw, but *sp*ared to *sp*eak." If the poet chose the word *spared* for any meaningful reason other than that it alliterates with *speak*, the reason is not clear.

As we have seen, to repeat the sound of a consonant is to produce alliteration, but to repeat the sound of a *vowel* is to produce **assonance.** Like alliteration, assonance may occur either initially—"*a*ll the *aw*ful *au*guries"[3]—or internally—Edmund Spenser's "Her goodly *eyes* l*i*ke sapph*i*res sh*i*ning br*i*ght, / Her forehead *i*vory wh*i*te . . ." and it can help make common phrases unforgettable: "eager beaver," "holy smoke." Like alliteration, it slows the reader down and focuses attention.

A. E. Housman (1859–1936)

Eight O'Clock

1922

He stood, and heard the steeple
  Sprinkle the quarters on the morning town.
One, two, three, four, to market-place and people
  It tossed them down.

[3] Some prefer to call the repetition of an initial vowel-sound by the name of alliteration: "apt alliteration's artful aid."

Strapped, noosed, nighing his hour,
He stood and counted them and cursed his luck;
And then the clock collected in the tower
Its strength, and struck.

Questions

1. Why does the protagonist in this brief drama curse his luck? What is his situation?
2. For so short a poem, "Eight O'Clock" carries a great weight of alliteration. What patterns of initial alliteration do you find? What patterns of internal alliteration? What effect is created by all this heavy emphasis?

Robert Herrick (1591–1674)

Upon Julia's Voice

1648

So smooth, so sweet, so silv'ry is thy voice,
As, could they hear, the damned would make no noise,
But listen to thee (walking in thy chamber)
Melting melodious words, to lutes of amber.

Upon Julia's Voice. 4. *amber:* either the fossilized resin from which pipestems are sometimes made today, and which might have inlaid the body of a lute; or an alloy of four parts silver and one part gold.

Questions

1. Is Julia speaking or singing? How do we know for sure?
2. In what moments in this brief poem does the sound of words especially help convey meaning?
3. Does Herrick's reference to *the damned* (presumably howling from Hell's torments) seem out of place?

Janet Lewis (b. 1899)

Girl Help

1927

Mild and slow and young,
She moves about the room,
And stirs the summer dust
With her wide broom.

In the warm, lofted air,
Soft lips together pressed,
Soft wispy hair,
She stops to rest,

And stops to breathe,
Amid the summer hum,
The great white lilac bloom
Scented with days to come.

QUESTIONS

1. What assonance and alliteration do you find in this poem? (Suggestion: It may help to read the poem aloud.)
2. In this particular poem, how are these repetitions (or echoes) of sound valuable?

EXERCISE: *Hearing How Sound Helps*

Which of these translations of the same passage from Petrarch do you think is better poetry? Why? What do assonance and alliteration have to do with your preference?

1. Love that liveth and reigneth in my thought,
   That built his seat within my captive breast,
   Clad in the arms wherein with me he fought,
   Oft in my face he doth his banner rest.
   —Henry Howard, Earl of Surrey (1517?–1547)

2. The long love that in my thought doth harbor,
   And in mine heart doth keep his residence,
   Into my face presseth with bold pretense
   And therein campeth, spreading his banner.
   —Sir Thomas Wyatt (1503?–1542)

EXPERIMENT: *Reading for Assonance*

Try reading aloud as rapidly as possible the following poem by Tennyson. From the difficulties you encounter, you may be able to sense the slowing effect of assonance. Then read the poem aloud a second time, with consideration.

Alfred, Lord Tennyson (1809–1892)

THE SPLENDOR FALLS ON CASTLE WALLS 1850

The splendor falls on castle walls
  And snowy summits old in story;
The long light shakes across the lakes,
  And the wild cataract leaps in glory.
Blow, bugle, blow, set the wild echoes flying,
Blow, bugle; answer, echoes, dying, dying, dying.

O hark, O hear! how thin and clear,
  And thinner, clearer, farther going!
O sweet and far from cliff and scar
  The horns of Elfland faintly blowing!
Blow, let us hear the purple glens replying:
Blow, bugle; answer, echoes, dying, dying, dying.

O love, they die in yon rich sky,
  They faint on hill or field or river;
Our echoes roll from soul to soul,
  And grow for ever and for ever.
Blow, bugle, blow, set the wild echoes flying,
And answer, echoes, answer, dying, dying, dying.

RIME

Isak Dinesen's tribesmen, to whom rime was a new phenomenon, recognized at once that rimed language is special language. So do we, for, although much English poetry is unrimed, rime is one means to set poetry apart from ordinary conversation and bring it closer to music. A **rime** (or rhyme), defined most narrowly, occurs when two or more words or phrases contain an identical or similar vowel-sound, usually accented, and the consonant-sounds (if any) that follow the vowel-sound are identical: *hay* and *sleigh, prairie schooner* and *piano tuner.*[4] From these examples it will be seen that rime depends not on spelling but on sound.

Excellent rimes surprise. It is all very well that a reader may anticipate which vowel-sound is coming next, for patterns of rime give pleasure by satisfying expectations; but riming becomes dull clunking if, at the end of each line, the reader can predict the word that will end the next. Hearing many a jukebox song for the first time, a listener can do so: *charms* lead to *arms, skies above* to *love.* As Alexander Pope observes of the habits of dull rimesters,

> Where'er you find "the cooling western breeze,"
> In the next line it "whispers through the trees";
> If crystal streams "with pleasing murmurs creep,"
> The reader's threatened (not in vain) with "sleep" . . .

But who—given the opening line of this children's jingle—could predict the lines that follow?

Anonymous (English)

JULIUS CAESAR (about 1940?)

Julius Caesar,
The Roman geezer,
Squashed his wife with a lemon-squeezer.

Here rimes combine things unexpectedly. Robert Herrick, too, made good use of rime to indicate a startling contrast:

> Then while time serves, and we are but decaying,
> Come, my Corinna, come, let's go a-Maying.

Though good rimes seem fresh, not all will startle, and probably few will call to mind things so unlike as *May* and *decay, Caesar* and *lemon-squeezer.* Some masters of rime often link words that, taken out of con-

[4] Some definitions of *rime* would apply the term to the repetition of any identical or similar sound, not only a vowel-sound. In this sense, assonance is a kind of rime; so is alliteration (called **initial rime**).

text, might seem common and unevocative. Here, for instance, is Alexander Pope's comment on a trifling courtier:

> Yet let me flap this bug with gilded wings,
> This painted child of dirt, that stinks and stings;
> Whose buzz the witty and the fair annoys,
> Yet wit ne'er tastes, and beauty ne'er enjoys:
> So well-bred spaniels civilly delight
> In mumbling of the game they dare not bite.
> Eternal smiles his emptiness betray,
> As shallow streams run dimpling all the way.

Pope's rime-words are not especially memorable—and yet these lines are, because (among other reasons) they rime. Wit may be driven home without rime, but it is rime that rings the doorbell. Admittedly, some rimes wear thin from too much use. More difficult to use freshly than before the establishment of Tin Pan Alley, rimes such as *moon, June, croon* seem leaden and to ring true would need an extremely powerful context. *Death* and *breath* are a rime that poets have used with wearisome frequency; another is *birth, earth, mirth.* And yet we cannot exclude these from the diction of poetry, for they might be the very words a poet would need in order to say something new and original. The following brief poem seems fresher than its rimes (if taken out of context) would lead us to expect.

William Blake (1757–1827)

The Angel that presided o'er my birth (1808–1811)

The Angel that presided o'er my birth
Said, "Little creature, formed of Joy and Mirth,
Go love without the help of any thing on earth."

What matters to rime is freshness—not of a word but of the poet's way of seeing.

Good poets, said John Dryden, learn to make their rime "so properly a part of the verse, that it should never mislead the sense, but itself be led and governed by it." The comment may remind us that skillful rime—unlike poor rime—is never a distracting ornament. "Rime the rudder is of verses, / With which, like ships, they steer their courses," wrote the seventeenth-century poet Samuel Butler. Like other patterns of sound, rime can help a poet to group ideas, emphasize particular words, and weave a poem together. It can start reverberations between words and can point to connections of meaning.

To have an **exact rime,** sounds following the vowel sound have to be the same: *red* and *bread, wealthily* and *stealthily, walk to her* and *talk to her.* If final consonant sounds are the same but the vowel sounds are different, the result is **slant rime,** also called **near rime, off rime,** or **partial rime:** *sun* riming with *bone, moon, rain, green, gone, thin.* By not satisfying the reader's expectation of an exact chime, but instead giving a clunk, a slant rime can help a poet say some things in a particular way. It works especially well for disappointed let-downs, negations, and denials, as in Blake's couplet:

He who the ox to wrath has moved
Shall never be by woman loved.

Consonance, a kind of slant rime, occurs when the rimed words or phrases have the same consonant sounds but a different vowel, as in *chitter* and *chatter.* It is used in a traditional nonsense poem, "The Cutty Wren": " 'O where are you going?' says *Milder* to *Malder.*" (W. H. Auden wrote a variation on it that begins, " 'O where are you going?' said *reader* to *rider,*" thus keeping the consonance.)

End rime, as its name indicates, comes at the ends of lines, **internal rime** within them. Most rime tends to be end rime. Few recent poets have used internal rime so heavily as Wallace Stevens in the beginning of "Bantams in Pine-Woods": "Chieftain Iffucan of Azcan in caftan / Of tan with henna hackles, halt!" (lines also heavy on alliteration). A poet may employ both end rime and internal rime in the same poem, as in Robert Burn's satiric ballad "The Kirk's Alarm":

Orthodox, Orthodox, wha believe in John Knox,
  Let me sound an alarm to your conscience:
There's a heretic blast has been blawn i' the wast°,   *west*
  "That what is not sense must be nonsense."

Masculine rime is a rime of one-syllable words (*jail, bail*) or (in words of more than one syllable) stressed final syllables: *di-VORCE, re-MORSE,* or *horse, re-MORSE.* **Feminine rime** is a rime of two or more syllables, with stress on a syllable other than the last: *TUR-tle, FER-tile,* or (to take an example from Byron) *in-tel-LECT-u-al, hen-PECKED you all.* Often it lends itself to comic verse, but can occasionally be valuable to serious poems, as in Wordsworth's "Resolution and Independence":

We poets in our youth begin in gladness,
But thereof come in the end despondency and madness.

or as in Anne Sexton's "Eighteen Days Without You":

and of course we're not married, we are a pair of scissors
who come together to cut, without towels saying His. Hers.

Serious poems containing feminine rimes of three syllables have been attempted, notably by Thomas Hood in "The Bridge of Sighs":

Take her up tenderly,
Lift her with care;
Fashioned so slenderly,
Young, and so fair!

But the pattern is hard to sustain without lapsing into unintended comedy, as in the same poem:

Still, for all slips of hers,
One of Eve's family—
Wipe those poor lips of hers,
Oozing so clammily.

It works better when comedy is wanted:

Hilaire Belloc (1870–1953)

The Hippopotamus — 1896

I shoot the Hippopotamus
  with bullets made of platinum,
Because if I use leaden ones
  his hide is sure to flatten 'em.

In **eye rime,** spellings look alike but pronunciations differ—*rough* and *dough, idea* and *flea.* Strictly speaking, eye rime is not rime at all.

In recent years American poetry has seen a great erosion of faith in rime, with Louis Simpson, James Wright, Robert Lowell, W. S. Merwin, and others quitting it for open forms. Indeed, it has been suggested that rime in the English language is exhausted. Such a view may be a reaction against the wearing-thin of rimes by overuse or the mechanical and meaningless application of a rime scheme. Yet anyone who listens to children skipping rope in the street, making up rimes to delight themselves as they go along, may doubt that the pleasures of rime are ended; and certainly the practice of Yeats and Emily Dickinson, to name only two, suggests that the possibilities of slant rime may be nearly infinite. If successfully employed, as it has been at times by a majority of English-speaking poets whose work we care to save, rime runs through its poem like a spine: the creature moves by means of it.

Robert Frost (1874–1963)

Desert Places — 1936

Snow falling and night falling fast, oh, fast
In a field I looked into going past,
And the ground almost covered smooth in snow,
But a few weeks and stubble showing last.

The woods around it have it—it is theirs.
All animals are smothered in their lairs,
I am too absent-spirited to count;
The loneliness includes me unawares.

And lonely as it is, that loneliness
Will be more lonely ere it will be less—
A blanker whiteness of benighted snow
With no expression, nothing to express.

They cannot scare me with their empty spaces
Between stars—on stars where no human race is.
I have it in me so much nearer home
To scare myself with my own desert places.

Questions

1. What are these desert places that the speaker finds in himself? (More than one theory is possible. What is yours?)
2. Notice how many times, within the short space of lines 8–10, Frost says *lonely* (or *loneliness*). What other words in the poem contain similar sounds that reinforce these words?
3. In the closing stanza, the feminine rimes *space, race is,* and *places* might well occur in light or comic verse. Does "Desert Places" leave you laughing? If not, what does it make you feel?

William Butler Yeats (1865–1939)

Leda and the Swan

1924

A sudden blow: the great wings beating still
Above the staggering girl, her thighs caressed
By the dark webs, her nape caught in his bill,
He holds her helpless breast upon his breast.

How can those terrified vague fingers push
The feathered glory from her loosening thighs?
And how can body, laid in that white rush,
But feel the strange heart beating where it lies?

A shudder in the loins engenders there
The broken wall, the burning roof and tower
And Agamemnon dead.
Being so caught up,
So mastered by the brute blood of the air,
Did she put on his knowledge with his power
Before the indifferent beak could let her drop?

Questions

1. According to Greek mythology, the god Zeus in the form of a swan descended upon Leda, a Spartan queen. Among the offspring of this union were Clytemnestra, Agamemnon's unfaithful wife who conspired in his murder, and Helen, on whose account the Trojan war was fought. What does a knowledge of these allusions contribute to our understanding of the poem's last two lines?

2. The slant rime *up / drop* (lines 11, 14) may seem accidental or inept. Is it? Would this poem have ended nearly so well if Yeats had made an exact rime like *up / cup* or like *stop / drop*?

Gerard Manley Hopkins (1844–1889)

God's Grandeur (1877)

The world is charged with the grandeur of God.
  It will flame out, like shining from shook foil;
  It gathers to a greatness, like the ooze of oil
Crushed. Why do men then now not reck his rod?
Generations have trod, have trod, have trod;
  And all is seared with trade; bleared, smeared with toil;
  And wears man's smudge and shares man's smell: the soil
Is bare now, nor can foot feel, being shod.

And for all this, nature is never spent;
  There lives the dearest freshness deep down things;
And though the last lights off the black West went
  Oh, morning, at the brown brink eastward, springs—
Because the Holy Ghost over the bent
  World broods with warm breast and with ah! bright wings.

Questions

1. In a letter Hopkins explained *shook foil* (line 2): "I mean foil in its sense of leaf or tinsel . . . . Shaken goldfoil gives off broad glares like sheet lightning and also, and this is true of nothing else, owing to its zigzag dints and creasings and network of small many cornered facets, a sort of fork lightning too." What do you think he meant by *ooze of oil* (line 3)? Is this phrase an example of alliteration?
2. What instances of internal rime does the poem contain? How would you describe their effects?
3. Point out some of the poet's uses of alliteration and assonance. Does Hopkins go too far in his heavy use of devices of sound, or would you defend his practice?
4. Why do you suppose Hopkins, in the last two lines, says *over the bent / World* instead of (as we might expect) *bent over the world*? How can the world be bent? Can you make any sense out of this wording, or is Hopkins just trying to get his rime scheme to work out?

Emily Dickinson (1830–1886)

The Soul selects her own Society (1862)

The Soul selects her own Society–
Then–shuts the Door–
To her divine Majority–
Present no more–

Unmoved–she notes the Chariots–pausing–
At her low Gate–
Unmoved–an Emperor be kneeling
Upon her Mat–

I've known her–from an ample nation–
Choose One–
Then–close the Valves of her attention–
Like Stone–

QUESTIONS

1. What kinds of rime do you find in this poem?
2. Try to describe the effect of the closing rime, *One / Stone*.
3. Who or what is the *One* chosen in line 10? Is this a living soul or a dying one? (Don't expect all readers of this poem to agree.)

READING AND HEARING POEMS ALOUD

Thomas Moore's "The light that lies in women's eyes"—a line rich in internal rime, alliteration, and assonance—is harder to forget than "The light burning in the gaze of a woman." Because of sound, it is possible to remember the obscure line Christopher Smart wrote while in an insane asylum: "Let Ross, house of Ross rejoice with the Great Flabber Dabber Flat Clapping Fish with hands." Such lines, striking as they are even when read silently, become still more effective when said out loud. Reading poems aloud is a way to understand them. For this reason, practice the art of lending poetry your voice.

Before trying to read a poem aloud to other people, understand its meaning as thoroughly as possible. If you know what the poet is saying and the poet's attitude toward it, you will be able to find an appropriate tone of voice and to give each part of the poem a proper emphasis.

Except in the most informal situations and in some class exercises, read a poem to yourself before trying it on an audience. No actor goes before the footlights without first having studied the script, and the language of poems usually demands even more consideration than the language of most contemporary plays. Prepare your reading in advance. Check pronunciations you are not sure of. Underline things to be emphasized.

Read deliberately, more slowly than you would read aloud from a newspaper. Keep in mind that you are saying something to somebody. Don't race through the poem as if you are eager to get it over with.

Don't lapse into singsong. A poem may have a definite swing, but swing should never be exaggerated at the cost of sense. If you understand what the poem is saying and utter the poem as if you do, the temptation to fall into such a mechanical intonation should not occur.

Observe the punctuation, making slight pauses for commas, longer pauses for full stops (periods, question marks, exclamation points).

If the poem is rimed, don't raise your voice and make the rimes stand out unnaturally. They should receive no more volume than other words in the poem, though a faint pause at the end of each line will call the listener's attention to them. This advice is contrary to a school that holds that, if a line does not end in any punctuation, one should not pause but run it together with the line following. The trouble is that, from such a reading, a listener may not be able to identify the rimes; besides, the line, that valuable unit of rhythm, is destroyed.

In some older poems rimes that look like slant rimes may have been exact rimes in their day:

> Still so perverse and opposite,
> As if they worshiped God for spite.
>
> —Samuel Butler, *Hudibras* (1663)

> Soft yielding minds to water glide away,
> And sip, with nymphs, their elemental tea.
>
> —Alexander Pope, "The Rape of the Lock" (1714)

You may wish to establish a consistent policy toward such shifting usage: is it worthwhile to distort current pronunciation for the sake of the rime?

Listening to a poem, especially if it is unfamiliar, calls for concentration. Merciful people seldom read poetry uninterruptedly to anyone for more than a few minutes at a time. Robert Frost, always kind to his audiences, used to intersperse poems with many silences and seemingly casual remarks—shrewdly giving his hearers a chance to rest from their labors and giving his poems a chance to settle in.

If, in first listening to a poem, you don't take in all its meaning, don't be discouraged. With more practice in listening, your attention span and your ability to understand poems read aloud will increase. Incidentally, following the text of poems in a book while hearing them read aloud may increase your comprehension, but it may not necessarily help you to *listen*. At least some of the time, close your book and let your ears make the poems welcome. That way, their sounds may better work for you.

Hearing recordings of poets reading their work can help both your ability to read aloud and your ability to listen. Not all poets read their poems well, but there is much to be relished in both the highly dramatic reading style of a Dylan Thomas and the quiet underplay of a Robert Frost. You need feel no obligation, of course, to imitate the poet's reading of a poem. You have to feel about the poem in your own way, in order to read it with conviction and naturalness.

Even if you don't have an audience, the act of speaking poetry can have its own rewards. Perhaps that is what James Wright is driving at in the following brief prose poem.

James Wright (1927–1980)

SAYING DANTE ALOUD 1976

You can feel the muscles and veins rippling in widening and rising circles,
like a bird in flight under your tongue.

EXERCISE: *Reading for Sound and Meaning*

Read these brief poems aloud. What devices of sound do you find in each of them? Try to explain what sound contributes to the total effect of the poem and how it reinforces what the poet is saying.

Michael Stillman (b. 1940)

IN MEMORIAM JOHN COLTRANE 1972

Listen to the coal
rolling, rolling through the cold
steady rain, wheel on

wheel, listen to the
turning of the wheels this night
black as coal dust, steel

on steel, listen to
these cars carry coal, listen
to the coal train roll.

IN MEMORIAM JOHN COLTRANE. John Coltrane (1926–1967) was the saxophonist whose originality, passion, and technical wizardry have had a deep influence on the history of modern jazz.

William Shakespeare (1564–1616)

FULL FATHOM FIVE THY FATHER LIES (ABOUT 1611)

Full fathom five thy father lies;
Of his bones are coral made;
Those are pearls that were his eyes:
Nothing of him that doth fade,
But doth suffer a sea change
Into something rich and strange.
Sea nymphs hourly ring his knell:
Ding-dong.
Hark! now I hear them—*Ding-dong, bell.*

FULL FATHOM FIVE THY FATHER LIES. The spirit Ariel sings this song in *The Tempest* to Ferdinand, prince of Naples, who mistakenly thinks his father is drowned.

Ebenezer Elliott (1781–1849)

On a Rose in December (about 1835)

Stay yet, pale flower. Though coming storms will tear thee,
My soul grows darker, and I cannot spare thee.

A. E. Housman (1859–1936)

With rue my heart is laden 1896

With rue my heart is laden
  For golden friends I had,
For many a rose-lipt maiden
  And many a lightfoot lad.

By brooks too broad for leaping
  The lightfoot boys are laid;
The rose-lipt girls are sleeping
  In fields where roses fade.

T. S. Eliot (1888–1965)

Virginia 1934

Red river, red river,
Slow flow heat is silence
No will is still as a river
Still. Will heat move
Only through the mocking-bird
Heard once? Still hills
Wait. Gates wait. Purple trees,
White trees, wait, wait,
Delay, decay. Living, living,
Never moving. Ever moving
Iron thoughts came with me
And go with me:
Red river, river, river.

Virginia. This poem is one of a series entitled "Landscapes."

Galway Kinnell (b. 1927)

Blackberry Eating 1980

I love to go out in late September
among the fat, overripe, icy, black blackberries
to eat blackberries for breakfast,

the stalks very prickly, a penalty
they earn for knowing the black art
of blackberry-making; and as I stand among them
lifting the stalks to my mouth, the ripest berries
fall almost unbidden to my tongue,
as words sometimes do, certain peculiar words
like *strengths* or *squinched,*
many-lettered, one-syllabled lumps,
which I squeeze, squinch open, and splurge well
in the silent, startled, icy, black language
of blackberry-eating in late September.

ḥythm

STRESSES AND PAUSES

Rhythms affect us powerfully. We are lulled by a hammock's sway, awakened by an alarm clock's repeated yammer. Long after we come home from a beach, the rising and falling of waves and tides continue in memory. How powerfully the rhythms of poetry also move us may be felt in folk songs of railroad workers and chain gangs whose words were chanted in time to the lifting and dropping of a sledgehammer, and in verse that marching soldiers shout, putting a stress on every word that coincides with a footfall:

> Your LEFT! TWO! THREE! FOUR!
> Your LEFT! TWO! THREE! FOUR!
> You LEFT your WIFE and TWEN-ty-one KIDS
> And you LEFT! TWO! THREE! FOUR!
> You'll NEV-er get HOME to-NIGHT!

A rhythm is produced by a series of recurrences: the returns and departures of the seasons, the repetitions of an engine's stroke, the beats of the heart. A rhythm may be produced by the recurrence of a sound (the throb of a drum, a telephone's busy-signal), but rhythm and sound are not identical. A totally deaf man at a parade can sense rhythm from the motions of the marchers' arms and feet, from the shaking of the pavement as they tramp. Rhythms inhere in the motions of the moon and stars, even though when they move we hear no sound.

In poetry, several kinds of recurrent *sound* are possible, including (as we saw in the last chapter) rime, alliteration, and assonance. But most often when we speak of the **rhythm** of a poem we mean the recurrence of stresses and pauses in it. When we hear a poem read aloud, stresses and pauses are, of course, part of its sound. It is possible to be aware of rhythms in poems read silently, too.

A **stress** (or **accent**) is a greater amount of force given to one syllable in speaking than is given to another. We favor a stressed syllable with a little more breath and emphasis, with the result that it comes out slightly louder, higher in pitch, or longer in duration than other syllables. In this manner we place a stress on the first syllable of words such as *eagle, impact, open,* and *statue,* and on the second syllable in *cigar, mystique, precise,* and *until.* Each word in English carries at least one stress, except (usually) for the articles *a, an,* and *the,* and one-syllable prepositions: *at, by, for, from, of, to, with.* Even these, however, take a stress once in a while: "Get WITH it!" "You're not THE Dolly Parton?" One word by itself is seldom long enough for us to notice a rhythm in it. Usually a sequence of at least a few words is needed for stresses to establish their pattern: a line, a passage, a whole poem. Strong rhythms may be seen in most Mother Goose rimes, to which children have been responding for hundreds of years. This rime is for an adult to chant while jogging a child up and down on a knee:

Here goes my lord
A trot, a trot, a trot, a trot!
Here goes my lady
A canter, a canter, a canter, a canter!
Here goes my young master
Jockey-hitch, jockey-hitch, jockey-hitch, jockey-hitch!
Here goes my young miss
An amble, an amble, an amble, an amble!
The footman lags behind to tipple ale and wine
And goes gallop, a gallop, a gallop, to make up his time.

More than one rhythm occurs in these lines, as the make-believe horse changes pace. How do these rhythms differ? From one line to the next, the interval between stresses lengthens or grows shorter. In "a TROT a TROT a TROT a TROT," the stress falls on every other syllable. But in the middle of the line "A CAN-ter a CAN-ter a CAN-ter a CAN-ter," the stress falls on every third syllable. When stresses recur at fixed intervals as in these lines, the result is called a **meter.** The line "A trot a trot a trot a trot" is in **iambic** meter, a succession of alternate unstressed and stressed syllables.[1] Of all rhythms in the English language, this one is most familiar; most of our traditional poetry is written in it and ordinary speech tends to resemble it. Most poems, less obvious in rhythm than nursery rimes are, rarely stick to their meters with such jog-trot regularity. The following lines also contain a horseback-riding rhythm. (The poet, Gerard Manley Hopkins, is comparing the pell-mell plunging of a burn—Scottish word for a brook—to the motion of a wild horse.)

This darksome burn, horseback brown,
His rollrock highroad roaring down,
In coop and in comb the fleece of his foam
Flutes and low to the lake falls home.

[1] Another kind of meter is possible, in which the intervals between stresses vary. This is **accentual** meter, not often found in contemporary poetry. It is discussed in the second part of this chapter.

In the third line, when the brook courses through coop and comb ("hollow" and "ravine"), the passage breaks into a gallop; then, with the two-beat *falls home,* almost seems reined to a sudden halt.

Stresses embody meanings. Whenever two or more fall side by side, words gain in emphasis. Consider these hard-hitting lines from John Donne, in which accent marks have been placed, dictionary-fashion, to indicate the stressed syllables:

Bat′ter my heart′, three′-per′soned God′, for You′
As yet′ but knock′, breathe′, shine′, and seek′ to mend′;
That I may rise′ and stand′, o′er′throw′ me, and bend′
Your force′ to break′, blow′, burn′, and make′ me new′.

Unstressed (or **slack**) syllables also can direct our attention to what the poet means. In a line containing few stresses and a great many unstressed syllables, there can be an effect not of power and force but of hesitation and uncertainty. Yeats asks in "Among School Children" what young mother, if she could see her baby grown to be an old man, would think him

A com′pen·sa′tion for the pang′ of his birth′
Or the un·cer′tain·ty of his set′ting forth′?

When unstressed syllables recur in pairs, the result is a rhythm that trips and bounces, as in Robert Service's rollicking line:

A bunch′ of the boys′ were whoop′ing it up′ in the Mal′a·mute sa·loon′. . .

or in Poe's lines—also light but probably supposed to be serious:

For the moon′ nev·er beams′ with·out bring′ing me dreams′
Of the beau′ti·ful An′na·bel Lee′.

Apart from the words that convey it, the rhythm of a poem has no meaning. There are no essentially sad rhythms, nor any essentially happy ones. But some rhythms enforce certain meanings better than others do. The bouncing rhythm of Service's line seems fitting for an account of a merry night in a Klondike saloon; but it may be distracting when encountered in Poe's wistful elegy.

Exercise: *Appropriate and Inappropriate Rhythms*

In each of the following passages, decide whether rhythm enforces meaning and tone or works against these elements and consequently against the poem's effectiveness.

1. Alfred, Lord Tennyson, "Break, break, break":

   Break, break, break,
   On thy cold gray stones, O Sea!

2. Edgar Allan Poe, "Ulalume":

Then my heart it grew ashen and sober
  As the leaves that were crispèd and sere—
  As the leaves that were withering and sere,
And I cried: "It was surely October
    On *this* very night of last year
    That I journey—I journeyed down here—
    That I brought a dread burden down here—
    On this night of all nights in the year,
    Ah, what demon has tempted me here?"

3. Greg Keeler, "There Ain't No Such Thing as a Montana Cowboy" (a song lyric):

I couldn't be cooler, I come from Missoula,
And I rope and I chew and I ride.
But I'm a heroin dealer, and I drive a four-wheeler
With stereo speakers inside.
My ol' lady Phoebe's out rippin' off C.B.'s
From the rigs at the Wagon Wheel Bar,
Near a Montana truck stop and a shit-outta-luck stop
For a trucker who's driven too far.

4. Eliza Cook, "Song of the Sea-Weed":

Many a lip is gaping for drink,
  And madly calling for rain;
And some hot brains are beginning to think
  Of a messmate's opened vein.

5. William Shakespeare, song from *The Tempest:*

The master, the swabber, the boatswain, and I,
The gunner and his mate
Loved Moll, Meg, and Marian, and Margery,
But none of us cared for Kate;
For she had a tongue with a tang
Would cry to a sailor "Go hang!"—
She loved not the savor of tar nor of pitch
Yet a tailor might scratch her where'er she did itch;
Then to sea, boys, and let her go hang!

Rhythms in poetry are due not only to stresses but also to pauses. "Every nice ear," observed Alexander Pope (*nice* meaning "finely tuned"), "must, I believe, have observed that in any smooth English verse of ten syllables, there is naturally a pause either at the fourth, fifth, or sixth syllable." Such a light but definite pause within a line is called a **cesura** (or caesura), "a cutting." More liberally than Pope, we apply the name to any pause in a line of any length, after any word in the line. In studying a poem, we often indicate a cesura by double lines (‖). Usually, a cesura will occur at a mark of punctuation, but there can be a cesura even if no punctuation is present. Sometimes you will find it at the end of a phrase or clause or, as in these lines by William Blake, after an internal rime:

And priests in black gowns‖were walking their rounds
And binding with briars‖my joys and desires.

Lines of ten or twelve syllables (as Pope knew) tend to have just one cesura, though sometimes there are more:

Cover her face:‖mine eyes dazzle:‖she died young.

Pauses also tend to recur at more prominent places—namely, after each line. At the end of a verse (from *versus,* "a turning"), the reader's eye, before turning to go on to the next line, makes a pause, however brief. If a line ends in a full pause—usually indicated by some mark of punctuation—we call it **end-stopped.** All the lines in this stanza by Theodore Roethke are end-stopped:

Let seed be grass and grass turn into hay:
I'm martyr to a motion not my own;
What's freedom for? To know eternity.
I swear she cast a shadow white as stone.
But who would count eternity in days?
These old bones live to learn her wanton ways:
(I measure time by how a body sways).[2]

A line that does not end in punctuation and that therefore is read with only a slight pause after it is called a **run-on line.** Because a run-on line gives us only part of a phrase, clause, or sentence, we have to read on to the line or lines following, in order to complete a thought. All these lines from Robert Browning are run-on lines:

. . . Sir, 'twas not
Her husband's presence only, called that spot
Of joy into the Duchess' cheek: perhaps
Frà Pandolf chanced to say "Her mantle laps
Over my lady's wrist too much," or "Paint
Must never hope to reproduce the faint
Half-flush that dies along her throat." Such stuff
Was courtesy, she thought . . .[3]

A passage in run-on lines has a rhythm different from that of a passage like Roethke's in end-stopped lines. When emphatic pauses occur in the quotation from Browning, they fall within a line rather than at the end of one. The passage by Roethke and that by Browning are in lines of the same meter (iambic) and the same length (ten syllables). What makes the big difference in their rhythms is the running on, or lack of it.

[2] The complete poem, "I Knew a Woman," appears on page 96.
[3] The complete poem, "My Last Duchess," appears on page 294.

To sum up: rhythm is recurrence. In poems, it is made of stresses and pauses. The poet can produce it by doing any of several things: making the intervals between stresses fixed or varied, long or short; indicating pauses (cesuras) within lines; end-stopping lines or running them over; writing in short or long lines. Rhythm in itself cannot convey meaning. And yet if a poet's words have meaning, their rhythm must be one with it.

Gwendolyn Brooks (b. 1917)

We Real Cool 1960

The Pool Players.
Seven at the Golden Shovel.

We real cool. We
Left school. We

Lurk late. We
Strike straight. We

Sing sin. We
Thin gin. We

Jazz June. We
Die soon.

Question

Describe the rhythms of this poem. By what techniques are they produced?

Robert Frost (1874–1963)

Never Again Would Birds' Song Be the Same 1942

He would declare and could himself believe
That the birds there in all the garden round
From having heard the daylong voice of Eve
Had added to their own an oversound,
Her tone of meaning but without the words.
Admittedly an eloquence so soft
Could only have had an influence on birds
When call or laughter carried it aloft.
Be that as may be, she was in their song.
Moreover her voice upon their voices crossed
Had now persisted in the woods so long
That probably it never would be lost.
Never again would birds' song be the same.
And to do that to birds was why she came.

Questions

1. Who is *he*?
2. In reading aloud line 9, do you stress *may*? (Do you say "as MAY be" or "as may BE"?) What guide do we have to the poet's wishes here?
3. Which lines does Frost cast mostly or entirely into monosyllables? How would you describe the impact of these lines?
4. In his *Essay on Criticism,* Alexander Pope made fun of poets who wrote mechanically, without wit: "And ten low words oft creep in one dull line." Do you think this criticism applicable to Frost's lines of monosyllables? Explain.

Ben Jonson (1573?–1637)

Slow, slow, fresh fount, keep time with my salt tears

1600

Slow, slow, fresh fount, keep time with my salt tears;
  Yet slower yet, oh faintly, gentle springs;
List to the heavy part the music bears,
  Woe weeps out her division° when she sings. *a part in a song*
    Droop herbs and flowers,
    Fall grief in showers;
    Our beauties are not ours;
      Oh, I could still,
Like melting snow upon some craggy hill,
  Drop, drop, drop, drop,
Since nature's pride is now a withered daffodil.

Slow, slow, fresh fount. The nymph Echo sings this lament over the youth Narcissus in Jonson's play *Cynthia's Revels.* In mythology, Nemesis, goddess of vengeance, to punish Narcissus for loving his own beauty, caused him to pine away and then transformed him into a narcissus (another name for a *daffodil,* line 11).

Questions

1. Read the first line aloud rapidly. Why is it difficult to do so?
2. Which lines rely most heavily on stressed syllables?
3. In general, how would you describe the rhythm of this poem? How is it appropriate to what is said?

Robert Lowell (1917–1977)

At the Altar

1946

I sit at a gold table with my girl
Whose eyelids burn with brandy. What a whirl
Of Easter eggs is colored by the lights,
As the Norwegian dancer's crystalled tights
Flash with her naked leg's high-booted skate,
Like Northern Lights upon my watching plate.

The twinkling steel above me is a star;
I am a fallen Christmas tree. Our car
Races through seven red-lights—then the road
Is unpatrolled and empty, and a load
Of ply-wood with a tail-light makes us slow.
I turn and whisper in her ear. You know
I want to leave my mother and my wife,
You wouldn't have me tied to them for life . . .
Time runs, the windshield runs with stars. The past
Is cities from a train, until at last
Its escalating and black-windowed blocks
Recoil against a Gothic church. The clocks
Are tolling. I am dying. The shocked stones
Are falling like a ton of bricks and bones
That snap and splinter and descend in glass
Before a priest who mumbles through his Mass
And sprinkles holy water; and the Day
Breaks with its lightning on the man of clay,
Dies amara valde. Here the Lord
Is Lucifer in harness: hand on sword,
He watches me for Mother, and will turn
The bier and baby-carriage where I burn.

AT THE ALTAR. In a public reading of this poem, Robert Lowell made some remarks cited by George P. Elliott in *Fifteen Modern American Poets* (New York: Holt, Rinehart & Winston, 1956). Lit up like a Christmas tree, the speaker finds himself in a Boston nightclub, watching a skating floorshow. Then he and his girl drive (or does he only dream they drive?) to a church where a priest saying a funeral Mass sprinkles a corpse with holy water. 23. *the Day:* the Day of Judgment. 25. *Dies amara valde:* "day bitter above all others," a phrase from a funeral hymn, the *Dies Irae,* in which sinners are warned to fear God's wrath. 28. *baby-carriage:* the undertaker's silver dolly, supporting a coffin.

QUESTIONS

1. Which lines in this poem are end-stopped?
2. What effects does Lowell obtain by so many run-on lines?
3. What else contributes to the rhythm of the poem?
4. How is this rhythm appropriate to what the poet is saying? Explain.

Alexander Pope (1688–1744)

ATTICUS 1735

How did they fume, and stamp, and roar, and chafe!
And swear, not Addison himself was safe.
  Peace to all such! but were there one whose fires
True genius kindles, and fair fame inspires;
Blest with each talent, and each art to please,
And born to write, converse, and live with ease,
Should such a man, too fond to rule alone,

Bear, like the Turk, no brother near the throne,
View him with scornful, yet with jealous eyes,
And hate for arts that caused himself to rise;
Damn with faint praise, assent with civil leer,
And, without sneering, teach the rest to sneer;
Willing to wound, and yet afraid to strike,
Just hint a fault, and hesitate dislike;
Alike reserved to blame, or to commend,
A timorous foe, and a suspicious friend;
Dreading e'en fools, by flatterers besieged,
And so obliging, that he ne'er obliged;
Like Cato, give his little Senate laws,
And sit attentive to his own applause:
While wits and Templars every sentence raise,
And wonder with a foolish face of praise—
Who but must laugh, if such a man there be?
Who would not weep, if Atticus were he?

ATTICUS. In this selection from "An Epistle to Dr. Arbuthnot," Pope has been referring to dull versifiers and their angry reception of his satiric thrusts at them. With *Peace to all such!* (line 3) he turns to his celebrated portrait of a rival man of letters, Joseph Addison. 19. *Cato:* Roman senator about whom Addison had written a tragedy. 21. *Templars:* London lawyers who dabbled in literature.

QUESTIONS

1. In these lines—one of the most famous damnations in English poetry—what positive virtues, in Pope's view, does Addison lack?
2. Read aloud from Robert Lowell's "At the Altar," then read aloud a few lines from Pope. Although both poets write in rimed couplets, in lines ten syllables long, how do the rhythms of the two poems compare? To what do you attribute the differences?

EXERCISE: *Two Kinds of Rhythm*

The following compositions in verse have lines of similar length, yet they differ greatly in rhythm. Explain how they differ and why.

Sir Thomas Wyatt (1503?–1542)

WITH SERVING STILL (1528–1536)

With serving still° — *continually*
  This have I won,
For my goodwill
  To be undone;

And for redress
  Of all my pain,
Disdainfulness
  I have again°; — *in return*

And for reward
  Of all my smart
Lo, thus unheard,
  I must depart!

Wherefore all ye
  That after shall
By fortune be,
  As I am, thrall,

Example take
  What I have won,
Thus for her sake
  To be undone!

Dorothy Parker (1893–1967)

RÉSUMÉ 1926

Razors pain you;
Rivers are damp;
Acids stain you;
And drugs cause cramp.
Guns aren't lawful;
Nooses give;
Gas smells awful;
You might as well live.

METER

To enjoy the rhythms of a poem, no special knowledge of meter is necessary. All you need do is pay attention to stresses and where they fall; and you will perceive the basic pattern, if there is any. However, there is nothing occult about the study of meter. Most people find they can master its essentials in no more time than it takes to learn a complicated game such as chess. If you take the time, you will then have the pleasure of knowing what is happening in the rhythms of many a fine poem, and pleasurable knowledge may even deepen your insight into poetry. The following discussion, then, will be of interest only to those who care to go deeper into **prosody,** the study of metrical structures in poetry.

Far from being artificial constructions found only in the minds of poets, meters occur in everyday speech and prose. As the following example will show, they may need only a poet to recognize them. The English satirist Max Beerbohm, after contemplating the title page of his first book, took his pen and added two more lines.

Max Beerbohm (1872–1956)

On the Imprint of the First English Edition of "The Works of Max Beerbohm" (1896)

"London: John Lane, *The Bodley Head*
  New York: Charles Scribner's Sons."
This plain announcement, nicely read,
  Iambically runs.

In everyday life, nobody speaks or writes in perfect iambic rhythm, except at moments: "a HAM on RYE and HIT the MUStard HARD!" (As we have seen, iambic rhythm consists of a series of syllables alternately unstressed and stressed.) Poets rarely speak in it for long, either—at least, not with absolute consistency. If you read aloud Max Beerbohm's lines, you'll hear an iambic rhythm, but not an unvarying one. And yet all of us speak with a rising and falling of stress *somewhat like* iambic meter. Perhaps, as the poet and scholar John Thompson has maintained, "The iambic metrical pattern has dominated English verse because it provides the best symbolic model of our language."[4]

To make ourselves aware of a meter, we need only listen to a poem, or sound its words to ourselves. If we care to work out exactly what a poet is doing, we *scan* a line or a poem by indicating the stresses in it. **Scansion,** the art of so doing, is not just a matter of pointing to syllables; it is also a matter of listening to a poem and making sense of it. To scan a poem is one way to indicate how to read it aloud; in order to see where stresses fall, you have to see the places where the poet wishes to put emphasis. That is why, when scanning a poem, you may find yourself suddenly understanding it.

An objection might be raised against scanning: isn't it too simple to pretend that all language (and poetry) can be divided neatly into stressed syllables and unstressed syllables? Indeed it is. As the linguist Otto Jespersen has said, "In reality there are infinite gradations of stress, from the most penetrating scream to the faintest whisper."[5] However, the idea in scanning a poem is not to reproduce the sound of a human voice. For that we would do better to buy a tape recorder. To scan a poem, rather, is to make a diagram of the stresses (and absences of stress) we find in it. Various marks are used in scansion; in this book we use ′ for a stressed syllable and ˘ for an unstressed syllable. Some scanners, wishing a little more precision, also use the **half-stress** (\`);

[4] *The Founding of English Metre* (New York: Columbia University Press, 1966), p. 12.
[5] "Notes on Metre," (1933), reprinted in *The Structure of Verse: Modern Essays on Prosody*, edited by Harvey Gross, second edition (New York: Echo Press, 1978).

this device can be helpful in many instances when a syllable usually not stressed comes at a place where it takes some emphasis, as in the last syllable in a line:

> ⏑ ′ ⏑ ′ ⏑ ′ ⏑ ⏑ ′⏑\
> Bound each to each with nat·u·ral pi·e·ty.

Here, with examples, are some of the principal meters we find in English poetry. Each is named for its basic **foot,** or molecule (usually one stressed and one or two unstressed syllables).

1. **Iambic** (foot: the **iamb,** ⏑ ′):

   ⏑ ′ ⏑ ′ ⏑ ′ ⏑ ′ ⏑ ′ ⏑ ′ ⏑ ′\
   The fall·ing out of faith·ful friends, re·new·ing is of love

2. **Anapestic** (foot: the **anapest,** ⏑ ⏑ ′):

   ⏑⏑ ′ ⏑ ⏑ ′ ⏑⏑ ′\
   I am mon·arch of all I sur·vey

3. **Trochaic** (foot: the **trochee,** ′ ⏑):

   ′ ⏑ ′ ⏑ ′ ⏑ ′ ⏑\
   Dou·ble, dou·ble, toil and trou·ble

4. **Dactylic** (foot: the **dactyl,** ′ ⏑ ⏑):

   ′ ⏑ ⏑ ′ ⏑ ⏑\
   Take her up ten·der·ly

Iambic and anapestic meters are called **rising** meters because their movement rises from unstressed syllable (or syllables) to stress; trochaic and dactylic meters are called **falling.** In the twentieth century, the bouncing meters—anapestic and dactylic—have been used more often for comic verse than for serious poetry. Called feet, though they contain no unaccented syllables, are the **monosyllabic foot** (′) and the **spondee** (″). Meters are not ordinarily made up of them; if one were, it would be like the steady impact of nails being hammered into a board—no pleasure to hear or to dance to. But inserted now and then, they can lend emphasis and variety to a meter, as Yeats well knew when he broke up the predominantly iambic rhythm of "Who Goes with Fergus?" (page 123) with the line,

> ⏑ ⏑ ′ ′ ⏑ ⏑ ′ ′\
> And the white breast of the dim sea,

in which occur two spondees. Meters are classified also by line lengths: *trochaic monometer,* for instance, is a line one trochee long, as in this anonymous brief comment on microbes:

> Adam\
> Had 'em.

A frequently heard metrical description is **iambic pentameter:** a line of five iambs, a meter especially familiar because it occurs in all blank verse (such as Shakespeare's plays and Milton's *Paradise Lost*), heroic couplets, and sonnets. The commonly used names for line lengths follow:

monometer	one foot	**pentameter**	five feet
dimeter	two feet	**hexameter**	six feet
trimeter	three feet	**heptameter**	seven feet
tetrameter	four feet	**octameter**	eight feet

Lines of more than eight feet are possible but are rare. They tend to break up into shorter lengths in the listening ear.

When Yeats chose the spondees *white breast* and *dim sea,* he was doing what poets who write in meter do frequently for variety—using a foot other than the expected one. Often such a substitution will be made at the very beginning of a line, as in the third line of this passage from Christopher Marlowe's *Tragical History of Doctor Faustus:*

> Was this the face that launched a thou·sand ships
> And burnt the top·less tow'rs of Il·i·um?
> Sweet Hel·en, make me im·mor·tal with a kiss.

How, we might wonder, can that last line be called iambic at all? But it is, just as a waltz that includes an extra step or two, or leaves a few steps out, remains a waltz. In the preceding lines the basic iambic pentameter is established, and though in the third line the regularity is varied from, it does not altogether disappear. It continues for a while to run on in the reader's mind, where (if the poet does not stay away from it for too long) the meter will be there when the poem comes back to it.

Like a basic dance step, a meter is not to be slavishly adhered to. The fun in reading a metrical poem often comes from watching the poet continually departing from perfect regularity, giving a few heel-kicks to display a bit of joy or ingenuity, then easing back into the basic step again. Because meter is orderly and the rhythms of living speech are unruly, poets can play one against the other, in a sort of counterpoint. Robert Frost, a master at pitting a line of iambs against a very natural-sounding and irregular sentence, declared, "I am never more pleased than when I can get these into strained relation. I like to drag and break the intonation across the meter as waves first comb and then break stumbling on a shingle."[6]

Evidently Frost's skilled effects would be lost to a reader who, scanning a Frost poem or reading it aloud, distorted its rhythms to fit the words exactly to the meter. With rare exceptions, a good poem can

[6] Letter to John Cournos in 1914, in *Selected Letters of Robert Frost,* edited by Lawrance Thompson (New York: Holt, Rinehart & Winston, 1964), p. 128.

be read and scanned the way we would speak its sentences if they were ours. This, for example, is an unreal scansion:

That's my last Duch·ess paint·ed on the wall.

—because no speaker of English would say that sentence in that way. We are likely to stress *That's* and *last.*

Variety in rhythm is not merely desirable in poetry, it is a necessity, and the poem that fails to depart often enough from absolute regularity is in trouble. If the beat of its words slips into a mechanical pattern, the poem marches robot-like right into its grave. Luckily, few poets, except writers of greeting cards, favor rhythms that go "a TROT a TROT a TROT a TROT" for very long. Robert Frost told an audience one time that if when writing a poem he found its rhythm becoming monotonous, he knew that the poem was going wrong and that he himself didn't believe what it was saying.

Although in good poetry we seldom meet a very long passage of absolute metrical regularity, we sometimes find (in a line or so) a monotonous rhythm that is effective. Words fall meaningfully in Macbeth's famous statement of world-weariness: "Tomorrow and tomorrow and tomorrow . . ." and in the opening lines of Thomas Gray's "Elegy":

The cur·few tolls the knell of part·ing day,
The low·ing herd wind slow·ly o'er the lea,
The plow·man home·ward plods his wear·y way,
And leaves the world to dark·ness and to me.[7]

Although certain unstressed syllables in these lines seem to call for more emphasis than others—you might, for instance, care to throw a little more weight on the second syllable of *curfew* in the opening line—we can still say the lines are notably iambic. Their almost unvarying rhythm seems just right to convey the tolling of a bell and the weary setting down of one foot after the other.

Besides the two rising meters (iambic, anapestic) and the two falling meters (trochaic, dactylic), English poets have another valuable meter. It is **accentual meter,** in which the poet does not write in feet (as in the other meters) but instead counts accents (stresses). The idea is to have the same number of stresses in every line. The poet may place them anywhere in the line and may include practically any number of unstressed syllables, which do not count. In "Christabel," for instance,

[7] The complete poem, "Elegy Written in a Country Churchyard," appears on page 267.

Coleridge keeps four stresses to a line, though the first line has only eight syllables and the last line has eleven:

> There is nót wind e·nóugh to twírl
> The óne red léaf, the lást of its clán,
> That dán·ces as óf·ten as dánce it cán,
> Háng·ing so líght, and háng·ing so hígh,
> On the tóp-most twíg that looks úp at theský.

The history of accentual meter is long and honorable. Old English poetry was written in a kind of accentual meter, but its line was more rule-bound than Coleridge's: four stresses arranged two on either side of a cesura, plus alliteration of three of the stressed syllables. In "Junk," Richard Wilbur revives the pattern:

> An áxe án·gles ‖ from my néigh·bor's ásh·can . . .

while Ezra Pound, in "The Seafarer" (page 352), also gives us an approximation of Old English poetry in modern English. Many poets, from the authors of Mother Goose rimes to Gerard Manley Hopkins, have sometimes found accentual meters congenial.

It has been charged that the importation of Greek names for meters and of the classical notion of feet was an unsuccessful attempt to make a Parthenon out of English wattles. The charge is open to debate, but at least it is certain that Greek names for feet cannot mean to us what they meant to Aristotle. Greek and Latin poetry is measured not by stressed and unstressed syllables but by long and short vowel sounds. An iamb in classical verse is one short syllable followed by a long syllable. Such a meter constructed on the principle of vowel length is called a **quantitative meter**. Campion's "Rose-cheeked Laura" was an attempt to demonstrate it in English, but probably we enjoy the rhythm of the poem's well-placed stresses whether or not we notice its vowel sounds.

Thomas Campion (1567–1620)

Rose-cheeked Laura, come — 1602

Rose-cheeked Laura, come,
Sing thou smoothly with thy beauty's
Silent music, either other
        Sweetly gracing.

Lovely forms do flow
From concent° divinely framèd; *harmony*
Heav'n is music, and thy beauty's
Birth is heavenly.

These dull notes we sing
Discords need for helps to grace them;
Only beauty purely loving
Knows no discord,

But still moves delight,
Like clear springs renewed by flowing,
Ever perfect, ever in them-
Selves eternal.

Although less popular among poets today than formerly, meter endures. Major poets from Shakespeare through Yeats have fashioned their work by it, and if we are to read their poems with full enjoyment, we need to be aware of it. To enjoy metrical poetry—even to write it—you do not have to slice lines into feet; you do need to recognize when a meter is present in a line, and when the line departs from it. An argument in favor of meter is that it reminds us of body rhythms such as breathing, walking, the beating of the heart. In an effective metrical poem, these rhythms cannot be separated from what the poet is saying—or, in the words of an old jazz song, "It doesn't mean a thing if you ain't got that swing." A critic, Paul Fussell, Jr., has put it: "No element of a poem is more basic—and I mean physical—in its effect upon the reader than the metrical element, and perhaps no technical triumphs reveal more readily than the metrical the poet's sympathy with that universal human nature . . . which exists outside his own."[8]

Walter Savage Landor (1775–1864)

On Seeing a Hair of Lucretia Borgia (1825)

Borgia, thou once wert almost too august
And high for adoration; now thou'rt dust.
All that remains of thee these plaits unfold,
Calm hair, meandering in pellucid gold.

Questions

1. Who was Lucretia Borgia and when did she live? What connotations that add meaning to Landor's poem has her name?
2. What does *meander* mean? How can a hair meander?

[8] *Poetic Meter and Poetic Form* (New York: Random House, 1965), p. 110.

3. Scan the poem, indicating stressed syllables. What is the basic meter of most of the poem? What happens to this meter in the last line? Note especially *meandering in pel-*. How many light, unstressed syllables are there in a row? Does rhythm in any way reinforce what Landor is saying?

EXERCISE: *Meaningful Variation*

At what place or places in each of these passages does the poet depart from basic iambic meter? How does each departure help underscore the meaning?

1. John Dryden, "Mac Flecknoe" (speech of Flecknoe, prince of Nonsense, referring to Thomas Shadwell, poet and playwright):

   Shadwell alone of all my sons is he
   Who stands confirmed in full stupidity.
   The rest to some faint meaning make pretense,
   But Shadwell never deviates into sense.

2. Alexander Pope, *An Essay on Criticism:*

   A needless Alexandrine ends the song
   That, like a wounded snake, drags its slow length along.

3. Henry King, "The Exequy" (an apostrophe to his wife):

   'Tis true, with shame and grief I yield,
   Thou like the van° first tookst the field, *vanguard*
   And gotten hath the victory
   In thus adventuring to die
   Before me, whose more years might crave
   A just precedence in the grave.
   But hark! my pulse like a soft drum
   Beats my approach, tells thee I come;
   And slow howe'er my marches be,
   I shall at last sit down by thee.

4. Henry Wadsworth Longfellow, "Mezzo Cammin":

   Half-way up the hill, I see the Past
   Lying beneath me with its sounds and sights,—
   A city in the twilight dim and vast,
   With smoking roofs, soft bells, and gleaming lights,—
   And hear above me on the autumnal blast
   The cataract of Death far thundering from the heights.

5. Wallace Stevens, "Sunday Morning":

   Deer walk upon our mountains, and the quail
   Whistle about us their spontaneous cries;
   Sweet berries ripen in the wilderness;
   And, in the isolation of the sky,
   At evening, casual flocks of pigeons make
   Ambiguous undulations as they sink,
   Downward to darkness, on extended wings.

EXERCISE: *Recognizing Rhythms*

Which of the following poems contain predominant meters? Which poems are not wholly metrical, but are metrical in certain lines? Point out any such lines. What reasons do you see, in such places, for the poet's seeking a metrical effect?

George Gordon, Lord Byron (1788–1824)

The Destruction of Sennacherib

1815

The Assyrian came down like the wolf on the fold,
And his cohorts were gleaming in purple and gold;
And the sheen of their spears was like stars on the sea,
When the blue wave rolls nightly on deep Galilee.

Like the leaves of the forest when summer is green,
That host with their banners at sunset were seen:
Like the leaves of the forest when autumn hath blown,
That host on the morrow lay withered and strown.

For the Angel of Death spread his wings on the blast,
And breathed in the face of the foe as he passed;
And the eyes of the sleepers waxed deadly and chill,
And their hearts but once heaved—and for ever grew still!

And there lay the steed with his nostril all wide,
But through it there rolled not the breath of his pride;
And the foam of his gasping lay white on the turf,
And cold as the spray of the rock-beating surf.

And there lay the rider distorted and pale,
With the dew on his brow, and the rust on his mail;
And the tents were all silent, the banners alone,
The lances unlifted, the trumpet unblown.

And the widows of Ashur are loud in their wail,
And the idols are broke in the temple of Baal;
And the might of the Gentile, unsmote by the sword,
Hath melted like snow in the glance of the Lord!

The Destruction of Sennacherib. Byron retells the Bible story of King Sennacherib of Assyria who, while leading an invasion of Jerusalem, suddenly lost his army: "And it came to pass that night, that the angel of the Lord went out, and smote in the camp of the Assyrians a hundred fourscore and five thousand: and when they arose early in the morning, behold, they were all dead corpses" (II Kings 19:35). 21–22: *Ashur . . . Baal:* Assyria and the Assyrian deity. 23. *Gentile:* Sennacherib (a non-Hebrew).

Edna St. Vincent Millay (1892–1950)

Counting-out Rhyme

1928

Silver bark of beech, and sallow
Bark of yellow birch and yellow
   Twig of willow.

Stripe of green in moosewood maple,
Colour seen in leaf of apple,
   Bark of popple.

Wood of popple pale as moonbeam,
Wood of oak for yoke and barn-beam,
  Wood of hornbeam.

Silver bark of beech, and hollow
Stem of elder, tall and yellow
  Twig of willow.

A. E. Housman (1859–1936)

When I was one-and-twenty 1896

When I was one-and-twenty
  I heard a wise man say,
"Give crowns and pounds and guineas
  But not your heart away;
Give pearls away and rubies
  But keep your fancy free."
But I was one-and-twenty,
  No use to talk to me.

When I was one-and-twenty
  I heard him say again,
"The heart out of the bosom
  Was never given in vain;
'Tis paid with sighs a plenty
  And sold for endless rue."
And I am two-and-twenty,
  And oh, 'tis true, 'tis true.

William Carlos Williams (1883–1963)

The Descent of Winter (section 10/30) 1934

To freight cars in the air

all the slow
  clank, clank
  clank, clank
moving about the treetops

the
  wha, wha
of the hoarse whistle

  pah, pah, pah
  pah, pah, pah, pah, pah
  piece and piece
  piece and piece
moving still trippingly
through the morningmist

long after the engine
has fought by
                and disappeared
in silence
                to the left

Ruth Pitter (b. 1897)

But for Lust — 1945

But for lust we could be friends,
  On each other's necks could weep:
In each other's arms could sleep
  In the calm the cradle lends:

Lends awhile, and takes away.
  But for hunger, but for fear,
Calm could be our day and year
  From the yellow to the grey:

From the gold to the grey hair,
  But for passion we could rest,
But for passion we could feast
  On compassion everywhere.

Even in this night I know
  By the awful living dead,
By this craving tear I shed,
  Somewhere, somewhere it is so.

Walt Whitman (1819–1892)

Beat! Beat! Drums! — (1861)

Beat! beat! drums!—blow! bugles! blow!
Through the windows—through doors—burst like a ruthless force,
Into the solemn church, and scatter the congregation,
Into the school where the scholar is studying;
Leave not the bridegroom quiet—no happiness must he have now with his bride,
Nor the peaceful farmer any peace, ploughing his field or gathering his grain,
So fierce you whirr and pound you drums—so shrill you bugles blow.

Beat! beat! drums!—blow! bugles! blow!
Over the traffic of cities—over the rumble of wheels in the streets;
Are beds prepared for sleepers at night in the houses? no sleepers must sleep in those beds,

No bargainer's bargains by day—no brokers or speculators—would they continue?
Would the talkers be talking? would the singer attempt to sing?
Would the lawyer rise in the court to state his case before the judge?
Then rattle quicker, heavier drums—you bugles wilder blow.

Beat! beat! drums!—blow! bugles! blow!
Make no parley—stop for no expostulation,
Mind not the timid—mind not the weeper or prayer,
Mind not the old man beseeching the young man,
Let not the child's voice be heard, nor the mother's entreaties,
Make even the trestles to shake the dead where they lie awaiting the hearses.
So strong you thump O terrible drums—so loud you bugles blow.

10 Closed Form, Open Form

Form, as a general idea, is the design of a thing as a whole, the configuration of all its parts. No poem can escape having some kind of form, whether its lines are as various in length as broomstraws, or all in hexameter. To put this point another way: if you were to listen to a poem read aloud in a language unknown to you, or if you saw the poem printed in that foreign language, whatever in the poem you could see or hear would be the form of it.[1]

Of late, poets and critics debating the relative merits of "closed" and "open" form have worn out many miles of typewriter ribbon. Writing in **closed form,** a poet follows (or finds) some sort of pattern, such as that of a sonnet with its rime scheme and its fourteen lines of iambic pentameter. On a page, poems in closed form tend to look regular and symmetrical. Along with William Butler Yeats, who held that a successful poem will "come shut with a click, like a closing box," the poet who writes in closed form apparently strives for a kind of perfection—seeking, perhaps, to lodge words so securely in place that no word can be budged without a worsening.

The poet who writes in **open form** usually seeks no final click. Often, such a poet views the writing of a poem as a process, rather than a quest for an absolute. Free to use white space for emphasis, able to shorten or lengthen lines as the sense seems to require, the poet lets the poem discover its shape as it goes along, moving as water flows downhill, adjusting to its terrain, engulfing obstacles.

Right now, most American poets prefer open form to closed. But although less fashionable than they were, rime and meter are still in evidence. Most poetry of the past is in closed form. The reader who seeks a wide understanding of poetry will want to know both closed and open varieties.

[1] For a good summary of the uses of the term **form** in criticism of poetry, see the article "Form" by G. N. G. Orsini in *Princeton Encyclopedia of Poetry and Poetics,* 2nd ed., eds. Preminger, Warnke, and Hardison (Princeton: Princeton University Press, 1975).

CLOSED FORM: BLANK VERSE, STANZA, SONNET

Closed form gives some poems a valuable advantage: it makes them more easily memorable. The **epic** poems of nations—long narratives tracing the adventures of popular heroes: the Greek *Iliad* and *Odyssey,* the French *Song of Roland,* the Spanish *Cid*—tend to occur in patterns of fairly consistent line length or number of stresses because these works were sometimes transmitted orally. Sung to the music of a lyre or chanted to a drumbeat, they may have been easier to memorize because of their patterns. If a singer forgot something, the song would have a noticeable hole in it, so rime or fixed meter probably helped prevent an epic from deteriorating when passed along from one singer to another. It is no coincidence that so many English playwrights of Shakespeare's day favored iambic pentameter. Companies of actors, often called upon to perform a different play daily, could count on a fixed line length to aid their burdened memories.

Some poets complain that closed form is a straitjacket, a limit to free expression. Other poets, however, feel that, like fires held fast in a narrow space, thoughts stated in a tightly binding form may take on a heightened intensity. "Limitation makes for power," according to one contemporary practitioner of closed form, Richard Wilbur; "the strength of the genie comes of his being confined in a bottle." Compelled by some strict pattern to arrange and rearrange words, delete, and exchange them, poets must focus on them the keenest attention. Often they stand a chance of discovering words more meaningful than the ones they started out with. And at times, in obedience to a rime scheme, the poet may be surprised by saying something quite unexpected. Composing a poem is like walking blindfolded down a dark road, with one's hand in the hand of an inexorable guide. With the conscious portion of the mind, the poet may wish to express what seems to be a good idea. But a line ending in *year* must be followed by another ending in *atmosphere, beer, bier, bombardier, cashier, deer, friction-gear, frontier,* or some other rime word that otherwise might not have entered the poem. That is why rime schemes and stanza patterns can be mighty allies and valuable disturbers of the unconscious. As Rolfe Humphries has said about a strict form: "It makes you think of better things than you would all by yourself."

The best-known one-line pattern for a poem in English is **blank verse:** unrimed iambic pentameter. (This pattern is not a stanza: stanzas have more than one line.) Most portions of Shakespeare's plays are in blank verse, and so are Milton's *Paradise Lost,* Tennyson's "Ulysses," certain dramatic monologues of Browning and Frost, and thousands of other poems. Here is a poem in blank verse that startles us by dropping out of its pattern in the final line. Keats appears to have written it late in his life to his fiancée Fanny Brawne.

John Keats (1795–1821)

THIS LIVING HAND, NOW WARM AND CAPABLE (1819?)

This living hand, now warm and capable
Of earnest grasping, would, if it were cold
And in the icy silence of the tomb,
So haunt thy days and chill thy dreaming nights
That thou wouldst wish thine own heart dry of blood
So in my veins red life might stream again,
And thou be conscience-calmed—see here it is—
I hold it towards you.

The **couplet** is a two-line stanza, usually rimed. Its lines often tend to be equal in length, whether short or long. Here are two examples:

Blow,
Snow!

As I in hoary winter's night stood shivering in the snow,
Surprised I was with sudden heat which made my heart to glow.

(Actually, any pair of rimed lines that contains a complete thought is called a couplet, even if it is not a stanza, such as the couplet that ends a sonnet by Shakespeare.) Unlike other stanzas, couplets are often printed solid, not separated one couplet from the next by white space. This practice is usual in printing the **heroic couplet**—or **closed couplet**—two rimed lines of iambic pentameter, the first ending in a light pause, the second more heavily end-stopped. George Crabbe, in *The Parish Register,* described a shotgun wedding:

Next at our altar stood a luckless pair,
Brought by strong passions and a warrant there:
By long rent cloak, hung loosely, strove the bride,
From every eye, what all perceived, to hide;
While the boy bridgegroom, shuffling in his place,
Now hid awhile and then exposed his face.
As shame alternately with anger strove
The brain confused with muddy ale to move,
In haste and stammering he performed his part,
And looked the rage that rankled in his heart.

Though employed by Chaucer, the heroic couplet was named from its later use by Dryden and others in poems, translations of classical epics, and verse plays of epic heroes. It continued in favor through most of the eighteenth century. Much of our pleasure in reading good heroic couplets comes from the seemingly easy precision with which a skilled poet unites statements and strict pattern. In doing so, the poet may place a pair of words, phrases, clauses, or sentences side by side in agreement or similarity, forming a **parallel,** or in contrast and opposition, forming an **antithesis.** The effect is neat. For such skill in manipulating parallels and antitheses, John Denham's lines on the river Thames were much admired:

O could I flow like thee, and make thy stream
My great example, as it is my theme!
Though deep, yet clear; though gentle, yet not dull;
Strong without rage, without o'erflowing full.

These lines were echoed by Pope, ridiculing a poetaster, in two heroic couplets in *The Dunciad:*

Flow, Welsted, flow! like thine inspirer, Beer:
Though stale, not ripe; though thin, yet never clear;
So sweetly mawkish, and so smoothly dull;
Heady, not strong; o'erflowing, though not full.

Reading long poems in so exact a form, one may feel like a spectator at a ping-pong match unless the poet skillfully keeps varying rhythms. (Among much else, this skill distinguishes the work of Dryden and Pope from that of a lockstep horde of coupleteers who followed them.) One way of escaping such metronome-like monotony is to keep the cesura (see page 539) shifting about from place to place—now happening early in a line, now happening late—and at times unexpectedly to hurl in a second or third cesura. Try working through George Crabbe's lines (on page 559) and observe where the cesuras fall.

The **tercet** is a three-line stanza that, if rimed, usually keeps to one rime sound. **Terza rima,** the form Dante employs for *The Divine Comedy,* is made of tercets linked together by the rime scheme *a b a, b c b, c d c, d e d, e f e,* and so on. Harder to do in English than in Italian—with its greater resources of riming words—the form nevertheless has been managed by Shelley in "Ode to the West Wind" (with the aid of some slant rimes):

Make me thy lyre, even as the forest is:
What if my leaves are falling like its own!
The tumult of thy mighty harmonies

Will take from both a deep, autumnal tone,
Sweet though in sadness. Be thou, spirit fierce,
My spirit! Be thou me, impetuous one!

The workhorse of English stanzas is the **quatrain,** used for more rimed poems than any other form. It comes in many line lengths, and sometimes contains lines of varying length, as in the ballad stanza (see Chapter Seven).

Longer and more complicated stanzas are, of course, possible, but couplet, tercet, and quatrain have been called the building blocks of our poetry because most longer stanzas are made up of them. What short stanzas does John Donne mortar together to make the longer stanza of his "Song"?

John Donne (1572–1631)

SONG 1633

Go and catch a falling star
  Get with child a mandrake root,
Tell me where all past years are,
  Or who cleft the Devil's foot,
Teach me to hear mermaids singing,
  Or to keep off envy's stinging,
    And find
    What wind
Serves to advance an honest mind.

If thou be'st borne to strange sights,
  Things invisible to see,
Ride ten thousand days and nights,
  Till age snow white hairs on thee,
Thou, when thou return'st, wilt tell me
  All strange wonders that befell thee,
    And swear
    Nowhere
Lives a woman true, and fair.

If thou findst one, let me know,
  Such a pilgrimage were sweet—
Yet do not, I would not go,
  Though at next door we might meet;
Though she were true, when you met her,
  And last, till you write your letter,
    Yet she
    Will be
False, ere I come, to two, or three.

Recently in vogue is a form known as **syllabic verse** in which the poet establishes a pattern of a certain number of syllables to a line. Either rimed or rimeless but usually stanzaic, syllabic verse has been hailed as a way for poets to escape "the tyranny of the iamb" and discover less conventional rhythms, since, if they take as their line length an *odd* number of syllables, then iambs, being feet of *two* syllables, cannot fit perfectly into it. Offbeat victories have been scored in syllabics by such poets as W. H. Auden, W. D. Snodgrass, Donald Hall, Thom Gunn, and Marianne Moore. A well-known syllabic poem is Dylan Thomas's "Fern Hill" (page 379). Notice its shape on the page, count the syllables in its lines, and you'll perceive its perfect symmetry. Although like playing a game, the writing of such a poem is apparently more than finger exercise: the discipline can help a poet to sing well, though (with Thomas) singing "in . . . chains like the sea."

Poets who write in demanding forms seem to enjoy taking on an arbitrary task for the fun of it, as ballet dancers do, or weightlifters. Much of our pleasure in reading such poems comes from watching words fall into a shape. It is the pleasure of seeing any hard thing done skillfully—a leap executed in a dance, a basketball swished through a basket. Still, to be excellent, a poem needs more than skill; and to enjoy a poem it isn't always necessary for the reader to be aware of the skill that went into it. Unknowingly, the editors of *The New Yorker* once printed an **acrostic**—a poem in which the initial letter of each line, read downwards, spells out a word or words—that named (and insulted) a well-known anthologist. Evidently, besides being ingenious, the acrostic was a printable poem. In the Old Testament book of Lamentations, profoundly moving songs tell of the sufferings of the Jews after the destruction of Jerusalem. Four of the songs are written as an alphabetical acrostic, every stanza beginning with a letter of the Hebrew alphabet. However ingenious, such sublime poetry cannot be dismissed as merely witty; nor can it be charged that a poet who writes in such a form does not express deep feeling.

Patterns of sound and rhythm can, however, be striven after in a dull mechanical way, for which reason many poets today think them dangerous. Swinburne, who loved alliterations and tripping meters, had enough detachment to poke fun at his own excessive patterning:

> From the depth of the dreamy decline of the dawn through a notable nimbus of nebulous noonshine,
> Pallid and pink as the palm of the flag-flower that flickers with fear of the flies as they float,
> Are the looks of our lovers that lustrously lean from a marvel of mystic miraculous moonshine,
> These that we feel in the blood of our blushes that thicken and threaten with throbs through the throat?

This is bad, but bad deliberately. If any good at all, a poem in a fixed pattern, such as a sonnet, is created not only by the craftsman's chipping away at it but by the explosion of a sonnet-shaped *idea*. Viewed mechanically, as so many empty boxes somehow to be filled up, stanzas can impose the most hollow sort of discipline, and a poem written in these stanzas becomes no more than finger-exercise. This comment (although on fiction) may be appropriate:

Roy Campbell (1901–1957)

On Some South African Novelists 1930

You praise the firm restraint with which they write—
  I'm with you there, of course.
They use the snaffle and the curb all right;
  But where's the bloody horse?

Not only firm restraint marks the rimed poems of Shakespeare, Emily Dickinson, and William Butler Yeats, but also strong emotion. Such poets ride with certain hand upon a sturdy horse.

Ronald Gross (b. 1935)

YIELD 1967

Yield.
No Parking.
Unlawful to Pass.
Wait for Green Light.
Yield.

Stop.
Narrow Bridge.
Merging Traffic Ahead
Yield.
Yield.

QUESTIONS

1. This poem by Ronald Gross is a "found poem." After reading it, how would you define **found poetry?**
2. Does "Yield" have a theme? If so, how would you state it?
3. What makes "Yield" mean more than traffic signs ordinarily mean to us?

Ronald Gross, who produces his "found poetry" by arranging prose from such unlikely places as traffic signs and news stories into poem-like lines, has told of making a discovery:

> As I worked with labels, tax forms, commercials, contracts, pin-up captions, obituaries, and the like, I soon found myself rediscovering all the traditional verse forms in found materials: ode, sonnet, epigram, haiku, free verse. Such finds made me realize that these forms are not mere artifices, but shapes that language naturally takes when carrying powerful thoughts or feelings.[2]

Though Gross is a playful experimenter, his remark is true of serious poetry. Traditional verse forms like sonnets and haiku aren't a lot of hollow pillowcases for a poet to stuff with verbiage. At best, in the hands of a skilled poet, they can be shapes into which living language seems to fall naturally.

It is fun to see words tumble gracefully into such a shape. Consider, for instance, one famous "found poem," a sentence discovered in a physics textbook: "And so no force, however great, can stretch a cord,

[2] "Speaking of Books: Found Poetry," *The New York Times Book Review,* June 11, 1967. See also Gross's *Pop Poems* (New York: Simon & Schuster, 1967).

however fine, into a horizontal line which shall be absolutely straight."[3] What a good clear sentence containing effective parallels ("however great . . . however fine"), you might say, taking pleasure in it. Yet this plain statement gives extra pleasure if arranged like this:

> And so no force, however great,
>   Can stretch a cord, however fine,
>   Into a horizontal line
> Which shall be absolutely straight.

So spaced, in lines that reveal its built-in rimes and rhythms, the sentence would seem one of those "shapes that language naturally takes" that Ronald Gross finds everywhere. (It is possible, of course, that the textbook writer was gleefully planting a quatrain for someone to find; but perhaps it is more likely that he knew much rimed, metrical poetry by heart and couldn't help writing it unconsciously.) Inspired by pop artists who reveal fresh vistas in Brillo boxes and comic strips, found poetry has had a recent flurry of activity. Earlier practitioners include William Carlos Williams, whose long poem *Paterson* quotes historical documents and statistics. Prose, wrote Williams, can be a "laboratory" for poetry: "It throws up jewels which may be cleaned and grouped." Such a jewel may be the sentence Rosmarie Waldrop found in *The Joy of Cooking* and arranged as verse.

Rosmarie Waldrop (b. 1935)

THE RELAXED ABALONE 1970

Abalone, like inkfish,
needs prodigious pounding
if it has died in a state
of tension.

EXPERIMENT: *Finding a Poem*

In a newspaper, magazine, catalogue, textbook, or advertising throwaway, find a sentence or passage that (with a little artistic manipulation on your part) shows promise of becoming a poem. Copy it into lines like poetry, being careful to place what seem to be the most interesting words at the ends of lines to give them greatest emphasis. According to the rules of found poetry, you may excerpt, delete, repeat, and rearrange elements but not add anything. What does this experiment tell you about poetric form? About ordinary prose?

When we speak, with Ronald Gross, of "traditional verse forms," we usually mean **fixed forms.** If written in a fixed form a poem inherits

[3] William Whewell, *Elementary Treatise on Mechanics* (Cambridge, England, 1819).

from other poems certain familiar elements of structure: an unvarying number of lines, say, or a stanza pattern. In addition, it may display certain **conventions:** expected features such as themes, subjects, attitudes, or figures of speech. In medieval folk ballads a "milk-white steed" is a conventional figure of speech; and if its rider be a cruel and beautiful witch who kidnaps mortals, she is a conventional character. (*Conventional* doesn't necessarily mean uninteresting.)

In the poetry of western Europe and America, the **sonnet** is the fixed form that has attracted for the longest time the largest number of noteworthy practitioners. Originally an Italian form (*sonnetto:* "little song"), the sonnet owes much of its prestige to Petrarch (1304–1374), who wrote in it of his love for the unattainable Laura. So great was the vogue for sonnets in England at the end of the sixteenth century that a gentleman might have been thought a boor if he couldn't turn out a decent one. Not content to adopt merely the sonnet's fourteen-line pattern, English poets also tried on its conventional mask of the tormented lover. They borrowed some of Petrarch's similes (a lover's heart, for instance, is like a storm-tossed boat) and invented others. (If you would like more illustrations of Petrarchan conventions, see pages 264–265.)

Soon after English poets imported the sonnet in the middle of the sixteenth century, they worked out their own rime scheme—one easier for them to follow than Petrarch's, which calls for a greater number of riming words than English can readily provide. (In Italian, according to an exaggerated report, practically everything rimes.) In the following **English sonnet,** sometimes called a **Shakespearean sonnet,** the rimes cohere in four clusters: *a b a b, c d c d, e f e f, g g.* Because a rime scheme tends to shape the poet's statements to it, the English sonnet has three places where the procession of thought is likely to turn in another direction. Within its form, a poet may pursue one idea throughout the three quatrains and then in the couplet end with a surprise.

Michael Drayton (1563–1631)

Since there's no help, come let us kiss and part

1619

Since there's no help, come let us kiss and part;
Nay, I have done, you get no more of me,
And I am glad, yea, glad with all my heart
That thus so cleanly I myself can free;
Shake hands for ever, cancel all our vows,
And when we meet at any time again,
Be it not seen in either of our brows
That we one jot of former love retain.
Now at the last gasp of Love's latest breath,

When, his pulse failing, Passion speechless lies,
When Faith is kneeling by his bed of death,
And Innocence is closing up his eyes,
  Now if thou wouldst, when all have given him over,
  From death to life thou mightst him yet recover.

Less frequently met in English poetry, the **Italian sonnet,** or **Petrarchan sonnet,** follows the rime scheme *a b b a, a b b a* in its first eight lines, the **octave,** and then adds new rime sounds in the last six lines, the **sestet.** The sestet may rime *c d c d c d, c d e c d e, c d c c d c,* or in almost any other variation that doesn't end in a couplet. This organization into two parts sometimes helps arrange the poet's thoughts. In the octave, the poet may state a problem, and then, in the sestet, may offer a resolution. A lover, for example, may lament all octave long that a loved one is neglectful, then in line 9 begin to foresee some outcome: the speaker will die, or accept unhappiness, or trust that the beloved will have a change of heart.

Elizabeth Barrett Browning (1806–1861)

Grief — 1844

I tell you, hopeless grief is passionless;
  That only men incredulous of despair,
  Half-taught in anguish, through the midnight air
Beat upward to God's throne in loud access
Of shrieking and reproach. Full desertness
  In souls, as countries, lieth silent-bare
  Under the blanching, vertical eye-glare
Of the absolute Heavens. Deep-hearted man, express
Grief for the Dead in silence like to death:
  Most like a monumental statue set
In everlasting watch and moveless woe
Till itself crumble to the dust beneath.
  Touch it: the marble eyelids are not wet—
If it could weep, it could arise and go.

In this Italian sonnet, the division in thought comes a bit early—in the middle of line 8. Few English-speaking poets who have used the form seem to feel strictly bound by it.

"The sonnet," in the view of Robert Bly, a modern critic, "is where old professors go to die." And yet the use of the form by such twentieth-century poets as Yeats, Frost, Auden, Thomas, Pound, Cummings, Berryman, and Lowell suggests that it may be far from exhausted. Like the hero of the popular ballad "Finnegan's Wake," literary forms (though not professors) declared dead have a habit of springing up again. No law compels sonnets to adopt an exalted tone, or confines them to an Elizabethan vocabulary.

Archibald MacLeish (1892–1982)

The End of the World — 1926

Quite unexpectedly as Vasserot
The armless ambidextrian was lighting
A match between his great and second toe,
And Ralph the lion was engaged in biting
The neck of Madame Sossman while the drum
Pointed, and Teeny was about to cough
In waltz-time swinging Jocko by the thumb–
Quite unexpectedly the top blew off:

And there, there overhead, there, there hung over
Those thousands of white faces, those dazed eyes,
There in the starless dark the poise, the hover,
There with vast wings across the canceled skies,
There in the sudden blackness the black pall
Of nothing, nothing, nothing–nothing at all.

Questions

1. Where does the action of this poem take place?
2. To see for yourself how the sonnet is organized, sum up what happens in the octave. Then sum up what happens in the sestet.
3. How does the tone of the octave contrast with that of the sestet? (If you need to review *tone*, see pages 10–15.) Comment in particular on the clause in line 8: *the top blew off*. How do those words make you feel? Grim? Horrified? Or what?
4. Now read the closing couplet aloud. Try to describe (and account for) its effectiveness. Suppose MacLeish had wanted to write an Italian sonnet; he might have arranged the lines in the sestet like this–

   And there, there overhead, there, there hung over
   Those thousands of white faces, those dazed eyes,
   There in the sudden blackness the black pall,
   There in the starless dark the poise, the hover,
   There with vast wings across the canceled skies
   Of nothing, nothing, nothing–nothing at all.

   Would that have been as effective?

Exercise: *Knowing Two Kinds of Sonnet*

Find other sonnets in this book. Which are English in form? Which are Italian? Which are variations on either form or combinations of the two? You may wish to try your hand at writing both kinds of sonnet and experience the difference for yourself.

Oscar Wilde said that a cynic is "a man who knows the price of everything and the value of nothing." Such a terse, pointed statement is called an epigram. In poetry, however, an **epigram** is a form: "A short poem ending in a witty or ingenious turn of thought, to which the rest of the composition is intended to lead up" (according to the *Oxford English Dictionary*). Often it is a malicious gibe with an unexpected stinger in the final line—perhaps in the very last word:

Alexander Pope (1688–1744)

Epigram Engraved on the Collar of a Dog Which I Gave to His Royal Highness

1738

I am his Highness' dog at Kew;
Pray tell me, sir, whose dog are you?

Cultivated by the Roman poet Martial—for whom the epigram was a short poem, sometimes satiric but not always—this form has been especially favored by English poets who love Latin. Few characteristics of the English epigram seem fixed. Its pattern tends to be brief and rimed, its tone playfully merciless.

Martial (A.D. 40?–102?)

You serve the best wines always, my dear sir

A.D. 90

You serve the best wines always, my dear sir,
And yet they say your wines are not so good.
They say you are four times a widower.
They say . . . A drink? I don't believe I would.

—Translated by J. V. Cunningham

Sir John Harrington (1561?–1612)

Of Treason

1618

Treason doth never prosper; what's the reason?
For if it prosper, none dare call it treason.

William Blake (1757–1827)

Her whole life is an epigram (1793)

Her whole life is an epigram: smack smooth°, and neatly penned, — *perfectly smooth*
Platted° quite neat to catch applause, with a sliding noose at the end. — *plaited, woven*

E. E. Cummings (1894–1962)

a politician 1944

a politician is an arse upon
which everyone has sat except a man

J. V. Cunningham (b. 1911)

This Humanist whom no beliefs constrained 1947

This *Humanist* whom no beliefs constrained
Grew so broad-minded he was scatter-brained.

John Frederick Nims (b. 1914)

Contemplation 1967

"I'm Mark's alone!" you swore. Given cause to doubt you,
I think less of you, dear. But more about you.

Keith Waldrop (b. 1932)

On Measure 1968

The delicate foot of
Phoebe Isolde Farmer
taps meters acceptable to, among others, the
* * * *Poetry Journal* and the
University of * * * * * * *Review* and to
her brother, a minister, who is paying
for the printing of a small
volume—while he should be
praying, "Lord, grant her
wings."

EXPERIMENT: *Expanding an Epigram*

Rewrite any of the preceding epigrams, taking them out of rime (if they are in rime) and adding a few more words to them. See if your revisions have nearly the same effect as the originals.

EXERCISE: *Reading for Couplets*

Read all the sonnets by Shakespeare in this book. How do the final couplets of some of them resemble epigrams? Does this similarity diminish their effect of "seriousness"?

In English the only other fixed form to rival the sonnet and the epigram in favor is the **limerick:** five anapestic lines usually riming *a a b b a*. Here is a sample, attributed to W. R. Inge (1860–1954):

There was an old man of Khartoum
Who kept a tame sheep in his room,
"To remind me," he said,
"Of someone who's dead,
But I never can recollect whom."

The limerick was made popular by Edward Lear (1812–1888), English painter and author of nonsense, whose own custom was to make the last line hark back to the first: "That oppressive old man of Khartoum."

William Harmon (b. 1938)

BUREAUCRATIC LIMERICK

1979

The Bureau of Labor Statistics
Has been taken over by mystics
Whose way is to say
That your pay for the day
Has no actual characteristics.

EXPERIMENT: *Contriving a Clerihew*

The **clerihew,** a fixed form named for its inventor, Edmund Clerihew Bentley (1875–1956), has straggled behind the limerick in popularity. Here are four examples: how would you define the form and what are its rules? Who or what is its conventional subject matter? Try writing your own example.

James Watt
Was the hard-boiled kind of Scot:
He thought any dream
Sheer waste of steam.

—W. H. Auden

Sir Christopher Wren
Said, "I am going to dine with some men.
If anybody calls
Say I am designing St. Paul's."
—Edmund Clerihew Bentley

Etienne de Silhouette
(It's a good bet)
Has the shadiest claim
To fame.
—Cornelius J. Ter Maat

Dylan Thomas
Showed early promise.
His name's no dimmer, man,
On old Bob Zimmerman.
—T. O. Maglow

Dylan Thomas (1914–1953)

Do not go gentle into that good night — 1952

Do not go gentle into that good night,
Old age should burn and rave at close of day;
Rage, rage against the dying of the light.

Though wise men at their end know dark is right,
Because their words had forked no lightning they
Do not go gentle into that good night.

Good men, the last wave by, crying how bright
Their frail deeds might have danced in a green bay,
Rage, rage against the dying of the light.

Wild men who caught and sang the sun in flight,
And learn, too late, they grieved it on its way,
Do not go gentle into that good night.

Grave men, near death, who see with blinding sight
Blind eyes could blaze like meteors and be gay,
Rage, rage against the dying of the light.

And you, my father, there on the sad height,
Curse, bless, me now with your fierce tears, I pray,
Do not go gentle into that good night.
Rage, rage against the dying of the light.

Questions

1. "Do not go gentle into that good night" is a **villanelle:** a fixed form originated by French courtly poets of the Middle Ages. (For another villanelle, see Theodore Roethke's "The Waking," page 362.) What are its rules?
2. Is Thomas's poem, like many another villanelle, just an elaborate and trivial exercise? Whom does the poet address? What is he saying?

OPEN FORM

Writing in **open form**, a poet seeks to discover a fresh and individual arrangement for words in every poem. Such a poem, generally speaking, has neither a rime scheme nor a basic meter informing the whole of it. Doing without those powerful (some would say hypnotic) elements, the poet who writes in open form relies on other means to engage and to sustain the reader's attention. Novice poets often think that open form looks easy, not nearly so hard as riming everything; but in truth, formally open poems are easy to write only if written carelessly. To compose lines with keen awareness of open form's demands, and of its infinite possibilities, calls for skill: at least as much as that needed to write in meter and rime, if not more. Should the poet succeed, then the discovered arrangement will seem exactly right for what the poem is saying. Words will seem at home in their positions, as naturally as the words of a decent sonnet.

Denise Levertov (b. 1923)

SIX VARIATIONS (PART III) 1961

Shlup, shlup, the dog
as it laps up
water
makes intelligent
music, resting
now and then to take breath in irregular
measure.

Open form, in this brief poem, affords Denise Levertov certain advantages. Able to break off a line at whatever point she likes (a privilege not available to the poet writing, say, a conventional sonnet, who has to break off each line after its tenth syllable), she selects her pauses artfully. Line-breaks lend emphasis: a word or phrase at the end of a line takes a little more stress (and receives a little more attention), because the ending of the line compels the reader to make a slight pause, if only for the brief moment it takes to sling back one's eyes (like a typewriter carriage) and fix them on the line following. Slight pauses, then, follow the words and phrases *the dog / laps up / water / intelligent / resting / irregular / measure*—all of these being elements that apparently the poet wishes to call our attention to. (The pause after a line-break also casts a little more weight upon the *first* word or phrase of each succeeding line.) Levertov makes the most of white space—another means of calling attention to things, as any good picture-framer knows. By setting a word all alone on a line (*water / measure*), she makes it stand out more than it would do in a line of pentameter. She feels free to include a bit of rime (*Shlup, shlup / up*). She creates rhythms: if you will read aloud the phrases *intelligent / music* and *irregular / measure,* you will sense that in each phrase the arrangement of pauses and stresses is identical. Like the dog's halts to take breath, the lengths of the lines seem naturally irregular. The result is a fusion of meaning and form: indeed, an "intelligent music."

Poetry in open form used to be called **free verse** (from the French **vers libre**), suggesting a kind of verse liberated from the shackles of rime and meter. "Writing free verse," said Robert Frost, who wasn't interested in it, "is like playing tennis with the net down." And yet, as Denise Levertov and many other poets demonstrate, high scores can be made in such an unconventional game, provided it doesn't straggle all over the court. For a successful poem in open form, the term *free verse* seems inaccurate. "Being an art form," said William Carlos Williams, "verse cannot be 'free' in the sense of having *no* limitations or guiding principles."[4] Various substitute names have been suggested: organic poetry, composition by field, raw (as against cooked) poetry, open form poetry. "But what does it matter what you call it?" remark the editors of an anthology called *Naked Poetry.* The best poems of the last twenty years "don't rhyme (usually) and don't move on feet of more or less equal duration (usually). That nondescription moves toward the only technical principle they all have in common."[5]

And yet many poems in open form have much more in common than absences and lacks. One positive principle has been Ezra Pound's famous suggestion that poets "compose in the sequence of the musical phrase, not in the sequence of the metronome" – good advice, perhaps, even for poets who write inside fixed forms. In Charles Olson's influential theory of **projective verse,** poets compose by listening to their own breathing. On paper, they indicate the rhythms of a poem by using a little white space or a lot, a slight indentation or a deep one, depending on whether a short pause or a long one is intended. Words can be grouped in clusters on the page (usually no more words than a lungful of air can accommodate). Heavy cesuras are sometimes shown by breaking a line in two and lowering the second part of it.[6] (An Olson poem appears on page 193.)

To the poet working in open form, no less than to the poet writing a sonnet, line length can be valuable. Walt Whitman, who loved to expand vast sentences for line after line, knew well that an impressive

[4] "Free Verse," article in *Princeton Encyclopedia of Poetry and Poetics.*
[5] Stephen Berg and Robert Mezey, eds., foreword to *Naked Poetry: Recent American Poetry in Open Forms* (Indianapolis: Bobbs-Merrill, 1969).
[6] See Olson's essays "Projective Verse" and "Letter to Elaine Feinstein" in *Selected Writings,* edited by Robert Creeley (New York: New Directions, 1966). Olson's letters to Cid Corman are fascinating: *Letters for Origin, 1950–1955,* edited by Albert Glover (New York: Grossman, 1970).

rhythm can accumulate if the poet will keep long lines approximately the same length, causing a pause to recur at about the same interval after every line. Sometimes, too, Whitman repeats the same words at each line's opening. An instance is the masterly sixth section of "When Lilacs Last in the Dooryard Bloom'd," an elegy for Abraham Lincoln:

> Coffin that passes through lanes and streets,
> Through day and night with the great cloud darkening the land,
> With the pomp of the inloop'd flags with the cities draped in black,
> With the show of the States themselves as of crape-veil'd women standing,
> With processions long and winding and the flambeaus of the night,
> With the countless torches lit, with the silent sea of faces and the unbared heads,
> With the waiting depot, the arriving coffin, and the somber faces,
> With dirges through the night, with the thousand voices rising strong and solemn,
> With all the mournful voices of the dirges pour'd around the coffin,
> The dim-lit churches and the shuddering organs—where amid these you journey,
> With the tolling tolling bells' perpetual clang,
> Here, coffin that slowly passes,
> I give you my sprig of lilac.

There is music in such solemn, operatic arias. Whitman's lines echo another model: the Hebrew **psalms,** or sacred songs, as translated in the King James Version of the Bible. In Psalm 150, repetition also occurs inside of lines:

> Praise ye the Lord. Praise God in his sanctuary: praise him in the firmament of his power.
>
> Praise him for his mighty acts: praise him according to his excellent greatness.
>
> Praise him with the sound of the trumpet: praise him with the psaltery and harp.
>
> Praise him with the timbrel and dance: praise him with stringed instruments and organs.
>
> Praise him upon the loud cymbals: praise him upon the high sounding cymbals.
>
> Let every thing that hath breath praise the Lord. Praise ye the Lord.

In Biblical Psalms, we are in the presence of (as Robert Lowell has said) "supreme poems, written when their translators merely intended prose and were forced by the structure of their originals to write poetry."[7]

Whitman was a more deliberate craftsman than he let his readers think, and to anyone interested in writing in open form, his work will

[7] "On Freedom in Poetry," in Berg and Mezey, *Naked Poetry.*

repay close study. He knew that repetitions of any kind often make memorable rhythms, as in this passage from "Song of Myself," with every line ending on an *-ing* word (a stressed syllable followed by an unstressed syllable):

> Here and there with dimes on the eyes walking,
> To feed the greed of the belly the brains liberally spooning,
> Tickets buying, taking, selling, but in to the feast never once going,
> Many sweating, ploughing, thrashing, and then the chaff for payment
>   receiving,
> A few idly owning, and they the wheat continually claiming.

Much more than simply repetition, of course, went into the music of those lines—the internal rime *feed, greed,* the use of assonance, the trochees that begin the third and fourth lines, whether or not they were calculated.

In such classics of open form poetry, sound and rhythm are positive forces. When speaking a poem in open form, you often may find that it makes a difference for the better if you pause at the end of each line. Try pausing there, however briefly; but don't allow your voice to drop. Read just as you would normally read a sentence in prose (except for the pauses, of course). Why do the pauses matter? Open form poetry usually has no meter to lend it rhythm. *Some* lines in an open form poem, as we have seen in Whitman's "dimes on the eyes" passage, do fall into metrical feet; sometimes the whole poem does. Usually lacking meter's aid, however, open form, in order to have more and more noticeable rhythms, has need of all the recurring pauses it can get. When reading their own work aloud, open form poets like Robert Creeley and Allen Ginsberg often pause very definitely at each line break. Such a habit makes sense only in reading artful poems.

Some poems, to be sure, seem more widely open in form than others. A poet, for instance, may employ rime, but have the rimes recur at various intervals; or perhaps rime lines of various lengths. (See T. S. Eliot's famous "Love Song of J. Alfred Prufrock" on page 310. Is it a closed poem left ajar or an open poem trying to slam itself?) No law requires a poet to split thoughts into verse lines at all. Charles Baudelaire, Rainer Maria Rilke, Jorge Luis Borges, Alexander Solzhenitsyn, T. S. Eliot, and many others have written **prose poems,** in which, without caring that eye appeal and some of the rhythm of a line structure may be lost, the poet prints words in a block like a prose paragraph. For an example see Karl Shapiro's "The Dirty Word" (page 366).[8]

The great majority of poems appearing at present in American literary magazines are in open form. "Farewell, pale skunky pentameters

[8] For more example see *The Prose Poem, An International Anthology,* edited by Michael Benedikt (New York: Dell, 1976).

(the only honest English meter, gloop! gloop!)," Kenneth Koch has gleefully exclaimed. Many poets have sought reasons for turning away from patterns and fixed forms. Some hold that it is wrong to fit words into any pattern that already exists and instead believe in letting a poem seek its own shape as it goes along. (Traditionalists might say that that is what all good poems do anyway: sonnets rarely know they are going to be sonnets until the third line has been written. However, there is no doubt that the sonnet form already exists, at least in the back of the head of any poet who has ever read sonnets.) Some open form poets offer a historical motive: they want to reflect the nervous, staccato, disconnected pace of our bumper-to-bumper society. Others see open form as an attempt to suit thoughts and words to a more spontaneous order than the traditional verse forms allow. "Better," says Gary Snyder, quoting from Zen, "the perfect, easy discipline of the swallow's dip and swoop, 'without east or west.' "[9]

E. E. Cummings (1894–1962)

Buffalo Bill's 1923

Buffalo Bill's
defunct
        who used to
        ride a watersmooth-silver
                                        stallion
and break onetwothreefourfive pigeonsjustlikethat
                                                    Jesus

he was a handsome man
                                and what i want to know is
how do you like your blueeyed boy
Mister Death

Question

Cummings's poem would look like this if given conventional punctuation and set in a solid block like prose:

Buffalo Bill's defunct, who used to ride a water-smooth silver stallion and break one, two, three, four, five pigeons just like that. Jesus, he was a handsome man. And what I want to know is: "How do you like your blue-eyed boy, Mister Death?"

If this were done, by what characteristics would it still be recognizable as poetry? But what would be lost?

[9] "Some Yips & Barks in the Dark," in Berg and Mezey, *Naked Poetry*.

Emily Dickinson (1830–1886)

VICTORY COMES LATE (1861)

Victory comes late–
And is held low to freezing lips–
Too rapt with frost
To take it–
How sweet it would have tasted–
Just a Drop–
Was God so economical?
His Table's spread too high for Us–
Unless We dine on tiptoe–
Crumbs–fit such little mouths–
Cherries–suit Robins–
The Eagle's Golden Breakfast strangles–Them–
God keep His Oath to Sparrows–
Who of little Love–know how to starve–

QUESTIONS

1. In this specimen of poetry in open form, can you see any other places at which the poet might have broken off any of her lines? To place a word last in a line gives it a greater emphasis; she might, for instance, have ended line 12 with *Breakfast* and begun a new line with the word *strangles*. Do you think she knows what she is doing here or does the pattern of this poem seem decided by whim? Discuss.
2. Read the poem aloud. Try pausing for a fraction of a second at every dash. Is there any justification for the poet's unorthodox punctuation?

Robert Herrick (1591–1674)

UPON A CHILD THAT DIED 1648

Here she lies, a pretty bud,
Lately made of flesh and blood.
Who as soon fell fast asleep
As her little eyes did peep.
Give her strewings, but not stir
The earth that lightly covers her.

Saint Geraud [Bill Knott] (b. 1940)

POEM 1968

The only response
to a child's grave is
to lie down before it and play dead

Question

What differences do you find between the effect of Herrick's poem and that of Saint Geraud's? Try to explain how the pattern (or lack of pattern) in each poem contributes to these differences.

William Carlos Williams (1883–1963)

The Dance

1944

In Breughel's great picture, The Kermess,
the dancers go round, they go round and
around, the squeal and the blare and the
tweedle of bagpipes, a bugle and fiddles
tipping their bellies (round as the thick-
sided glasses whose wash they impound)
their hips and their bellies off balance
to turn them. Kicking and rolling about
the Fair Grounds, swinging their butts, those
shanks must be sound to bear up under such
rollicking measures, prance as they dance
in Breughel's great picture, The Kermess.

The Dance. Pieter Breughel (1520?–1569), a Flemish painter known for his scenes of peasant activities, represented in "The Kermess" a celebration on the feast day of a local patron saint.

Questions

1. Scan this poem and try to describe the effect of its rhythms.
2. Williams, widely admired for his free verse, insisted for many years that what he sought was a form not in the least bit free. What effect does he achieve by ending lines on such weak words as the articles *and* and *the*? By splitting *thick- / sided*? By splitting a prepositional phrase with the break at the end of line 8? By using line breaks to split *those* and *such* from what they modify? What do you think he is trying to convey?
3. Is there any point in his making line 12 a repetition of the opening line?
4. Look at the reproduction of Breughel's painting "The Kermess" (also called "Peasants Dancing"). Aware that the rhythms of dancers, the rhythms of a painting, and the rhythms of a poem are not all the same, can you put in your own words what Breughel's dancing figures have in common with Williams's descriptions of them?
5. Compare with "The Dance" another poem that refers to a Breughel painting: W. H. Auden's "Musée des Beaux Arts" on page 289. What seems to be each poet's main concern: to convey in words a sense of the painting, or to visualize the painting in order to state some theme?

Stephen Crane (1871–1900)

The Heart

1895

In the desert
I saw a creature, naked, bestial,
Who, squatting upon the ground,
Held his heart in his hands,
And ate of it.

I said, "Is it good, friend?"
"It is bitter—bitter," he answered;
"But I like it
Because it is bitter,
And because it is my heart."

Walt Whitman (1819–1892)

Cavalry Crossing a Ford

(1865)

A line in long array where they wind betwixt green islands,
They take a serpentine course, their arms flash in the sun—hark to the musical clank,
Behold the silvery river, in it the splashing horses loitering stop to drink,
Behold the brown-faced men, each group, each person a picture, the negligent rest on the saddles,
Some emerge on the opposite bank, others are just entering the ford—while,
Scarlet and blue and snowy white,
The guidon flags flutter gayly in the wind.

Questions

The following nit-picking questions are intended to help you see exactly what makes these two open form poems by Crane and Whitman so different in their music.

1. What devices of sound occur in Whitman's phrase *silvery river* (line 3)? Where else in his poem do you find these devices?
2. Does Crane use any such devices?
3. In number of syllables, Whitman's poem is almost twice as long as Crane's. Which poem has more pauses in it? (Count pauses at the ends of lines, at marks of punctuation.)
4. Read the two poems aloud. In general, how would you describe the effect of their sounds and rhythms? Is Crane's poem necessarily an inferior poem for having less music?

Gary Gildner (b. 1938)

First Practice 1969

After the doctor checked to see
we weren't ruptured,
the man with the short cigar took us
under the grade school,
where we went in case of attack
or storm, and said
he was Clifford Hill, he was
a man who believed dogs
ate dogs, he had once killed
for his country, and if
there were any girls present
for them to leave now.
                                        No one
left. OK, he said, he said I take
that to mean you are hungry
men who hate to lose as much
as I do. OK. Then
he made two lines of us
facing each other,
and across the way, he said,
is the man you hate most
in the world,
and if we are to win
that title I want to see how.
But I don't want to see
any marks when you're dressed,
he said. He said, *Now*.

Questions

1. What do you make of Hill and his world-view?

2. How does the speaker reveal his own view? Why, instead of quoting Hill directly ("This is a dog-eat-dog world"), does he call him *a man who believed dogs ate dogs* (lines 8–9)?
3. What effect is made by breaking off and lowering *No one* at the end of line 12?
4. What is gained by having a rime on the poem's last word?
5. For the sake of understanding how right the form of Gildner's poem is for it, imagine the poem in meter and a rime scheme, and condensed into two stanzas:

   Then he made two facing lines of us
   And he said, Across the way,
   Of all the men there are in the world
   Is the man you most want to slay,

   And if we are to win that title, he said,
   I want you to show me how.
   But I don't want to see any marks when you're dressed,
   He said. Go get him. *Now.*

   Why would that rewrite be so unfaithful to what Gildner is saying?
6. How would you answer someone who argued, "This can't be a poem—its subject is ugly and its language isn't beautiful"?

Leonard Cohen (b. 1934)

ALL THERE IS TO KNOW ABOUT ADOLPH EICHMANN — 1964

EYES: ....Medium
HAIR: ....Medium
WEIGHT: ....Medium
HEIGHT: ....Medium
DISTINGUISHING FEATURES: ....None
NUMBER OF FINGERS: ....Ten
NUMBER OF TOES: ....Ten
INTELLIGENCE: ....Medium

What did you expect?

Talons?

Oversize incisors?

Green saliva?

Madness?

ALL THERE IS TO KNOW ABOUT ADOLPH EICHMANN. During World War II Eichmann, a colonel in Hitler's secret police, directed the deportation to concentration camps of some 6,000,000 Jews from Germany and Nazi-occupied countries. After the war Eichmann was arrested in Argentina by Israeli agents. Tried in Israel on charges of mass murder, he was found guilty, sentenced to death, and hanged in 1962.

Questions

1. How does this work resemble a "found poem"?
2. How does it recall poetry in closed form? (Suggestion: Read it aloud.)
3. What is it saying? Try to state its theme.

Bruce Guernsey (b. 1944)

Louis B. Russell

1976

Louis B. Russell, a shop teacher from Indianapolis, died Wednesday after living for more than six years with a transplanted heart—longer than anyone else in history . . . he had received the heart of a 17 year-old boy killed in a hunting accident.

—The Associated Press

At night
he'd lie in bed
listening
to his new heart thump,
the blood pumping like strong legs
in a race
around the body's track,
its quick steps the echo
of his own young heart
as he reached for her hand
years ago,
that first kiss.

And falling asleep
he'd dream of the rifle, lifting it
slowly, slowly,
to his cheek,
his heart wild with death:
his first buck
square in the crosshairs
as he squeezes forever the blue steel
of the trigger,
his own head in another's sights
exploding like a melon
under the blood-bright cap.

Suddenly awake,
he'd listen for hours to the clock's tick
quick as a sprinter's breath,
its bright circle of numbers
grinning in the dark,
and think
of the shop class he'd teach tomorrow,
the powerful young men,
hammers
tight in their fists.

Questions

1. What does the poet indicate by dividing his poem into three parts?
2. In the third part, what comparison is implied in the image of *the clock's tick?* In the young men's *hammers tight in their fists?*
3. "It doesn't make sense for a poem about a heart to be written in jerky little short uneven lines like these. Guernsey ought to have written it in meter, in lines with a regular heart-like beat." Would you side with this critic, or with the poet? Why?

FOR REVIEW AND FURTHER STUDY

Leigh Hunt (1784–1859)

Rondeau

1838

Jenny kissed me when we met,
  Jumping from the chair she sat in;
Time, you thief, who love to get
  Sweets into your list, put that in:
Say I'm weary, say I'm sad,
  Say that health and wealth have missed me,
Say I'm growing old, but add,
  Jenny kissed me.

Question

Here is a fresh contemporary version of Hunt's "Rondeau" that yanks open the form of the rimed original:

Jenny kissed me when we met,
jumping from her chair;
Time, you thief, who love to add
sweets into your list, put that in:
say I'm weary, say I'm sad,
say I'm poor and in ill health,
say I'm growing old—but note, too,
Jenny kissed me.

That revised version says approximately the same thing as Hunt's original, doesn't it? Why is it less effective?

Stevie Smith (1902–1971)

I Remember

1957

It was my bridal night I remember,
An old man of seventy-three
I lay with my young bride in my arms,
A girl with t.b.

It was wartime, and overhead
The Germans were making a particularly heavy raid on Hampstead.
What rendered the confusion worse, perversely
Our bombers had chosen that moment to set out for Germany.
Harry, do they ever collide?
I do not think it has ever happened,
Oh my bride, my bride.

QUESTIONS

1. From the opening three lines, you might expect a rollicking, roughly metrical ballad or song. But as this poem goes on, how does its form surprise you?
2. What besides form, by the way, is odd or surprising here? Why can't this be called a conventional love lyric?
3. Lewis Turco has proposed the name *Nashers* for a certain kind of line (or couplet) found in the verse of Ogden Nash (whose "Very Like a Whale" appears on page 98). Nashers, according to Turco, are "usually long, of flat free verse or prose with humorous, often multisyllabic endings utilizing wrenched rhymes" (Lewis Turco, *The Book of Forms*, New York: E. P. Dutton, 1968). What Nashers can you find in "I Remember"?
4. What does the poet achieve by ending her poem in an exact rime (*collide/bride*)? Suppose she had ended it with another long, sprawling, unrimed line; for example, "As far as I know from reading the newspapers, O my poor coughing dear." What would be lost?
5. What do you understand to be the *tone* of this poem (the poet's implied attitude toward her material)? Would you call it tender and compassionate? Sorrowful? Grim? Playful and humorous? Earnest?
6. How does noticing the form of this poem help you to understand the tone of it?

Thomas Hardy (1840–1928)

AT A HASTY WEDDING 1901

If hours be years the twain are blest,
For now they solace swift desire
By bonds of every bond the best,
If hours be years. The twain are blest
Do eastern stars slope never west,
Nor pallid ashes follow fire:
If hours be years the twain are blest,
For now they solace swift desire.

QUESTIONS

1. A challenge that a poet faces in writing a **triolet** (another French courtly form) is that, obliged to devote five out of eight lines to repetitions, the poet has little room to say anything. In this triolet, what has Hardy succeeded in saying? Sum up his theme.
2. Why is the image of fire that dies to "pallid ashes" especially appropriate? (Compare the effect of this image to that of other images of pale things in Hardy's "Neutral Tones," page 208, a poem about the aftermath of a love affair.)

Geoffrey Chaucer (1340?–1400)

Your ÿen two wol slee me sodenly (late fourteenth century)

Your ÿen two wol slee° me sodenly; *eyes, slay*
I may the beautee of hem° not sustene°, *them, resist*
So woundeth hit thourghout my herte kene.

And but° your word wol helen° hastily *unless, heal*
My hertes wounde, while that hit is grene°, *new*
  Your ÿen two wol slee me sodenly;
  I may the beautee of hem not sustene.

Upon my trouthe° I sey you feithfully *word*
That ye ben of my lyf and deeth the quene;
For with my deeth the trouthe° shal be sene. *truth*
  Your ÿen two wol slee me sodenly;
  I may the beautee of hem not sustene,
  So woundeth it thourghout my herte kene.

Your ÿen two wol slee me sodenly. This poem is one of a group of three in the same fixed form, entitled "Merciles Beaute." 3. *so woundeth . . . kene:* "So deeply does it wound me through the heart."

Questions

1. This is a **roundel** (or **rondel**), an English form. What are its rules? How does it remind you of French courtly forms such as the villanelle and the triolet?
2. Try writing a roundel of your own in modern English. Although tricky, the form isn't extremely difficult: write only three lines and your poem is already eight-thirteenths finished. Here are some possible opening lines:

   Baby, your eyes will slay me. Shut them tight.
   Against their glow, I can't hold out for long. . . .

   Your eyes present a pin to my balloon:
   One pointed look and I start growing small. . . .

   Since I escaped from love, I've grown so fat,
   I barely can remember being thin. . . .

Wallace Stevens (1879–1955)

Thirteen Ways of Looking at a Blackbird 1923

I

Among twenty snowy mountains,
The only moving thing
Was the eye of the blackbird.

II

I was of three minds,
Like a tree
In which there are three blackbirds.

III

The blackbird whirled in the autumn winds.
It was a small part of the pantomime.

IV

A man and a woman
Are one.
A man and a woman and a blackbird
Are one.

V

I do not know which to prefer,
The beauty of inflections
Or the beauty of innuendoes,
The blackbird whistling
Or just after.

VI

Icicles filled the long window
With barbaric glass.
The shadow of the blackbird
Crossed it, to and fro.
The mood
Traced in the shadow
An indecipherable cause.

VII

O thin men of Haddam,
Why do you imagine golden birds?
Do you not see how the blackbird
Walks around the feet
Of the women about you?

VIII

I know noble accents
And lucid, inescapable rhythms;
But I know, too,
That the blackbird is involved
In what I know.

IX

When the blackbird flew out of sight,
It marked the edge
Of one of many circles.

X

At the sight of blackbirds
Flying in a green light,
Even the bawds of euphony
Would cry out sharply.

XI

He rode over Connecticut
In a glass coach.
Once, a fear pierced him,
In that he mistook
The shadow of his equipage
For blackbirds.

XII

The river is moving.
The blackbird must be flying.

XIII

It was evening all afternoon.
It was snowing
And it was going to snow.
The blackbird sat
In the cedar-limbs.

THIRTEEN WAYS OF LOOKING AT A BLACKBIRD. 25. *Haddam:* This Biblical-sounding name is that of a town in Connecticut.

QUESTIONS

1. What is the speaker's attitude toward the men of Haddam? What attitude toward this world does he suggest they lack? What is implied by calling them *thin* (line 25)?
2. What do the landscapes of winter contribute to the poem's effectiveness? If Stevens had chosen images of summer lawns, what would have been lost?
3. In which sections of the poem does Stevens suggest that a unity exists between human being and blackbird, between blackbird and the entire natural world? Can we say that Stevens "philosophizes"? What role does imagery play in Stevens's statement of his ideas?
4. What sense can you make of Part X? Make an enlightened guess.
5. Consider any one of the thirteen parts. What patterns of sound and rhythm do you find in it? What kind of structure does it have?
6. If the thirteen parts were arranged in some different order, would the poem be just as good? Or can we find a justification for its beginning with Part I and ending with Part XIII?
7. Does the poem seem an arbitrary combination of thirteen separate poems? Or is there any reason to call it a whole?

EXERCISE: *Seeing the Logic of Open Form Verse*

Read the following poems in open form silently to yourself, noticing what each poet does with white space, repetitions, line breaks, and indentations. Then read the poems aloud, trying to indicate by slight pauses where lines end and also pausing slightly at any space inside a line. Can you see any reasons for the poet's placing his words in this arrangement rather than in a prose paragraph? Do any of these poets seem to care also about visual effect? (As is the case with other kinds of poetry, there may not be any obvious logical reason for everything that happens in these poems.)

E. E. Cummings (1894–1962)

IN JUST- 1923

in Just-
spring when the world is mud-
luscious the little
lame balloonman

whistles far and wee

and eddieandbill come
running from marbles and
piracies and it's
spring

when the world is puddle-wonderful

the queer
old balloonman whistles
far and wee
and bettyandisbel come dancing

from hop-scotch and jump-rope and

it's
spring
and
the

goat-footed

balloonMan whistles
far
and
wee

Myra Cohn Livingston (b. 1926)

DRIVING 1972

Smooth it feels
wheels
in the groove of the gray
roadway
speedway
freeway

long along the in and out
of gray car
red car
blue car

catching up and overtaking into
one lane
two lane
three lane
it feels
over and over and ever and along

Donald Finkel (b. 1929)

Gesture 1970

My arm sweeps down
a pliant arc
whatever I am
streams through my
negligent wrist:

the poem
uncoils
like a
whip, and
snaps
softly an inch from your enchanted face.

Charles Olson (1910–1970)

La Chute 1967

my drum, hollowed out thru the thin slit,
carved from the cedar wood, the base I took
when the tree was felled

o my lute, wrought from the tree's crown

my drum, whose lustiness
was not to be resisted
my lute,
from whose pulsations
not one could turn away

They
are where the dead are, my drum fell
where the dead are, who
will bring it up, my lute
who will bring it up where it fell in the face of them
where they are, where my lute and drum have fallen?

La Chute. The French title means "The Fall."

11 Poems for the Eye

Let's look at a famous poem with a distinctive visible shape. In the seventeenth century, ingenious poets trimmed their lines into the silhouettes of altars and crosses, pillars and pyramids. Here is one. Is it anything more than a demonstration of ingenuity?

George Herbert (1593–1633)

Easter Wings 1633

Lord, who createdst man in wealth and store,
Though foolishly he lost the same,
Decaying more and more
Till he became
Most poor;
With thee
Oh, let me rise
As larks, harmoniously,
And sing this day thy victories;
Then shall the fall further the flight in me.

My tender age in sorrow did begin;
And still with sicknesses and shame
Thou didst so punish sin,
That I became
Most thin.
With thee
Let me combine,
And feel this day thy victory;
For if I imp my wing on thine,
Affliction shall advance the flight in me.

In the next-to-last line, *imp* is a term from falconry meaning to repair the wing of an injured bird by grafting feathers into it.

If we see it merely as a picture, we will have to admit that Herbert's word design does not go far. It renders with difficulty shapes that a sketcher's pencil could set down in a flash. The pencil sketch might have more detail, might be more accurate. Was Herbert's effort wasted? It might have been, were there not more to his poem than meets the eye. The mind, too, is engaged by the visual pattern, by the realization that the words *most thin* are given emphasis by their narrow form. Here, visual pattern points out meaning. Heard aloud, too, "Easter Wings" takes on additional depths. Its rimes, its pattern of rhythm are perceptible. It gives pleasure as any poem in a symmetrical stanza may do: by establishing a pattern that leads the reader to anticipate when another rime or a pause will arrive and then fulfilling that expectation.

Ever since the invention of the alphabet, poems have existed not only as rhythmic sounds upon the air but also as visual patterns made of words. At least some of our pleasure in silently reading a poem derives from the way it looks upon its page. A poem in an open form can engage the eye with snowfields of white space and thickets of close-set words. A poem in stanzas can please us by its visual symmetry. And, far from being merely decorative, the visual devices of a poem can be meaningful, too. White space—as poets demonstrate who work in open forms—can indicate pauses. If white space entirely surrounds a word or phrase or line, then that portion of the poem obviously takes special emphasis. Typographical devices such as capital letters and italics also can lay stress upon words. In most traditional poems, a capital letter at the beginning of each new line helps indicate the importance the poet places upon line-divisions, whose regular intervals make a rhythm out of pauses. And the poet may be trying to show us that certain lines rime by indenting them.

Ever since George Herbert's day, writers have continued to experiment with the appearances of printed poetry. Notable efforts to entertain the eye are Lewis Carroll's rimed mouse's tail in *Alice in Wonderland;* and the *Calligrammes* of Guillaume Apollinaire, who arranged words in the shapes of a necktie, of the Eiffel Tower, and of spears of falling rain. Here is a bird-shaped poem of more recent inspiration than Herbert's. What does its visual form have to do with what the poet is saying?

John Hollander (b. 1929)

Swan and Shadow — 1969

Dusk
Above the
water hang the
loud
flies
Here
O so
gray
then
What A pale signal will appear
When Soon before its shadow fades
Where Here in this pool of opened eye
In us No Upon us As at the very edges
of where we take shape in the dark air
this object bares its image awakening
ripples of recognition that will
brush darkness up into light
even after this bird this hour both drift by atop the perfect sad instant now
already passing out of sight
toward yet-untroubled reflection
this image bears its object darkening
into memorial shades Scattered bits of
light No of water Or something across
water Breaking up No Being regathered
soon Yet by then a swan will have
gone Yes out of mind into what
vast
pale
hush
of a
place
past
sudden dark as
if a swan
sang

A whole poem doesn't need to be such a verbal silhouette, of course, for its appearance on the page to seem meaningful. In some lines of a longer poem, William Carlos Williams has conveyed the way an energetic bellhop (or hotel porter) runs downstairs:

ta tuck a
ta tuck a
ta tuck a
ta tuck a
ta tuck a

This is not only good onomatopoeia and an accurate description of a rhythm; the steplike appearance of the lines goes together with their meaning.

Sometimes an unconventional-looking poem represents no familiar object but is an attempt to make the eye follow an unaccustomed path, as in this experiment by E. E. Cummings.

E. E. Cummings (1894–1962)

R-P-O-P-H-E-S-S-A-G-R 1935

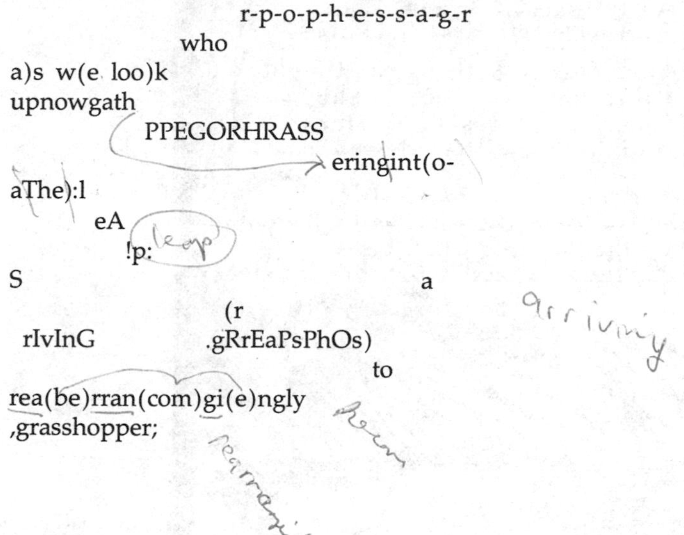

r-p-o-p-h-e-s-s-a-g-r
who
a)s w(e loo)k
upnowgath
PPEGORHRASS
eringint(o-
aThe):l
eA
!p:
S a
(r
rIvInG .gRrEaPsPhOs)
to
rea(be)rran(com)gi(e)ngly
,grasshopper;

However startling it may be to eyes accustomed to poems in conventional line arrangements, this experiment is not a shaped poem. What matters is the grasshopperish leaps and backtracks that our eyes must make in unscrambling letters and words, rearranging them into a more usual order.

Though too much importance can be given to the visual element of poetry and though many poets seem hardly to care about it, it can be another dimension that sets apart poetry from prose. It is at least arguable that some of Walt Whitman's long-line, page-filling descriptions of the wide ocean, open landscapes, and broad streets of his America, which meet the eye as wide expanses of words, would lose something—besides rhythm—if couched in lines only three or four syllables long. Another poet who deeply cared about visual appearance was William Blake (1757–1827), graphic artist and engraver as well as a master artist in words. By publishing his *Songs of Innocence* and *Songs of Experience* (among other works) with illustrations and accompanying hand-lettered poems, often interwoven with the lines of the poems, Blake apparently strove to make poem and appearance of poem a unity, striking mind and eye at the same time.

Some poets who write in English have envied poets who write in Chinese, a language in which certain words look like the things they represent. Consider this Chinese poem:

Wang Wei (701–761)

BIRD-SINGING STREAM (about 750)

人 閒 桂 花 落
靜 夜 春 山 空
月 出 驚 山 鳥
時 鳴 春 澗 中

Substituting English words for ideograms, the poem becomes:

man	leisure	cassia	flower	fall
quiet	night	spring	mountain	empty
moon	rise	startle	mountain	bird
at times	sing	spring	stream	middle

Even without the aid of English crib-notes, all of us can read some Chinese if we can recognize a picture of a man. What resemblances can you see between any of the other ideograms and the things they stand for?[1]

Wai-lim Yip, the poet and critic who provided the Chinese text and translation, has also translated the poem into more usual English word order, still keeping close to the original sequence of ideas:

Man at leisure. Cassia flowers fall.
Quiet night. Spring mountain is empty.
Moon rises. Startles—a mountain bird.
It sings at times in the spring stream.

One envious Western poet was Ezra Pound, who included a few Chinese ideograms in his *Cantos* as illustrations. From the scholar Ernest Fenollosa, Pound said he had come to understand why a language written in ideograms "simply *had to stay poetic;* simply couldn't help being and staying poetic in a way that a column of English type might very well not stay poetic."[2] Having an imperfect command of Chinese, Pound greatly overestimated the tendency of the language to depict things. (Only a small number of characters in modern Chinese are pictures; Chinese characters, like Western alphabets, also indicate the sounds of words.) Still, Pound's misunderstanding was fruitful. Thanks to his influence, many other recent poets were encouraged to consider the appearance of words.[3] E. E. Cummings, in a poem that begins "mOOn Over tOwns mOOn," has reveled in the fact that O's are moon-shaped. Aram Saroyan, in a poem entitled "crickets," makes capital of the fact that the word *cricket* somewhat resembles the snub-nosed insect of approximately the same length. The poem begins,

crickets
crickets
crickets
crickets

[1] To help you compare English and Chinese, the Chinese original has been arranged in Western word-order. (Ordinarily, in Chinese, the word for "man" would appear at the upper right.)
[2] *The ABC of Reading* (Norfolk, Conn., 1960), p. 22.
[3] For a brief discussion of Pound's misunderstanding and its influence, see Milton Klonsky's introduction to his anthology *Speaking Pictures: A Gallery of Pictorial Poetry from the Sixteenth Century to the Present* (New York: Harmony, 1975).

and goes on down its page like that, for thirty-seven lines. (Read aloud, by the way, the poem sounds somewhat like crickets chirping!) In recent years, a movement called **concrete poetry** has traveled far and wide. Though practitioners of the art disagree over its definition, what most concretists seem to do is make designs out of letters and words.

Reinhard Döhl (b. 1934)

1965

ApfelApfel
pfelApfelApfelApfelA
pfelApfelApfelApfelApfelA
felApfelApfelApfelApfelApfe
ApfelApfelApfelApfelApfelApf
pfelApfelApfelApfelApfelApfelA
lApfelApfelApfelApfelApfelApfe
pfelApfelApfelApfelApfelApfelA
ApfelApfelApfelApfelApfelApfe
pfelApfelApfelApfelApfelApfel
ApfelApfelApfelApfelApfelApf
elApfelApfelApfelWurmAp
felApfelApfelApfelApfel
pfelApfelApfelApfel
pfelApfelApfelA
pfelApfel

QUESTIONS

1. Translate this concrete poem.
2. Do you think we should call it a poem? Why? Or why not?

Other concrete poets wield typography like a brush dipped in paint, using such techniques as blow-up, montage, and superimposed elements (the same words printed many times on top of the same impression, so that the result is blurriness). They may even keep words in a usual order, perhaps employing white space as freely as any writer of open form verse. According to Mary Ellen Solt, an American concretist, we can tell a concrete poem by its "concentration upon the physical material from which the poem or text is made."[4] Still another practitioner, Richard Kostelanetz, has suggested that a more accurate name for

[4] Introduction to her anthology *Concrete Poetry: A World View* (Bloomington, Ind.: Indiana University Press, 1969).

concrete poetry might be "word-imagery." He sees it occupying an area somewhere between conventional poetry and visual art.[5]

What makes concretism look foolish or impossible to understand (to those who approach it as if it ought to be traditional poetry) may be that concretists often use words without placing them in context with any other words. Aram Saroyan has a concrete poem consisting of a page blank except for one word: *oxygen.*

Much concrete poetry is clearly "something to look at rather than to read," Louis Untermeyer has said unsympathetically. And yet certain concrete poems can please as good poems always do: by their connotations, figures of speech, sounds, and metaphors—not to mention their rewards to the eye.

Admittedly, some concrete poems mean less than meets the eye. In this fact, they seem more rigidly confined to the printed page than shaped poems such as "Easter Wings." A good shaped poem, though it would lose much if heard and not seen, still might be a satisfying poem. That many pretentious doodlers have taken up concretism may have caused a *Time* writer to sneer: did Joyce Kilmer miss all that much by never having seen a poem lovely as a

t
ttt
rrrrr
rrrrrrr
eeeeeeeee
???

However, like other structures of language, concrete poems evidently can have the effect of poetry, if written by poets. Whether or not it ought to be dubbed "poetry," this art can do what poems traditionally have done: use language in delightful ways that reveal meanings to us.

Edwin Morgan (b. 1920)

SIESTA OF A HUNGARIAN SNAKE 1968

s sz sz SZ sz SZ sz ZS zs ZS zs zs z

QUESTIONS

1. What do you suppose Morgan is trying to indicate by reversing the order of the two letters in mid line?
2. What, if anything, about this snake seems Hungarian?
3. Does the sound of its consonants matter?

[5] Introduction to his anthology *Imaged Words and Worded Images* (New York: Outerbridge and Dienstfrey, 1970).

Richard Kostelanetz (b. 1940)

1970

DISINTEGRATION

DISINTEGRATION

Dorthi Charles (b. 1963)

Concrete Cat

1971

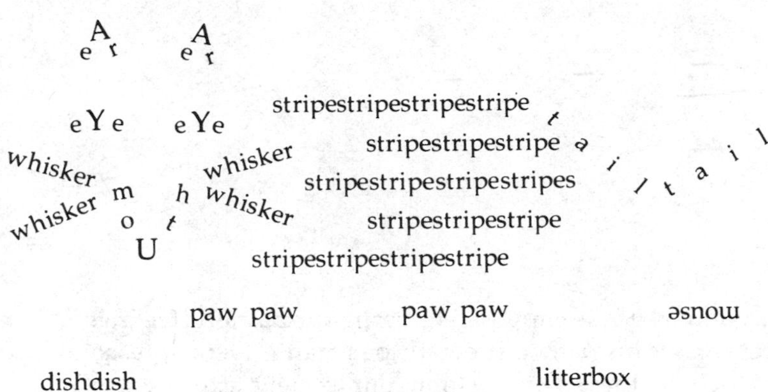

A A
e r e r
eYe eYe
stripestripestripestripe
whisker whisker
stripestripestripe
stripestripestripestripes
whisker m h whisker
o t
U
stripestripestripe
stripestripestripestripe
t a i l t a i l
paw paw paw paw
əsnoɯ
dishdish
litterbox
litterbox

Questions

1. What does this writer indicate by capitalizing the *a* in *ear*? The *y* in *eye*? The *u* in mouth? By using spaces between the letters in the word *tail*?
2. Why is the word *mouse* upside down?
3. What possible pun might be seen in the cat's middle stripe?
4. What is the tone of "Concrete Cat"? How is it made evident?
5. Do these words seem chosen for their connotations or only for their denotations? Would you call this work of art a poem?

Experiment: *Do It Yourself*

Make a concrete poem of your own. If you need inspiration, pick some familiar object or animal and try to find words that look like it. For more ideas, study the typography of a magazine or newspaper; cut out interesting letters and numerals and try pasting them into arrangements. What (if anything) do your experiments tell you about familiar letters and words?

12 Symbol

The national flag is supposed to bestir our patriotic feelings. When a black cat crosses his path, a superstitious man shivers, foreseeing bad luck. To each of these, by custom, our society expects a standard response. A flag, a black cat's crossing one's path – each is a **symbol:** a visible object or action that suggests some further meaning in addition to itself. In literature, a symbol might be the word *flag* or the words *a black cat crossed his path* or every description of flag or cat in an entire novel, story, play, or poem.

A flag and the crossing of a black cat may be called **conventional symbols,** since they can have a conventional or customary effect on us. Conventional symbols are also part of the language of poetry, as we know when we meet the red rose, emblem of love, in a lyric, or the Christian cross in the devotional poems of George Herbert. More often, however, symbols in literature have no conventional, long-established meaning, but particular meanings of their own. In Melville's novel *Moby Dick,* to take a rich example, whatever we associate with the great white whale is *not* attached unmistakably to white whales by custom. Though Melville tells us that men have long regarded whales with awe and relates Moby Dick to the celebrated fish that swallowed Jonah, the reader's response is to one particular whale, the creature of Herman Melville. Only the experience of reading the novel in its entirety can give Moby Dick his particular meaning.

We should say *meanings,* for as Eudora Welty has observed, it is a good thing Melville made Moby Dick a whale, a creature large enough to contain all that critics have found in him. A symbol in literature, if not conventional, has more than just one meaning. In "The Raven," by Edgar Allan Poe, the appearance of a strange black bird in the narrator's study is sinister; and indeed, if we take the poem seriously, we may even respond with a sympathetic shiver of dread. Does the bird mean death, fate, melancholy, the loss of a loved one, knowledge in the service of evil? All these, perhaps. Like any well-chosen symbol, Poe's raven sets going within the reader an unending train of feelings and associations.

We miss the value of a symbol, however, if we think it can mean absolutely anything we wish. If a poet has any control over our reactions, the poem will guide our responses in a certain direction.

T. S. Eliot (1888–1965)

The Boston Evening Transcript 1917

The readers of the *Boston Evening Transcript*
Sway in the wind like a field of ripe corn.

When evening quickens faintly in the street,
Wakening the appetites of life in some
And to others bringing the *Boston Evening Transcript,*
I mount the steps and ring the bell, turning
Wearily, as one would turn to nod good-bye to La Rochefoucauld,
If the street were time and he at the end of the street,
And I say, "Cousin Harriet, here is the *Boston Evening Transcript.*"

The newspaper, whose name Eliot purposely repeats so monotonously, indicates what this poem is about. Now defunct, the *Transcript* covered in detail the slightest activity of Boston's leading families and was noted for the great length of its obituaries. Eliot, then, uses the newspaper as a symbol for an existence of boredom, fatigue (*Wearily*), petty and unvarying routine (since an evening newspaper, like night, arrives on schedule). The *Transcript* evokes a way of life without zest or passion, for, opposed to people who read it, Eliot sets people who do not: those whose desires revive, not expire, when the working day is through. Suggestions abound in the ironic comparison of the *Transcript*'s readers to a cornfield late in summer. To mention only a few: the readers sway because they are sleepy; they vegetate; they are drying up; each makes a rattling sound when turning a page. It is not necessary that we know the remote and similarly disillusioned friend to whom the speaker might nod: La Rochefoucauld, whose cynical *Maxims* entertained Parisian society under Louis XIV (sample: "All of us have enough strength to endure the misfortunes of others"). We understand that the nod is symbolic of an immense weariness of spirit. We know nothing about Cousin Harriet, whom the speaker addresses, but imagine from the greeting she inspires that she is probably a bore.

If Eliot wishes to say that certain Bostonians lead lives of sterile boredom, why does he couch his meaning in symbols? Why doesn't he tell us directly what he means? These questions imply two assumptions not necessarily true: first, that Eliot has a message to impart; second, that he is concealing it. We have reason to think that Eliot did not usually have a message in mind when beginning a poem, for as he once told a critic: "The conscious problems with which one is concerned in the actual writing are more those of a quasi musical nature . . . than of a conscious exposition of ideas." Poets sometimes discover what they have to say while in the act of saying it. And it may be that in his *Transcript* poem, Eliot is saying exactly what he means. By communicating his meaning through symbols instead of statements, he may be choosing the only kind of language appropriate to an idea of great subtlety and complexity. (The paraphrase "Certain Bostonians are bored" hardly begins to describe the poem in all its possible meaning.) And by his use of symbolism, Eliot affords us the pleasure of finding our own entrances to his poem. Another great strength of a symbol is that, like some figures of speech, it renders the abstract in concrete terms, and, like any other image, refers to what we can perceive – an object like a newspaper, a gesture like a nod. Eliot might, like Robert Frost, have called himself a "synecdochist." Frost explained: "Always a larger significance. A little thing touches a larger thing."

This power of suggestion that a symbol contains is, perhaps, its greatest advantage. Sometimes, as in the following poem by Emily Dickinson, a symbol will lead us from a visible object to something too vast to be perceived.

Emily Dickinson (1830–1886)

The Lightning is a yellow Fork (about 1870)

The Lightning is a yellow Fork
From Tables in the sky
By inadvertent fingers dropt
The awful Cutlery

Of mansions never quite disclosed
And never quite concealed
The Apparatus of the Dark
To ignorance revealed.

If the lightning is a fork, then whose are the fingers that drop it, the table from which it slips, the household to which it belongs? The poem implies this question without giving an answer. An obvious answer is "God," but can we be sure? We wonder, too, about these partially lighted mansions: if our vision were clearer, what would we behold?[1]

[1] In its suggestion of an infinite realm that mortal eyes cannot quite see, but whose nature can be perceived fleetingly through things visible, Emily Dickinson's poem, by coincidence, resembles the work of late-nineteenth-century French poets called **symbolists.** To a symbolist the shirt-tail of Truth is continually seen disappearing around a corner. With their Neoplatonic view of ideal realities existing in a great beyond, whose corresponding symbols are the perceptible cats that bite us and tangible stones we stumble over, French poets such as Charles Baudelaire, Jules Laforgue, and Stéphane Mallarmé were profoundly to affect poets writing in English, notably Yeats (who said a poem "entangles . . . a part of the Divine essence") and Eliot. But we consider in this chapter symbolism as an element in certain poems, not Symbolism, the literary movement.

"But how am I supposed to know a symbol when I see one?" The best approach is to read poems closely, taking comfort in the likelihood that it is better not to notice symbols at all than to find significance in every literal stone and huge meanings in every thing. In looking for the symbols in a poem, pick out all the references to concrete objects—newspapers, black cats, twisted pins. Consider these with special care. Note any that the poet emphasizes by detailed description, by repetition, or by placing at the very beginning or end of the poem. Ask: What is the poem about, what does it add up to? If, when the poem is paraphrased, the paraphrase depends primarily upon the meaning of certain concrete objects, these richly suggestive objects may be the symbols.

There are some things a literary symbol usually is *not*. A symbol is not an abstraction. Such terms as *truth, death, love,* and *justice* cannot work as symbols (unless personified, as in the traditional figure of Justice holding a scale). Most often, a symbol is something we can see in the mind's eye: a newspaper, a lightning bolt, a gesture of nodding good-bye.

In narratives, a well-developed character who speaks much dialogue and is not the least bit mysterious is usually not a symbol. But watch out for an executioner in a black hood; a character, named for a Biblical prophet, who does little but utter a prophecy; a trio of old women who resemble the Three Fates. (It has been argued, with good reason, that Milton's fully rounded character of Satan in *Paradise Lost* is a symbol embodying evil and human pride, but a narrower definition of symbol is more frequently useful.) A symbol *may* be a part of a person's body (the baleful eye of the murder victim in Poe's story "The Tell-Tale Heart") or a look, a voice, a mannerism.

A symbol usually is not the second term of a metaphor. In the line "The lightning is a yellow fork," the symbol is the lightning, not the fork.

Sometimes a symbol addresses a sense other than sight: the sound of a mysterious harp at the end of Chekhov's play *The Cherry Orchard;* or, in William Faulkner's tale "A Rose for Emily," the odor of decay that surrounds the house of the last survivor of a town's leading family—suggesting not only physical dissolution but also the decay of a social order. A symbol is a special kind of image, for it exceeds the usual image in the richness of its connotations. The dead wife's cold comb in the haiku of Buson (discussed on pages 69–70) works symbolically, suggesting among other things the chill of the grave, the contrast between the living and the dead.

Holding a narrower definition than that used in this book, some readers of poetry prefer to say that a symbol is always a concrete object, never an act. They would deny the label "symbol" to Ahab's breaking his tobacco pipe before setting out to pursue Moby Dick (suggesting, perhaps, his determination to allow no pleasure to distract him from the chase) or to any large motion (as Ahab's whole quest). This distinction, while confining, does have the merit of sparing one from seeing all motion to be possibly symbolic. Some would call Ahab's gesture not a symbol but a **symbolic act.**

To sum up: a symbol radiates hints or casts long shadows (to use Henry James's metaphor). We are unable to say it "stands for" or "represents" a meaning. It evokes, it suggests, it manifests. It demands no single necessary interpretation, such as the interpretation a driver gives to a red traffic light. Rather, like Emily Dickinson's lightning bolt, it points toward an indefinite meaning, which may lie in part beyond the reach of words. In a symbol, as Thomas Carlyle said in *Sartor Resartus,* "the Infinite is made to blend with the Finite, to stand visible, and as it were, attainable there."

Thomas Hardy (1840–1928)

Neutral Tones

1898

We stood by a pond that winter day,
And the sun was white, as though chidden of God,
And a few leaves lay on the starving sod;
  —They had fallen from an ash, and were gray.

Your eyes on me were as eyes that rove
Over tedious riddles of years ago;
And some words played between us to and fro
  On which lost the more by our love.

The smile on your mouth was the deadest thing
Alive enough to have strength to die;
And a grin of bitterness swept thereby
  Like an ominous bird a-wing. . . .

Since then, keen lessons that love deceives,
And wrings with wrong, have shaped to me
Your face, and the God-curst sun, and a tree,
  And a pond edged with grayish leaves.

Questions

1. Sum up the story told in this poem. In lines 1–12, what is the dramatic situation? What has happened in the interval between the experience related in these lines and the reflection in the last stanza?
2. What meanings do you find in the title?
3. Explain in your own words the metaphor in line 2.
4. What connotations appropriate to this poem does the *ash* (line 4) have, that *oak* or *maple* would lack?
5. What visible objects in the poem function symbolically? What actions or gestures?

If we read of a ship, its captain, its sailors, and the rough seas, and we realize we are reading about a commonwealth and how its rulers and workers keep it going even in difficult times, then we are reading an **allegory.** Closely akin to symbolism, allegory is a description—usually narrative—in which persons, places, and things are employed in a continuous system of equivalents.

Although more strictly limited in its suggestions than symbolism, allegory need not be thought inferior. Few poems continue to interest readers more than Dante's allegorical *Divine Comedy*. Sublime evidence of the appeal of allegory may be found in Christ's use of the **parable:** a brief narrative—usually allegorical but sometimes not—that teaches a moral.

Matthew 13:24–30 (Authorized or King James Version, 1611)

The Parable of the Good Seed

The kingdom of heaven is likened unto a man which sowed good seed in his field:

But while men slept, his enemy came and sowed tares among the wheat, and went his way.

But when the blade was sprung up, and brought forth fruit, then appeared the tares also.

So the servants of the householder came and said unto him, Sir, didst not thou sow good seed in thy field? From whence then hath it tares?

He said unto them, An enemy hath done this. The servants said unto him, Wilt thou then that we go and gather them up?

But he said, Nay; lest while ye gather up the tares, ye root up also the wheat with them.

Let both grow together until the harvest: and in the time of harvest I will say to the reapers, Gather ye together first the tares, and bind them in bundles to burn them: but gather the wheat into my barn.

The sower is the Son of man, the field is the world, the good seed are the children of the Kingdom, the tares are the children of the wicked one, the enemy is the devil, the harvest is the end of the world, the reapers are angels. "As therefore the tares are gathered and burned in the fire; so shall it be in the end of this world" (Matthew 13:36–42).

Usually, as in this parable, the meanings of an allegory are plainly labeled or thinly disguised. In John Bunyan's allegorical narrative *The Pilgrim's Progress,* it is clear that the hero Christian, on his journey through places with such pointed names as Vanity Fair, the Valley of the Shadow of Death, and Doubting Castle, is the soul, traveling the road of life on the way toward Heaven. An allegory, when carefully built, is systematic. It makes one principal comparison, the working out of whose details may lead to further comparisons, then still further comparisons: Christian, thrown by Giant Despair into the dungeon of Doubting Castle, escapes by means of a key called Promise. Such a complicated design may take great length to unfold, as in Spenser's *Faerie Queene;* but, the method may be seen in a short poem:

George Herbert (1593–1633)

REDEMPTION

1633

Having been tenant long to a rich Lord,
  Not thriving, I resolvèd to be bold,
And make a suit unto him to afford
  A new small-rented lease and cancel th' old.
In Heaven at his manor I him sought.
  They told me there that he was lately gone
About some land which he had dearly bought
  Long since on earth, to take possessiòn.
I straight returned, and knowing his great birth,
  Sought him accordingly in great resorts,
  In cities, theaters, gardens, parks, and courts.
At length I heard a ragged noise and mirth
  Of thieves and murderers; there I him espied,
  Who straight "Your suit is granted," said, and died.

QUESTIONS

1. In this allegory, what equivalents does Herbert give each of these terms: *tenant, Lord, not thriving, suit, new lease, old lease, manor, land, dearly bought, take possession, his great birth*?
2. What scene is depicted in the last three lines?

An object in allegory is like a bird whose cage is clearly lettered with its identity—"RAVEN, *Corvus corax;* habitat of specimen, Maine." A symbol, by contrast, is a bird with piercing eyes that mysteriously appears one evening in your library. It is there; you can touch it. But what does it mean? You look at it. It continues to look at you.

Whether an object in literature is a symbol, part of an allegory, or no such thing at all, it has at least one sure meaning. Moby Dick is first a whale, the *Boston Evening Transcript* a newspaper. Besides deriving a multitude of intangible suggestions from the title symbol in Eliot's long poem *The Waste Land,* its readers cannot fail to carry away a sense of the land's physical appearance: a river choked with sandwich papers and cigarette ends, London Bridge "under the brown fog of a winter dawn." A virtue of *The Pilgrim's Progress* is that its walking abstractions are no mere abstractions but are also human: Giant Despair is a henpecked husband. The most vital element of a literary work may pass us by, unless before seeking further depths in a thing, we look to the thing itself.

Sir Philip Sidney (1554–1586)

YOU THAT WITH ALLEGORY'S CURIOUS FRAME — 1591

You that with allegory's curious frame
  Of others' children changelings use to make,
  With me those pains, for God's sake, do not take;
I list not° dig so deep for brazen fame. — *I do not choose to*
When I say Stella, I do mean the same
  Princess of beauty for whose only sake
  The reins of love I love, though never slake,
And joy therein, though nations count it shame.
I beg no subject to use eloquence,
  Nor in hid ways do guide philosophy;
Look at my hands for no such quintessence,
  But know that I in pure simplicity
  Breathe out the flames which burn within my heart,
  Love only reading unto me this art.

Emily Dickinson (1830–1886)

I HEARD A FLY BUZZ—WHEN I DIED — (about 1862)

I heard a Fly buzz–when I died–
The Stillness in the Room
Was like the Stillness in the Air–
Between the Heaves of Storm–

The Eyes around–had wrung them dry–
And Breaths were gathering firm
For that last Onset–when the King
Be witnessed–in the Room–

I willed my Keepsakes–Signed away
What portion of me be
Assignable–and then it was
There interposed a Fly–

With Blue–uncertain stumbling Buzz–
Between the light–and me–
And then the Windows failed–and then
I could not see to see–

QUESTIONS

1. Why is the poem written in the past tense? Where is the speaker at present?
2. What do you understand from the repetition of the word *see* in the last line?
3. What does the poet mean by *Eyes around* (line 5), *that last Onset* (line 7), *the King* (line 7), and *What portion of me be / Assignable* (lines 10–11)?
4. In line 13, how can a sound be called *Blue* and *stumbling*?
5. What further meaning might *the Windows* (line 15) suggest, in addition to denoting the windows of the room?

6. What connotations of the word *fly* seem relevant to an account of a death?
7. Summarize your interpretation of the poem. What does the fly mean?

Philip Dow (b. 1937)

Drunk Last Night With Friends, I Go To Work Anyway

1979

The boss knows what shape I'm in. He tells me
about the twenties, when he was my age,
how he drank all night and woke up in strange rooms
with strange dolls. He tells me *Get lost.*

Out back, a weedbank I'd never noticed—
I head for it in cold air, remembering
dogs and cats eating grass when sick.

I sit shoulder deep in weeds. Beneath the leaves
in green air black beetles shoulder
enormous stems, dew quivering
between stalk and leaf. In the pale moss I see
ants the size of salt grains,
and budding red flowers
smaller than these ants. A snail
dreaming in the throat of an old wine bottle.

Questions

Is the snail in the throat of a wine bottle a symbol? A simple image from nature? An implied metaphor expressing how the speaker himself feels?

Exercise: *Symbol Hunting*

After you have read each of these poems, decide which description best suits it:

1. The poem has a central symbol.
2. The poem contains no symbolism, but is to be taken literally.

William Carlos Williams (1883–1963)

Poem

1934

As the cat
climbed over
the top of

the jamcloset
first the right
forefoot

carefully
then the hind
stepped down

into the pit of
the empty
flowerpot

Theodore Roethke (1908–1963)

Night Crow

1948

When I saw that clumsy crow
Flap from a wasted tree,
A shape in the mind rose up:
Over the gulfs of dream
Flew a tremendous bird
Further and further away
Into a moonless black,
Deep in the brain, far back.

John Donne (1572–1631)

A Burnt Ship

1633

Out of a fired ship which by no way
But drowning could be rescued from the flame
Some men leaped forth, and ever as they came
Near the foe's ships, did by their shot decay;
So all were lost, which in the ship were found,
They in the sea being burnt, they in the burnt ship drowned.

Wallace Stevens (1879–1955)

Anecdote of the Jar

1923

I placed a jar in Tennessee,
And round it was, upon a hill.
It made the slovenly wilderness
Surround that hill.

The wilderness rose up to it,
And sprawled around, no longer wild.
The jar was round upon the ground
And tall and of a port in air.

It took dominion everywhere.
The jar was gray and bare.
It did not give of bird or bush,
Like nothing else in Tennessee.

13 Myth

Poets have long been fond of retelling **myths,** narrowly defined as traditional stories of immortal beings. Such stories taken collectively may also be called **myth** or **mythology.** In one of the most celebrated collections of myth ever assembled, the *Metamorphoses,* the poet Ovid has told—to take one example from many—how Phaeton, child of the sun god, rashly tried to drive his father's fiery chariot on its daily round, lost control of the horses, and caused disaster both to himself and to the world. Our use of the term *myth* in discussing poetry, then, differs from its use in expressions such as "the myth of communism" and "the myth of democracy." In these examples, myth, in its broadest sense, is any idea people believe in, whether true or false. Nor do we mean—to take another familiar use of the word—a cock-and-bull story: "Judge Rapp doesn't roast speeders alive; that's just a *myth.*" In the following discussion, *myth* will mean—as critic Northrop Frye has put it—"the imitation of actions near or at the conceivable limits of desire." Myths tell us of the exploits of the gods—their battles, the ways in which they live, love, and perhaps suffer—all on a scale of magnificence larger than our life. We envy their freedom and power; they enact our wishes and dreams. Whether we believe in them or not, their adventures are myths: Ovid, it seems, placed no credence in the stories he related, for he declared, "I prate of ancient poets' monstrous lies."

And yet it is characteristic of a myth that it *can* be believed. Throughout history, myths have accompanied religious doctrines and rituals. They have helped sanction or recall the reasons for religious observances. A sublime instance is the New Testament account of the Last Supper. Because of it and its record of the words of Jesus, "This do in remembrance of Me," Christians have continued to re-enact the offering and partaking of the body and blood of their Lord, under the appearances of bread and wine. It is essential to recall that, just because a myth narrates the acts of a god, we do not necessarily mean by the term a false or fictitious narrative. When we speak of the "myth of Islam" or "the Christian myth," we do so without implying either belief or disbelief. Myths can also help sanction customs and institutions other than religious ones. At the same time the baking of bread was introduced to ancient Greece—one theory goes—there was introduced the myth of Demeter, goddess of grain, who had kindly sent her emissary Triptolemus to teach humankind this valuable art—thus helping to persuade the distrustful that bread was a good thing. Some myths seem made to divert and regale, not to sanction anything. Such may be the story of the sculptor Pygmalion, who fell in love with his statue of a woman; so exquisite was his work, so deep was his feeling, that Aphrodite brought the statue to life. And yet perhaps the story goes deeper than mere diversion: perhaps it is a way of saying that works of art achieve a reality of their own, that love can transform or animate its object.

How does a myth begin? Several theories have been proposed, none universally accepted. One is that a myth is a way to explain some natural phenomenon. Winter comes and the vegetation perishes because Persephone, child of Demeter, must return to the underworld for four months every year. This theory, as classical scholar Edith Hamilton has pointed out, may lead us to think incorrectly that Greek mythology was the creation of a primitive people. Tales of the gods of Mount Olympus may reflect an earlier inheritance, but Greek myths known to us were transcribed in an era of high civilization. Anthropologists have questioned whether primitive people generally find beauty in the mysteries of nature. "From my own study of living myths among savages," wrote Bronislaw Malinowski, "I should say that primitive man has to a very limited extent the purely artistic or scientific interest in nature; there is but little room for symbolism in his ideas and tales; and myth, in fact, is not an idle rhapsody . . . but a hard-working, extremely important cultural force."[1] Such a practical function was seen by Sir James Frazer in *The Golden Bough:* myths were originally expressions of human hope that nature would be fertile. Still another theory is that, once upon a time, heroes of myth were human prototypes. The Greek philosopher Euhemerus declared myths to be tales of real persons, which poets had exaggerated. Most present-day historians of myth would seek no general explanation but would say that different myths probably have different origins.

Poets have many coherent mythologies on which to draw; perhaps those most frequently consulted by British and American poets are the classical, the Christian, the Norse, and folk myth of the American frontier (embodying the deeds of superhuman characters such as Paul Bunyan). Some poets have taken inspiration from other myths as well: T. S. Eliot's *The Waste Land,* for example, is enriched by allusions to Buddhism and to pagan vegetation-cults.

As a tour through any good art museum will demonstrate, myth

[1] Bronislaw Malinowski, *Myth in Primitive Psychology* (1926); reprinted in *Magic, Science and Religion* (New York: Doubleday, 1954), p. 97.

pervades much of the graphic art of Western civilization. In literature, one evidence of its continuing value to recent poets and storytellers is the frequency with which myths—both primitive and civilized—are retold. William Faulkner's story "The Bear" recalls tales of Indian totem animals; John Updike's novel *The Centaur* presents the horse-man Chiron as a modern high school teacher; Hart Crane's poem "For the Marriage of Faustus and Helen" unites two figures of different myths, who dance to jazz; T. S. Eliot's plays bring into the drawing-room the myths of Alcestis (*The Cocktail Party*) and the Eumenides (*The Family Reunion*); Jean Cocteau's film *Orphée* shows us Eurydice riding to the underworld with an escort of motorcycles. Popular interest in such works may testify to the profound appeal myths continue to hold for us. Like any other large body of knowledge that can be alluded to, myth offers the poet an instant means of communication—if the reader also knows the particular myth cited. Writing "Lycidas," John Milton could depend upon his readers—mostly persons of similar classical learning—to understand him without footnotes. Today, a poet referring to a traditional myth must be sure to choose a reasonably well known one, or else write as well as T. S. Eliot, whose work has compelled his readers to single out his allusions and look them up. Like other varieties of poetry, myth is a kind of knowledge, not at odds with scientific knowledge but existing in addition to it.

D. H. Lawrence (1885–1930)

Bavarian Gentians

1932

Not every man has gentians in his house
In soft September, at slow, sad Michaelmas.

Bavarian gentians, big and dark, only dark
darkening the daytime, torch-like with the smoking blueness of Pluto's gloom,
ribbed and torch-like, with their blaze of darkness spread blue
down flattening into points, flattened under the sweep of white day
torch-flower of the blue-smoking darkness, Pluto's dark-blue daze,
black lamps from the halls of Dis, burning dark blue,
giving off darkness, blue darkness, as Demeter's pale lamps give off light,
lead me then, lead the way.

Reach me a gentian, give me a torch!
let me guide myself with the blue, forked torch of this flower
down the darker and darker stairs, where blue is darkened on blueness
even where Persephone goes, just now, from the frosted September
to the sightless realm where darkness is awake upon the dark

and Persephone herself is but a voice
or a darkness invisible enfolded in the deeper dark
of the arms Plutonic, and pierced with the passion of dense gloom,
among the splendor of torches of darkness, shedding darkness on the lost
bride and her groom.

BAVARIAN GENTIANS. 4. *Pluto:* Roman name for Hades, in Greek mythology the ruler of the underworld, who abducted Persephone to be his bride. Each spring Persephone returns to earth and is welcomed by her mother Demeter, goddess of fruitfulness; each winter she departs again, to dwell with her husband below. 8. *Dis:* Pluto's realm.

QUESTIONS

1. Read this poem aloud. What devices of sound do you hear in it?
2. What characteristics of gentians appear to remind Lawrence of the story of Persephone? What significance do you attach to the poem's being set in September? How does the fact of autumn matter to the gentians and to Persephone?

Thomas Hardy (1840–1928)

THE OXEN 1915

Christmas Eve, and twelve of the clock.
"Now they are all on their knees,"
An elder said as we sat in a flock
By the embers in hearthside ease.

We pictured the meek mild creatures where
They dwelt in their strawy pen,
Nor did it occur to one of us there
To doubt they were kneeling then.

So fair a fancy few would weave
In these years! Yet, I feel,
If someone said on Christmas Eve,
"Come; see the oxen kneel

"In the lonely barton° by yonder coomb° *farmyard; a hollow*
Our childhood used to know,"
I should go with him in the gloom,
Hoping it might be so.

THE OXEN. This ancient belief has had wide currency among peasants and farmers of western Europe. Some also say that on Christmas eve the beasts can speak.

QUESTIONS

1. What body of myth is Hardy's subject and what are his speaker's attitudes toward it? Perhaps, in Hardy's view, the pious report about oxen is only part of it.

2. Read this poem aloud and notice its sound and imagery. What contrast do you find between the sounds of the first stanza and the sounds of the last stanza? Which words make the difference? What images enforce a contrast in tone between the beginning of the poem and its ending?
3. G. K. Chesterton, writing as a defender of Christian faith, called Hardy's writings "the mutterings of the village atheist." See other poems by Hardy (particularly "Channel Firing," page 322). What do you think Chesterton might have meant? Can "The Oxen" be called a hostile mutter?

William Wordsworth (1770–1850)

The World Is Too Much with Us 1807

The world is too much with us; late and soon,
Getting and spending, we lay waste our powers;
Little we see in Nature that is ours;
We have given our hearts away, a sordid boon!
This Sea that bares her bosom to the moon;
The winds that will be howling at all hours,
And are up-gathered now like sleeping flowers;
For this, for everything, we are out of tune;
It moves us not. Great God! I'd rather be
A Pagan suckled in a creed outworn;
So might I, standing on this pleasant lea,
Have glimpses that would make me less forlorn;
Have sight of Proteus rising from the sea;
Or hear old Triton blow his wreathèd horn.

Questions

1. In this sonnet by Wordsworth what condition does the poet complain about? To what does he attribute this condition?
2. How does it affect him as an individual?

When Plato in *The Republic* relates the Myth of Er, he introduces supernatural characters he himself originated. Poets, too, have been inspired to make up myths of their own, for their own purposes. "I must create a system or be enslaved by another man's," said William Blake, who in his "prophetic books" peopled the cosmos with supernatural beings having names like Los, Urizen, and Vala (side by side with recognizable figures from the Old Testament and New Testament). This kind of system-making probably has advantages and drawbacks. T. S. Eliot, in his essay on Blake, wishes that the author of *The Four Zoas* had accepted traditional myths, and he compares Blake's thinking to a piece of homemade furniture whose construction diverted valuable energy from the writing of poems. Others have found Blake's untraditional cosmos an achievement—notably William Butler Yeats, himself the author of an elaborate personal mythology. Although we need not know all of Yeats's mythology to enjoy his poems, to know of its existence can make a few great poems deeper for us and less difficult.

William Butler Yeats (1865–1939)

THE SECOND COMING 1921

Turning and turning in the widening gyre° *spiral*
The falcon cannot hear the falconer;
Things fall apart; the center cannot hold;
Mere anarchy is loosed upon the world,
The blood-dimmed tide is loosed, and everywhere
The ceremony of innocence is drowned;
The best lack all conviction, while the worst
Are full of passionate intensity.

Surely some revelation is at hand;
Surely the Second Coming is at hand;
The Second Coming! Hardly are those words out
When a vast image out of *Spiritus Mundi*
Troubles my sight: somewhere in sands of the desert
A shape with lion body and the head of a man,
A gaze blank and pitiless as the sun,
Is moving its slow thighs, while all about it
Reel shadows of the indignant desert birds.
The darkness drops again; but now I know
That twenty centuries of stony sleep
Were vexed to nightmare by a rocking cradle,
And what rough beast, its hour come round at last,
Slouches towards Bethlehem to be born?

What kind of Second Coming does Yeats expect? Evidently it is not to be a Christian one. Yeats saw human history as governed by the turning of a Great Wheel, whose phases influence events and determine human personalities—rather like the signs of the Zodiac in astrology. Every two thousand years comes a horrendous moment: the Wheel completes a turn; one civilization ends and another begins. Strangely, a new age is always announced by birds and by acts of violence. Thus the Greek-Roman world arrives with the descent of Zeus in swan's form and the burning of Troy, the Christian era with the descent of the Holy Spirit—traditionally depicted as a dove—and the Crucifixion. In 1919 when Yeats wrote "The Second Coming," his Ireland was in the midst of turmoil and bloodshed; the Western Hemisphere had been severely shaken by World War I. A new millennium seemed imminent. What sphinxlike, savage deity would next appear, with birds proclaiming it angrily? Yeats thinks he imagines it emerging from *Spiritus Mundi*, Soul of the World, a collective unconscious from which a human being (since the individual soul touches it) receives dreams, nightmares, and racial memories.[2]

It is hard to say whether a poet who discovers a personal myth does so to have something to live by or to have something to write about. Robert Graves, who professes his belief in a White Goddess ("Mother of All Living, the ancient power of love and terror"), has said that he has written poetry in a trance, inspired by his Goddess-Muse.[3] Luckily, we do not have to know a poet's religious affiliation before we can read the poems. Perhaps most personal myths that enter poems are not acts of faith but works of art: stories that resemble traditional mythology.

Barry Spacks (b. 1931)

Teaching the Penguins to Fly

1975

The penguins must have had it once,
some drive and wingspan, back before
they joined up in committees to waddle
on slow-moving ice floes, flapping rhetorical
vans°. My daughter's first ambition *wings (archaic)*
was teaching them to fly, and she hasn't
forgotten: a poster of Emperor penguins
hangs on her bedroom wall where Beatles
still remain, and Aquarius,
her sign—the fuzzy young and vaguely
gazing adults, all of them look
like kids who've lost their expedition
leader. Emperors. Most of them show
color enough at the neck for the mythseeking
eye to propose, from vestigial yellows,
ancestor roc-macaws. Fifteen,
already the culture-heroine knows
it's nothing like easy to start them moving;
she'll leap and flap her arms to teach
the huge idea: up on the toes,
higher, higher, lift those wings!—
trials down ice-slicked runways, lengthy
political sessions, building the Movement,

[2] Yeats fully explains his system in *A Vision* (1938; reprinted New York: Macmillan, 1956).
[3] See Graves's *The White Goddess*, rev. ed. (New York: Farrar, Straus & Giroux, 1966), or for a terser statement of his position, see his lecture "The Personal Muse" in *On Poetry: Collected Talks and Essays* (New York: Doubleday, 1969).

until the strongest risk the winter
sky, shedding their dickies, becoming
through generations enormous budgies
who sing in the jungle, in general bird,
the epic tale of the odd liberator
in shirt and jeans who beat the air
with her arms, who sang them
Woody Guthrie, who
brought the revolution
uncramping their lives.

QUESTIONS

1. A roc is a legendary, gigantic bird encountered by Sinbad in *The Arabian Nights.* What then is a *roc-macaw* (line 16)? Whose is the *mythseeking eye?*
2. Why do you suppose the fifteen-year-old daughter hasn't yet relinquished the posters on her wall and her fanciful ambition to teach the penguins? (Is she merely being childish?)
3. What is the speaker's attitude toward his daughter's ambition? Describe the general tone of the poem.
4. What is suggested by the detail that the daughter's astrological sign is Aquarius? What other recollections of American life in the 1960s and early 1970s does this poem contain?
5. Discuss: Is the poet trying to draw a parallel between the idealism of some Americans in recent years and his daughter's endeavor? Or isn't that his concern?
6. Explain *culture-heroine* (line 17) and *epic tale* (line 28). If the daughter succeeds, what will become of her?

Earlier, looking at symbols, we saw that certain concrete objects in poetry can convey suggestions to which we respond without quite being able to tell why. Such, perhaps, are Emily Dickinson's forked lightning bolt dropped from celestial tables and her buzzing fly that arrives with death. Indefinite power may be present also in an **archetype** (Greek: "first-molded"), which can mean "an original model or pattern from which later things are made." The word acquired a special denotation through the work of the Swiss psychologist Carl Gustav Jung (1875–1961). Recently, it has occurred so frequently in literary criticism that students of poetry may wish to be aware of it.

An archetype, in Jung's view, is generally a story, character, symbol, or situation that recurs again and again in worldwide myth, literature, and dream. Some of these – as defined by Jung and others – might be figures such as the cruel mother (Cinderella's stepmother), the creature half human and half animal (centaurs, satyrs, mermaids), the beautiful garden (Eden, Arcadia, the myth of the Golden Age), the story of the hero who by slaying a monster delivers a country from its curse (the romance of Parsifal, the Old English heroic narrative *Beowulf,* the myth of Perseus, the legend of Saint George and the dragon), the story of the beast who yearns for the love of a woman (the fairy tale of "Beauty and the Beast," the movie *King Kong*), the story of the fall from innocence and initiation into life (the account in Genesis of the departure from Eden, J. D. Salinger's novel *The Catcher in the Rye*).

Like Sigmund Freud, Jung saw myth as an aid to the psychiatrist seeking to understand patients' dreams. But Jung went further and postulated the existence of a "collective unconscious" or racial memory in which archetypes lie. "These fantasy-images," said Jung, referring to dreams not traceable to anything a patient has ever experienced, "correspond to certain *collective* (not personal) structural elements in the human psyche in general, and, like the morphological elements of the human body, are *inherited*. . . . The archetype—let us never forget this—is a psychic organ present in all of us."[4]

What this means to the study of poetry is that, if we accept Jung's view, poems containing recognizable archetypes are likely to stir us more profoundly than those that do not. Archetypes being our inheritance from what Shakespeare called "the dark backward and abysm of time," most people can perceive them and respond to them. Some critics have found Jung's theory helpful in fathoming poems. In *Archetypal Patterns in Poetry* (1934), Maud Bodkin found similar archetypes in such dissimilar poems as "Kubla Khan" and *Paradise Lost*.

Recall Yeats's poem "The Second Coming," only one manifestation of the monstrous Sphinx in literature. There are clear resemblances between the *Spiritus Mundi* in Yeats's poem and Jung's idea of the collective unconscious. As early as 1900, Yeats felt sure of the existence of symbols much like archetypes:

> Any one who has any experience of any mystical state of the soul knows how there float up in the mind profound symbols, whose meaning, if indeed they do not delude one into the dream that they are meaningless, one does not perhaps understand for years. Nor I think has anyone, who has known that experience with any constancy, failed to find some day, in some old book or on some old monument, a strange or intricate image that had floated up before him, and to grow perhaps dizzy with the sudden conviction that our little memories are but part of some great Memory that renews the world and men's thoughts age after age, and that our thoughts are not, as we suppose, the deep, but a little foam upon the deep.[5]

Not all psychologists and students of literature agree with Jung. Some maintain that archetypes, because they tend to disappear with the disintegration of a culture in which they had prospered, are transmitted

[4] Carl Jung, "The Psychology of the Child Archetype," in *Psyche and Symbol*, edited by Violet S. de Laszlo (New York: Doubleday, 1958), pp. 117, 123.

[5] W. B. Yeats, "The Philosophy of Shelley's Poetry," *Essays and Introductions* (New York: Macmillan, 1968), pp. 78–79.

by word of mouth, not by racial memory.[6] Not all poets are as fond of the notion of great Memory as Yeats was. Recently the English poet Philip Larkin has observed:

> As a guiding principle I believe that every poem must be its own sole freshly created universe, and therefore have no belief in "tradition" or a common myth-kitty. . . . To me the whole of the ancient world, the whole of classical and biblical mythology means very little, and I think that using them today not only fills poems full of dead spots but dodges the writer's duty to be original.[7]

Larkin is probably reacting against bookishness. However, even readers who took no stock in Jung's theories may find *archetype* a useful name for something that, since antiquity, has exerted appeal to makers of myth – including some poets and storytellers.

John Keats (1795–1821)

La Belle Dame sans Merci (1819)

O what can ail thee, knight-at-arms,
  Alone and palely loitering?
The sedge has withered from the lake,
  And no birds sing.

O what can ail thee, knight-at-arms,
  So haggard and so woe-begone?
The squirrel's granary is full,
  And the harvest's done.

I see a lily on thy brow
  With anguish moist and fever dew,
And on thy cheek a fading rose
  Fast withereth too.

"I met a lady in the meads,
  Full beautiful – a faery's child;
Her hair was long, her foot was light,
  And her eyes were wild.

"I made a garland for her head,
  And bracelets too, and fragrant zone°; *belt, sash*
She looked at me as she did love,
  And made sweet moan.

[6] See J. S. Lincoln, *The Dream in Primitive Cultures* (1935, p. 24; reprinted New York: Johnson Reprints, 1970).
[7] Statements made on two different occasions, quoted by John Press, *A Map of Modern English Verse* (New York: Oxford University Press, 1969), pp. 258–59.

"I set her on my pacing steed,
And nothing else saw all day long,
For sidelong would she bend, and sing
A faery's song.

"She found me roots of relish sweet,
And honey wild, and manna dew,
And sure in language strange she said—
'I love thee true!'

"She took me to her elfin grot,
And there she wept and sighed full sore,
And there I shut her wild wild eyes
With kisses four.

"And there she lullèd me asleep,
And there I dreamed—ah! woe betide!
The latest dream I ever dreamed
On the cold hill's side.

"I saw pale kings and princes too,
Pale warriors, death-pale were they all;
They cried—'La Belle Dame sans Merci
Hath thee in thrall!'

"I saw their starved lips in the gloam,
With horrid warning gapèd wide,
And I awoke and found me here,
On the cold hill's side.

"And this is why I sojourn here,
Alone and palely loitering,
Though the sedge is withered from the lake
And no birds sing."

La Belle Dame sans Merci. Keats borrowed this title, "The Lovely Merciless Lady," from a medieval French poem. The text given above is his earliest version.

Questions

1. What happens in this ballad? What is indicated by the contrast between the imagery from nature in lines 17, 18, 25, and 26 and that in lines 3–4, 7–8, 44, and 47–48? How do you interpret the knight's *latest dream* (line 35)?
2. What do we know about this beautiful lady without pity? What supernatural powers does she possess?
3. What other *dames sans merci* do you find in other poems in this book? In what respects are they similar? In what respects, if any, is Keats's lady an individual?
4. What other relentless beauties with supernatural powers do you know from myth, folklore, literature, movies, or television? In what respects, if any, do they resemble the *Belle Dame?*

John Milton (1608–1674)

Lycidas

1637

In this monody the author bewails a learned friend, unfortunately drowned in his passage from Chester on the Irish Seas, 1637. And by occasion foretells the ruin of our corrupted clergy then in their height.

Yet once more, O ye laurels, and once more,
Ye myrtles brown°, with ivy never sere, *dark*
I come to pluck your berries harsh and crude°, *immature*
And with forced fingers rude
Shatter your leaves before the mellowing year.
Bitter constraint and sad occasion dear
Compels me to disturb your season due;
For Lycidas is dead, dead ere his prime,
Young Lycidas, and hath not left his peer.
Who would not sing for Lycidas? he knew
Himself to sing, and build the lofty rhyme.
He must not float upon his wat'ry bier
Unwept, and welter° to the parching wind, *toss about*
Without the meed° of some melodious tear. *tribute*
  Begin, then, Sisters of the Sacred Well
That from beneath the seat of Jove doth spring,
Begin, and somewhat loudly sweep the string.
Hence with denial vain and coy excuse:
So may some gentle Muse° *poet*
With lucky words favor my destined urn,
And, as he passes, turn,
And bid fair peace be to my sable shroud!
For we were nursed upon the self-same hill,
Fed the same flocks, by fountain, shade, and rill;
  Together both, ere the high lawns appeared
Under the opening eyelids of the Morn,
We drove a-field, and both together heard
What time the gray-fly winds° her sultry horn, *sounds*
Batt'ning° our flocks with the fresh dews of night, *feeding*
Oft till the star that rose at evening bright
Toward Heav'n's descent had sloped his westering wheel.
Meanwhile the rural ditties were not mute,
Tempered to the oaten° flute, *made of an oat stalk*
Rough satyrs danced, and fauns with cloven heel

Lycidas. A *monody* is a song for a single voice, generally a lament. Milton's *learned friend* was Edward King, scholar and poet, a fellow student at Cambridge University, where King had been preparing for the ministry. In calling him Lycidas, Milton employs a conventional name for a young shepherd in **pastoral poetry** (which either portrays the world of shepherds with some realism, as in Virgil's *Eclogues,* or makes it a prettified Eden, as in Marlowe's "The Passionate Shepherd to His Love"). 1–2. *laurels, myrtles:* Evergreens in the crowns traditionally bestowed upon poets.

From the glad sound would not be absent long;
And old Damoetas loved to hear our song.
But, O the heavy change, now thou art gone,
Now thou art gone, and never must return!
Thee, Shepherd, thee the woods and desert caves,
With wild thyme and the gadding° vine o'ergrown, *wandering*
And all their echoes mourn.
The willows, and the hazel copses green,
Shall now no more be seen
Fanning their joyous leaves to thy soft lays.
As killing as the canker to the rose,
Or taint-worm to the weanling herds that graze,
Or frost to flowers, that their gay wardrobe wear
When first the white thorn blows°; *blossoms*
Such, Lycidas, thy loss to shepherd's ear.
Where were ye, Nymphs, when the remorseless deep
Closed o'er the head of your loved Lycidas?
For neither were ye playing on the steep
Where your old bards, the famous Druids, lie,
Nor on the shaggy top of Mona high,
Nor yet where Deva spreads her wizard stream.
Ay me! I fondly° dream! *foolishly*
"Had ye been there"—for what could that have done?
What could the Muse herself that Orpheus bore,
The Muse herself, for her enchanting son,
Whom universal Nature did lament,
When, by the rout° that made the hideous roar, *mob*
His gory visage down the stream was sent,
Down the swift Hebrus to the Lesbian shore?
Alas! What boots it° with uncessant care *what good does it do*
To tend the homely, slighted shepherd's trade,
And strictly meditate the thankless Muse?
Were it not better done, as others use°, *do*
To sport with Amaryllis in the shade,
Or with the tangles of Neaera's hair?
Fame is the spur that the clear spirit doth raise
(That last infirmity of noble mind)
To scorn delights and live laborious days;
But the fair guerdon when we hope to find,
And think to burst out into sudden blaze,
Comes the blind Fury with th' abhorrèd shears,
And slits the thin-spun life. "But not the praise,"

36. *Damoetas:* Perhaps some Cambridge tutor. 53. *Druids:* priests and poets of the Celts in pre-Christian Britain. 54. *Mona:* Roman name for the Isle of Man, near which King was drowned. 55. *Deva:* the River Dee, flowing between England and Wales. Its shifts in course were said to augur good luck for one country or the other. 68–69. *Amaryllis, Neaera:* conventional names for shepherdesses. 70. *the clear spirit doth raise:* doth raise the clear spirit.

Phoebus replied, and touched my trembling ears:
"Fame is no plant that grows on mortal soil,
Nor in the glistering° foil, *glittering*
Set off to the world, nor in broad rumor° lies, *reputation*
But lives and spreads aloft by those pure eyes
And perfect witness of all-judging Jove;
As he pronounces lastly on each deed,
Of so much fame in Heav'n expect thy meed."
O fountain Arethuse, and thou honored flood,
Smooth-sliding Mincius, crowned with vocal reeds,
That strain I heard was of a higher mood:
But now my oat proceeds,
And listens to the Herald of the Sea,
That came in Neptune's plea.
He asked the waves, and asked the felon winds,
What hard mishap hath doomed this gentle swain?
And questioned every gust of rugged wings
That blows from off each beakèd promontory:
They knew not of his story;
And sage Hippotades their answer brings,
That not a blast was from his dungeon strayed:
The air was calm, and on the level brine
Sleek Panope with all her sisters played.
It was that fatal and perfidious bark,
Built in th' eclipse, and rigged with curses dark,
That sunk so low that sacred head of thine.
Next, Camus, reverend sire, went footing slow,
His mantle hairy, and his bonnet sedge,
Inwrought with figures dim, and on the edge
Like to that sanguine flower inscribed with woe.
"Ah! who hath reft," quoth he, "my dearest pledge?"
Last came, and last did go,
The pilot of the Galilean lake;
Two massy keys he bore of metals twain
(The golden opes, the iron shuts amain°). *with force*
He shook his mitered locks, and stern bespake:—
"How well could I have spared for thee, young swain,
Enow° of such as for their bellies' sake, *enough*

77. *touched . . . ears:* gesture signifying "Remember!" 79. *foil:* a setting of gold or silver leaf, used to make a gem appear more brilliant. 85–86. *Arethuse, Minicius:* a fountain and river near the birthplaces of Theocritus and Virgil, respectively, hence recalling the most celebrated writer of pastorals in Greek and the most celebrated in Latin. 90. *in Neptune's plea:* bringing the sea-god's plea, "not guilty." 99. *Panope:* a sea nymph. Her name means "one who sees all." 101. *eclipse:* thought to be an omen of evil fortune. 103. *Camus:* spirit of the river Cam and personification of Cambridge University. 109–112. *pilot:* Saint Peter, once a fisherman in Galilee, to whom Christ gave the *keys* of Heaven (Matthew 16:19). As first Bishop of Rome, he wears the miter, a bishop's emblematic head-covering.

Creep, and intrude, and climb into the fold!
Of other care they little reck'ning make
Than how to scramble at the shearers' feast,
And shove away the worthy bidden guest.
Blind mouths! that scarce themselves know how to hold
A sheep-hook, or have learned aught else the least
That to the faithful herdsman's art belongs!
What recks it them? What need they? they are sped°; *prosperous*
And, when they list°, their lean and flashy songs *so incline*
Grate on their scrannel° pipes of wretched straw; *feeble, harsh*
The hungry sheep look up, and are not fed,
But, swoll'n with wind and the rank mist they draw,
Rot inwardly, and foul contagion spread;
Besides what the grim wolf with privy° paw *stealthy*
Daily devours apace, and nothing said;
But that two-handed engine at the door
Stands ready to smite once, and smite no more."

Return, Alpheus; the dread voice is past
That shrunk thy streams; return, Sicilian Muse,
And call the vales, and bid them hither cast
Their bells and flow'rets of a thousand hues.
Ye valleys low, where the mild whispers use° *resort*
Of shades, and wanton winds, and gushing brooks,
On whose fresh lap the swart star sparely looks,
Throw hither all your quaint enameled eyes,
That on the green turf suck the honied showers,
And purple all the ground with vernal flowers.
Bring the rathe° primrose that forsaken dies, *early*
The tufted crow-toe, and pale jessamine,
The white pink, and the pansy freaked° with jet, *streaked*
The glowing violet,
The musk-rose, and the well-attired woodbine,
With cowslips wan that hang the pensive head,
And every flower that sad embroidery wears;
Bid amaranthus all his beauty shed,
And daffadillies fill their cups with tears,
To strew the laureate hearse where Lycid lies.
For so, to interpose a little ease,
Let our frail thoughts dally with false surmise,

115. *fold:* the Church of England. 120. *sheep-hook:* a bishop's staff or crozier, which resembles a shepherd's crook. 128. *wolf:* probably the Church of Rome. Jesuits in England at the time were winning converts. 130. *two-handed engine:* This disputed phrase may refer (among other possibilities) to the punishing sword of The Word of God (Revelation 19:13–15 and Hebrews 4:12). Perhaps Milton sees it as a lightning bolt, as does Spenser, to whom Jove's wrath is a "three-forked engine" (*Faerie Queene,* VIII, 9). 131. *smite once . . . no more:* Because, in the proverb, lightning never strikes twice in the same place. 133. *Sicilian Muse:* who inspired Theocritus, a native of Sicily. 138. *swart star:* Sirius, at its zenith in summer, was thought to turn vegetation black. 153. *false surmise:* futile hope that the body of Lycidas could be recovered.

Ay me! whilst thee the shores and sounding seas
Wash far away, where'er thy bones are hurled;
Whether beyond the stormy Hebrides,
Where thou, perhaps, under the whelming tide
Visit'st the bottom of the monstrous° world; *full of sea monsters*
Or whether thou, to our moist vows° denied, *prayers*
Sleep'st by the fable of Bellerus old,
Where the great Vision of the guarded mount
Looks toward Namancos and Bayona's hold°: *stronghold*
Look homeward, angel, now, and melt with ruth°; *pity*
And, O ye dolphins, waft the hapless youth.
  Weep no more, woeful shepherds, weep no more,
For Lycidas, your sorrow, is not dead,
Sunk though he be beneath the wat'ry floor:
So sinks the day-star in the ocean bed
And yet anon repairs his drooping head,
And tricks° his beams, and with new-spangled ore° *arrays; gold*
Flames in the forehead of the morning sky:
So Lycidas sunk low, but mounted high,
Through the dear might of Him that walked the waves,
Where, other groves and other streams along,
With nectar pure his oozy locks he laves,
And hears the unexpressive nuptial song,
In the blest kingdoms meek of Joy and Love.
There entertain him all the Saints above,
In solemn troops, and sweet societies,
That sing, and singing in their glory move,
And wipe the tears forever from his eyes.
Now, Lycidas, the shepherds weep no more;
Henceforth thou art the Genius° of the shore, *guardian spirit*
In thy large recompense, and shalt be good
To all that wander in that perilous flood.

  Thus sang the uncouth° swain to th' oaks and rills, *rustic (or little-known)*
While the still Morn went out with sandals gray;
He touched the tender stops of various quills°, *reeds of a shepherd's pipe*
With eager thought warbling his Doric lay:
And now the sun had stretched out all the hills,
And now was dropped into the western bay.
At last he rose, and twitched° his mantle blue: *donned*
Tomorrow to fresh woods and pastures new.

160. *Bellerus:* legendary giant of Land's End, the far tip of Cornwall. 161. *guarded mount:* Saint Michael's Mount, off Land's End, said to be under the protection of the archangel. 162. *Namancos, Bayona:* on the coast of Spain. 164. *dolphins:* In Greek legend, these kindly mammals carried the spirits of the dead to the Blessed Isles. 176. *unexpressive nuptial song:* inexpressibly beautiful song for the marriage feast of the Lamb (Revelation 19:9). 189. *Doric lay:* pastoral poem. Doric is the dialect of Greek employed by Theocritus.

Questions and Exercises

1. With the aid of an encyclopedia or a handbook of classical mythology (such as Bulfinch's *Mythology*, Edith Hamilton's *Mythology*, or H. J. Rose's *Handbook of Greek Mythology*) learn more about the following myths or mythical figures and places to which Milton alludes:

Line 15	Sisters of the Sacred Well (Muses)
16	seat of Jove (Mount Olympus)
58	the Muse . . . that Orpheus bore (Calliope)
61–63	(the death of Orpheus)
75	Fury with the . . . shears (Atropos, one of the three Fates)
77	Phoebus
89	Herald of the Sea (Triton)
90	Neptune
96	Hippotades
106	(Hyacinthus)
132	Alpheus

   Then reread Milton's poem. As a result of your familiarity with these myths, what details become clear?

2. Read the parable of the Good Shepherd (John 10:1–18). What relationships does Milton draw between the Christian idea of the shepherd and pastoral poetry?
3. "With these trifling fictions [allusions to classical mythology]," wrote Samuel Johnson about "Lycidas," "are mingled the most awful and sacred truths, such as ought never to be polluted with such irreverend combinations." Does this mingling of paganism and Christianity detract from Milton's poem? Discuss.
4. In "Lycidas" does Milton devise any new myth or myths?

14 Alternatives

THE POET'S REVISIONS

"He / Who casts to write a living line must sweat, / . . . and strike the second heat / Upon the Muse's anvil," wrote Ben Jonson. Indeed, few if any immortal poems can have been perfected with the first blow. As a result, a poet may leave us two or more versions of a poem—perhaps (as Robert Graves has said of his work drafts) "hatched and cross-hatched by puzzling layers of ink."

We need not, of course, rummage the poet's wastebasket in order to evaluate a poem. If we wish, we can follow a suggestion of the critic Austin Warren: take any fine poem and make changes in it. Then compare the changes with the original. We may then realize why the poem is as it is instead of something else. However, there is a certain undeniable pleasure in watching a poem go through its growth stages. Some readers have claimed that the study of successive versions gives them insight into the process by which poems come to be. More important to a reader whose concern is to read poems with appreciation, we stand to learn something about the rightness of a finished poem from seeing what alternatives occurred to the poet. To a critic who protested two lines in Wordsworth's "The Thorn," a painfully flat description of an infant's grave,

> I've measured it from side to side;
> 'Tis three feet long and two feet wide,

Wordsworth retorted, "They ought to be liked." However, he thought better of them and later made this change:

> Though but of compass small, and bare
> To thirsty suns and parching air.

William Butler Yeats, who enjoyed revision, kept trying to improve the poems of his youth. A merciless self-critic, Yeats discarded lines that a lesser poet would have been grateful for. In some cases his final version was practically a new poem.

William Butler Yeats (1865–1939)

The Old Pensioner 1890

I had a chair at every hearth,
When no one turned to see
With "Look at that old fellow there;
And who may he be?"
And therefore do I wander on,
And the fret is on me.

The road-side trees keep murmuring—
Ah, wherefore murmur ye
As in the old days long gone by,
Green oak and poplar tree!
The well-known faces are all gone,
And the fret is on me.

The Lamentation of the Old Pensioner 1939

Although I shelter from the rain
Under a broken tree
My chair was nearest to the fire
In every company
That talked of love or politics,
Ere Time transfigured me.

Though lads are making pikes again
For some conspiracy,
And crazy rascals rage their fill
At human tyranny,
My contemplations are of Time
That has transfigured me.

There's not a woman turns her face
Upon a broken tree,
And yet the beauties that I loved
Are in my memory;
I spit into the face of Time
That has transfigured me.

Questions

1. "The Old Pensioner" is this poem's first printed version; "Lamentation," its last. From the original, what elements has Yeats in the end retained?
2. What does the final version add to our knowledge of the old man (his character, attitudes, circumstances)?
3. Compare in sound and rhythm the refrain in the "Lamentation" with the original refrain.
4. Why do the statements in the final version seem to follow one another more naturally, and the poem as a whole seem more tightly woven together?

Yeats's practice seems to document the assertion of critic A. F. Scott that "the work of correction is often quite as inspired as the first onrush of words and ideas." Yeats made a revealing comment on his methods of revision:

> In dream poetry, in "Kubla Khan," . . . every line, every word can carry its unanalyzable, rich associations; but if we dramatize some possible singer or speaker we remember that he is moved by one thing at a time, certain words must be dull and numb. Here and there in correcting my early poems I have introduced such numbness and dullness, turned, for instance, the "curd-pale moon" into the "brilliant moon," that all might seem, as it were, remembered with indifference, except some one vivid image. When I began to rehearse a play I had the defects of my early poetry; I insisted upon obvious all-pervading rhythm. Later on I found myself saying that only in those lines or words where the beauty of the passage came to its climax, must rhythm be obvious.[1]

In changing words for "dull and numb" ones, in breaking up and varying rhythms, Yeats evidently is trying for improvement not necessarily in a particular line, but in an entire poem.

Not all revisions are successful. An instance might be the alterations Keats made in "La Belle Dame sans Merci," in which the stanza with the "wild wild eyes" and the exactly counted kisses,

She took me to her elfin grot,
  And there she wept and sighed full sore,
And there I shut her wild wild eyes
  With kisses four.

was scrapped in favor of:

She took me to her elfin grot,
  And there she gazed and sighèd deep,
And there I shut her wild sad eyes—
  So kissed to sleep.

When Mark Antony begins his funeral oration, "Friends, Romans, countrymen: lend me your ears," Shakespeare makes him ask something quite different from the modernized version in one high school English textbook: "Friends, Romans, countrymen: listen to me." Strictly speaking, any revised version of a poem is a different poem, even if its only change is a single word.

Exercise: *Early and Late Versions*

In each of the following pairs, which details of the revised version show an improvement of the earlier one? Exactly what makes the poet's second thoughts seem better (if you agree that they are)? Italics indicate words of one text not

[1] "Dramatis Personae, 1896–1902," in *The Autobiography of William Butler Yeats* (New York: Macmillan, 1953).

found in the other. Notice that in some cases, the poet has also changed word order.

1. Samuel Taylor Coleridge, "The Rime of the Ancient Mariner," from Part III:

   a. One after one, by the hornèd Moon
      (Listen, O Stranger! to me)
   Each turn'd his face with a ghastly pang
      And curs'd me with his *ee*. *(1799 version)*

   b. One after one, by the *star-dogged* Moon,
   Too quick for groan or sigh,
   Each turned his face with a ghastly pang
   And cursed me with his *eye*. *(1817 version)*

2. William Blake, last stanza of "London" (complete poem given on page 68):

   a. But most the midnight harlot's curse
   From every *dismal* street I hear,
   Weaves around the marriage hearse
   And blasts the new born infant's tear. *(first draft, 1793)*

   b. But most *through* midnight streets I hear
   How the *youthful* harlot's curse
   Blasts the new born infant's tear
   And *blights with plagues* the marriage hearse. *(1794 version)*

3. Edward FitzGerald, *The Rubáiyát of Omar Khayyám*, a quatrain:

   a. *For in and out, above, about, below,*
   'Tis nothing but a Magic Shadow-show,
      Play'd in a Box whose Candle is the Sun,
   Round *which* we *Phantom Figures* come and go.
   (first version, 1859 edition)

   b. We *are no other than a moving row*
   Of Magic Shadow-*shapes that* come and go
      Round *with* the Sun-*illumined Lantern held*
   In Midnight by the Master of the Show; . . .
   (fifth version, 1889 edition)

Walt Whitman (1819–1892)

A Noiseless Patient Spider

A noiseless patient spider,
I mark'd where on a little promontory it stood isolated,
Mark'd how to explore the vacant vast surrounding,
It launch'd forth filament, filament, filament, out of itself,
Ever unreeling them, ever tirelessly speeding them.
And you O my soul where you stand,
Surrounded, detached, in measureless oceans of space,
Ceaselessly musing, venturing, throwing, seeking the spheres to connect
      them,
Till the bridge you will need be form'd, till the ductile anchor hold,
Till the gossamer thread you fling catch somewhere, O my soul.

The Soul, reaching, throwing out for love

The Soul, reaching, throwing out for love,
As the spider, from some little promontory, throwing out filament after
filament, tirelessly out of itself, that one at least may catch and form
a link, a bridge, a connection
O I saw one passing along, saying hardly a word—yet full of love I de-
tected him, by certain signs
O eyes wishfully turning! O silent eyes!
For then I thought of you o'er the world,
O latent oceans, fathomless oceans of love!
O waiting oceans of love! yearning and fervid! and of you sweet souls
perhaps in the future, delicious and long:
But Death, unknown on the earth—ungiven, dark here, unspoken, never
born:
You fathomless latent souls of love—you pent and unknown oceans of
love!

Questions

1. One of these two versions of a poem by Whitman is an early draft from the poet's notebook. The other is the final version completed in 1871, about ten years later. Which is the final version?
2. In the final version, what has Whitman done to render his central metaphor (the comparison of soul and spider) more vivid and exact? What proportion of the final version is devoted to this metaphor?
3. In the early draft, what lines seem distracting or nonessential?

Donald Hall (b. 1928)

My Son, My Executioner 1955

My son, my executioner,
I take you in my arms,
Quiet and small and just astir,
And whom my body warms.

Sweet death, small son, our instrument
Of immortality,
Your cries and hungers document
Our bodily decay.

We twenty-five and twenty-two,
Who seemed to live forever,
Observe enduring life in you
And start to die together.

Questions

1. The first line introduces a paradoxical truth, the basic theme of the poem. How would you sum up this truth in your own words?

2. Exactly what do these words denote: *instrument* (line 5), *document* (line 7)?
3. When first published, this poem had a fourth stanza:

I take into my arms the death
  Maturity exacts,
And name with my imperfect breath
  The mortal paradox.

Do you think the poet right or wrong to omit this stanza? Explain.

TRANSLATIONS

Poetry, said Robert Frost, is what gets lost in translation. If absolutely true, the comment is bad news for most of us, who have to depend on translations for our only knowledge of great poems in some other languages. However, some translators seem able to save a part of their originals and bring it across the language gap. At times they may even add more poetry of their own, as if to try to compensate for what is lost.

Unlike the writer of an original poem, the translator begins with a meaning that already exists. To convey it, the translator may decide to stick closely to the denotations of the original words or else to depart from them, more or less freely, after something he or she values more. The latter aim is evident in the *Imitations* of Robert Lowell, who said he had been "reckless with literal meaning" and instead had "labored hard to get the tone." Particularly defiant of translation are poems in dialect, uneducated speech, and slang: what can be used for English equivalents? Ezra Pound, in a bold move, translates the song of a Chinese peasant in *The Classic Anthology Defined by Confucius:*

Yaller bird, let my corn alone,
Yaller bird, let my crawps alone,
These folks here won't let me eat,
I wanna go back whaar I can meet
the folks I used to know at home,
              I got a home an' I wanna' git goin'.

Here, it is our purpose to judge a translation not by its fidelity to its original, but by the same standards we apply to any other poem written in English. To do so may be another way to see the difference between appropriate and inappropriate words.

Federico García Lorca (1899–1936)

LA GUITARRA (1921)	GUITAR 1967
Empieza el llanto de la guitarra.	Begins the crying of the guitar.

Se rompen las copas
de la madrugada.
Empieza el llanto
de la guitarra.
Es inútil
callarla.
Es imposible
callarla.
Llora monótona
como llora el agua,
como llora el viento
sobre la nevada.
Es imposible
callarla.
Llora por cosas
lejanas.
Arena del Sur caliente
que pide camelias blancas.
Llora flecha sin blanco,
la tarde sin mañana,
y el primer pájaro muerto
sobre la rama.
¡Oh, guitarra!
Corazón malherido
por cinco espadas.

From earliest dawn
the strokes are breaking.
Begins the crying
of the guitar.
It is futile
to stop its sound.
It is impossible
to stop its sound.
It is crying a monotone
like the crying of water,
like the crying of wind
over fallen snow.
It is impossible
to stop its sound.
It is crying over things
far off.
Burning sand of the South
which covets white camelias.
It is crying the arrow without aim,
the evening without tomorrow,
and the first dead bird on the branch.
O guitar!
Heart heavily wounded
by five sharp swords.

—Translated by Keith Waldrop

Questions

1. Someone who knows Spanish should read aloud the original and the translation. Although it is impossible for any translation fully to capture the resonance of García Lorca's poem, in what places is the English version most nearly able to approximate it?
2. Another translation renders line 21: "It mourns for the targetless arrow." What is the difference between mourning for something and being the cry of it?
3. Throughout his translation, Waldrop closely follows the line divisions of the original, but in line 23 he combines García Lorca's lines 23 and 24. Can you see any point in his doing so? Would "on the branch" by itself be a strong line of English poetry?

Exercise: *Comparing Translations*

Which English translation of each of the following poems is the best poetry? The originals may be of interest to some. For those who do not know the foreign language, the editor's line-by-line prose paraphrases may help indicate what the translator had to work with and how much of the translation is the translator's own idea. In which do you find the diction most felicitous? In which do pattern and structure best move as one? What differences in tone are apparent? It is doubtful that any one translation will surpass the others in every detail.

Horace (65–8 B.C.)

ODES I (38) (about 20 B.C.)

Persicos odi, puer, apparatus,
Displicent nexae philyra coronae;
Mitte sectari, rosa quo locorum
Sera moretur.
Simplici myrto nihil allabores
Sedulus curo: neque te ministrum
Dedecet myrtus neque me sub arta
Vite bibentem.

ODES I (38). Prose translation: (1) Persian pomp, boy, I detest, (2) garlands woven of linden bark displease me; (3–4) give up searching for the place where the late-blooming rose is. (5–6) Put no laborious trimmings on simple myrtle: (6–7) for myrtle is unbecoming neither to you, a servant, nor to me, under the shade of this (8) vine, drinking.

1. SIMPLICITY (about 1782)

Boy, I hate their empty shows,
Persian garlands I detest,
Bring me not the late-blown rose
Lingering after all the rest:
Plainer myrtle pleases me
Thus outstretched beneath my vine,
Myrtle more becoming thee,
Waiting with thy master's wine.

—William Cowper

2. FIE ON EASTERN LUXURY! (about 1830)

Nay, nay, my boy—'tis not for me,
This studious pomp of Eastern luxury;
Give me no various garlands—fine
With linden twine,
Nor seek, where latest lingering blows,
The solitary rose.

Earnest I beg—add not with toilsome pain,
One far-sought blossom to the myrtle plain,
For sure, the fragrant myrtle bough
Looks seemliest on thy brow;
Nor me mis-seems, while, underneath the vine,
Close interweaved, I quaff the rosy wine.

—Hartley Coleridge

3. THE PREFERENCE DECLARED 1892

Boy, I detest the Persian pomp;
I hate those linden-bark devices;
And as for roses, holy Moses!
They can't be got at living prices!
Myrtle is good enough for us,—
For *you*, as bearer of my flagon;
For *me*, supine beneath this vine,
Doing my best to get a jag on!

—Eugene Field

Charles Baudelaire (1821–1867)

Recueillement 1866

Sois sage, ô ma Douleur, et tiens-toi plus tranquille.
Tu réclamais le Soir; il descend; le voici:
Une atmosphère obscure enveloppe la ville,
Aux uns portant la paix, aux autres le souci.

Pendant que des mortels la multitude vile,
Sous le fouet du Plaisir, ce bourreau sans merci,
Va cueillir des remords dans la fête servile,
Ma Douleur, donne-moi la main; viens par ici,

Loin d'eux. Vois se pencher les défuntes Années,
Sur les balcons du ciel, en robes surannées;
Surgir du fond des eaux le Regret souriant;

Le Soleil moribond s'endormir sous une arche,
Et, comme un long linceul trainant à l'Orient,
Entends, ma chère, entends la douce Nuit qui marche.

"Meditation." Prose translation: (1) Behave yourself [as a mother would say to her child], O my Sorrow, and keep calmer. (2) You called for Evening; it descends; here it is: (3) a dim atmosphere envelops the city, (4) Bringing peace to some; to others anxiety. (5) While the vile multitude of mortals (6) under the whip of Pleasure, that merciless executioner, (7) go to gather remorse in the servile festival, (8) my Sorrow, give me your hand; come this way, (9) far from them. See the dead years lean (10) on the balconies of the sky, in old-fashioned dresses; (11) [see] Regret, smiling, emerge from the depths of the waters; (12) [see] the dying Sun go to sleep under an arch; (13) and like a long shroud trailing in the East, (14) hear, my darling, hear the soft Night who is walking.

1. Peace, be at peace, O thou my heaviness 1919

Peace, be at peace, O thou my heaviness,
Thou callèdst for the evening, lo! 'tis here,
The City wears a somber atmosphere
That brings repose to some, to some distress.
Now while the heedless throng make haste to press
Where pleasure drives them, ruthless charioteer,
To pluck the fruits of sick remorse and fear,
Come thou with me, and leave their fretfulness.
See how they hang from heaven's high balconies,
The old lost years in faded garments dressed,
And see Regret with faintly smiling mouth;
And while the dying sun sinks in the west,
Hear how, far off, Night walks with velvet tread,
And her long robe trails all about the south.

—Lord Alfred Douglas

2. Inward Conversation 1961

Be reasonable, my pain, and think with more detachment.
You asked to see the dusk; it descends; it is here:
A sheath of dark light robes the city,
To some bringing peace, to some the end of peace.

Now while the rotten herds of mankind,
Flogged by pleasure, that lyncher without touch,
Go picking remorse in their filthy holidays,
Let us join hands, my pain; come this way,

Far from them. Look at the dead years that lean on
The balconies of the sky, in their clothes long out of date;
The sense of loss that climbs from the deep waters with a smile;

The sun, nearly dead, that drops asleep beneath an arch;
And listen to the night, like a long shroud being dragged
Toward the east, my love, listen, the soft night is moving.

—Robert Bly

3. MEDITATION 1961

Calm down, my Sorrow, we must move with care.
You called for evening; it descends; it's here.
The town is coffined in its atmosphere,
bringing relief to some, to others care.

Now while the common multitude strips bare,
feels pleasure's cat o' nine tails on its back,
and fights off anguish at the great bazaar,
give me your hand, my Sorrow. Let's stand back;

back from these people! Look, the dead years dressed
in old clothes crowd the balconies of the sky.
Regret emerges smiling from the sea,

the sick sun slumbers underneath an arch,
and like a shroud strung out from east to west,
listen, my Dearest, hear the sweet night march!

—Robert Lowell

PARODY

In a **parody,** one writer imitates—and pokes fun at—another. Skillfully wrought, a parody can be a devastating form of literary criticism. Usually the parodist imitates the characteristic tone, form, language, and other elements of the original model, but sometimes applies them to a ludicrously uncharacteristic subject—as in E. B. White's parody of Walt Whitman, "A Classic Waits for Me" (page 244).

Rather than merely flinging abuse at another poet, the wise parodist imitates with understanding—perhaps with sympathy. The many crude parodies of T. S. Eliot's difficult poem *The Waste Land* show parodists mocking what they cannot fathom, with the result that, instead of illuminating the original, they belittle it (and themselves). Good parodists have an ear for the sounds and rhythms of their originals, as does James Camp, who echoes Walt Whitman's stately "Out of the Cradle Endlessly Rocking" in his line "Out of the crock endlessly ladling" (what a weary teacher feels he is doing). William Harmon has imagined Emily Dickinson as a college student keeping a diary that begins:

The Soul selects her own Sorority –
Then – shuts the Dorm –
From her elite Majority
Black balls – eclectic – swarm –

(Compare Emily Dickinson's original on page 134.) Parody can be aimed at poems good or bad; yet there are poems of such splendor and dignity that no parodist seems able to touch them without looking like a small dog defiling a cathedral, and others so illiterate that good parody would be squandered on them. In the following original by T. E. Brown, what failings does the parodist, J. A. Lindon, jump upon? (*God wot,* by the way, is an archaism for "God knows.")

T. E. Brown (1830–1897)

My Garden — 1887

A garden is a lovesome thing,
  God wot!
Rose plot,
Fringed pool,
Ferned grot—
The veriest school
Of peace; and yet the fool
Contends that God is not—
Not God! in gardens! when the eve
  is cool?
Nay, but I have a sign;
'Tis very sure God walks in mine.

J. A. Lindon (b. 1914)

My Garden — 1959

A garden is a *lovesome* thing?
  What rot!
Weed plot,
Scum pool,
Old pot,
Snail-shiny stool
In pieces; yet the fool
Contends that snails are not—
Not snails! in gardens! when the
  eve is cool?
Nay, but I see their trails!
'Tis very sure *my* garden's full of
  snails!

Hugh Kingsmill
[Hugh Kingsmill Lunn] (1889–1949)

What, still alive at twenty-two — (about 1920)

What, still alive at twenty-two,
A clean, upstanding chap like you?
Sure, if your throat 'tis hard to slit,
Slit your girl's, and swing for it.

Like enough, you won't be glad
When they come to hang you, lad:

But bacon's not the only thing
That's cured by hanging from a string.

So, when the spilt ink of the night
Spreads o'er the blotting-pad of light,
Lads whose job is still to do
Shall whet their knives, and think of you.

QUESTIONS

1. A. E. Housman considered this the best of many parodies of his poetry. Read his poems in this book, particularly "Terence, this is stupid stuff" and "To an Athlete Dying Young" (pages 329–331). What characteristics of theme, form, and language does Hugh Kingsmill's parody convey?
2. What does Kingsmill exaggerate?

Kenneth Koch (b. 1925)

MENDING SUMP

1960

"Hiram, I think the sump is backing up.
The bathroom floor boards for above two weeks
Have seemed soaked through. A little bird, I think,
Has wandered in the pipes, and all's gone wrong."
"Something there is that doesn't hump a sump,"
He said; and through his head she saw a cloud
That seemed to twinkle. "Hiram, well," she said,
"Smith is come home! I saw his face just now
While looking through your head. He's come to die
Or else to laugh, for hay is dried-up grass
When you're alone." He rose, and sniffed the air.
"We'd better leave him in the sump," he said.

QUESTIONS

1. What poet is the object of this parody? Which of his poems are echoed in it?
2. Koch gains humor by making outrageous statements in the tone and language of his original. Looking at other poems in this book by the poet being parodied, how would you describe their tone? Their language?
3. Suppose, instead of casting his parody into blank verse, Koch had written:

   "Hiram, the sump is backing up.
   The bathroom floor boards
   For above two weeks
   Have been soaking through. A little bird,
   I think, has wandered in
   The pipes, and all's gone wrong."

   Why would the biting edge of his parody have been blunted?
4. What, by the way, is a *sump*?

EXERCISE: *Spotting the Originals*

In each of the following three parodies, what poem or poet is being kidded? In each, does the parodist seem only to be having fun, or is he making any critical point?

Desmond Skirrow (1924–1976)

ODE ON A GRECIAN URN SUMMARIZED 1960

Gods chase
Round vase.
What say?
What play?
Don't know.
Nice, though.

John Ciardi (b. 1916)

BY A BUSH IN HALF TWILIGHT 1980

A cow came over the wall New England style,
Its hind end first. As if it knew
There was more in what it was coming from
Than in what it was going to.

George Starbuck (b. 1931)

MARGARET ARE YOU DRUG 1966

Cool it Mag.
Sure it's a drag
With all that green flaked out.
Next thing you know they'll be changing the color of bread.

But look, Chick,
Why panic?
Sevennyeighty years, we'll *all* be dead.

Roll with it, Kid.
I did.
Give it the old benefit of the doubt.

I mean leaves
Schmeaves.
You sure you aint just feeling sorry for yourself?

MARGARET ARE YOU DRUG. This is one of a series of "Translations from the English."

E. B. White (b. 1899)

A Classic Waits for Me

1944

(With apologies to Walt Whitman, plus a trial membership in the Classics Club)

A classic waits for me, it contains all, nothing is lacking,
Yet all were lacking if taste were lacking, or if the endorsement of the right man were lacking.
O clublife, and the pleasures of membership,
O volumes for sheer fascination unrivalled.
Into an armchair endlessly rocking,
Walter J. Black my president,
I, freely invited, cordially welcomed to membership,
My arm around John Kieran, Pearl S. Buck,
My taste in books guarded by the spirits of William Lyon Phelps, Hendrik Willem van Loon,
(From your memories, sad brothers, from the fitful risings and callings I heard),
I to the classics devoted, brother of rough mechanics, beauty-parlor technicians, spot welders, radio-program directors
(It is not necessary to have a higher education to appreciate these books),
I, connoisseur of good reading, friend of connoisseurs of good reading everywhere,
I, not obliged to take any specific number of books, free to reject any volume, perfectly free to reject Montaigne, Erasmus, Milton,
I, in perfect health except for a slight cold, pressed for time, having only a few more years to live,
Now celebrate this opportunity.
Come, I will make the club indissoluble,
I will read the most splendid books the sun ever shone upon,
I will start divine magnetic groups,
  With the love of comrades,
  With the life-long love of distinguished committees.

I strike up for an Old Book.
Long the best-read figure in America, my dues paid, sitter in armchairs everywhere, wanderer in populous cities, weeping with Hecuba and with the late William Lyon Phelps,
Free to cancel my membership whenever I wish,
Turbulent, fleshy, sensible,
Never tiring of clublife,
Always ready to read another masterpiece provided it has the approval of my president, Walter J. Black,
Me imperturbe, standing at ease among writers,
Rais'd by a perfect mother and now belonging to a perfect book club,
Bearded, sunburnt, gray-neck'd, astigmatic,
Loving the masters and the masters only

(I am mad for them to be in contact with me),
My arm around Pearl S. Buck, only American woman to receive the Nobel
    Prize for Literature,
I celebrate this opportunity.
And I will not read a book nor the least part of a book but has the approval
    of the Committee,
For all is useless without that which you may guess at many times and not
    hit, that which they hinted at,
All is useless without readability.
By God! I will accept nothing which all cannot have their counterpart of
    on the same terms (89¢ for the Regular Edition or $1.39 for the De
    Luxe Edition, plus a few cents postage).
I will make inseparable readers with their arms around each other's necks,
  By the love of classics,
  By the manly love of classics.

A CLASSIC WAITS FOR ME. Advertisements for the Classics Club used to proclaim that its books were selected by a committee of the popular writers and interpreters of culture named in lines 8–9. 10. *your memories, sad brothers:* Phelps and van Loon had died shortly before White's satire was first printed in 1944. 23. *Hecuba:* in Homer's *Iliad,* the wife of Priam, defeated king of Troy, and mother of Hector, Trojan hero slain by Achilles. 28. *Me imperturbe:* Whitman's poem by this title begins, "Me imperturbe, standing at ease in Nature . . ." (The Latinate phrase could be roughly translated, "I, the unflappable.")

QUESTIONS

1. What is E. B. White making fun of, besides Walt Whitman's poetry? How timely does White's satire remain? (Have you noticed any recent book club ads?)
2. Compare White's opening lines with those of Whitman's "A Woman Waits for Me," a celebration of the joys of reproduction:

   A woman waits for me, she contains all, nothing is lacking,
   Yet all were lacking if sex were lacking, or if the
      moisture of the right man were lacking.

   In White's lines, how does the phrase *nothing is lacking* change in meaning? The phrase *the right man*?
3. What traits of Whitman's style does White imitate? (See other poems by Whitman in this book.)
4. The more you read of Whitman, the more you will appreciate White's parody. Look up "A Woman Waits for Me" in Whitman's *Leaves of Grass.* See also "Out of the Cradle Endlessly Rocking" and "Song of Myself." What further echoes of Whitman do you find in White's take-off? How closely does White remind you of Whitman's attitudes toward himself and toward the world?

EXPERIMENT: *Writing an Imitation or a Parody*

Write a poem in the manner of Emily Dickinson, William Carlos Williams, E. E. Cummings, or any other modern poet whose work interests you and which you feel able to imitate. Decide, before you start, whether to write a serious imitation (that could be slipped into the poet's *Collected Poems* without anyone being the wiser), or a humorous parody. Read all the poet's poems included in this book; perhaps you will find it helpful also to consult a larger selection or collection of the poet's work. It might be simplest to choose a particular poem as your model; but, if you like, you may echo any number of poems. Choose a model within the range of your own skill: to imitate a sonnet, for instance, you need to be able to rime and to write in meter. Probably, if your imitation is serious, and not a parody like E. B. White's parody of Whitman, it is a good idea to pick a subject or theme characteristic of the poet. This is a difficult project, but if you can do it even fairly well, you will know a great deal more about poetry and your poet.

15 Telling Good from Bad

"The bulk of English poetry is bad," a critic has said,[1] referring to all verse printed over the past six hundred years, not only that which survives in anthologies. As his comment reminds us, excellent poetry is at least as scarce as gold. Though readers who seek it for themselves can expect to pan through much shale, such labor need not discourage them from prospecting. Only the naïve reader assumes, "This poem must be good, or else why would it appear in a leading magazine?" Only the reader whose mind is coasting in neutral says, "Who knows if this poem is good? Who cares? It all depends upon your point of view." Open-minded, skeptical, and alert, the critical reader will make independent evaluations.

Why do we call some poems "bad"? We are not talking about their moral implications. Rather, we mean that, for one or more of many possible reasons, the poem has failed to move us or to engage our sympathies. Instead, it has made us doubt that the poet is in control of language and vision; perhaps it has aroused our antipathies or unwittingly appealed to our sense of the comic, though the poet is serious. Some poems can be said to succeed despite burdensome faults. But in general such faults are symptoms of deeper malady: some weakness in a poem's basic conception or in the poet's competence.

Nearly always, a bad poem reveals only a dim and distorted awareness of its probable effect on an alert reader. Perhaps the sound of words may clash with what a poem is saying, as in the jarring last word of this opening line of a tender lyric (author unknown, quoted by Richard Wilbur): "Come into the tent, my love, and close the flap." Perhaps a metaphor may fail by calling to mind more differences than similarities, as in Emily Dickinson's lines "Our lives are Swiss-- / So still--so cool." A bad poem usually overshoots or falls short of its mark by the poet's thinking too little or too much. Thinking much, a poet contrives such an excess of ingenuity as that quoted by Alexander Pope in

[1] Christopher Adams in the preface to his anthology, *The Worst English Poets* (London: Allan Wingate, 1958).

Peri Bathous, or *Of the Art of Sinking in Poetry:* a hounded stag who "Hears his own feet, and thinks they sound like more; / And fears the hind feet will o'ertake the fore." Thinking little, a poet writes redundantly, as Wordsworth in "The Thorn": "And they had fixed the wedding-day, / The morning that must wed them both."

In a poem that has a rime scheme or a set line length, when all is well, pattern and structure move inseparably with the rest of their poem, the way a tiger's skin and bones move with their tiger. But sometimes, in a poem that fails, the poet evidently has had difficulty in persuading statements to fit a formal pattern. English poets have long felt free to invert word order for a special effect, but the poet having trouble keeping to a rime scheme may invert words for no apparent reason but convenience. Needing a rime for *barge* may lead to ending a line with a *policedog large* instead of *a large policedog*. Another sign of trouble is a profusion of adjectives. If a line of iambic pentameter reads, "Her lovely skin, like dear sweet white old silk," we suspect the poet of stuffing the line to make it long enough. Whenever two or more adjectives stand together (in poetry or in good prose), they need to be charged with meaning. No one suspects Matthew Arnold of padding the last line of "To Marguerite": "The unplumbed, salt, estranging sea."

Because, over his dead body, even a poet's slightest and feeblest efforts may be collected, some lines in the canon of celebrated bards make us wonder, "How could he have written this?" Wordsworth, Shelley, Whitman, and Browning are among the great whose failures can be painful, and lapses of awareness may occur even in poems that, taken entire, are excellent. To be unwilling to read them, though, would be as ill advised as to refuse to see Venice just because the Grand Canal is said to contain impurities. The seasoned reader of poetry thinks no less of Tennyson for having written, "Form, Form, Riflemen Form! . . . Look to your butts, and take good aims!" The collected works of a duller poet may contain no such lines of unconscious double meaning, but neither do they contain, perhaps, any poem as good as "Ulysses." If the duller poet never had a spectacular failure, it may be because of failure to take risks.

We flatter ourselves if we think all imprecise poetry the work of times gone by. Poetry editors of current magazines find that about nine hundred out of a thousand unsolicited poems are, at a glance, unworthy of a second reading. Although editors may have nightmares in which they ignorantly reject the poems of some new Gerard Manley Hopkins or Emily Dickinson, they nonetheless send them back with a printed "thank you" slip, then turn to the hundred that look interesting. How are the poems winnowed so quickly? Often, inept poems fall into familiar categories. At one extreme is the poem written entirely in conventional diction, dimly echoing Shakespeare, Wordsworth, and the Bible, but garbling them. Couched in a rhythm that ticks along like a metronome, this kind of poem shows no sign that its author has ever taken a hard look at anything that can be tasted, handled, and felt. It employs loosely and thoughtlessly the most abstract of words: *love, beauty, life, death, time, eternity*. Littered with old-fashioned contractions (*'tis, o'er, where'er*), it may end in a simple platitude or preachment, as if the poet expected us to profit from his or her wisdom and moral superiority. George Orwell's complaint against much contemporary writing (not only poetry) is applicable: "As soon as certain topics are raised" – and one thinks of such standard topics for poetry as spring, a first kiss, and stars – "the concrete melts into the abstract and no one seems able to think of turns of speech that are not hackneyed." Writers, Orwell charged, too often make their sentences out of tacked-together phrases "like the sections of a prefabricated hen-house."[2] Versifiers often do likewise.

At the opposite extreme is the poem that displays no acquaintance with poetry of the past but manages, instead, to fabricate its own clichés. Slightly paraphrased, a manuscript once submitted to *The Paris Review* began:

Vile
        rottenflush
                        o   – *screaming* –
                        f CORPSEBLOOD!!   ooze
    STRANGLE my
                        eyes . . .   HELL's
                              O, ghastly   stench**!!!

At most, such a work has only a private value. The writer has vented personal frustrations upon words, instead of kicking stray dogs. In its way, "Vile Rottenflush" is as self-indulgent as the oldfangled "first kiss in spring" kind of poem. Both offend, both inspire distrust. "I dislike," said John Livingston Lowes, "poems that black your eyes, or put up their mouths to be kissed."

As jewelers tell which of two diamonds is fine by seeing which scratches the other, two poems may be tested by comparing them. This method works only on poems similar in length and kind: an epigram cannot rival an epic. Most poems we meet are neither sheer trash nor obvious masterpieces. Since, however, good diamonds to be proven need softer ones to scratch, in this chapter you will find a few clear-cut gems and a few clinkers. "In poetry," said Ronsard, "mediocrity is the greatest vice."

[2] George Orwell, "Politics and the English Language," from *Shooting an Elephant and Other Essays* (New York: Harcourt Brace Jovanovich, 1945).

Anonymous (English)

O MOON, WHEN I GAZE ON THY BEAUTIFUL FACE (about 1900)

O Moon, when I gaze on thy beautiful face,
Careering along through the boundaries of space,
The thought has often come into my mind
If I ever shall see thy glorious behind.

O MOON. Sir Edmund Gosse, the English critic (1849–1928), offered this quatrain as the work of his maidservant, but there is reason to suspect him of having written it.

QUESTIONS

1. To what fact of astronomy does the last line refer?
2. Which words seem chosen with too little awareness of their denotations and connotations?
3. Even if you did not know that these lines probably were deliberately bad, how would you argue with someone who maintained that the opening *O* in the poem was admirable as a bit of concrete poetry? (See the quotation from E. E. Cummings on page 199.)

Grace Treasone

LIFE (about 1963)

Life is like a jagged tooth
that cuts into your heart;
fix the tooth and save the root,
and laughs, not tears, will start.

William Ernest Henley (1849–1903)

MADAM LIFE'S A PIECE IN BLOOM 1908

Madam Life's a piece in bloom
  Death goes dogging everywhere:
She's the tenant of the room,
  He's the ruffian on the stair.

You shall see her as a friend,
  You shall bilk him once or twice;
But he'll trap you in the end,
  And he'll stick you for her price.

With his kneebones at your chest,
  And his knuckles in your throat,
You would reason — plead — protest!
  Clutching at her petticoat;

But she's heard it all before,
  Well she knows you've had your fun,
Gingerly she gains the door,
  And your little job is done.

Questions

1. Try to paraphrase the two preceding poems. What is the theme of each?
2. Which statement of theme do you find more convincing? Why?
3. Which poem is the more consistent in working out its metaphor?

Stephen Tropp (b. 1930)

My Wife Is My Shirt 1960

My wife is my shirt
I put my hands through her armpits
slide my head through her mouth
& finally button her blood around my hands

Questions

1. How consistently is the metaphor elaborated?
2. Why can this metaphor be said to work in exactly the opposite way from a personification?
3. A paraphrase might discover this simile: "My wife is as intimate, familiar, and close to me as the shirt on my back." If this is the idea and the poem is supposed to be a love poem, how precisely is its attitude expressed?

Emily Dickinson (1830–1886)

A Dying Tiger–moaned for Drink (about 1862)

A Dying Tiger–moaned for Drink–
I hunted all the Sand–
I caught the Dripping of a Rock
And bore it in my Hand–

His Mighty Balls–in death were thick–
But searching–I could see
A Vision on the Retina
Of Water–and of me–

'Twas not my blame–who sped too slow–
'Twas not his blame–who died
While I was reaching him–
But 'twas–the fact that He was dead–

Question

How does this poem compare in success with other poems of Emily Dickinson that you know? Justify your opinion by pointing to some of this poem's particulars.

Exercise: *Seeing What Went Wrong*

Here is a small anthology of bad moments in poetry. For what reasons does each selection fail? In which passages do you attribute the failure to inappropriate sound or diction? To awkward word order? To inaccurate metaphor? To excessive overstatement? To forced rime? To monotonous rhythm? To redundancy? To simple-mindedness or excessive ingenuity?

1. "I'm Glad," in its entirety, author unknown:

   I'm glad the sky is painted blue,
   And the earth is painted green,
   With such a lot of nice fresh air
   All sandwiched in between.

2. A lover's lament from Harry Edward Mills's *Select Sunflowers:*

   I see her in my fondest moods,
     She haunts the parlor hallway;
   And yet her form my clasp eludes,
     Her lips my kisses alway.

3. A suffering swain makes a vow, from "the poem of a young tradesman" quoted by Coleridge in *Biographia Literaria:*

   No more will I endure love's pleasing pain,
   Or round my heart's leg tie his galling chain.

4. From an elegy for Queen Victoria by one of her subjects:

   Dust to dust, and ashes to ashes,
   Into the tomb the Great Queen dashes.

5. The opening lines of Alice Meynell's "The Shepherdess":

   She walks—the lady of my delight—
   A shepherdess of sheep.

6. From a juvenile poem of John Dryden, "Upon the Death of the Lord Hastings" (a victim of smallpox):

   Blisters with pride swelled; which through's flesh did sprout
   Like rose-buds, stuck i' th'lily-skin about.
   Each little pimple had a tear in it,
   To wail the fault its rising did commit . . .

7. From "The Abbey Mason" by Thomas Hardy:

   —When longer yet dank death had wormed
   The brain wherein the style had germed

   From Gloucester church it flew afar—
   The style called Perpendicular.—

   To Winston and to Westminster
   It ranged, and grew still beautifuller . . .

8. From a classified advertisement on the obituary page, Boston *Globe,* January 8, 1980:

1977—ELVIS PRESLEY—1980

Today is your birthday
And although you're not here,
There are, no doubt, many more
Than I who still miss you and care.
And every time we see your pictures
Or hear your special songs,
We'll feel a pain deep
In our hearts, still so strong.
We will never forget you.
You remain on our minds.
Forever, our love, Elvis.
You were one of a kind.
A loving fan.
Diane.

9. A metaphor from Edgar A. Guest's "The Crucible of Life":

Sacred and sweet is the joy that must come
From the furnace of life when you've poured off the scum.

10. A stanza composed by Samuel Johnson as a deliberately bad example:

I put my hat upon my head
And walked into the Strand;
And there I met another man
Whose hat was in his hand.

11. A lover describes his lady, from Thomas Holley Chivers's "Rosalie Lee":

Many mellow Cydonian suckets,
  Sweet apples, anthosmial, divine,
From the ruby-rimmed beryline buckets,
  Star-gemmed, lily-shaped, hyaline:
Like the sweet golden goblet found growing
  On the wild emerald cucumber-tree,
Rich, brilliant, like chrysoprase glowing,
  Was my beautiful Rosalie Lee.

12. Lines on a sick gypsy, author unknown, quoted in *The Stuffed Owl, an Anthology of Bad Verse,* edited by D. B. Wyndham Lewis and Charles Lee:

    There we leave her,
    There we leave her,
Far from where her swarthy kindred roam,
    In the Scarlet Fever,
    Scarlet Fever,
Scarlet Fever Convalescent Home.

Sentimentality is the failure of writers who imply that they feel great emotion but who fail to give us sufficient grounds for sharing it. The emotion may be an anger greater than its object seems to call for, as in these lines to a girl who caused scandal (the exact nature of her act never being specified): "The gossip in each hall / Will curse your name . . . / Go! better cast yourself right down the falls!"[3] Or it may be an enthusiasm quite unwarranted by its subject: in *The Fleece* John Dyer temptingly describes the pleasures of life in a workhouse for the poor. The sentimental poet is especially prone to tenderness. Great tears fill this poet's eyes at a glimpse of an aged grandmother sitting by a hearth. For all the poet knows, she may be the well-to-do manager of a casino in Las Vegas, who would be startled to find herself an object of pity, but the sentimentalist seems not to care to know much about the woman herself. She is employed as a general excuse for feeling maudlin. Any other conventional object will serve as well: a faded valentine, the strains of an old song, a baby's cast-off pacifier. A celebrated instance of such emotional self-indulgence is "The Old Oaken Bucket," by Samuel Woodworth, a stanza of which goes:

> How sweet from the green, mossy brim to receive it,
> As, poised on the curb, it inclined to my lips!
> Not a full-flushing goblet could tempt me to leave it,
> Tho' filled with the nectar that Jupiter sips.
> And now, far removed from the loved habitation,
> The tear of regret will intrusively swell,
> As fancy reverts to my father's plantation,
> And sighs for the bucket that hung in the well.

As a symbol, the bucket might conceivably be made to hold the significance of the past and the speaker's regret at being caught in the destroying grip of time. But the staleness of the phrasing and imagery (Jove's nectar, *tear of regret*) suggests that the speaker is not even seeing the actual physical bucket, and the tripping meter of the lines is inappropriate to an expression of tearful regret. Perhaps the poet's nostalgia is genuine. We need not doubt it; indeed, as Keith Waldrop has put it, "a bad poem is always sincere." However sincere in their feelings, sentimental poets are insincere in their art—otherwise, wouldn't they trouble to write better poems, or at least not print the ones they write? Woodworth, by the vagueness of his language and the monotony of his rhythms, fails to persuade us that we ought to care. Wet-eyed and sighing for a bucket, he achieves not pathos but **bathos:** a description that can move us to laughter instead of tears.[4]

[3] Ali. S. Hilmi, "The Preacher's Sermon," in *Verse at Random* (Larnaca, Cyprus: Ohanian Press, 1953).

[4] *Bathos* in poetry can also mean an abrupt fall from the sublime to the trivial or incongruous. A sample, from Nicholas Rowe's play *The Fair Penitent:* "Is it the voice of thunder, or my father?" Another, from John Close, a minor Victorian: "Around their heads a dazzling halo shone, / No need of mortal robes, or any hat." When, however, such a letdown is used for a *desirable* effect of humor or contrast, it is usually called an **anticlimax:** as in Alexander Pope's lines on the queen's palace, "Here thou, great Anna! whom three realms obey, / Dost sometimes counsel take—and sometimes tea."

Tears, of course, can be shed for good reason. A piece of sentimentality is not be confused with a well-wrought poem whose tone is tenderness. At first glance, the following poem by Burns might strike you as sentimental. If so, your suspicions are understandable, for it is a rare poet who can speak honestly or effectively on the theme that love grows deeper as lovers grow old. Many a popular song-writer has seen the process of aging as valuable: "Darling, I am growing old, / Silver threads among the gold." According to such songs, to grow decrepit is a privilege. What is fresh in Burns's poem, however, is that no attempt is made to gloss over the ravages of age and the inevitability of death. The speaker expresses no self-pity, no comment *about* her feelings, only a simple account of what has befallen her and her John and what is still to follow.

Robert Burns (1759–1796)

John Anderson my jo, John (1790)

John Anderson my jo°, John, *dear*
When we were first acquent°, *acquainted*
Your locks were like the raven,
Your bonny brow was brent°; *unwrinkled*
But now your brow is beld°, John, *bald*
Your locks are like the snaw;
But blessings on your frosty pow°, *head*
John Anderson my jo.

John Anderson my jo, John,
We clamb the hill thegither;
And mony a canty° day, John, *happy*
We've had wi' ane anither:
Now we maun° totter down, John, *must*
And hand in hand we'll go,
And sleep together at the foot,
John Anderson my jo.

EXERCISE: *Fine or Shoddy Tenderness*

Which of the following three poems do you find sentimental? Which would you defend? At least one kind of evidence to look for is minute, detailed observation of physical objects. In a successful poem, the poet is likely at least occasionally to notice the world beyond his or her own skin; in a sentimental poem, this world is likely to be ignored.

Hart Crane (1899–1932)

My Grandmother's Love Letters 1926

There are no stars to-night
But those of memory.
Yet how much room for memory there is
In the loose girdle of soft rain.

There is even room enough
For the letters of my mother's mother,
Elizabeth,
That have been pressed so long
Into a corner of the roof
That they are brown and soft,
And liable to melt as snow.

Over the greatness of such space
Steps must be gentle.
It is all hung by an invisible white hair.
It trembles as birch limbs webbing the air.

And I ask myself:

"Are your fingers long enough to play
Old keys that are but echoes:
Is the silence strong enough
To carry back the music to its source
And back to you again
As though to her?"

Yet I would lead my grandmother by the hand
Through much of what she would not understand;
And so I stumble. And the rain continues on the roof
With such a sound of gently pitying laughter.

Eliza Cook (1818–1889)

The Old Arm-Chair

I love it, I love it! and who shall dare
To chide me for loving that old arm-chair?
I've treasured it long as a sainted prize,
I've bedewed it with tears, I've embalmed it with sighs,
'Tis bound by a thousand bands to my heart;
Not a tie will break, not a link will start.
Would you know the spell?—a mother sat there!
And a sacred thing is that old arm-chair.

In childhood's hour I lingered near
The hallowed seat with listening ear;
And gentle words that mother would give

To fit me to die and teach me to live.
She told me that shame would never betide
With truth for my creed, and God for my guide;
She taught me to lisp my earliest prayer,
As I knelt beside that old arm-chair.

I sat and watched her many a day,
When her eyes grew dim, and her locks were gray;
And I almost worshipped her when she smiled,
And turned from her Bible to bless her child.
Years rolled on, but the last one sped,—
My idol was shattered, my earth-star fled!
I learned how much the heart can bear,
When I saw her die in her old arm-chair.

'Tis past, 'tis past! but I gaze on it now,
With quivering breath and throbbing brow;
'Twas there she nursed me, 'twas there she died,
And memory flows with a lava tide.
Say it is folly, and deem me weak,
Whilst scalding drops start down my cheek;
But I love it, I love it! and cannot tear
My soul from a mother's old arm-chair.

D. H. Lawrence (1885–1930)

Piano 1918

Softly, in the dusk, a woman is singing to me;
Taking me back down the vista of years, till I see
A child sitting under the piano, in the boom of the tingling strings
And pressing the small, poised feet of a mother who smiles as she sings.

In spite of myself, the insidious mastery of song
Betrays me back, till the heart of me weeps to belong
To the old Sunday evenings at home, with winter outside
And hymns in the cozy parlor, the tinkling piano our guide.

So now it is vain for the singer to burst into clamor
With the great black piano appassionato. The glamor
Of childish days is upon me, my manhood is cast
Down in the flood of remembrance, I weep like a child for the past.

Rod McKuen (b. 1933)

Thoughts on Capital Punishment 1954

There ought to be capital punishment for cars
that run over rabbits and drive into dogs
and commit the unspeakable, unpardonable crime
of killing a kitty cat still in his prime.

Purgatory, at the very least
should await the driver
driving over a beast.

Those hurrying headlights coming out of the dark
that scatter the scampering squirrels in the park
should await the best jury that one might compose
of fatherless chipmunks and husbandless does.

And then found guilty, after too fair a trial
should be caged in a cage with a hyena's smile
or maybe an elephant with an elephant gun
should shoot out his eyes when the verdict is done.

There ought to be something, something that's fair
to avenge Mrs. Badger as she waits in her lair
for her husband who lies with his guts spilling out
cause he didn't know what automobiles are about.

Hell on the highway, at the very least
should await the driver
driving over a beast.

Who kills a man kills a bit of himself
But a cat too is an extension of God.

William Stafford (b. 1914)

Traveling Through the Dark 1962

Traveling through the dark I found a deer
dead on the edge of the Wilson River road.
It is usually best to roll them into the canyon:
that road is narrow; to swerve might make more dead.

By glow of the tail-light I stumbled back of the car
and stood by the heap, a doe, a recent killing;
she had stiffened already, almost cold.
I dragged her off; she was large in the belly.

My fingers touching her side brought me the reason—
her side was warm; her fawn lay there waiting,
alive, still, never to be born.
Beside that mountain road I hesitated.

The car aimed ahead its lowered parking lights;
under the hood purred the steady engine.
I stood in the glare of the warm exhaust turning red;
around our group I could hear the wilderness listen.

I thought hard for us all—my only swerving—
then pushed her over the edge into the river.

Questions

1. Compare these poems by Rod McKuen and William Stafford. How are they similar?
2. Explain Stafford's title. Who are all those traveling through the dark?
3. Comment on McKuen's use of language. Consider especially: *unspeakable, unpardonable crime* (line 3), *kitty cat* (4), *scatter the scampering squirrels* (9), and *cause he didn't know* (19).
4. Compare the meaning of Stafford's last two lines and McKuen's last two. Does either poem have a moral? Can either poem be said to moralize?
5. Which poem might be open to the charge of sentimentality? Why?
6. Compare these two poems with another poem similar in subject matter: Gerald Stern's "Behaving Like a Jew" (page 372). Evaluate Stern's poem by comparison with McKuen's poem and Stafford's.

16 Knowing Excellence

How can we tell an excellent poem from any other? To give reasons for excellence in poetry is harder than to give reasons for failure in poetry (so often due to familiar, old-hat sorts of imprecision and sentimentality). A bad poem tends to be stereotyped, an excellent poem unique. In judging either, we can have no absolute preexisting specifications. A poem is not a simple mechanism like an electric toaster that an inspector in a factory can test by a check-off list. It has to be judged on the basis of what it evidently is trying to be and how well it succeeds in its effort. Nor is excellence simply due to regularity and symmetry. For the sake of meaning, a competent poet often will depart from a pattern. There is satisfaction, said Robert Frost, in things not mechanically straight: "We enjoy the straight crookedness of a good walking stick."

To judge a poem, we first have to understand it. At least, we need to understand it *almost* all the way; there is, to be sure, a poem such as Hopkins's "The Windhover" (page 329), which most readers probably would call excellent even though its meaning is still being debated. While it is a good idea to give a poem at least a couple of considerate readings before judging it, sometimes our first encounter with a poem starts turning into an act of evaluation. Moving along into the poem, becoming more deeply involved in it, we may begin forming an opinion. In general, the more a poem contains for us to understand, the more rewarding we are likely to find it. This does not mean that an obscure and highly demanding poem is always to be preferred to a relatively simple one. Difficult poems can be pretentious and incoherent, but there is something to be said for the poem complicated enough to leave us something to discover on our fifteenth reading (unlike most limericks, which yield their all at a single look). Here is such a poem, one not readily fathomed and exhausted.

William Butler Yeats (1865–1939)

Sailing to Byzantium — 1927

That is no country for old men. The young
In one another's arms, birds in the trees
—Those dying generations—at their song,

The salmon-falls, the mackerel-crowded seas,
Fish, flesh, or fowl, commend all summer long
Whatever is begotten, born, and dies.
Caught in that sensual music all neglect
Monuments of unaging intellect.

An aged man is but a paltry thing,
A tattered coat upon a stick, unless
Soul clap its hands and sing, and louder sing
For every tatter in its mortal dress,
Nor is there singing school but studying
Monuments of its own magnificence;
And therefore I have sailed the seas and come
To the holy city of Byzantium.

O sages standing in God's holy fire
As in the gold mosaic of a wall,
Come from the holy fire, perne in a gyre°, *spin down a spiral*
And be the singing-masters of my soul.
Consume my heart away; sick with desire
And fastened to a dying animal
It knows not what it is; and gather me
Into the artifice of eternity.

Once out of nature I shall never take
My bodily form from any natural thing,
But such a form as Grecian goldsmiths make
Of hammered gold and gold enameling
To keep a drowsy Emperor awake;
Or set upon a golden bough to sing
To lords and ladies of Byzantium
Of what is past, or passing, or to come.

SAILING TO BYZANTIUM. Byzantium was the capital of the Byzantine Empire, the city now called Istanbul. Yeats means, though, not merely the physical city. Byzantium is also a name for his conception of paradise.

Though *salmon-falls* (line 4) suggests Yeats's native Ireland, the poem, as we find out in line 25, is about escaping from the entire natural world. If the poet desires this escape, then probably the *country* mentioned in the opening line is no political nation but the cycle of birth and death in which human beings are trapped; and, indeed, the poet says his heart is "fastened to a dying animal." Imaginary landscapes, it would seem, are merging with the historical Byzantium. Lines 17-18 refer to mosaic images, adornments of the Byzantine cathedral of St. Sophia, in which the figures of saints are inlaid against backgrounds of gold. The clockwork bird of the last stanza is also a reference to something actual. Yeats noted: "I have read somewhere that in the Emperor's palace at Byzantium was a tree made of gold and silver, and artificial birds that sang." This description of the role the poet would seek—that of a changeless, immortal singer—directs us back to the earlier references to music and singing. Taken all together, they point toward the central metaphor of the poem: the craft of poetry can be a kind of singing. One kind of everlasting monument is a great poem. To study masterpieces of poetry is the only "singing school"—the only way to learn to write a poem.

We have no more than skimmed through a few of this poem's suggestions, enough to show that, out of allusion and imagery, Yeats has woven at least one elaborate metaphor. Surely one thing the poem achieves is that, far from merely puzzling us, it makes us aware of relationships between what a person can imagine and the physical world. There is the statement that a human heart is bound to the body that perishes, and yet it is possible to see consciousness for a moment independent of flesh, to sing with joy at the very fact that the body is crumbling away. Expressing a similar view of mortality, the Japanese artist Hokusai has shown a withered tree letting go of its few remaining leaves, while under it two graybeards shake with laughter. Like Hokusai's view, that of Yeats is by no means simple. Much of the power of Yeats's poem comes from the physical terms with which he states the ancient quarrel between body and spirit, body being a "tattered coat upon a stick." There is all the difference in the world between the work of the poet like Yeats whose eye is on the living thing and whose mind is awake and passionate, and that of the slovenly poet whose dull eye and sleepy mind focus on nothing more than some book read hastily long ago. The former writes a poem out of compelling need, the latter as if it seems a nice idea to write something.

Yeats's poem has the three qualities essential to beauty, according to the definition of Thomas Aquinas: wholeness, harmony, and radiance. The poem is all one; its parts move in peace with one another; it shines with emotional intensity. There is an orderly progression going on in it: from the speaker's statement of his discontent with the world of "sensual music," to his statement that he is quitting this world, to his prayer that the sages will take him in, and his vision of future immortality. And the images of the poem relate to one another—*dying generations* (line 3), *dying animal* (line 22), and the undying golden bird (lines 27-32)—to mention just one series of related things. "Sailing to Byzantium" is not the kind of poem that has, in Pope's words, "One simile, that solitary shines / In the dry desert of a thousand lines." Rich in figurative language, Yeats's whole poem develops a metaphor, with further metaphors as its tributaries.

"Sailing to Byzantium" has a theme that matters to us. What human being does not long, at times, to shed timid, imperfect flesh, to live in a state of absolute joy, unperishing? Being human, perhaps we too are stirred by Yeats's prayer: "Consume my heart away, sick with desire / And fastened to a dying animal. . . ." If it is true that in poetry (as Ezra Pound declared) "only emotion endures," then Yeats's poem ought to endure. (No reasons to be moved by a poem, however, can be of much use. If you happen not to feel moved by this particular poem, try another—but come back to "Sailing to Byzantium" after a while.)

Most excellent poems, it might be argued, contain significant themes, as does "Sailing to Byzantium." But the presence of such a theme is not enough to render a poem excellent. That classic tear-jerker "The Old Arm-Chair" (page 256) expresses in its way, too, faith in a kind of immortality. Not theme alone makes an excellent poem, but how well a theme is stated.

Yeats's poem, some would say, is the match of any lyric in our language. Some might call it inferior to an epic (to Milton's *Paradise Lost*, say, or to the *Iliad*), but this is to lead us into a different argument: whether certain genres are innately better than others. Such an argument usually leads to a dead end. Evidently, *Paradise Lost* has greater range, variety, matter, length, and ambitiousness. But any poem—whether an epic or an epigram—may be judged by how well it fulfills the design it undertakes. God, who created both fleas and whales, pronounced all good. Fleas, like epigrams, have no reason to feel inferior.

Exercise: *Two Poems to Compare*

Here are two poems with a similar theme. Which contains more qualities of excellent poetry? Decide whether the other is bad or whether it may be praised for achieving something different.

Arthur Guiterman (1871–1943)

On the Vanity of Earthly Greatness — 1936

The tusks that clashed in mighty brawls
Of mastodons, are billiard balls.

The sword of Charlemagne the Just
Is ferric oxide, known as rust.

The grizzly bear whose potent hug
Was feared by all, is now a rug.

Great Caeser's bust is on the shelf,
And I don't feel so well myself.

Percy Bysshe Shelley (1792–1822)

Ozymandias — 1818

I met a traveler from an antique land
Who said: Two vast and trunkless legs of stone
Stand in the desert. Near them, on the sand,
Half sunk, a shattered visage lies, whose frown,
And wrinkled lip, and sneer of cold command,
Tell that its sculptor well those passions read

Which yet survive, stamped on these lifeless things,
The hand that mocked° them and the heart that fed; *imitated*
And on the pedestal these words appear:
"My name is Ozymandias, king of kings:
Look on my works, ye Mighty, and despair!"
Nothing beside remains. Round the decay
Of that colossal wreck, boundless and bare
The lone and level sands stretch far away.

Some excellent poems of the past will remain sealed to us unless we are willing to sympathize with their conventions. Pastoral poetry, for instance—Marlowe's "Passionate Shepherd" and Milton's "Lycidas"—asks us to accept certain conventions and situations that may seem old-fashioned: idle swains, oaten flutes. We are under no grim duty, of course, to admire poems whose conventions do not appeal to us. But there is no point in blaming a poet for playing a particular game or for observing its rules.

Bad poems, of course, can be woven together out of conventions, like patchwork quilts made of old unwanted words. In Shakespeare's England, poets were busily imitating the sonnets of Petrarch, the Italian poet whose praise of his beloved Laura had become well known. The result of their industry was a surplus of Petrarchan **conceits,** or elaborate comparisons (from the Italian *concetto:* concept, bright idea). In the following sonnet, Shakespeare, who at times helped himself generously from the Petrarchan stockpile, pokes fun at poets who thoughtlessly use such handed-down figures of speech.

William Shakespeare (1564–1616)

My mistress' eyes are nothing like the sun — 1609

My mistress' eyes are nothing like the sun;
Coral is far more red than her lips' red;
If snow be white, why then her breasts are dun;
If hairs be wires, black wires grow on her head.
I have seen roses damasked red and white,
But no such roses see I in her cheeks;
And in some perfumes is there more delight
Than in the breath that from my mistress reeks.
I love to hear her speak, yet well I know
That music hath a far more pleasing sound;
I grant I never saw a goddess go:
My mistress, when she walks, treads on the ground.
  And yet, by heaven, I think my love as rare
  As any she°, belied with false compare. *woman*

Contrary to what you might expect, for years after Shakespeare's time, poets continued to write fine poems with the aid of such conventions.

Thomas Campion (1567–1620)

THERE IS A GARDEN IN HER FACE 1617

There is a garden in her face
Where roses and white lilies grow;
A heav'nly paradise is that place
Wherein all pleasant fruits do flow.
There cherries grow which none may buy
Till "Cherry-ripe" themselves do cry.

Those cherries fairly do enclose
Of orient pearl a double row,
Which when her lovely laughter shows,
They look like rose-buds filled with snow;
Yet them nor° peer nor prince can buy, *neither*
Till "Cherry-ripe" themselves do cry.

Her eyes like angels watch them still;
Her brows like bended bows do stand,
Threat'ning with piercing frowns to kill
All that attempt, with eye or hand
Those sacred cherries to come nigh
Till "Cherry-ripe" themselves do cry.

THERE IS A GARDEN IN HER FACE. 6. *"Cherry-ripe":* cry of fruit-peddlers in London streets.

QUESTIONS

1. What does Campion's song owe to Petrarchan tradition?
2. What in it strikes you as fresh observation of actual life?
3. Comment in particular on the last stanza. Does the comparison of eyebrows to threatening bowmen seem too silly or far-fetched? What sense do you find in it?
4. Try to describe the tone of this poem. What do you understand, from this portrait of a young girl, to be the poet's feelings?

Excellent poetry might be easier to recognize if each poet had a fixed position on the slopes of Mount Parnassus, but from one century to the next, the reputations of some poets have taken humiliating slides, or made impressive clambers. We decide for ourselves which poems to call excellent, but readers of the future may reverse our opinions. Most of us no longer would share this popular view of Walt Whitman by one of his contemporaries:

> Walt Whitman (1819-1892), by some regarded as a great poet; by others, as no poet at all. Most of his so-called poems are mere catalogues of things, without meter or rime, but in a few more regular poems and in lines here and there he is grandly poetical, as in "O Captain! My Captain!"[1]

[1] J. Willis Westlake, A.M., in *Common-school Literature, English and American, with Several Hundred Extracts to be Memorized* (Philadelphia, 1898).

Walt Whitman (1819–1892)

O Captain! My Captain! 1865

O Captain! my Captain! our fearful trip is done,
The ship has weather'd every rack, the prize we sought is won,
The port is near, the bells I hear, the people all exulting,
While follow eyes the steady keel, the vessel grim and daring;
But O heart! heart! heart!
O the bleeding drops of red,
Where on the deck my Captain lies,
Fallen cold and dead.

O Captain! my Captain! rise up and hear the bells;
Rise up—for you the flag is flung—for you the bugle trills,
For you bouquets and ribbon'd wreaths—for you the shores a-crowding,
For you they call, the swaying mass, their eager faces turning;
Here Captain! dear father!
This arm beneath your head!
It is some dream that on the deck,
You've fallen cold and dead.

My Captain does not answer, his lips are pale and still,
My father does not feel my arm, he has no pulse nor will,
The ship is anchor'd safe and sound, its voyage closed and done,
From fearful trip the victor ship comes in with object won;
Exult O shores, and ring O bells!
But I with mournful tread,
Walk the deck my Captain lies,
Fallen cold and dead.

O Captain! My Captain! Written soon after the death of Abraham Lincoln, this was, in Whitman's lifetime, by far the most popular of his poems.

Questions

1. Compare this with other Whitman poems. (See another elegy for Lincoln, "When Lilacs Last in the Dooryard Bloom'd," quoted in part on page 178.) In what ways is "O Captain! My Captain!" uncharacteristic of his works? Do you agree with J. Willis Westlake that this is one of the few occasions on which Whitman is "grandly poetical"?
2. Comment on the appropriateness to its subject of the poem's rhythms.
3. Do you find any evidence in this poem than an excellent poet wrote it?

There is nothing to do but commit ourselves and praise or blame and, if need be, let time erase our error. In a sense, all readers of poetry are constantly reexamining the judgments of the past by choosing those poems they care to go on reading. In the end, we have to admit that the critical principles set forth in this chapter are all very well for admiring excellent poetry we already know, but they cannot be carried like a yardstick in the hand, to go out looking for it. As Ezra Pound said in his *ABC of Reading,* "A classic is classic not because it conforms to certain structural rules, or fits certain definitions (of which its author had quite probably never heard). It is classic because of a certain eternal and irrepressible freshness."

The best poems, like "Sailing to Byzantium," may offer a kind of religious experience. In the eighth decade of the twentieth century, some of us rarely set foot outside an artificial environment. Whizzing down four-lane superhighways, we observe lakes and trees in the distance. In a way our cities are to us as anthills are to ants, as Frost reminds us in "Departmental." No less than anthills, they are "natural" structures. But the "unnatural" world of school or business is, as Wordsworth says, too much with us. Locked in the shells of our ambitions, our self-esteem, we forget our kinship to earth and sea. We fabricate self-justifications. But a great poem shocks us into another order of perception. It points beyond language to something still more essential. It ushers us into an experience so moving and true that we feel (to quote King Lear) "cut to the brain." In bad or indifferent poetry, words are all there is.

Matthew Arnold (1822–1888)

BELOW THE SURFACE-STREAM, SHALLOW AND LIGHT 1869

Below the surface-stream, shallow and light,
Of what we *say* we feel—below the stream,
As light, of what we *think* we feel—there flows
With noiseless current strong, obscure and deep,
The central stream of what we feel indeed.

QUESTIONS

1. Speaking of himself and his fellow poets, W. D. Snodgrass has expressed the opinion that:

   our only hope as artists is to continually ask ourselves, "Am I writing what I *really* think? Not what is acceptable; not what my favorite intellectual would think in this situation; not what I wish I felt. Only what I cannot help thinking." ("Finding a Poem," *In Radical Pursuit,* New York, Harper & Row, 1974.)

   Compare Snodgrass's statement and the statement that Arnold makes in his brief poem.
2. Of what value is Arnold's observation to readers of poetry?

Thomas Gray (1716–1771)

ELEGY WRITTEN IN A COUNTRY CHURCHYARD 1753

The curfew tolls the knell of parting day,
  The lowing herd wind slowly o'er the lea,
The plowman homeward plods his weary way,
  And leaves the world to darkness and to me.

Now fades the glimmering landscape on the sight,
And all the air a solemn stillness holds,
Save where the beetle wheels his droning flight,
And drowsy tinklings lull the distant folds;

Save that from yonder ivy-mantled tower
The moping owl does to the moon complain
Of such, as wand'ring near her secret bower,
Molest her ancient solitary reign.

Beneath those rugged elms, that yew tree's shade,
Where heaves the turf in many a mold'ring heap,
Each in his narrow cell forever laid,
The rude° forefathers of the hamlet sleep. *simple, ignorant*

The breezy call of incense-breathing morn,
The swallow twitt'ring from the straw-built shed,
The cock's shrill clarion, or the echoing horn°, *fox-hunters' horn*
No more shall rouse them from their lowly bed.

For them no more the blazing hearth shall burn,
Or busy housewife ply her evening care;
No children run to lisp their sire's return,
Or climb his knees the envied kiss to share.

Oft did the harvest to their sickle yield,
Their furrow oft the stubborn glebe° has broke; *turf*
How jocund did they drive their team afield!
How bowed the woods beneath their sturdy stroke!

Let not Ambition mock their useful toil,
Their homely joys, and destiny obscure;
Nor Grandeur hear with a disdainful smile
The short and simple annals of the poor.

The boast of heraldry°, the pomp of pow'r, *noble birth*
And all that beauty, all that wealth e'er gave,
Awaits alike th' inevitable hour.
The paths of glory lead but to the grave.

Nor you, ye proud, impute to these the fault,
If Mem'ry o'er their tomb no trophies raise,
Where through the long-drawn aisle and fretted° vault *inlaid with designs*
The pealing anthem swells the note of praise.

Can storied urn or animated bust
Back to its mansion call the fleeting breath?
Can Honor's voice provoke the silent dust,
Or Flatt'ry soothe the dull cold ear of Death?

Perhaps in this neglected spot is laid
Some heart once pregnant with celestial fire;
Hands that the rod of empire might have swayed,
Or waked to ecstasy the living lyre.

But knowledge to their eyes her ample page
Rich with the spoils of time did ne'er unroll;
Chill Penury° repressed their noble rage, *Poverty*
And froze the genial current of the soul.

Full many a gem of purest ray serene,
The dark unfathomed caves of ocean bear:
Full many a flower is born to blush unseen,
And waste its sweetness on the desert air.

Some village Hampden, that with dauntless breast
The little tyrant of his field withstood;
Some mute inglorious Milton here may rest,
Some Cromwell, guiltless of his country's blood.

Th' applause of list'ning senates to command,
The threats of pain and ruin to despise,
To scatter plenty o'er a smiling land,
And read their hist'ry in a nation's eyes,

Their lot forbade; nor circumscribed alone
Their growing virtues, but their crimes confined;
Forbade to wade through slaughter to a throne,
And shut the gates of mercy on mankind,

The struggling pangs of conscious truth to hide,
To quench the blushes of ingenuous° shame, *innocent*
Or heap the shrine of Luxury and Pride
With incense kindled at the Muse's flame.

Far from the madding° crowd's ignoble strife, *frenzied*
Their sober wishes never learned to stray;
Along the cool sequestered vale of life
They kept the noiseless tenor° of their way. *ongoing motion*

Yet ev'n these bones from insult to protect
Some frail memorial still erected nigh,
With uncouth rhymes and shapeless sculpture decked,
Implores the passing tribute of a sigh.

Their name, their years, spelt by th' unlettered Muse,
The place of fame and elegy supply:
And many a holy text around she strews,
That teach the rustic moralist to die.

For who to dumb Forgetfulness a prey,
This pleasing anxious being e'er resigned,
Left the warm precincts of the cheerful day,
Nor cast one longing ling'ring look behind?

On some fond breast the parting soul relies,
Some pious drops the closing eye requires;
Ev'n from the tomb the voice of Nature cries,
Ev'n in our ashes live their wonted° fires. *customary*

For thee, who mindful of th' unhonored dead
Dost in these lines their artless tale relate;
If chance°, by lonely contemplation led, — *if by chance*
Some kindred spirit shall inquire thy fate,

Haply° some hoary-headed swain° may say, — *perhaps; gray-haired shepherd*
"Oft have we seen him at the peep of dawn
Brushing with hasty steps the dews away
To meet the sun upon the upland lawn.

"There at the foot of yonder nodding beech
That wreathes its old fantastic roots so high,
His listless length at noontide would he stretch,
And pore upon the brook that babbles by.

"Hard by yon wood, now smiling as in scorn,
Mutt'ring his wayward fancies he would rove,
Now drooping, woeful wan, like one forlorn,
Or crazed with care, or crossed in hopeless love.

"One morn I missed him, on the customed hill,
Along the heath and near his fav'rite tree;
Another came; not yet beside the rill°, — *brook*
Nor up the lawn, nor at the wood was he;

"The next with dirges due in sad array
Slow though the churchway path we saw him borne.
Approach and read (for thou canst read) the lay°, — *song or poem*
Graved on the stone beneath yon aged thorn."

The Epitaph

Here rests his head upon the lap of Earth
A youth to Fortune and to Fame unknown.
Fair Science° frowned not on his humble birth, — *Knowledge*
And Melancholy marked him for her own.

Large was his bounty, and his soul sincere,
Heav'n did a recompense as largely send:
He gave to Mis'ry all he had, a tear,
He gained from Heav'n ('twas all he wished) a friend.

No farther seek his merits to disclose,
Or draw his frailties from their dread abode,
(There they alike in trembling hope repose),
The bosom of His Father and his God.

Elegy Written in a Country Churchyard. In English poetry, an **elegy** has come to mean a lament or a sadly meditative poem, sometimes written on the occasion of a death. Other elegies in this book include Chidiock Tichborne's "Elegy," Milton's "Lycidas," A. E. Housman's "To an Athlete Dying Young," and in more recent poetry, "The Rites for Cousin Vit" by Gwendolyn Brooks and "Elegy for Jane" by Theodore Roethke. 41. *storied urn:* vessel holding the ashes of the dead after cremation. *Storied* can mean (1) decorated with scenes; (2) inscribed with a life's story; or (3) celebrated in story or history. The *animated bust* is a lifelike sculpture of the dead, placed on a tomb. 57. *Hampden:* John

Hampden (1594–1643), member of Parliament, had resisted illegal taxes on his lands imposed by Charles I. 60. *Cromwell . . . his country's blood:* Gray blames Oliver Cromwell (1599–1658) for strife and tyranny. As general of the armies of Parliament, Cromwell had won the Civil War against Charles I and had signed the king's death warrant. As Lord Protector of England (1653–1658), he had ruled with an iron hand. 71–72: *heap the shrine . . . Muse's flame:* Gray chides mercenary poets who write poems to please their rich, high-living patrons.

Questions

1. In contrasting the unknown poor buried in this village churchyard and famous men buried in cathedrals (in *fretted vault*, line 39), what is Gray's theme? What do you understand from the line, *The paths of glory lead but to the grave*?
2. Carl J. Weber thinks that Gray's compassion for the village poor anticipates the democratic sympathies of the American Revolution: "Thomas Gray is the pioneer literary spokesman for the Ordinary Man." But another critic, Lyle Glazier, argues that the "Elegy" isn't political at all: that we misread if we think the poet meant "to persuade the poor and obscure that their barren lives are meaningful"; and also misread if we think he meant to assure the privileged classes "in whose ranks Gray was proud to consider himself" that they need not worry about the poor, "who have already all essential riches." How much truth do you find in either of these views?
3. Cite lines and phrases that show Gray's concern for the musical qualities of words.
4. Who is the *youth* of the closing Epitaph? By *thee* (line 93) does Gray mean himself? Does he mean some fictitious poet supposedly writing the "Elegy" —the first-person speaker (line 4)? Does he mean some village stonecutter, a crude poet whose illiterate Muse (line 81) inspired him to compose tombstone epitaphs? Or could the Epitaph possibly refer to Gray's close friend of school and undergraduate days, the promising poet Richard West, who had died in 1742? Which interpretation seems to you the most reasonable? (Does our lack of absolute certainty negate the value of the poem?)
5. Walter Savage Landor called the Epitaph a tin kettle tied to the tail of a noble dog. Do you agree that the Epitaph is inferior to what has gone before it? What is its function in Gray's poem?
6. Many sources for Gray's phrases and motifs have been found in earlier poets: Virgil, Horace, Dante, Milton, and many more. Even if it could be demonstrated that Gray's poem has not one original line in it, would it be possible to dismiss the "Elegy" as a mere rag-bag of borrowings, like John Lyly's "Daphne"?
7. Gray's poem, a pastoral elegy, is in the same genre as another famous English poem: John Milton's "Lycidas." What conventions are common to both?
8. In the earliest surviving manuscript of Gray's poem, lines 73–76 read:

   No more with Reason and thyself at strife;
   Give anxious cares and endless wishes room
   But through the cool sequester'd vale of Life
   Pursue the silent tenor of thy doom.

   In what ways does the final version of those lines seem superior?
9. Perhaps the best-known poem in English, Gray's "Elegy" has inspired hundreds of imitations, countless parodies, and translations into eighteen

or more languages. (Some of these languages contain dozens of attempts to translate it.) To what do you attribute the poem's fame? What do you suppose has proved so universally appealing in it?

10. Compare Gray's "Elegy" with Shelley's "Ozymandias" and Arthur Guiterman's "On the Vanity of Earthly Greatness." What do the three poems have in common? How would you rank them in order of excellence?

David Bottoms (b. 1949)

Smoking in an Open Grave

1980

We bury ourselves to get high.
Huddled in this open crypt we lay the bottle,
the lantern, the papers, the bag on a marble slab,
tune the guitar to a mouth harp
and choir out the old spirituals.
When the shadows of this life have grown, I'll fly away.

Across Confederate Row an owl hoots our departure
and half-fallen brick becomes a porthole filled with stars.
We lay our ears against the clay wall;
at the foot of the hill the river whispers on its track.
It's a strange place where graves go,
so much of us already geared for the journey.

Questions

1. What ironies do you detect in this poem? What contrasts between past and present?
2. "Like Thomas Gray, David Bottoms speaks for the Graveyard School in poetry. As does Gray in his celebrated 'Elegy,' Bottoms both affirms truth about the dead and appears to be making his own personal statement." Discuss this critical opinion.
3. How would you evaluate "Smoking in an Open Grave"—good, bad, indifferent, or excellent? Refer to the poem in supporting your evaluation.

27 What Is Poetry?

Archibald MacLeish (1892–1982)

ARS POETICA° *Art of Poetry* 1926

A poem should be palpable and mute
As a globed fruit,

Dumb
As old medallions to the thumb,

Silent as the sleeve-worn stone
Of casement ledges where the moss has grown—

A poem should be wordless
As the flight of birds.

A poem should be motionless in time
As the moon climbs,

Leaving, as the moon releases
Twig by twig the night-entangled trees,

Leaving, as the moon behind the winter leaves,
Memory by memory the mind—

A poem should be motionless in time
As the moon climbs.

A poem should be equal to:
Not true.

For all the history of grief
An empty doorway and a maple leaf.

For love
The leaning grasses and two lights above the sea—

A poem should not mean
But be.

What is poetry? By now, perhaps, you have formed your own idea, whether or not you feel able to define it. Just in case further efforts at definition can be useful, here are a few memorable ones (including, for a second look, some given earlier):

> the art of uniting pleasure with truth by calling imagination to the help of reason.
>
> —Samuel Johnson

> the best words in the best order.
>
> —Samuel Taylor Coleridge

> the record of the best and happiest moments of the happiest and best minds.
>
> —Percy Bysshe Shelley

> musical Thought.
>
> —Thomas Carlyle

> at bottom a criticism of life.
>
> —Matthew Arnold

> If I read a book and it makes my whole body so cold no fire can ever warm me, I know that it is poetry. If I feel physically as if the top of my head were taken off, I know that it is poetry. Is there any other way?
>
> —Emily Dickinson

> speech framed . . . to be heard for its own sake and interest even over and above its interest of meaning.
>
> —Gerard Manley Hopkins

> a revelation in words by means of the words.
>
> —Wallace Stevens

> not the assertion that something is true, but the making of that truth more fully real to us.
>
> —T. S. Eliot

> the body of linguistic constructions that men usually refer to as poems.
>
> —J. V. Cunningham

> the clear expression of mixed feelings.
>
> —W. H. Auden

A poem differs from most prose in several ways. For one, both writer and reader tend to regard it differently. The poet's attitude is something like this: I offer this piece of writing to be read not as prose but as a poem—that is, more perceptively, thoughtfully, and considerately, with more attention to sounds and connotations. This is a great deal to expect, but in return, the reader, too, has a right to certain expectations. Approaching the poem in the anticipation of out-of-the-ordinary knowledge and pleasure, the reader assumes that the poet may use certain enjoyable devices not available to prose: rime, alliteration, meter, and rhythms—definite, various, or emphatic. (The poet may not *always* choose to employ these things.) The reader expects the poet to make greater use, perhaps, of resources of meaning such as figurative language, allusion, symbol, and imagery. As readers of prose we might seek no more than meaning: no more than what could be paraphrased without serious loss. Meeting any figurative language or graceful turns of word order, we think them pleasant extras. But in poetry all these "extras" matter as much as the paraphraseable content, if not more. For, when we finish reading a good poem, we cannot explain precisely to ourselves of what we have experienced—without repeating, word for word, the language of the poem itself.

"Poetry is to prose as dancing is to walking," remarked Paul Valéry. It is doubtful, however, that anyone can draw an immovable boundary between poetry and prose. Certain prose needs only to be arranged in lines to be seen as poetry—especially prose that conveys strong emotion in vivid, physical imagery and in terse, figurative, rhythmical language. Even in translation the words of Chief Joseph of the Nez Percé tribe, at the moment of his surrender to the U.S. Army in 1877, still move us and are memorable:

Hear me, my warriors, my heart is sick and sad:
Our chiefs are killed,
The old men all are dead,
It is cold and we have no blankets.

The little children freeze to death.

Hear me, my warriors, my heart is sick and sad:
From where the sun now stands I will fight no more forever.

It may be that a poem can point beyond words to something still more essential. Language has its limits, and probably Edgar Allan Poe was the only poet ever to claim he could always find words for whatever he wished to express. For, of all a human being can experience and imagine, words say only part. "Human speech," said Flaubert, who strove after the best of it, "is like a cracked kettle on which we hammer out tunes to make bears dance, when what we long for is the compassion of the stars."

Like Yeats's chestnut-tree in "Among School Children" (which when asked whether it is leaf, blossom, or bole, has no answer), a poem is to be seen not as a confederation of form, rime, image, metaphor, tone, and theme, but as a whole. We study a poem one element at a time because the intellect best comprehends what it can separate. But only our total attention, involving the participation of our blood and marrow, can see all elements in a poem fused, all dancing together. Yeats knew how to make poems and how to read them:

God guard me from those thoughts men think
In the mind alone;
He that sings a lasting song
Thinks in a marrow-bone.

Throughout this book, we have been working on the assumption that the patient and conscious explication of poems will sharpen unconscious perceptions. We can only hope that it will; the final test lies in whether you care to go on by yourself, reading other poems, finding in them pleasure and enlightenment. Pedagogy must have a stop; so must the viewing of poems as if their elements fell into chapters. For the total experience of reading a poem surpasses the mind's categories. The wind in the grass, says a proverb, cannot be taken into the house.

Anthology: Poetry

Sit a while dear son,
Here are biscuits to eat and here is milk to drink,
But as soon as you sleep and renew yourself in sweet clothes,
I kiss you with a good-by kiss and open the gates for your egress hence.

Long enough have you dream'd contemptible dreams,
Now I wash the gum from your eyes,
You must habit yourself to the dazzle of the light and of every moment of
your life.

Long have you timidly waded holding a plank by the shore,
Now I will you to be a bold swimmer,
To jump off in the midst of the sea, rise again, nod to me, shout, and
laughingly dash with your hair.

—Walt Whitman, "Song of Myself"

Anthology: Poetry

Anonymous (English lyric)

I Have a Young Sister (fifteenth century)

I have a young sister
  Far beyonden the sea.
Many be the drowries° *love-tokens*
  That she sente me.

She sente me the cherry
  Withouten any stone
And so she did the dove
  Withouten any bone.

She sente me the briar
  Withouten any rind,° *bark*
She bade me love my lemman° *lover*
  Without longing.

How should any cherry
  Be withoute stone?
And how should any dove
  Be withoute bone?

How should any briar
  Be withoute rind?
How should I love my lemman
  Without longing?

When the cherry was a flower
  Then hadde it no stone,
When the dove was an egg
  Then hadde it no bone,

When the briar was unbred° *not yet sown*
  Then hadde it no rind,
When the maiden hath that she loveth
  She is without longing.

I Have a Young Sister. Joan Baez and other popular singers have made this medieval lyric, in American versions, a standard in the repertoire of folk balladeers today.

Anonymous (traditional Scottish ballad)

EDWARD

"Why dois your brand° sae° drap wi' bluid, *sword; so*
Edward, Edward?
Why dois your brand sae drap wi' bluid?
And why sae sad gang° yee, O?" *go*
"O, I hae killed my hauke sae guid,
Mither, mither,
O, I hae killed my hauke sae guid,
And I had nae mair bot° hee, O." *but*

"Your haukis bluid was nevir sae reid,
Edward, Edward,
Your haukis bluid was nevir sae reid,
My deir son I tell thee, O."
"O, I hae killed my reid-roan steid,
Mither, mither,
O, I hae killed my reid-roan steid,
That erst° was sa fair and frie°, O." *once; free*

"Your steid was auld, and ye hae gat mair,
Edward, Edward,
Your steid was auld, and ye hae gat mair,
Sum other dule° ye drie°, O." *sorrow; suffer*
"O, I hae killed my fadir deir,
Mither, mither,
O, I hae killed my fadir deir,
Alas, and wae° is mee, O!" *woe*

"And whatten penance wul ye drie for that,
Edward, Edward?
And whatten penance will ye drie for that?
My deir son, now tell me, O."
"Ile set my feit in yonder boat,
Mither, mither,
Ile set my feit in yonder boat,
And Ile fare ovir the sea, O."

"And what wul ye doe wi' your towirs and your ha'°, *hall*
Edward, Edward,
And what wul ye doe wi' your towirs and your ha',
That were sae fair to see, O?"
"Ile let thame stand tul they doun fa',
Mither, mither,
Ile let thame stand tul they doun fa',
For here nevir mair maun° I bee, O." *must*

"And what wul ye leive to your bairns° and your wife, *children*
Edward, Edward?

And what wul ye leive to your bairns and your wife,
  When ye gang ovir the sea, O?"
"The warldis° room, late° them beg thrae° life, *world's; let; through*
      Mither, mither
The warldis room, late them beg thrae life,
  For thame nevir mair wul I see, O."

"And what wul ye leive to your ain° mither deir, *own*
      Edward, Edward?
And what wul ye leive to your ain mither deir?
  My deir son, now tell me, O."
"The curse of hell frae me sall ye beir,
      Mither, mither,
The curse of hell frae me sall ye beir,
  Sic° counseils° ye gave to me, O." *such; counsel*

Anonymous (traditional Scottish ballad)

Sir Patrick Spence

The king sits in Dumferling toune,
  Drinking the blude-reid wine:
"O whar will I get guid sailor
  To sail this schip of mine?"

Up and spak an eldern knicht,
  Sat at the kings richt kne:
"Sir Patrick Spence is the best sailor
  That sails upon the se."

The king has written a braid letter,
  And signed it wi' his hand,
And sent it to Sir Patrick Spence,
  Was walking on the sand.

The first line that Sir Patrick red,
  A loud lauch lauchèd he;
The next line that Sir Patrick red,
  The teir blinded his ee.

"O wha° is this has don this deid, *who*
  This ill deid don to me,
To send me out this time o' the yeir,
  To sail upon the se!

"Mak haste, mak haste, my mirry men all,
  Our guid schip sails the morne."
"O say na sae°, my master deir, *so*
  For I feir a deadlie storme.

"Late late yestreen I saw the new moone,
Wi' the auld moone in hir arme,
And I feir, I feir, my deir master,
That we will cum to harme."

O our Scots nobles wer richt laith° — *loath*
To weet° their cork-heild schoone°; — *wet; shoes*
Bot lang owre° a' the play wer playd, — *before*
Their hats they swam aboone°. — *above (their heads)*

O lang, lang may their ladies sit,
Wi' their fans into their hand,
Or ere° they se Sir Patrick Spence — *long before*
Cum sailing to the land.

O lang, lang may the ladies stand,
Wi' their gold kems° in their hair, — *combs*
Waiting for their ain° deir lords, — *own*
For they'll se thame na mair.

Haf owre°, haf owre to Aberdour, — *halfway over*
It's fiftie fadom deip,
And thair lies guid Sir Patrick Spence,
Wi' the Scots lords at his feit.

SIR PATRICK SPENCE. 9. *braid:* Broad, but broad in what sense? Among guesses are *plain-spoken, official,* and *on wide paper.*

Anonymous (traditional English ballad)

THE THREE RAVENS

There were three ravens sat on a tree,
Down a down, hay down, hay down,
There were three ravens sat on a tree,
With a down,
There were three ravens sat on a tree,
They were as black as they might be.
With a down derry, derry, derry, down, down.

The one of them said to his mate,
"Where shall we our breakfast take?"

"Down in yonder greene field,
There lies a knight slain under his shield.

"His hounds they lie down at his feet,
So well they can their master keep.

"His hawks they fly so eagerly,
There's no fowl dare him come nigh."

Down there comes a fallow doe,
As great with young as she might go.

She lift up his bloody head,
And kist his wounds that were so red.

She got him up upon her back,
And carried him to earthen lake°. *the grave*

She buried him before the prime,
She was dead herself ere evensong time.

God send every gentleman
Such hawks, such hounds, and such a leman°. *lover*

THE THREE RAVENS. The lines of refrain are repeated in each stanza. "Perhaps in the folk mind the doe is the form the soul of a human mistress, now dead, has taken," Albert B. Friedman has suggested (in *The Viking Book of Folk Ballads*). "Most probably the knight's beloved was understood to be an enchanted woman who was metamorphosed at certain times into an animal." 22–23. *prime, evensong:* two of the canonical hours set aside for prayer and worship. Prime is at dawn, evensong at dusk.

Anonymous (traditional Scottish ballad)

THE TWA CORBIES

As I was walking all alane,
I heard twa corbies° making a mane°; *ravens; moan*
The tane° unto the t'other say, *one*
"Where sall we gang° and dine today?" *go*

"In behint yon auld fail dyke°, *turf wall*
I wot° there lies a new slain knight; *know*
And naebody kens° that he lies there, *knows*
But his hawk, his hound, and lady fair.

"His hound is to the hunting gane,
His hawk to fetch the wild-fowl hame,
His lady's ta'en another mate,
So we may mak our dinner sweet.

"Ye'll sit on his white hause-bane°, *neck bone*
And I'll pike out his bonny blue een;
Wi' ae° lock o' his gowden hair *one*
We'll theek° our nest when it grows bare. *thatch*

"Mony a one for him makes mane,
But nane sall ken where he is gane;
O'er his white banes, when they are bare,
The wind sall blaw for evermair."

THE TWA CORBIES. Sir Walter Scott, the first to print this ballad in his *Minstrelsy of the Scottish Border* (1802–1803), calls it "rather a counterpart than a copy" of "The Three Ravens." M. J. C. Hodgart and other scholars think he may have written most of it himself.

Anonymous (English lyric)

SUMER IS ICUMEN IN (thirteenth century)

Sumer is icumen in
Lhude sing cuccu
Groweþ sed and bloweþ med
and springþ þe wde nu
Sing cuccu

Awe bleteþ after lomb
lhouþ after calue cu
Bulluc sterteþ bucke uerteþ
Murie sing cuccu
Cuccu cuccu
Wel singes þu cuccu
ne swik þu nauer nu

Sing cuccu nu Sing cuccu
Sing cuccu Sing cuccu nu

Summer is acoming in—
Loudly sing, cuckoo!
Groweth seed and bloweth mead
And springeth the wood new.
Sing, cuckoo!

Ewe bleateth after lamb,
Loweth after calf cow,
Bullock starteth, buck farteth—
Merrily sing, cuckoo!
Cuckoo, cuckoo,
Well singest thou, cuckoo!
Cease thou never now.

Sing, cuckoo now! Sing, cuckoo!
Sing, cuckoo! Sing, cuckoo, now!

SUMER IS ICUMEN IN. On the left, this famous song is printed as it appears in a thirteenth-century manuscript: a commonplace book, or book of songs and obituaries set down by various monks at Reading Abbey (Harley manuscript 978, now in the British Museum). On the right, words and spellings have been modernized and punctuation added, but word-order kept unaltered. In the opening line, *acoming* is not quite a faithful translation: *is icumen* means "has come." Summer is already here. The character þ is called a *thorn*, and is pronounced like the spelling *th*. 8. *starteth:* starts, jumps up and runs.

Anonymous (English lyric)

I SING OF A MAIDEN (fifteenth century)

I sing of a maiden   that is makeless°,   *matchless (or mateless)*
King of alle kinges   to° her son che ches°.   *to be; she chose*

He cam all so stille   there° his moder was   *where*
As dew in Aprille   that falleth on the grass.

He cam all so stille   to his moderes bower
As dew in Aprille   that falleth on the flower.

He cam all so stille   there his moder lay
As dew in Aprille   that falleth on the spray.

Moder and maiden   was never none but she—
Well may swich° a lady   Godes moder be.   *such*

I SING OF A MAIDEN. To keep the rhythm, pronounce the final *e* in *alle, stille,* and *Aprille* like *e* in *the*. 5. *bower:* dwelling place, room, or bedchamber.

Anonymous (English lyric)

WESTERN WIND (about 1500)

Western wind, when wilt thou blow,
The° small rain down can rain? *(so that) the*
Christ, if my love were in my arms,
And I in my bed again!

James Agee (1909–1955)

SUNDAY: OUTSKIRTS OF KNOXVILLE, TENNESSEE 1937

There, in the earliest and chary spring, the dogwood flowers.

Unharnessed in the friendly sunday air
By the red brambles, on the river bluffs,
Clerks and their choices pair.

Thrive by, not near, masked all away by shrub and juniper,
The ford v eight, racing the chevrolet.

They can not trouble her:

Her breasts, helped open from the afforded lace,
Lie like a peaceful lake;
And on his mouth she breaks her gentleness:

Oh, wave them awake!

They are not of the birds. Such innocence
Brings us whole to break us only.
Theirs are not happy words.

We that are human cannot hope.
Our tenderest joys oblige us most.
No chain so cuts the bone; and sweetest silk most shrewdly strangles.

How this must end, that now please love were ended,
In kitchens, bedfights, silences, women's-pages,
Sickness of heart before goldlettered doors,
Stale flesh, hard collars, agony in antiseptic corridors,
Spankings, remonstrances, fishing trips, orange juice,
Policies, incapacities, a chevrolet,
Scorn of their children, kind contempt exchanged,
Recalls, tears, second honeymoons, pity,
Shouted corrections of missed syllables,
Hot water bags, gallstones, falls down stairs,
Stammerings, soft foods, confusion of personalities,

Oldfashioned christmases, suspicions of theft,
Arrangements with morticians taken care of by sons in law,
Small rooms beneath the gables of brick bungalows,
The tumbler smashed, the glance between daughter and husband,
The empty body in the lonely bed
And, in the empty concrete porch, blown ash
Grandchildren wandering the betraying sun

Now, on the winsome crumbling shelves of the horror
God show, God blind these children!

Matthew Arnold (1822–1888)

Dover Beach — 1867

The sea is calm tonight.
The tide is full, the moon lies fair
Upon the straits;—on the French coast the light
Gleams and is gone; the cliffs of England stand,
Glimmering and vast, out in the tranquil bay.
Come to the window, sweet is the night-air!
Only, from the long line of spray
Where the sea meets the moon-blanched land,
Listen! you hear the grating roar
Of pebbles which the waves draw back, and fling,
At their return, up the high strand,
Begin, and cease, and then again begin,
With tremulous cadence slow, and bring
The eternal note of sadness in.

Sophocles long ago
Heard it on the Aegean, and it brought
Into his mind the turbid ebb and flow
Of human misery; we
Find also in the sound a thought,
Hearing it by this distant northern sea.

The Sea of Faith
Was once, too, at the full, and round earth's shore
Lay like the folds of a bright girdle furled.
But now I only hear
Its melancholy, long, withdrawing roar,
Retreating, to the breath
Of the night-wind, down the vast edges drear
And naked shingles° of the world. *gravel beaches*

Ah, love, let us be true
To one another! for the world, which seems
To lie before us like a land of dreams,
So various, so beautiful, so new,

Hath really neither joy, nor love, nor light,
Nor certitude, nor peace, nor help for pain;
And we are here as on a darkling° plain *darkened or darkening*
Swept with confused alarms of struggle and flight,
Where ignorant armies clash by night.

John Ashbery (b. 1927)

City Afternoon 1975

A veil of haze protects this
Long-ago afternoon forgotten by everybody
In this photograph, most of them now
Sucked screaming through old age and death.

If one could seize America
Or at least a fine forgetfulness
That seeps into our outline
Defining our volumes with a stain
That is fleeting too
But commemorates
Because it does define, after all:
Gray garlands, that threesome
Waiting for the light to change,
Air lifting the hair of one
Upside down in the reflecting pool.

W. H. Auden (1907–1973)

As I Walked Out One Evening 1940

As I walked out one evening,
  Walking down Bristol Street,
The crowds upon the pavement
  Were fields of harvest wheat.

And down by the brimming river
  I heard a lover sing
Under an arch of the railway:
  "Love has no ending.

"I'll love you, dear, I'll love you
  Till China and Africa meet,
And the river jumps over the mountain
  And the salmon sing in the street,

"I'll love you till the ocean
  Is folded and hung up to dry
And the seven stars go squawking
  Like geese about the sky.

"The years shall run like rabbits,
  For in my arms I hold
The Flower of the Ages,
  And the first love of the world."

But all the clocks in the city
  Began to whirr and chime:
"O let not Time deceive you,
  You cannot conquer Time.

"In the burrows of the Nightmare
  Where Justice naked is,
Time watches from the shadow
  And coughs when you would kiss.

"In headaches and in worry
  Vaguely life leaks away,
And Time will have his fancy
  Tomorrow or today.

"Into many a green valley
  Drifts the appalling snow;
Time breaks the threaded dances
  And the diver's brilliant bow.

"O plunge your hands in water,
  Plunge them in up to the wrist;
Stare, stare in the basin
  And wonder what you've missed.

"The glacier knocks in the cupboard,
  The desert sighs in the bed,
And the crack in the teacup opens
  A lane to the land of the dead.

"Where the beggars raffle the banknotes
  And the Giant is enchanting to Jack,
And the Lily-white Boy is a Roarer,
  And Jill goes down on her back.

"O look, look in the mirror,
  O look in your distress;
Life remains a blessing
  Although you cannot bless.

"O stand, stand at the window
  As the tears scald and start;
You shall love your crooked neighbor
  With your crooked heart."

It was late, late in the evening,
  The lovers they were gone;
The clocks had ceased their chiming,
  And the deep river ran on.

W. H. Auden (1907–1973)

Musée des Beaux Arts

1940

About suffering they were never wrong,
The Old Masters: how well they understood
Its human position; how it takes place
While someone else is eating or opening a window or just walking dully
along;
How, when the aged are reverently, passionately waiting
For the miraculous birth, there always must be
Children who did not specially want it to happen, skating
On a pond at the edge of the wood:
They never forgot
That even the dreadful martyrdom must run its course
Anyhow in a corner, some untidy spot
Where the dogs go on with their doggy life and the torturer's horse
Scratches its innocent behind on a tree.

In Brueghel's *Icarus,* for instance: how everything turns away
Quite leisurely from the disaster; the ploughman may
Have heard the splash, the forsaken cry,
But for him it was not an important failure; the sun shone
As it had to on the white legs disappearing into the green
Water; and the expensive delicate ship that must have seen
Something amazing, a boy falling out of the sky,
Had somewhere to get to and sailed calmly on.

COMPARE:

"Musée des Beaux Arts" with "The Dance" by William Carlos Williams (page 578) and the painting by Pieter Breughel (1502?–1569) to which each poem refers.

Amiri Baraka [LeRoi Jones] (b. 1934)

PREFACE TO A TWENTY VOLUME SUICIDE NOTE 1961

For Kellie Jones, Born 16 May 1959

Lately, I've become accustomed to the way
The ground opens up and envelopes me
Each time I go out to walk the dog.
Or the broad edged silly music the wind
Makes when I run for a bus . . .

Things have come to that.

And now, each night I count the stars,
And each night I get the same number.
And when they will not come to be counted,
I count the holes they leave.

Nobody sings anymore.

And then last night I tiptoed up
To my daughter's room and heard her
Talking to someone, and when I opened
The door, there was no one there . . .
Only she on her knees, peeking into

Her own clasped hands.

COMPARE:

"Preface to a Twenty Volume Suicide Note" with "Morning Song" by Sylvia Plath (page 747) and "My Son, My Executioner" by Donald Hall (page 631).

Wendell Berry (b. 1934)

THE PEACE OF WILD THINGS 1968

When despair for the world grows in me
and I wake in the night at the least sound
in fear of what my life and my children's lives may be,
I go and lie down where the wood drake
rests in his beauty on the water, and the great heron feeds.
I come into the peace of wild things
who do not tax their lives with forethought
of grief. I come into the presence of still water.

And I feel above me the day-blind stars
waiting with their light. For a time
I rest in the grace of the world, and am free.

COMPARE:

"The Peace of Wild Things" with "Skunk Hour" by Robert Lowell (page 342).

Elizabeth Bishop (b. 1911–1979)

FILLING STATION 1965

Oh, but it is dirty!
—this little filling station,
oil-soaked, oil-permeated
to a disturbing, over-all
black translucency.
Be careful with that match!

Father wears a dirty,
oil-soaked monkey suit
that cuts him under the arms,
and several quick and saucy
and greasy sons assist him
(it's a family filling station),
all quite thoroughly dirty.

Do they live in the station?
It has a cement porch
behind the pumps, and on it
a set of crushed and grease-
impregnated wickerwork;
on the wicker sofa
a dirty dog, quite comfy.

Some comic books provide
the only note of color—
of certain color. They lie
upon a big dim doily
draping a taboret
(part of the set), beside
a big hirsute begonia.

Why the extraneous plant?
Why the taboret?
Why, oh why, the doily?
(Embroidered in daisy stitch
with marguerites, I think,
and heavy with gray crochet.)

Somebody embroidered the doily.
Somebody waters the plant,
or oils it, maybe. Somebody
arranges the rows of cans
so that they softly say:
ESSO — SO — SO — SO
to high-strung automobiles.
Somebody loves us all.

William Blake (1757–1827)

THE SICK ROSE 1794

O Rose, thou art sick!
The invisible worm
That flies in the night,
In the howling storm,

Has found out thy bed
Of crimson joy,
And his dark secret love
Does thy life destroy.

William Blake (1757–1827)

THE TYGER 1794

Tyger! Tyger! burning bright
In the forests of the night,
What immortal hand or eye
Could frame thy fearful symmetry?

In what distant deeps or skies
Burnt the fire of thine eyes?
On what wings dare he aspire?
What the hand dare seize the fire?

And what shoulder, and what art,
Could twist the sinews of thy heart?
And when thy heart began to beat,
What dread hand? and what dread feet?

What the hammer? what the chain?
In what furnace was thy brain?
What the anvil? what dread grasp
Dare its deadly terrors clasp?

When the stars threw down their spears,
And watered heaven with their tears,
Did he smile his work to see?
Did he who made the Lamb make thee?

Tyger! Tyger! burning bright
In the forests of the night,
What immortal hand or eye
Dare frame thy fearful symmetry?

Mark Alexander Boyd (1563–1601)

Cupid and Venus (late sixteenth century)

Fra bank to bank, fra wood to wood I rin°, *run*
  Ourhailit° with my feeble fantasie, *overcome*
  Like til° a leaf that fallis from a tree *to*
Or til a reed ourblawin with the win.
Twa gods guides me: the ane of them is blin,
  Yea, and a bairn° brocht up in vanitie, *child*
  The next a wife ingenrit° of the sea, *engendered*
And lichter nor° a dauphin° with her fin. *than; dolphin*

Unhappy is the man for evermair
That tills the sand and sawis° in the air; *sows*
  But twice unhappier is he, I lairn,
That feidis° in his hairt a mad desire *feeds*
And follows on a woman thro the fire,
  Led by a blind and teachit by a bairn.

Gwendolyn Brooks (b. 1917)

The Rites for Cousin Vit 1949

Carried her unprotesting out the door.
Kicked back the casket-stand. But it can't hold her,
That stuff and satin aiming to enfold her,
The lid's contrition nor the bolts before.
Oh oh. Too much. Too much. Even now, surmise,
She rises in the sunshine. There she goes,
Back to the bars she knew and the repose
In love-rooms and the things in people's eyes.
Too vital and too squeaking. Must emerge.
Even now she does the snake-hips with a hiss,
Slops the bad wine across her shantung, talks
Of pregnancy, guitars and bridgework, walks
In parks or alleys, comes haply on the verge
Of happiness, haply hysterics. Is.

Sterling A. Brown (b. 1901)

Effie 1932

She who was easy for any chance lover,
Whose frequent laugh rang flaccid and shrill;
She, finding death at last, the dazed fret over,
Lies here so oddly stern for once, and still.

Put her away, and put away with her
What she has now of harshness and strength,
She who was clay for any clumsy sculptor
Becomes inflexible; fixed of form at length.

She who would veer with any passing wind
Like a rusty vane with rickety ways,
She is aloof now, and seems—oh, so determined;
And that is the Paradise crowning her days.

Compare:

"Effie" with "The Rites for Cousin Vit" by Gwendolyn Brooks (page 293).

Robert Browning (1812–1889)

My Last Duchess 1842

Ferrara

That's my last Duchess painted on the wall,
Looking as if she were alive. I call
That piece a wonder, now; Frà Pandolf's hands
Worked busily a day, and there she stands.
Will 't please you sit and look at her? I said
"Frà Pandolf" by design, for never read
Strangers like you that pictured countenance,
The depth and passion of its earnest glance,
But to myself they turned (since none puts by
The curtain I have drawn for you, but I)
And seemed as they would ask me, if they durst,
How such a glance came there; so, not the first
Are you to turn and ask thus. Sir, 'twas not
Her husband's presence only, called that spot
Of joy into the Duchess' cheek; perhaps
Frà Pandolf chanced to say, "Her mantle laps
Over my lady's wrist too much," or "Paint
Must never hope to reproduce the faint
Half-flush that dies along her throat." Such stuff
Was courtesy, she thought, and cause enough
For calling up that spot of joy. She had
A heart—how shall I say?—too soon made glad,
Too easily impressed; she liked whate'er

She looked on, and her looks went everywhere.
Sir, 'twas all one! My favor at her breast,
The dropping of the daylight in the West,
The bough of cherries some officious fool
Broke in the orchard for her, the white mule
She rode with round the terrace—all and each
Would draw from her alike the approving speech,
Or blush, at least. She thanked men,—good! but thanked
Somehow—I know not how—as if she ranked
My gift of a nine-hundred-years' old name
With anybody's gift. Who'd stoop to blame
This sort of trifling? Even had you skill
In speech—which I have not—to make your will
Quite clear to such an one, and say "Just this
Or that in you disgusts me; here you miss,
Or there exceed the mark"—and if she let
Herself be lessoned so, nor plainly set
Her wits to yours, forsooth, and made excuse—
E'en then would be some stooping; and I choose
Never to stoop. Oh, sir, she smiled, no doubt,
Whene'er I passed her; but who passed without
Much the same smile? This grew; I gave commands;
Then all smiles stopped together. There she stands
As if alive. Will 't please you rise? We'll meet
The company below, then. I repeat,
The Count your master's known munificence
Is ample warrant that no just pretense
Of mine for dowry will be disallowed;
Though his fair daughter's self, as I avowed
At starting, is my object. Nay, we'll go
Together down, sir. Notice Neptune, though,
Taming a sea-horse, thought a rarity,
Which Claus of Innsbruck cast in bronze for me!

MY LAST DUCHESS. Ferrara, a city in northern Italy, is the scene. Browning may have modeled his speaker after Alonzo, Duke of Ferrara (1533-1598). 3. *Frà Pandolf* and 56. *Claus of Innsbruck:* fictitious names of artists.

Robert Browning (1812–1889)

SOLILOQUY OF THE SPANISH CLOISTER — 1842

Gr-r-r—there go, my heart's abhorrence!
  Water your damned flower-pots, do!
If hate killed men, Brother Lawrence,
  God's blood, would not mine kill you!
What? your myrtle-bush wants trimming?
  Oh, that rose has prior claims—
Needs its leaden vase filled brimming?
  Hell dry you up with its flames!

At the meal we sit together;
Salve tibi!° I must hear *Hail to thee!*
Wise talk of the kind of weather,
Sort of season, time of year:
Not a plenteous cork-crop: scarcely
Dare we hope oak-galls, I doubt;
What's the Latin name for "parsley"?
What's the Greek name for "swine's snout"?

Whew! We'll have our platter burnished,
Laid with care on our own shelf!
With a fire-new spoon we're furnished,
And a goblet for ourself,
Rinsed like something sacrificial
Ere 'tis fit to touch our chaps—
Marked with L. for our initial!
(He-he! There his lily snaps!)

Saint, forsooth! While Brown Dolores
Squats outside the Convent bank
With Sanchicha, telling stories,
Steeping tresses in the tank,
Blue-black, lustrous, thick like horsehairs,
—Can't I see his dead eye glow,
Bright as 'twere a Barbary corsair's?
(That is, if he'd let it show!)

When he finishes refection,
Knife and fork he never lays
Cross-wise, to my recollection,
As I do, in Jesu's praise.
I the Trinity illustrate,
Drinking watered orange-pulp—
In three sips the Arian frustrate;
While he drains his at one gulp!

Oh, those melons! if he's able
We're to have a feast; so nice!
One goes to the Abbot's table,
All of us get each a slice.
How go on your flowers? None double?
Not one fruit-sort can you spy?
Strange!—And I, too, at such trouble,
Keep them close-nipped on the sly!

There's a great text in Galatians,
Once you trip on it, entails
Twenty-nine distinct damnations,
One sure, if another fails;
If I trip him just a-dying,
Sure of heaven as sure can be,
Spin him round and send him flying
Off to hell, a Manichee?

Or, my scrofulous French novel
  On grey paper with blunt type!
Simply glance at it, you grovel
  Hand and foot in Belial's gripe;
If I double down its pages
  At the woeful sixteenth print,
When he gathers his greengages,
  Ope a sieve and slip it in't?

Or, there's Satan!—one might venture
  Pledge one's soul to him, yet leave
Such a flaw in the indenture
  As he'd miss till, past retrieve,
Blasted lay that rose-acacia
  We're so proud of! *Hy, Zy, Hine. . . .*
'St, there's Vespers! *Plena gratia*
Ave, Virgo!° Gr-r-r—you swine! *Hail, Virgin, full of grace!*

SOLILOQUY OF THE SPANISH CLOISTER. 3. *Brother Lawrence:* one of the speaker's fellow monks. 31. *Barbary corsair:* a pirate operating off the Barbary coast of Africa. 39. *Arian:* a follower of Arius, heretic who denied the doctrine of the Trinity. 49. *a great text in Galatians:* a difficult verse in this book of the Bible. Brother Lawrence will be damned as a heretic if he wrongly interprets it. 56. *Manichee:* another kind of heretic, one who (after the Persian philosopher Mani) sees in the world a constant struggle between good and evil, neither able to win. 60. *Belial:* Here, not specifically Satan but (as used in the Old Testament) a name for wickedness. 70. *Hy, Zy, Hine:* Possibly the sound of a bell to announce evening devotions, possibly the beginning of a formula to summon the Devil.

Thomas Carew (1594?–1640)

ASK ME NO MORE WHERE JOVE BESTOWS 1640

Ask me no more where Jove bestows,
When June is past, the fading rose;
For in your beauty's orient deep
These flowers, as in their causes, sleep.

Ask me no more whither do stray
The golden atoms of the day;
For in pure love heaven did prepare
Those powders to enrich your hair.

Ask me no more whither doth haste
The nightingale when May is past,
For in your sweet dividing throat
She winters, and keeps warm her note.

Ask me no more where those stars light
That downwards fall in dead of night,
For in your eyes they sit, and there
Fixèd become, as in their sphere.

Ask me no more if east or west
The phoenix builds her spicy nest,
For unto you at last she flies
And in your fragrant bosom dies.

ASK ME NO MORE WHERE JOVE BESTOWS. 3. *orient:* radiant, glowing. (In our time, this sense of the word is obsolete.) 4. *These flowers . . . sleep:* as they slept before they came into existence. (A *cause,* that which gives being, is a term from Aristotle and the Scholastic philosophers.) 11. *dividing:* singing, uttering a "**division**" or melodic phrase added to a basic tune. 18. *phoenix:* In legend, an Arabian bird believed to subsist on incense and perfumes. It was supposed to reproduce by going up in flames, to rise again out of its ashes.

G. K. Chesterton (1874–1936)

THE DONKEY 1900

When fishes flew and forests walked
  And figs grew upon thorn,
Some moment when the moon was blood
  Then surely I was born;

With monstrous head and sickening cry
  And ears like errant wings,
The devil's walking parody
  On all four-footed things.

The tattered outlaw of the earth,
  Of ancient crooked will;
Starve, scourge, deride me: I am dumb,
  I keep my secret still.

Fools! For I also had my hour;
  One far fierce hour and sweet:
There was a shout about my ears,
  And palms before my feet.

THE DONKEY. For more details of the donkey's hour of triumph see Matthew 21:1–8.

Samuel Taylor Coleridge (1772–1834)

KUBLA KHAN (1797–1798)

Or, a Vision in a Dream. A Fragment.

In Xanadu did Kubla Khan
A stately pleasure-dome decree:
Where Alph, the sacred river, ran
Through caverns measureless to man
  Down to a sunless sea.
So twice five miles of fertile ground

With walls and towers were girdled round;
And there were gardens bright with sinuous rills,
Where blossomed many an incense-bearing tree;
And here were forests ancient as the hills,
Enfolding sunny spots of greenery.

But oh! that deep romantic chasm which slanted
Down the green hill athwart a cedarn cover!
A savage place! as holy and enchanted
As e'er beneath a waning moon was haunted
By woman wailing for her demon-lover!
And from this chasm, with ceaseless turmoil seething,
As if this earth in fast thick pants were breathing,
A mighty fountain momently was forced:
Amid whose swift half-intermitted burst
Huge fragments vaulted like rebounding hail,
Or chaffy grain beneath the thresher's flail:
And 'mid these dancing rocks at once and ever
It flung up momently the sacred river.
Five miles meandering with a mazy motion
Through wood and dale the sacred river ran,
Then reached the caverns measureless to man,
And sank in tumult to a lifeless ocean:
And 'mid this tumult Kubla heard from far
Ancestral voices prophesying war!

The shadow of the dome of pleasure
Floated midway on the waves;
Where was heard the mingled measure
From the fountain and the caves.
It was a miracle of rare device,
A sunny pleasure-dome with caves of ice!

A damsel with a dulcimer
In a vision once I saw:
It was an Abyssinian maid,
And on her dulcimer she played,
Singing of Mount Abora.
Could I revive within me
Her symphony and song,
To such a deep delight 'twould win me,
That with music loud and long,
I would build that dome in air,
That sunny dome! those caves of ice!
And all who heard should see them there,
And all should cry, Beware! Beware!
His flashing eyes, his floating hair!
Weave a circle round him thrice,
And close your eyes with holy dread,
For he on honey-dew hath fed,
And drunk the milk of Paradise.

KUBLA KHAN. There was an actual Kublai Khan, a thirteenth-century Mongol emperor, and a Chinese city of Xamdu; but Coleridge's dream vision also borrows from travelers' descriptions of such other exotic places as Abyssinia and America. 51. *circle:* a magic circle drawn to keep away evil spirits.

William Cowper (1731–1800)

PRAISE FOR THE FOUNTAIN OPENED

1779

There is a fountain filled with blood
  Drawn from Emmanuel's veins;
And sinners, plunged beneath that flood,
  Lose all their guilty stains.

The dying thief rejoiced to see
  That fountain in his day;
And there have I, as vile as he,
  Washed all my sins away.

Dear dying Lamb, thy precious blood
  Shall never lose its pow'r;
Till all the ransomed church of God
  Be saved, to sin no more.

E'er since, by faith, I saw the stream
  Thy flowing wounds supply,
Redeeming love has been my theme
  And shall be till I die.

Then in a nobler sweeter song
  I'll sing thy power to save;
When this poor lisping stammering tongue
  Lies silent in the grave.

Lord, I believe thou hast prepared
  (Unworthy though I be)
For me a blood-bought free reward,
  A golden harp for me!

'Tis strung, and tuned, for endless years,
  And formed by pow'r divine
To sound in God the Father's ears
  No other name but thine.

PRAISE FOR THE FOUNTAIN OPENED. This hymn is based on the Biblical prophecy of the cleansing fountain (Zechariah 13:1): "In that day there shall be a fountain opened to the house of David and to the inhabitants of Jerusalem for sin and for uncleanness." Cowper, although his works were various, was most widely famed in late eighteenth-century England as the poet of a new evangelical religious movement, Methodism. For a collection, the *Olney Hymns,* written together with the Reverend John Newton, Cowper supplied this and sixty-six other hymns including "Oh! For a Closer Walk with God" and "Light Shining Out of Darkness" ("God moves in a mysterious way,/His wonders to perform").

COMPARE:

"Praise for the Fountain Opened" and "A Prayer, Living and Dying" by Augustus M. Toplady (page 116). Compare the language and stanza form of Cowper's hymn with "Because I could not stop for Death" (below) and other poems by Emily Dickinson.

Emily Dickinson (1830–1886)

BECAUSE I COULD NOT STOP FOR DEATH (1863)

Because I could not stop for Death–
He kindly stopped for me–
The Carriage held but just Ourselves–
And Immortality.

We slowly drove–He knew no haste
And I had put away
My labor and my leisure too,
For His Civility–

We passed the School, where Children strove
At Recess–in the Ring–
We passed the Fields of Gazing Grain–
We passed the Setting Sun–

Or rather–He passed Us–
The Dews drew quivering and chill–
For only Gossamer, my Gown–
My Tippet°–only Tulle– *cape*

We paused before a House that seemed
A Swelling of the Ground–
The Roof was scarcely visible–
The Cornice – in the Ground–

Since then–'tis Centuries–and yet
Feels shorter than the Day
I first surmised the Horses' Heads
Were toward Eternity–

BECAUSE I COULD NOT STOP FOR DEATH. In the version of this poem printed by Emily Dickinson's first editors in 1890, stanza four was left out. In line 9 *strove* was replaced by *played;* line 10 was made to read "Their lessons scarcely done"; line 20, "The cornice but a mound"; line 21, "Since then 'tis centuries, but each"; and capitalization and punctuation were made conventional.

COMPARE:

"Because I could not stop for Death" and other poems in common meter by Emily Dickinson (such as "I heard a Fly buzz–when I died," page 211, and "My Life had stood–a Loaded Gun," page 302) with "Praise for the Fountain Opened" by William Cowper (page 300).

Emily Dickinson (1830–1886)

I started Early—Took my Dog (1862)

I started Early–Took my Dog–
And visited the Sea–
The Mermaids in the Basement
Came out to look at me–

And Frigates–in the Upper Floor
Extended Hempen Hands–
Presuming Me to be a Mouse–
Aground–upon the Sands–

But no Man moved Me–till the Tide
Went past my simple Shoe–
And past my Apron–and my Belt
And past my Bodice–too–

And made as He would eat me up–
As wholly as a Dew
Upon a Dandelion's Sleeve–
And then–I started–too–

And He–He followed–close behind–
I felt His Silver Heel
Upon my Ankle–Then my Shoes
Would overflow with Pearl–

Until We met the Solid Town–
No One He seemed to know–
And bowing–with a Mighty look–
At me–The Sea withdrew–

Emily Dickinson (1830–1886)

My Life had stood–a Loaded Gun (about 1863)

My Life had stood–a Loaded Gun–
In Corners–till a Day
The Owner passed–identified–
And carried Me away–

And now We roam in Sovreign Woods–
And now We hunt the Doe–
And every time I speak for Him–
The Mountains straight reply–

And do I smile, such cordial light
Upon the Valley glow–
It is as a Vesuvian face
Had let its pleasure through–

And when at Night–Our good Day done–
I guard My Master's Head–
'Tis better than the Eider-Duck's
Deep Pillow–to have shared–

To foe of His–I'm deadly foe–
None stir the second time–
On whom I lay a Yellow Eye–
Or an emphatic Thumb–

Though I than He–may longer live
He longer must–than I–
For I have but the power to kill,
Without–the power to die–

Emily Dickinson (1830–1886)

Safe in their Alabaster Chambers (1859–1861)

Safe in their Alabaster Chambers–
Untouched by Morning–
And untouched by Noon–
Lie the meek members of the Resurrection–
Rafter of Satin–and Roof of Stone!

Light laughs the breeze
In her Castle above them–
Babbles the Bee in a stolid Ear,
Pipe the Sweet Birds in ignorant cadence–
Ah, what sagacity perished here!

Grand go the Years–in the Crescent–above them–
Worlds scoop their Arcs–
And Firmaments–row–
Diadems–drop–and Doges–surrender–
Soundless as dots–on a Disc of Snow–

Safe in their Alabaster Chambers. "It is unlikely," according to Thomas H. Johnson, who first edited the poet's complete poems, "that Emily Dickinson ever completed this poem in a version that entirely satisfied her." Two versions of the poem exist, and we print here that of 1861, with the inclusion of lines 6–10, written in 1859. If you care to read only the poet's later version, ignore the middle stanza.

John Donne (1572–1631)

The Bait (about 1600?)

Come live with me and be my love,
And we will some new pleasures prove°, *try*
Of golden sands and crystal brooks,
With silken lines and silver hooks.

There will the river whispering run,
Warmed by thy eyes more than the sun;
And there the enamored fish will stay,
Begging themselves they may betray.

When thou wilt swim in that live bath,
Each fish, which every channel hath,
Will amorously to thee swim,
Gladder to catch thee, than thou him.

If thou to be so seen be'st loath,
By sun or moon, thou dark'nest both;
And if myself have leave to see,
I need not their light, having thee.

Let others freeze with angling reeds°, *rods*
And cut their legs with shells and weeds,
Or treacherously poor fish beset
With strangling snare or windowy net.

Let coarse bold hands from slimy nest
The bedded fish in banks out-wrest,
Or curious traitors, sleave-silk flies,
Bewitch poor fishes' wand'ring eyes.

For thee, thou need'st no such deceit,
For thou thyself art thine own bait;
That fish that is not catched thereby,
Alas, is wiser far than I.

COMPARE:

"The Bait" with "The Passionate Shepherd to His Love" by Christopher Marlowe (page 343).

John Donne (1572–1631)

DEATH BE NOT PROUD (about 1610)

Death be not proud, though some have callèd thee
Mighty and dreadful, for thou art not so;
For those whom thou think'st thou dost overthrow
Die not, poor death, nor yet canst thou kill me.
From rest and sleep, which but thy pictures be,
Much pleasure, then from thee much more must flow,
And soonest our best men with thee do go,
Rest of their bones, and soul's delivery.
Thou art slave to fate, chance, kings, and desperate men,
And dost with poison, war, and sickness dwell,
And poppy, or charms can make us sleep as well,
And better than thy stroke; why swell'st thou then?
One short sleep past, we wake eternally,
And death shall be no more; death, thou shalt die.

John Donne (1572–1631)

A Valediction: Forbidding Mourning (1611)

As virtuous men pass mildly away,
  And whisper to their souls to go,
Whilst some of their sad friends do say
  The breath goes now, and some say no:

So let us melt, and make no noise,
  No tear-floods, nor sigh-tempests move;
'Twere profanation of our joys
  To tell the laity° our love. *common people*

Moving of th' earth° brings harms and fears; *earthquake*
  Men reckon what it did and meant;
But trepidation of the spheres,
  Though greater far, is innocent°. *harmless*

Dull sublunary lovers' love
  (Whose soul is sense) cannot admit
Absence, because it doth remove
  Those things which elemented° it. *constituted*

But we, by a love so much refined
  That ourselves know not what it is,
Inter-assurèd of the mind,
  Care less, eyes, lips, and hands to miss.

Our two souls, therefore, which are one,
  Though I must go, endure not yet
A breach, but an expansiòn,
  Like gold to airy thinness beat.

If they be two, they are two so
  As stiff twin compasses are two:
Thy soul, the fixed foot, makes no show
  To move, but doth, if th' other do.

And though it in the center sit,
  Yet when the other far doth roam,
It leans and harkens after it,
  And grows erect as that comes home.

Such wilt thou be to me, who must,
  Like th' other foot, obliquely run;
Thy firmness makes my circle just°, *perfect*
  And makes me end where I begun.

A Valediction: Forbidding Mourning. According to Donne's biographer Izaak Walton, Donne's wife received this poem as a gift before the poet departed on a journey to France. 11. *spheres:* In Ptolemaic astronomy, the concentric spheres surrounding the earth. The trepidation or motion of the ninth sphere was thought to change the date of the equinox. 19. *Inter-assurèd of the mind:* each sure in mind that the other is faithful. 24. *gold to airy thinness:* Gold is so malleable that, if beaten to the thickness of gold leaf (1/250,000 of one inch), one ounce of gold would cover 250 square feet.

John Dryden (1631–1700)

To the Memory of Mr. Oldham

1684

Farewell, too little and too lately known,
Whom I began to think and call my own;
For sure our souls were near allied, and thine
Cast in the same poetic mold with mine.
One common note on either lyre did strike,
And knaves and fools we both abhorred alike.
To the same goal did both our studies drive:
The last set out the soonest did arrive.
Thus Nissus fell upon the slippery place,
While his young friend performed and won the race.
O early ripe! to thy abundant store
What could advancing age have added more?
It might (what Nature never gives the young)
Have taught the numbers° of thy native tongue. *meters*
But satire needs not those, and wit will shine
Through the harsh cadence of a rugged line.
A noble error, and but seldom made,
When poets are by too much force betrayed.
Thy gen'rous fruits, though gathered ere their prime,
Still showed a quickness; and maturing time
But mellows what we write to the dull sweets of rhyme.
Once more, hail, and farewell! farewell, thou young
But ah! too short, Marcellus of our tongue!
Thy brows with ivy and with laurels bound;
But fate and gloomy night encompass thee around.

To the Memory of Mr. Oldham. John Oldham, poet best remembered for his *Satires upon the Jesuits,* had died at thirty. 9–10. *Nissus; his young friend:* These two close friends, as Virgil tells us in the *Aeneid,* ran a race for the prize of an olive crown. 23. *Marcellus:* Had he not died in his twentieth year, he would have succeeded the Roman emperor Augustus. 25. This line echoes the *Aeneid* (VI, 886), in which Marcellus is seen walking under the black cloud of his impending doom.

Compare:

"To the Memory of Mr. Oldham" with "To an Athlete Dying Young" by A. E. Housman (page 331).

Alan Dugan (b. 1923)

Love Song: I and Thou

1961

Nothing is plumb, level or square:
  the studs are bowed, the joists
are shaky by nature, no piece fits
  any other piece without a gap

or pinch, and bent nails
  dance all over the surfacing
like maggots. By Christ
  I am no carpenter, I built
the roof for myself, the walls
  for myself, the floors
for myself, and got
  hung up in it myself. I
danced with a purple thumb
  at this house-warming, drunk
with my prime whiskey: rage.
  Oh I spat rage's nails
into the frame-up of my work:
  it held. It settled plumb,
level, solid, square and true
  for that great moment. Then
it screamed and went on through,
  skewing as wrong the other way.
God damned it. This is hell,
  but I planned it, I sawed it,
I nailed it, and I
  will live in it until it kills me.
I can nail my left palm
  to the left-hand cross-piece but
I can't do everything myself.
  I need a hand to nail the right,
a help, a love, a you, a wife.

COMPARE:

"Love Song: I and Thou" with "Love Poem" by John Frederick Nims (page 348).

Bob Dylan (b. 1941)

SUBTERRANEAN HOMESICK BLUES — 1965

Johnny's in the basement
Mixing up the medicine
I'm on the pavement
Thinking about the government
The man in the trenchcoat
Badge out, laid off
Says he's got a bad cough
Wants to get paid off

SUBTERRANEAN HOMESICK BLUES by Bob Dylan. Dylan performs this song on *Bringing It All Back Home* (Columbia Records, stereo CS 9128, mono CL 2328), also on *Bob Dylan's Greatest Hits* (Columbia, stereo KCS 9463, mono KCL 2663).

Look out kid
It's something you did
God knows when
But you're doin' it again
You better duck down the alley way
Lookin' for a new friend
The man in the coonskin cap
By the pig pen
Wants eleven dollar bills
You only got ten.

Maggie comes fleet foot
Face full of black soot
Talkin' that the heat° put *police*
Plants° in the bed but *microphones*
The phone's tapped anyway
Maggie says that many say
They must bust in early May
Orders from the D.A.
Look out kid
Don't matter what you did
Walk on your tip toes
Don't try No-Doz
Better stay away from those
That carry around a fire hose° *syringe*
Keep a clean nose
Watch the plain clothes
You don't need a weather man
To tell which way the wind blows.

Get sick get well
Hang around an ink well
Ring bell, hard to tell
If anything is goin' to sell
Try hard, get barred
Get back, write braille
Get jailed, jump bail
Join the army, if you fail
Look out kid, you're gonna get hit
But users, cheaters
Six time losers
Hang around the theatres
Girl by the whirl pool's
Lookin' for a new fool
Don't follow leaders
Watch the parkin' meters.

Ah, get born, keep warm
Short pants, romance, learn to dance
Get dressed, get blessed

Try to be a success
Please her, please him, buy gifts
Don't steal, don't lift
Twenty years of schoolin'
And they put you on the day shift
Look out kid, they keep it all hid
Better jump down a manhole
Light yourself a candle, don't wear sandals
Try to avoid the scandals
Don't wanna be a bum
You better chew gum
The pump don't work
'Cause the vandals took the handles.

T. S. Eliot (1888–1965)

Journey of the Magi — 1927

"A cold coming we had of it,
Just the worst time of the year
For a journey, and such a long journey:
The ways deep and the weather sharp,
The very dead of winter."
And the camels galled, sore-footed, refractory,
Lying down in the melting snow.
There were times we regretted
The summer palaces on slopes, the terraces,
And the silken girls bringing sherbet.
Then the camel men cursing and grumbling
And running away, and wanting their liquor and women,
And the night-fires going out, and the lack of shelters,
And the cities hostile and the towns unfriendly
And the villages dirty and charging high prices:
A hard time we had of it.
At the end we preferred to travel all night,
Sleeping in snatches,
With the voices singing in our ears, saying
That this was all folly.

Then at dawn we came down to a temperate valley,
Wet, below the snow line, smelling of vegetation;
With a running stream and a water-mill beating the darkness,
And three trees on the low sky,
And an old white horse galloped away in the meadow.
Then we came to a tavern with vine-leaves over the lintel,
Six hands at an open door dicing for pieces of silver,
And feet kicking the empty wine-skins.
But there was no information, and so we continued
And arrived at evening, not a moment too soon

Finding the place; it was (you may say) satisfactory.
All this was a long time ago, I remember,
And I would do it again, but set down
This set down
This: were we led all that way for
Birth or Death? There was a Birth, certainly,
We had evidence and no doubt. I had seen birth and death,
But had thought they were different; this Birth was
Hard and bitter agony for us, like Death, our death.
We returned to our places, these Kingdoms,
But no longer at ease here, in the old dispensation,
With an alien people clutching their gods.
I should be glad of another death.

JOURNEY OF THE MAGI. The story of the Magi, the three wise men who traveled to Bethlehem to behold the Christ child, is told in Matthew 2:1–12. That the three were kings is a later tradition. 1–5. *A cold coming . . . winter:* Eliot quotes with slight changes from a sermon preached on Christmas day, 1622, by Bishop Lancelot Andrewes. 24. *three times:* foreshadowing the three crosses on Calvary (see Luke 23:32–33). 25. *white horse:* perhaps the steed that carried the conquering Christ in the vision of St. John the Divine (Revelation 19:11–16). 41. *old dispensation:* older, pagan religion about to be displaced by Christianity.

COMPARE:

"Journey of the Magi" with "The Magi" by William Butler Yeats (page 396).

T. S. Eliot (1888–1965)

THE LOVE SONG OF J. ALFRED PRUFROCK 1917

S'io credessi che mia risposta fosse
A persona che mai tornasse al mondo,
Questa fiamma staria senza piu scosse.
Ma perciocche giammai di questo fondo
Non torno vivo alcun, s'i'odo il vero,
Senza tema d'infamia ti rispondo.

Let us go then, you and I,
When the evening is spread out against the sky
Like a patient etherized upon a table;
Let us go, through certain half-deserted streets,
The muttering retreats
Of restless nights in one-night cheap hotels
And sawdust restaurants with oyster-shells:
Streets that follow like a tedious argument
Of insidious intent
To lead you to an overwhelming question . . .
Oh, do not ask, "What is it?"
Let us go and make our visit.

In the room the women come and go
Talking of Michelangelo.

The yellow fog that rubs its back upon the window-panes,
The yellow smoke that rubs its muzzle on the window-panes
Licked its tongue into the corners of the evening,
Lingered upon the pools that stand in drains,
Let fall upon its back the soot that falls from chimneys,
Slipped by the terrace, made a sudden leap,
And seeing that it was a soft October night,
Curled once about the house, and fell asleep.

And indeed there will be time
For the yellow smoke that slides along the street,
Rubbing its back upon the window-panes;
There will be time, there will be time
To prepare a face to meet the faces that you meet;
There will be time to murder and create,
And time for all the works and days of hands
That lift and drop a question on your plate;
Time for you and time for me,
And time yet for a hundred indecisions,
And for a hundred visions and revisions,
Before the taking of a toast and tea.

In the room the women come and go
Talking of Michelangelo.

And indeed there will be time
To wonder, "Do I dare?" and, "Do I dare?"
Time to turn back and descend the stair,
With a bald spot in the middle of my hair—
[They will say: "How his hair is growing thin!"]
My morning coat, my collar mounting firmly to the chin,
My necktie rich and modest, but asserted by a simple pin—
[They will say: "But how his arms and legs are thin!"]
Do I dare
Disturb the universe?
In a minute there is time
For decisions and revisions which a minute will reverse.

For I have known them all already, known them all:—
Have known the evenings, mornings, afternoons,
I have measured out my life with coffee spoons;
I know the voices dying with a dying fall
Beneath the music from a farther room.
  So how should I presume?

And I have known the eyes already, known them all—
The eyes that fix you in a formulated phrase,
And when I am formulated, sprawling on a pin,

When I am pinned and wriggling on the wall,
Then how should I begin
To spit out all the butt-ends of my days and ways?
  And how should I presume?

And I have known the arms already, known them all—
Arms that are braceleted and white and bare
[But in the lamplight, downed with light brown hair!]
Is it perfume from a dress
That makes me so digress?
Arms that lie along a table, or wrap about a shawl.
  And should I then presume?
  And how should I begin?

. . . . .

Shall I say, I have gone at dusk through narrow streets
And watched the smoke that rises from the pipes
Of lonely men in shirt-sleeves, leaning out of windows? . . .

I should have been a pair of ragged claws
Scuttling across the floors of silent seas.

. . . . .

And the afternoon, the evening, sleeps so peacefully!
Smoothed by long fingers,
Asleep . . . tired . . . or it malingers,
Stretched on the floor, here beside you and me.
Should I, after tea and cakes and ices,
Have the strength to force the moment to its crisis?
But though I have wept and fasted, wept and prayed,
Though I have seen my head [grown slightly bald] brought in upon a platter,
I am no prophet—and here's no great matter;
I have seen the moment of my greatness flicker,
And I have seen the eternal Footman hold my coat, and snicker,
And in short, I was afraid.

And would it have been worth it, after all,
After the cups, the marmalade, the tea,
Among the porcelain, among some talk of you and me,
Would it have been worth while,
To have bitten off the matter with a smile,
To have squeezed the universe into a ball
To roll it toward some overwhelming question,
To say: "I am Lazarus, come from the dead,
Come back to tell you all, I shall tell you all"—
If one, settling a pillow by her head,
  Should say: "That is not what I meant at all.
  That is not it, at all."

And would it have been worth it, after all,
Would it have been worth while,

After the sunsets and the dooryards and the sprinkled streets,
After the novels, after the teacups, after the skirts that trail along the
floor—
And this, and so much more?—
It is impossible to say just what I mean!
But as if a magic lantern threw the nerves in patterns on a screen:
Would it have been worth while
If one, settling a pillow or throwing off a shawl,
And turning toward the window, should say:
"That is not it at all,
That is not what I meant, at all."

. . . . .

No! I am not Prince Hamlet, nor was meant to be;
Am an attendant lord, one that will do
To swell a progress, start a scene or two,
Advise the prince; no doubt, an easy tool,
Deferential, glad to be of use,
Politic, cautious, and meticulous;
Full of high sentence, but a bit obtuse;
At times, indeed, almost ridiculous—
Almost, at times, the Fool.

I grow old . . . I grow old . . .
I shall wear the bottoms of my trousers rolled.

Shall I part my hair behind? Do I dare to eat a peach?
I shall wear white flannel trousers, and walk upon the beach.
I have heard the mermaids singing, each to each.

I do not think that they will sing to me.

I have seen them riding seaward on the waves
Combing the white hair of the waves blown back
When the wind blows the water white and black.

We have lingered in the chambers of the sea
By sea-girls wreathed with seaweed red and brown
Till human voices wake us, and we drown.

THE LOVE SONG OF J. ALFRED PRUFROCK. The epigraph, from Dante's *Inferno*, is the speech of one dead and damned, who thinks that his hearer also is going to remain in Hell. Count Guido da Montefeltro, whose sin has been to give false counsel after a corrupt prelate had offered him prior absolution and whose punishment is to be wrapped in a constantly burning flame, offers to tell Dante his story: "If I thought my reply were to someone who could ever return to the world, this flame would waver no more. But since, I'm told, nobody ever escapes from this pit, I'll tell you without fear of ill fame." 29. *works and days:* title of a poem by Hesiod (eighth century B.C.), depicting his life as a hard-working Greek farmer and exhorting his brother to be like him. 82. *head . . . platter:* like that of John the Baptist, prophet and praiser of chastity, whom King Herod beheaded at the demand of Herodias, his unlawfully wedded wife (see Mark 6:17–28). 92–93. *squeezed . . . To roll it:* an echo from Marvell's "To His Coy Mistress," lines 41–42 (see p. 8) 94. *Lazarus:* Probably the Lazarus whom Jesus called forth from the tomb (John 11:1–44), but possibly the beggar seen in Heaven by the rich man in Hell (Luke 16:19–25).

Ralph Waldo Emerson (1803–1882)

DAYS

1867

Daughters of Time, the hypocritic Days,
Muffled and dumb like barefoot dervishes,
And marching single in an endless file,
Bring diadems and fagots in their hands.
To each they offer gifts after his will,
Bread, kingdom, stars, and sky that holds them all.

I, in my pleachèd garden, watched the pomp°, *solemn procession*
Forgot my morning wishes, hastily
Took a few herbs and apples, and the Day
Turned and departed silent. I, too late,
Under her solemn fillet° saw the scorn. *headband*

DAYS. 1. *hypocritic:* Our word *hypocrite* comes from Greek: "one who plays a part" (as in a play or a procession). 2. *dervishes:* members of a Moslem religious order, whose vows of poverty obliged them to give away their possessions. 7. *pleachèd:* To pleach is to bend and interweave—a stylized, artificial method of prettifying natural branches.

Robert Frost (1874–1963)

MENDING WALL

1914

Something there is that doesn't love a wall,
That sends the frozen-ground-swell under it,
And spills the upper boulders in the sun;
And makes gaps even two can pass abreast.
The work of hunters is another thing:
I have come after them and made repair
Where they have left not one stone on a stone,
But they would have the rabbit out of hiding,
To please the yelping dogs. The gaps I mean,
No one has seen them made or heard them made,
But at spring-mending time we find them there.
I let my neighbor know beyond the hill;
And on a day we meet to walk the line
And set the wall between us once again.
We keep the wall between us as we go.
To each the boulders that have fallen to each.
And some are loaves and some so nearly balls
We have to use a spell to make them balance:
'Stay where you are until our backs are turned!'
We wear our fingers rough with handling them.
Oh, just another kind of outdoor game,
One on a side. It comes to little more:
There where it is we do not need the wall:

He is all pine and I am apple orchard.
My apple trees will never get across
And eat the cones under his pines, I tell him.
He only says, 'Good fences make good neighbors.'
Spring is the mischief in me, and I wonder
If I could put a notion in his head:
'*Why* do they make good neighbors? Isn't it
Where there are cows? But here there are no cows.
Before I built a wall I'd ask to know
What I was walling in or walling out,
And to whom I was like to give offense.
Something there is that doesn't love a wall,
That wants it down.' I could say 'Elves' to him,
But it's not elves exactly, and I'd rather
He said it for himself. I see him there
Bringing a stone grasped firmly by the top
In each hand, like an old-stone savage armed.
He moves in darkness as it seems to me,
Not of woods only and the shade of trees.
He will not go behind his father's saying,
And he likes having thought of it so well
He says again, 'Good fences make good neighbors.'

COMPARE:

"Mending Wall" with "Mending Sump" by Kenneth Koch (page 242).

Robert Frost (1874–1963)

STOPPING BY WOODS ON A SNOWY EVENING 1923

Whose woods these are I think I know.
His house is in the village though;
He will not see me stopping here
To watch his woods fill up with snow.

My little horse must think it queer
To stop without a farmhouse near
Between the woods and frozen lake
The darkest evening of the year.

He gives his harness bells a shake
To ask if there is some mistake.
The only other sound's the sweep
Of easy wind and downy flake.

The woods are lovely, dark and deep,
But I have promises to keep,
And miles to go before I sleep,
And miles to go before I sleep.

COMPARE:

"Stopping by Woods on a Snowy Evening" with "Desert Places" by Robert Frost (page 132).

Robert Frost (1874–1963)

THE WITCH OF COÖS

1923

I stayed the night for shelter at a farm
Behind the mountain, with a mother and son,
Two old-believers. They did all the talking.

MOTHER. Folks think a witch who has familiar spirits
She could call up to pass a winter evening,
But won't, should be burned at the stake or something.
Summoning spirits isn't 'Button, button,
Who's got the button,' I would have them know.

SON. Mother can make a common table rear
And kick with two legs like an army mule.

MOTHER. And when I've done it, what good have I done?
Rather than tip a table for you, let me
Tell you what Ralle the Sioux Control once told me.
He said the dead had souls, but when I asked him
How could that be—I thought the dead were souls,
He broke my trance. Don't that make you suspicious
That there's something the dead are keeping back?
Yes, there's something the dead are keeping back.

SON. You wouldn't want to tell him what we have
Up attic, mother?

MOTHER. Bones—a skeleton.

SON. But the headboard of mother's bed is pushed
Against the attic door: the door is nailed.
It's harmless. Mother hears it in the night
Halting perplexed behind the barrier
Of door and headboard. Where it wants to get
Is back into the cellar where it came from.

MOTHER. We'll never let them, will we, son! We'll never!

SON. It left the cellar forty years ago
And carried itself like a pile of dishes
Up one flight from the cellar to the kitchen,
Another from the kitchen to the bedroom,
Another from the bedroom to the attic,
Right past both father and mother, and neither stopped it.
Father had gone upstairs; mother was downstairs.
I was a baby: I don't know where I was.

MOTHER. The only fault my husband found with me—
I went to sleep before I went to bed,
Especially in winter when the bed
Might just as well be ice and the clothes snow.
The night the bones came up the cellar-stairs
Toffile had gone to bed alone and left me,
But left an open door to cool the room off
So as to sort of turn me out of it.
I was just coming to myself enough
To wonder where the cold was coming from,
When I heard Toffile upstairs in the bedroom
And thought I heard him downstairs in the cellar.
The board we had laid down to walk dry-shod on
When there was water in the cellar in spring
Struck the hard cellar bottom. And then someone
Began the stairs, two footsteps for each step,
The way a man with one leg and a crutch,
Or a little child, comes up. It wasn't Toffile:
It wasn't anyone who could be there.
The bulkhead double-doors were double-locked
And swollen tight and buried under snow.
The cellar windows were banked up with sawdust
And swollen tight and buried under snow.
It was the bones. I knew them—and good reason.
My first impulse was to get to the knob
And hold the door. But the bones didn't try
The door; they halted helpless on the landing,
Waiting for things to happen in their favor.
The faintest restless rustling ran all through them.
I never could have done the thing I did
If the wish hadn't been too strong in me
To see how they were mounted for this walk.
I had a vision of them put together
Not like a man, but like a chandelier.
So suddenly I flung the door wide on him.
A moment he stood balancing with emotion,
And all but lost himself. (A tongue of fire
Flashed out and licked along his upper teeth.
Smoke rolled inside the sockets of his eyes.)
Then he came at me with one hand outstretched,
The way he did in life once; but this time
I struck the hand off brittle on the floor,
And fell back from him on the floor myself.
The finger-pieces slid in all directions.
(Where did I see one of those pieces lately?
Hand me my button-box—it must be there.)
I sat up on the floor and shouted. "Toffile,
It's coming up to you.' It had its choice
Of the door to the cellar or the hall.

It took the hall door for the novelty,
And set off briskly for so slow a thing,
Still going every which way in the joints, though,
So that it looked like lightning or a scribble,
From the slap I had just now given its hand.
I listened till it almost climbed the stairs
From the hall to the only finished bedroom,
Before I got up to do anything;
Then ran and shouted, "Shut the bedroom door,
Toffile, for my sake!' 'Company?' he said,
'Don't make me get up; I'm too warm in bed.'
So lying forward weakly on the handrail
I pushed myself upstairs, and in the light
(The kitchen had been dark) I had to own
I could see nothing. 'Toffile, I don't see it.
It's with us in the room though. It's the bones.'
'What bones?' 'The cellar bones—out of the grave.'
That made him throw his bare legs out of bed
And sit up by me and take hold of me.
I wanted to put out the light and see
If I could see it, or else mow the room,
With our arms at the level of our knees,
And bring the chalk-pile down. 'I'll tell you what—
It's looking for another door to try.
The uncommonly deep snow has made him think
Of his old song, *The Wild Colonial Boy,*
He always used to sing along the tote road.
He's after an open door to get outdoors.
Let's trap him with an open door up attic.'
Toffile agreed to that, and sure enough,
Almost the moment he was given an opening,
The steps began to climb the attic stairs.
I heard them. Toffile didn't seem to hear them.
'Quick!' I slammed to the door and held the knob.
'Toffile, get nails.' I made him nail the door shut
And push the headboard of the bed against it.
Then we asked was there anything
Up attic that we'd ever want again.
The attic was less to us than the cellar.
If the bones liked the attic, let them have it.
Let them stay in the attic. When they sometimes
Come down the stairs at night and stand perplexed
Behind the door and headboard of the bed,
Brushing their chalky skull with chalky fingers,
With sounds like the dry rattling of a shutter,
That's what I sit up in the dark to say—
To no one any more since Toffile died.
Let them stay in the attic since they went there.
I promised Toffile to be cruel to them
For helping them to be cruel once to him.

SON. We think they had a grave down in the cellar.

MOTHER. We know they had a grave down in the cellar.

SON. We never could find out whose bones they were.

MOTHER. Yes, we could too, son. Tell the truth for once.
They were a man's his father killed for me.
I mean a man he killed instead of me.
The least I could do was to help dig their grave.
We were about it one night in the cellar.
Son knows the story: but 'twas not for him
To tell the truth, suppose the time had come.
Son looks surprised to see me end a lie
We'd kept all these years between ourselves
So as to have it ready for outsiders.
But tonight I don't care enough to lie—
I don't remember why I ever cared.
Toffile, if he were here, I don't believe
Could tell you why he ever cared himself. . . .

She hadn't found the finger-bone she wanted
Among the buttons poured out in her lap.
I verified the name next morning: Toffile.
The rural letter box said Toffile Lajway.

THE WITCH OF COÖS. Coös is the northernmost county in New Hampshire. 13. *Ralle the Sioux Control:* the spirit of a dead Indian. In spiritualism, a control is a spirit who serves as a contact between a medium and other spirits of the departed.

Tess Gallagher (b. 1943)

UNDER STARS 1978

The sleep of this night deepens
because I have walked coatless from the house
carrying the white envelope.
All night it will say one name
in its little tin house by the roadside.

I have raised the metal flag
so its shadow under the roadlamp
leaves an imprint on the rain-heavy bushes.
Now I will walk back
thinking of the few lights still on
in the town a mile away.

In the yellowed light of a kitchen
the millworker has finished his coffee,
his wife has laid out the white slices of bread
on the counter. Now while the bed they have left
is still warm, I will think of you, you

who are so far away
you have caused me to look up at the stars.

Tonight they have not moved
from childhood, those games played after dark.
Again I walk into the wet grass
toward the starry voices. Again, I
am the found one, intimate, returned
by all I touch on the way.

Allen Ginsberg (b. 1926)

A Supermarket in California 1956

What thoughts I have of you tonight, Walt Whitman, for I walked down the sidestreets under the trees with a headache self-conscious looking at the full moon.
In my hungry fatigue, and shopping for images, I went into the neon fruit supermarket, dreaming of your enumerations!
What peaches and what penumbras! Whole families shopping at night! Aisles full of husbands! Wives in the avocados, babies in the tomatoes! — and you, Garcia Lorca, what were you doing down by the watermelons?

I saw you, Walt Whitman, childless, lonely old grubber, poking among the meats in the refrigerator and eyeing the grocery boys.
I heard you asking questions of each: Who killed the pork chops? What price bananas? Are you my Angel?
I wandered in and out of the brilliant stacks of cans following you, and followed in my imagination by the store detective.
We strode down the open corridors together in our solitary fancy tasting artichokes, possessing every frozen delicacy, and never passing the cashier.

Where are we going, Walt Whitman? The doors close in an hour. Which way does your beard point tonight?
(I touch your book and dream of our odyssey in the supermarket and feel absurd.)
Will we walk all night through solitary streets? The trees add shade to shade, lights out in the houses, we'll both be lonely.
Will we stroll dreaming of the lost America of love past blue automobiles in driveways, home to our silent cottage?
Ah, dear father, graybeard, lonely old courage-teacher, what America did you have when Charon quit poling his ferry and you got out on a smoking bank and stood watching the boat disappear on the black waters of Lethe?

Berkeley 1955

A Supermarket in California. 2. *enumerations:* Many of Whitman's poems contain lists of observed details. 3. *Garcia Lorca:* modern Spanish poet who wrote an "Ode to Walt

Whitman" in his booklength sequence *Poet in New York.* (A poem by Lorca appears on page 236.) 12. *Charon . . . Lethe:* Is the poet confusing two underworld rivers? Charon, in Greek and Roman mythology, is the boatman who ferries the souls of the dead across the River Styx. The River Lethe also flows through Hades, and a drink of its waters makes the dead lose their painful memories of loved ones thay have left behind.

COMPARE:

"A Supermarket in California" with Walt Whitman's "To a Locomotive in Winter" (page 13) and "I Saw in Louisiana a Live-Oak Growing" (page 385).

Donald Hall (b. 1928)

THE TOWN OF HILL

1975

Back of the dam, under
a flat pad

of water, church
bells ring

in the ears of lilies,
a child's swing

curls in the current
of a yard, horned

pout sleep
in a green

mailbox, and
a boy walks

from a screened
porch beneath

the man-shaped
leaves of an oak

down the street looking
at the town

of Hill that water
covered forty

years ago,
and the screen

door shuts
under dream water.

The Town of Hill. Hill today is a town of about 500 a few miles from Danbury, New Hampshire; but the present town replaced an older one that, as part of a flood control project, had to be destroyed. As a child, the poet visited the old town shortly before it was evacuated.

Thomas Hardy (1840–1928)

Channel Firing

1914

That night your great guns, unawares,
Shook all our coffins as we lay,
And broke the chancel window-squares,
We thought it was the Judgment-day

And sat upright. While drearisome
Arose the howl of wakened hounds:
The mouse let fall the altar-crumb,
The worms drew back into the mounds,

The glebe cow drooled. Till God called, "No;
It's gunnery practice out at sea
Just as before you went below;
The world is as it used to be:

"All nations striving strong to make
Red war yet redder. Mad as hatters
They do no more for Christés sake
Than you who are helpless in such matters.

"That this is not the judgment-hour
For some of them's a blessed thing,
For if it were they'd have to scour
Hell's floor for so much threatening . . .

"Ha, ha. It will be warmer when
I blow the trumpet (if indeed
I ever do; for you are men,
And rest eternal sorely need)."

So down we lay again. "I wonder,
Will the world ever saner be,"
Said one, "than when He sent us under
In our indifferent century!"

And many a skeleton shook his head.
"Instead of preaching forty year,"
My neighbor Parson Thirdly said,
"I wish I had stuck to pipes and beer."

Again the guns disturbed the hour,
Roaring their readiness to avenge,
As far inland as Stourton Tower,
And Camelot, and starlit Stonehenge.

Channel Firing. 9. *glebe:* land belonging to the church, used for grazing. 35. *Stourton Tower:* a monument to the defeat of the Danes by Alfred the Great in 879 A.D. 36. *Camelot:* where King Arthur held court; *Stonehenge:* circle of huge stones thought to be the ruins of a prehistoric place of worship.

Compare:

"Channel Firing" with "The Fury of Aerial Bombardment" by Richard Eberhart (page 55).

Thomas Hardy (1840–1928)

The Convergence of the Twain

1912

Lines on the Loss of the "Titanic"

I

In a solitude of the sea
Deep from human vanity,
And the Pride of Life that planned her, stilly couches she.

II

Steel chambers, late the pyres
Of her salamandrine fires,
Cold currents thrid°, and turn to rhythmic tidal lyres. *thread*

III

Over the mirrors meant
To glass the opulent
The sea-worm crawls—grotesque, slimed, dumb, indifferent.

IV

Jewels in joy designed
To ravish the sensuous mind
Lie lightless, all their sparkles bleared and black and blind.

V

Dim moon-eyed fishes near
Gaze at the gilded gear
And query: "What does this vaingloriousness down here?"

VI

Well: while was fashioning
This creature of cleaving wing,
The Immanent Will that stirs and urges everything

VII

Prepared a sinister mate
For her—so gaily great—
A Shape of Ice, for the time far and dissociate.

VIII

And as the smart ship grew
In stature, grace, and hue,
In shadowy silent distance grew the Iceberg too.

IX

Alien they seemed to be:
No mortal eye could see
The intimate welding of their later history,

X

Or sign that they were bent
By paths coincident
On being anon twin halves of one august event.

XI

Till the Spinner of the Years
Said "Now!" And each one hears,
And consummation comes, and jars two hemispheres.

THE CONVERGENCE OF THE TWAIN. The luxury liner *Titanic,* supposedly unsinkable, went down in 1912 after striking an iceberg, on its first Atlantic voyage. 5. *salamandrine:* like the salamander, a lizard that supposedly thrives in fires, or like a spirit of the same name that inhabits fire (according to alchemists).

Seamus Heaney (b. 1939)

SUNLIGHT

1975

There was a sunlit absence.
The helmeted pump in the yard
heated its iron,
water honeyed

in the slung bucket
and the sun stood
like a griddle cooling
against the wall

of each long afternoon.
So, her hands scuffled
over the bakeboard,
the reddening stove

sent its plaque of heat
against her where she stood
in a floury apron
by the window.

Now she dusts the board
with a goose's wing,

now sits, broad-lapped,
with whitened nails

and measling shins:
here is a space
again, the scone rising
to the tick of two clocks.

And here is love
like a tinsmith's scoop
sunk past its gleam
in the meal-bin.

SUNLIGHT. This portrait of a woman at work in an Irish country kitchen comes from "Mossbawn: Two Poems in Dedication for Mary Heaney." Mossbawn is the farm in Derry, Northern Ireland, where the poet was born. 23. *scone:* a quick, faintly sweet bread made of oatmeal and barley flour. Usually rolled, cut into quarters, and baked on a hot griddle, it looks like a baking-powder biscuit.

Anthony Hecht (b. 1923)

THE VOW 1967

In the third month, a sudden flow of blood.
The mirth of tabrets ceaseth, and the joy
Also of the harp. The frail image of God
Lay spilled and formless. Neither girl nor boy,
But yet blood of my blood, nearly my child.
All that long day
Her pale face turned to the window's mild
Featureless grey.

And for some nights she whimpered as she dreamed
The dead thing spoke, saying: "Do not recall
Pleasure at my conception. I am redeemed
From pain and sorrow. Mourn rather for all
Who breathlessly issue from the bone gates,
The gates of horn,
For truly it is best of all the fates
Not to be born.

"Mother, a child lay gasping for bare breath
On Christmas Eve when Santa Claus had set
Death in the stocking, and the lights of death
Flamed in the tree. O, if you can, forget
You were the child, turn to my father's lips
Against the time
When his cold hand puts forth its fingertips
Of jointed lime."

Doctors of Science, what is man that he
Should hope to come to a good end? *The best*
Is not to have been born. And could it be
That Jewish diligence and Irish jest
The consent of flesh and a midwinter storm
        Had reconciled,
Was yet too bold a mixture to inform
        A simple child?

Even as gold is tried, Gentile and Jew.
If that ghost was a girl's, I swear to it:
Your mother shall be far more blessed than you.
And if a boy's, I swear: The flames are lit
That shall refine us; they shall not destroy
        A living hair.
Your younger brothers shall confirm in joy
        This that I swear.

THE VOW. 2. *tabrets:* small drums used to accompany traditional Jewish dances. 14. *gates of horn:* According to Homer and Virgil pleasant, lying dreams emerge from the underworld through gates of ivory; ominous, truth-telling dreams, through gates of horn.

George Herbert (1593–1633)

LOVE

1633

Love bade me welcome; yet my soul drew back,
        Guilty of dust and sin.
But quick-eyed Love, observing me grow slack
        From my first entrance in,
Drew nearer to me, sweetly questioning
        If I lacked anything.

"A guest," I answered, "worthy to be here";
        Love said, "You shall be he."
"I, the unkind, ungrateful? Ah, my dear,
        I cannot look on Thee."
Love took my hand, and smiling did reply,
        "Who made the eyes but I?"

"Truth, Lord, but I have marred them; let my shame
        Go where it doth deserve."
"And know you not," says Love, "who bore the blame?"
        "My dear, then I will serve."
"You must sit down," says Love, "and taste My meat."
        So I did sit and eat.

COMPARE

"Love" with "Batter my heart, three-personed God, for You" by John Donne (page 39).

Robert Herrick (1591–1674)

DELIGHT IN DISORDER 1648

A sweet disorder in the dress
Kindles in clothes a wantonness.
A lawn° about the shoulders thrown *linen*
Into a fine distractión;
An erring lace, which here and there
Enthralls the crimson stomacher;
A cuff neglectful, and thereby
Ribbons to flow confusedly;
A winning wave, deserving note,
In the tempestuous petticoat;
A careless shoestring, in whose tie
I see a wild civility;
Do more bewitch me than when art
Is too precise in every part.

Robert Herrick (1591–1674)

TO THE VIRGINS, TO MAKE MUCH OF TIME 1648

Gather ye rose-buds while ye may,
  Old Time is still a-flying;
And this same flower that smiles today,
  Tomorrow will be dying.

The glorious lamp of heaven, the sun,
  The higher he's a-getting,
The sooner will his race be run,
  And nearer he's to setting.

That age is best which is the first,
  When youth and blood are warmer;
But being spent, the worse, and worst
  Times still succeed the former.

Then be not coy, but use your time,
  And while ye may, go marry;
For having lost but once your prime,
  You may for ever tarry.

COMPARE:

"To the Virgins, to Make Much of Time" with "To His Coy Mistress" by Andrew Marvell (page 8) and "Go, Lovely Rose" by Edmund Waller (page 383).

A. D. Hope (b. 1907)

The Brides

1955

Down the assembly line they roll and pass
Complete at last, a miracle of design;
Their chromium fenders, the unbreakable glass,
The fashionable curve, the air-flow line.

Grease to the elbows Mum and Dad enthuse,
Pocket their spanners° and survey the bride; *wrenches*
Murmur: 'A sweet job! All she needs is juice!
Built for a life-time—sleek as a fish. Inside

'He will find every comfort: the full set
Of gadgets; knobs that answer to the touch
For light or music; a place for his cigarette;
Room for his knees; a honey of a clutch.'

Now slowly through the show-room's flattering glare
See her wheeled in to love, console, obey,
Shining and silent! Parson with a prayer
Blesses the number-plate, she rolls away

To write her numerals in his book of life;
And now, at last, stands on the open road,
Triumphant, perfect, every inch a wife,
While the corks pop, the flash-light bulbs explode.

Her heavenly bowser-boy assumes his seat;
She prints the soft dust with her brand-new treads,
Swings towards the future, purring with a sweet
Concatenation of the poppet heads.

The Brides. 21. *bowser-boy:* gasoline-pump attendant (British and Australian slang). 24. *Concatenation:* coupling, linking together. *poppet heads:* valve heads. *Poppet* can also mean puppet or little person.

Gerard Manley Hopkins (1844–1889)

Spring and Fall

(1880)

To a Young Child

Márgarét, are you grieving
Over Goldengrove unleaving°? *shedding its leaves*
Leáves, like the things of man, you
With your fresh thoughts care for, can you?
Ah! ás the heart grows older
It will come to such sights colder
By and by, nor spare a sigh
Though worlds of wanwood leafmeal lie;

And yet you will weep and know why.
Now no matter, child, the name:
Sórrow's springs áre the same.
Nor mouth had, no nor mind, expressed
What heart heard of, ghost° guessed: *spirit*
It is the blight man was born for,
It is Margaret you mourn for.

COMPARE:

"Spring and Fall" with "Janet Waking" by John Crowe Ransom (page 355). Also with "Margaret Are You Drug" by George Starbuck (page 243).

Gerard Manley Hopkins (1844–1889)

THE WINDHOVER (1877)

To Christ Our Lord

I caught this morning morning's minion, king-
  dom of daylight's dauphin, dapple-dawn-drawn Falcon, in his riding
  Of the rolling level underneath him steady air, and striding
High there, how he rung upon the rein of a wimpling wing
In his ecstasy! then off, off forth on swing,
  As a skate's heel sweeps smooth on a bow-bend: the hurl and gliding
  Rebuffed the big wind. My heart in hiding
Stirred for a bird,—the achieve of, the mastery of the thing!

Brute beauty and valor and act, oh, air, pride, plume, here
  Buckle! and the fire that breaks from thee then, a billion
Times told lovelier, more dangerous, O my chevalier!

  No wonder of it: shéer plód makes plow down sillion° *furrow*
Shine, and blue-bleak embers, ah my dear,
  Fall, gall themselves, and gash gold-vermilion.

THE WINDHOVER. A windhover is a kestrel, or small falcon, so called because it can hover upon the wind. 4. *rung . . . wing:* A horse is "rung upon the rein" when its trainer holds the end of a long rein and has the horse circle him. The possible meanings of *wimpling* include (1) curving; (2) pleated, arranged in many little folds one on top of another; (3) rippling or undulating like the surface of a flowing stream.

A. E. Housman (1859–1936)

TERENCE, THIS IS STUPID STUFF 1896

"Terence, this is stupid stuff:
You eat your victuals fast enough;
There can't be much amiss, 'tis clear,
To see the rate you drink your beer.
But oh, good Lord, the verse you make,

It gives a chap the belly-ache.
The cow, the old cow, she is dead;
It sleeps well, the horned head:
We poor lads, 'tis our turn now
To hear such tunes as killed the cow.
Pretty friendship 'tis to rhyme
Your friends to death before their time
Moping melancholy mad:
Come, pipe a tune to dance to, lad.''

Why, if 'tis dancing you would be,
There's brisker pipes than poetry.
Say, for what were hop-yards meant,
Or why was Burton built on Trent?
Oh many a peer of England brews
Livelier liquor than the Muse,
And malt does more than Milton can
To justify God's ways to man.
Ale, man, ale's the stuff to drink
For fellows whom it hurts to think:
Look into the pewter pot
To see the world as the world's not.
And faith, 'tis pleasant till 'tis past:
The mischief is that 'twill not last.
Oh I have been to Ludlow fair
And left my necktie God knows where,
And carried half-way home, or near,
Pints and quarts of Ludlow beer:
Then the world seemed none so bad,
And I myself a sterling lad;
And down in lovely muck I've lain,
Happy till I woke again.
Then I saw the morning sky:
Heigho, the tale was all a lie;
The world, it was the old world yet,
I was I, my things were wet,
And nothing now remained to do
But begin the game anew.

Therefore, since the world has still
Much good, but much less good than ill,
And while the sun and moon endure
Luck's a chance, but trouble's sure,
I'd face it as a wise man would,
And train for ill and not for good.
'Tis true, the stuff I bring for sale
Is not so brisk a brew as ale:
Out of a stem that scored the hand
I wrung it in a weary land.
But take it: if the smack is sour,
The better for the embittered hour;

It should do good to heart and head
When your soul is in my soul's stead;
And I will friend you, if I may,
In the dark and cloudy day.

There was a king reigned in the East:
There, when kings will sit to feast,
They get their fill before they think
With poisoned meat and poisoned drink.
He gathered all that springs to birth
From the many-venomed earth;
First a little, thence to more,
He sampled all her killing store;
And easy, smiling, seasoned sound,
Sate the king when healths went round.
They put arsenic in his meat
And stared aghast to watch him eat;
They poured strychnine in his cup
And shook to see him drink it up:
They shook, they stared as white's their shirt:
Them it was their poison hurt.
—I tell the tale that I heard told.
Mithridates, he died old.

TERENCE, THIS IS STUPID STUFF. 1. *Terence:* As a name for himself, Housman takes that of a Roman poet, author of satiric comedies. 18. *why was Burton built on Trent?* The answer is: to use the river's water in the town's brewing industry.

A. E. Housman (1859–1936)

To an Athlete Dying Young 1896

The time you won your town the race
We chaired you through the market-place;
Man and boy stood cheering by,
And home we brought you shoulder-high.

Today, the road all runners come,
Shoulder-high we bring you home,
And set you at your threshold down,
Townsman of a stiller town.

Smart lad, to slip betimes away
From fields where glory does not stay,
And early though the laurel grows
It withers quicker than the rose.

Eyes the shady night has shut
Cannot see the record cut,
And silence sounds no worse than cheers
After earth has stopped the ears.

Now you will not swell the rout
Of lads that wore their honors out,
Runners whom renown outran
And the name died before the man.

So set, before its echoes fade,
The fleet foot on the sill of shade,
And hold to the low lintel up
The still-defended challenge-cup.

And round that early-laureled head
Will flock to gaze the strengthless dead,
And find unwithered on its curls
The garland briefer than a girl's.

COMPARE:

"To an Athlete Dying Young" with "To the Memory of Mr. Oldham" by John Dryden (page 306).

Langston Hughes (1902–1967)

DREAM DEFERRED

1951

What happens to a dream deferred?

Does it dry up
like a raisin in the sun?
Or fester like a sore—
And then run?
Does it stink like rotten meat?
Or crust and sugar over—
like a syrupy sweet?

Maybe it just sags
like a heavy load.

Or does it explode?

COMPARE:

"Dream Deferred" with "Ballad of Birmingham" by Dudley Randall (page 354).

Langston Hughes (1902–1967)

SONG FOR A DARK GIRL

1927

Way Down South in Dixie
(Break the heart of me)
They hung my black young lover
To a cross roads tree.

Way Down South in Dixie
  (Bruised body high in air)
I asked the white Lord Jesus
  What was the use of prayer.

Way Down South in Dixie
  (Break the heart of me)
Love is a naked shadow
  On a gnarled and naked tree.

David Ignatow (b. 1914)

Get the Gasworks 1948

Get the gasworks into a poem,
and you've got the smoke and smokestacks,
the mottled red and yellow tenements,
and grimy kids who curse with the pungency
of the odor of gas. You've got America, boy.

Sketch in the river and barges,
all dirty and slimy.
How do the seagulls stay so white?
And always cawing like little mad geniuses?
You've got the kind of living
that makes the kind of thinking we do:
gaswork smokestack whistle tooting wisecracks.
They don't come because we like it that way,
but because we find it outside our window each morning,
in soot on the furniture,
and trucks carrying coal for gas,
the kid hot after the ball under the wheel.
He gets it over the belly, all right.
He dies there.

So the kids keep tossing the ball around
after the funeral.
So the cops keep chasing them,
so the mamas keep hollering,
and papa flings his newspaper outward,
in disgust with discipline.

Randall Jarrell (1914–1965)

The Death of the Ball Turret Gunner 1945

From my mother's sleep I fell into the State
And I hunched in its belly till my wet fur froze.
Six miles from earth, loosed from its dream of life,

I woke to black flak and the nightmare fighters.
When I died they washed me out of the turret with a hose.

THE DEATH OF THE BALL TURRET GUNNER. Jarrell has written: "A ball turret was a plexiglass sphere set into the belly of a B-17 or B-24, and inhabited by two .50 caliber machine-guns and one man, a short small man. When this gunner tracked with his machine-guns a fighter attacking his bomber from below, he revolved with the turret; hunched upside-down in his little sphere, he looked like the fetus in the womb. The fighters which attacked him were armed with cannon firing explosive shells. The hose was a steam hose."

COMPARE:

"The Death of the Ball Turret Gunner" with "Dulce et Decorum Est" by Wilfred Owen (page 29).

Randall Jarrell (1914–1965)

THE WOMAN AT THE WASHINGTON ZOO 1960

The saris go by me from the embassies.

Cloth from the moon. Cloth from another planet.
They look back at the leopard like the leopard.

And I. . . .
                    this print of mine, that has kept its color
Alive through so many cleanings; this dull null
Navy I wear to work, and wear from work, and so
To my bed, so to my grave, with no
Complaints, no comment: neither from my chief,
The Deputy Chief Assistant, nor his chief—
Only I complain. . . . this serviceable
Body that no sunlight dyes, no hand suffuses
But, dome-shadowed, withering among columns,
Wavy beneath fountains—small, far-off, shining
In the eyes of animals, these beings trapped
As I am trapped but not, themselves, the trap,
Aging, but without knowledge of their age,
Kept safe here, knowing not of death, for death—
Oh, bars of my own body, open, open!

The world goes by my cage and never sees me.
And there come not to me, as come to these,
The wild beasts, sparrows pecking the llamas' grain,
Pigeons settling on the bears' bread, buzzards
Tearing the meat the flies have clouded. . . .
                                                                        Vulture,
When you come for the white rat that the foxes left,
Take off the red helmet of your head, the black
Wings that have shadowed me, and step to me as man:
The wild brother at whose feet the white wolves fawn,
To whose hand of power the great lioness

Stalks, purring. . . .
You know what I was,
You see what I am: change me, change me!

John Keats (1795–1821)

Ode on a Grecian Urn 1820

Thou still unravished bride of quietness,
Thou foster-child of silence and slow time,
Sylvan historian, who canst thus express
A flowery tale more sweetly than our rhyme:
What leaf-fringed legend haunts about thy shape
Of deities or mortals, or of both,
In Tempe or the dales of Arcady?
What men or gods are these? What maidens loth?
What mad pursuit? What struggle to escape?
What pipes and timbrels? What wild ecstasy?

Heard melodies are sweet, but those unheard
Are sweeter; therefore, ye soft pipes, play on;
Not to the sensual° ear, but, more endeared, *physical*
Pipe to the spirit ditties of no tone:
Fair youth, beneath the trees, thou canst not leave
Thy song, nor ever can those trees be bare;
Bold Lover, never, never canst thou kiss,
Though winning near the goal—yet, do not grieve;
She cannot fade, though thou hast not thy bliss,
For ever wilt thou love, and she be fair!

Ah, happy, happy boughs! that cannot shed
Your leaves, nor ever bid the Spring adieu;
And, happy melodist, unweariѐd,
For ever piping songs for ever new;
More happy love! more happy, happy love!
For ever warm and still to be enjoyed,
For ever panting, and for ever young;
All breathing human passion far above,
That leaves a heart high-sorrowful and cloyed,
A burning forehead, and a parching tongue.

Who are these coming to the sacrifice?
To what green altar, O mysterious priest,
Lead'st thou that heifer lowing at the skies,
And all her silken flanks with garlands drest?
What little town by river or sea shore,
Or mountain-built with peaceful citadel,
Is emptied of this folk, this pious morn?
And, little town, thy streets for evermore
Will silent be; and not a soul to tell
Why thou art desolate, can e'er return.

O Attic shape! Fair attitude! with brede° *design*
Of marble men and maidens overwrought,
With forest branches and the trodden weed;
Thou, silent form, dost tease us out of thought
As doth Eternity: Cold Pastoral!
When old age shall this generation waste,
Thou shalt remain, in midst of other woe
Than ours, a friend to man, to whom thou say'st,
Beauty is truth, truth beauty,—that is all
Ye know on earth, and all ye need to know.

ODE ON A GRECIAN URN. An **ode** was originally a song in praise of gods, heroes, or victorious athletes, and in the hands of the Greek poet Pindar (522–443 B.C.) is laid out in intricate stanzas, bound by formal rules. For nineteenth-century English Romantic poets Keats, Wordsworth, and Shelley, the ode is a less rule-bound, more personal thing: in general, a lyric poem of a page or more, with a serious, lofty tone, in which the poet sets forth a thoughtful meditation. For the Roman poet Horace (see page 238) an ode is a lyric not necessarily lofty: it may be a drinking song. 7. *Tempe, dales of Arcady:* valleys in Greece. 41. *Attic:* Athenian, possessing classical simplicity and grace. 49–50: If Keats had put the urn's words in quotation marks, critics might have been spared much ink. Does the urn say just "beauty is truth, truth beauty," or does its statement take in the whole of the last two lines?

COMPARE:

"Ode on a Grecian Urn" with "Lapis Lazuli" by William Butler Yeats (page 394) and "Anecdote of the Jar" by Wallace Stevens (page 213). Then compare "Ode on a Grecian Urn summarized" by Desmond Skirrow (page 243).

John Keats (1795–1821)

ON FIRST LOOKING INTO CHAPMAN'S HOMER — 1816

Much have I traveled in the realms of gold,
And many goodly states and kingdoms seen;
Round many western islands have I been
Which bards in fealty to Apollo hold.
Oft of one wide expanse had I been told
That deep-browed Homer ruled as his demesne°, *domain*
Yet did I never breathe its pure serene
Till I heard Chapman speak out loud and bold.
Then felt I like some watcher of the skies
When a new planet swims into his ken;
Or like stout Cortez when with eagle eyes
He stared at the Pacific—and all his men
Looked at each other with a wild surmise—
Silent, upon a peak in Darien.

ON FIRST LOOKING INTO CHAPMAN'S HOMER. When one evening in October 1816 Keats's friend and former teacher Cowden Clarke introduced the young poet to George Chapman's vigorous Elizabethan translations of the *Iliad* and the *Odyssey*, Keats stayed up all night reading and discussing them in high excitement; then went home at dawn to compose this sonnet, which Clarke received at his breakfast table. 4. *fealty:* in feudalism, the loyalty of a vassal to his lord; *Apollo:* classical god of poetic inspiration. 11. *stout Cortez:* the best-known boner in English poetry. (What Spanish explorer *was* the first European to view the Pacific?) 14. *Darien:* old name for the Isthmus of Panama.

John Keats (1795–1821)

To Autumn

1820

I

Season of mists and mellow fruitfulness,
  Close bosom-friend of the maturing sun;
Conspiring with him how to load and bless
  With fruit the vines that round the thatch-eves run;
To bend with apples the mossed cottage-trees,
  And fill all fruit with ripeness to the core;
    To swell the gourd, and plump the hazel shells
With a sweet kernel; to set budding more,
  And still more, later flowers for the bees,
  Until they think warm days will never cease,
    For Summer has o'er-brimmed their clammy cells.

II

Who hath not seen thee oft amid thy store?
  Sometimes whoever seeks abroad may find
Thee sitting careless on a granary floor,
  Thy hair soft-lifted by the winnowing wind;
Or on a half-reaped furrow sound asleep,
  Drowsed with the fume of poppies, while thy hook
    Spares the next swath and all its twinèd flowers:
And sometimes like a gleaner thou dost keep
  Steady thy laden head across a brook;
  Or by a cider-press, with patient look,
    Thou watchest the last oozings hours by hours.

III

Where are the songs of Spring? Ay, where are they?
  Think not of them, thou hast thy music too,—
While barrèd clouds bloom the soft-dying day,
  And touch the stubble-plains with rosy hue;
Then in a wailful choir the small gnats mourn
  Among the river sallows°, borne aloft *willows*
    Or sinking as the light wind lives or dies;
And full-grown lambs loud bleat from hilly bourn;
  Hedge-crickets sing; and now with treble soft
  The red-breast whistles from a garden-croft°; *garden plot*
    And gathering swallows twitter in the skies.

Compare:

"To Autumn" with "In the Elegy Season" by Richard Wilbur (page 41).

Maxine Kumin (b. 1925)

Woodchucks

1972

Gassing the woodchucks didn't turn out right.
The knockout bomb from the Feed and Grain Exchange
was featured as merciful, quick at the bone
and the case we had against them was airtight,
both exits shoehorned shut with puddingstone,
but they had a sub-sub-basement out of range.

Next morning they turned up again, no worse
for the cyanide than we for our cigarettes
and state-store Scotch, all of us up to scratch.
They brought down the marigolds as a matter of course
and then took over the vegetable patch
nipping the broccoli shoots, beheading the carrots.

The food from our mouths, I said, righteously thrilling
to the feel of the .22, the bullets' neat noses.
I, a lapsed pacifist fallen from grace
puffed with Darwinian pieties for killing,
now drew a bead on the littlest woodchuck's face.
He died down in the everbearing roses.

Ten minutes later I dropped the mother. She
flipflopped in the air and fell, her needle teeth
still hooked in a leaf of early Swiss chard.
Another baby next. O one-two-three
the murderer inside me rose up hard,
the hawkeye killer came on stage forthwith.

There's one chuck left. Old wily fellow, he keeps
me cocked and ready day after day after day.
All night I hunt his humped-up form. I dream
I sight along the barrel in my sleep.
If only they'd all consented to die unseen
gassed underground the quiet Nazi way.

Compare:

"Woodchucks" with "The Bull Calf" by Irving Layton (page 340).

Philip Larkin (b. 1922)

Vers de Société

1974

My wife and I have asked a crowd of craps
To come and waste their time and ours: perhaps
You'd care to join us? In a pig's arse, friend.
Day comes to an end.

The gas fire breathes, the trees are darkly swayed.
And so *Dear Warlock-Williams: I'm afraid—*

Funny how hard it is to be alone.
I could spend half my evenings, if I wanted,
Holding a glass of washing sherry, canted
Over to catch the drivel of some bitch
Who's read nothing but *Which;*
Just think of all the spare time that has flown

Straight into nothingness by being filled
With forks and faces, rather than repaid
Under a lamp, hearing the noise of wind,
And looking out to see the moon thinned
To an air-sharpened blade.
A life, and yet how sternly it's instilled

All solitude is selfish. No one now
Believes the hermit with his gown and dish
Talking to God (who's gone too); the big wish
Is to have people nice to you, which means
Doing it back somehow.
Virtue is social. Are, then, these routines

Playing at goodness, like going to church?
Something that bores us, something we don't do well
(Asking that ass about his fool research)
But try to feel, because, however crudely,
It shows us what should be?
Too subtle, that. Too decent, too. Oh, hell,

Only the young can be alone freely.
The time is shorter now for company,
And sitting by a lamp more often brings
Not peace, but other things.
Beyond the light stand failure and remorse.
Whispering *Dear Warlock-Williams: Why, of course—*

VERS DE SOCIÉTÉ. The title is a French term for light verse, especially that written for social occasions. 9. *washing sherry:* sherry the quality of washing liquid, or dish detergent. 11. *Which:* British equivalent of *Consumer Reports.*

D. H. Lawrence (1885–1930)

A YOUTH MOWING 1917

There are four men mowing down by the Isar;
I can hear the swish of the scythe-strokes, four
Sharp breaths taken: yea, and I
Am sorry for what's in store.

The first man out of the four that's mowing
Is mine, I claim him once and for all;
Though it's sorry I am, on his young feet, knowing
None of the trouble he's led to stall.

As he sees me bringing the dinner, he lifts
His head as proud as a deer that looks
Shoulder-deep out of the corn; and wipes
His scythe-blade bright, unhooks

The scythe-stone and over the stubble to me.
Lad, thou hast gotten a child in me,
Laddie, a man thou'lt ha'e to be,
Yea, though I'm sorry for thee.

A YOUTH MOWING. 1. *Isar:* river in Austria and Germany that flows into the Danube.

Irving Layton (b. 1912)

THE BULL CALF

1959

The thing could barely stand. Yet taken
from his mother and the barn smells
he still impressed with his pride,
with the promise of sovereignty in the way
his head moved to take us in.
The fierce sunlight tugging the maize from the ground
licked at his shapely flanks.
He was too young for all that pride.
I thought of the deposed Richard II.

"No money in bull calves," Freeman had said.
The visiting clergyman rubbed the nostrils
now snuffing pathetically at the windless day.
"A pity," he sighed.
My gaze slipped off his hat toward the empty sky
that circled over the black knot of men,
over us and the calf waiting for the first blow.

Struck,
the bull calf drew in his thin forelegs
as if gathering strength for a mad rush . . .
tottered . . . raised his darkening eyes to us,
and I saw we were at the far end
of his frightened look, growing smaller and smaller
till we were only the ponderous mallet
that flicked his bleeding ear
and pushed him over on his side, stiffly,
like a block of wood.

Below the hill's crest
the river snuffled on the improvised beach.
We dug a deep pit and threw the dead calf into it.
It made a wet sound, a sepulchral gurgle,
as the warm sides bulged and flattened.
Settled, the bull calf lay as if asleep,
one foreleg over the other,
bereft of pride and so beautiful now,
without movement, perfectly still in the cool pit,
I turned away and wept.

COMPARE:

"The Bull Calf" with "Woodchucks" by Maxine Kumin (page 338).

Denise Levertov (b. 1923)

SUNDAY AFTERNOON 1958

After the First Communion
and the banquet of mangoes and
bridal cake, the young daughters
of the coffee merchant lay down
for a long siesta, and their white dresses
lay beside them in quietness
and the white veils floated
in their dreams as the flies buzzed.
But as the afternoon
burned to a close they rose
and ran about the neighborhood
among the halfbuilt villas
alive, alive, kicking a basketball, wearing
other new dresses, of bloodred velvet.

COMPARE:

"Sunday Afternoon" with "Disillusionment of Ten O'Clock" by Wallace Stevens (page 63).

Philip Levine (b. 1928)

TO A CHILD TRAPPED IN A BARBER SHOP 1966

You've gotten in through the transom
        and you can't get out
till Monday morning or, worse,
        till the cops come.

That six-year-old red face
    calling for mama
is yours; it won't help you
    because your case

is closed forever, hopeless.
    So don't drink
the Lucky Tiger, don't
    fill up on grease

because that makes it a lot worse,
    that makes it a crime
against property and the state
    and that costs time.

We've all been here before,
    we took our turn
under the electric storm
    of the vibrator

and stiffened our wills to meet
    the close clippers
and heard the true blade mowing
    back and forth

on a strip of dead skin,
    and we stopped crying.
You think your life is over?
    It's just begun.

Robert Lowell (1917–1977)

Skunk Hour 1959

For Elizabeth Bishop

Nautilus Island's hermit
heiress still lives through winters in her Spartan cottage;
her sheep still graze above the sea.
Her son's a bishop. Her farmer
is first selectman in our village;
she's in her dotage.

Thirsting for
the hierarchic privacy
of Queen Victoria's century,
she buys up all
the eyesores facing her shore,
and lets them fall.

The season's ill—
we've lost our summer millionaire,
who seemed to leap from an L. L. Bean

catalogue. His nine-knot yawl
was auctioned off to lobstermen.
A red fox stain covers Blue Hill.

And now our fairy
decorator brightens his shop for fall;
his fishnet's filled with orange cork,
orange, his cobbler's bench and awl;
there is no money in his work,
he'd rather marry.

One dark night,
my Tudor Ford climbed the hill's skull;
I watched for love-cars. Lights turned down,
they lay together, hull to hull,
where the graveyard shelves on the town. . . .
My mind's not right.

A car radio bleats,
"Love, O careless Love. . . ." I hear
my ill-spirit sob in each blood cell,
as if my hand were at its throat. . . .
I myself am hell;
nobody's here—

only skunks, that search
in the moonlight for a bite to eat.
They march on their soles up Main Street:
white stripes, moonstruck eyes' red fire
under the chalk-dry and spar spire
of the Trinitarian Church.

I stand on top
of our back steps and breathe the rich air—
a mother skunk with her column of kittens swills the garbage pail.
She jabs her wedge-head in a cup
of sour cream, drops her ostrich tail,
and will not scare.

COMPARE:

"Skunk Hour" with "The Peace of Wild Things" by Wendell Berry (page 290).

Christopher Marlowe (1564–1593)

THE PASSIONATE SHEPHERD TO HIS LOVE 1600

Come live with me and be my love,
And we will all the pleasures prove
That valleys, groves, hills, and fields,
Woods, or steepy mountain yields.

And we will sit upon the rocks,
Seeing the shepherds feed their flocks
By shallow rivers, to whose falls
Melodious birds sing madrigals.

And I will make thee beds of roses
And a thousand fragrant posies,
A cap of flowers and a kirtle° *skirt*
Embroidered all with leaves of myrtle;

A gown made of the finest wool
Which from our pretty lambs we pull;
Fair-linèd slippers for the cold,
With buckles of the purest gold;

A belt of straw and ivy buds,
With coral clasps and amber studs.
And if these pleasures may thee move,
Come live with me and be my love.

The shepherds' swains shall dance and sing
For thy delight each May morning.
If these delights thy mind may move,
Then live with me and be my love.

COMPARE:

"The Passionate Shepherd to His Love" with "The Bait" by John Donne (page 303).

George Meredith (1828–1909)

LUCIFER IN STARLIGHT

1883

On a starred night Prince Lucifer uprose,
  Tired of his dark dominion, swung the fiend
  Above the rolling ball in cloud part screened,
Where sinners hugged their specter of repose.
Poor prey to his hot fit of pride were those.
  And now upon his western wing he leaned,
  Now his huge bulk o'er Afric's sands careened,
Now the black planet shadowed Arctic snows.
Soaring through wider zones that pricked his scars
  With memory of the old revolt from Awe,
He reached a middle height, and at the stars,
Which are the brain of heaven, he looked, and sank.
Around the ancient track marched, rank on rank,
  The army of unalterable law.

James Merrill (b. 1926)

Laboratory Poem 1958

Charles used to watch Naomi, taking heart
And a steel saw, open up turtles, live.
While she swore they felt nothing, he would gag
At blood, at the blind twitching, even after
The murky dawn of entrails cleared, revealing
Contours he knew, egg-yellows like lamps paling.

Well then. She carried off the beating heart
To the kymograph and rigged it there, a rag
In fitful wind, now made to strain, now stopped
By her solutions tonic or malign
Alternately in which it would be steeped.
What the heart bore, she noted on a chart,

For work did not stop only with the heart.
He thought of certain human hearts, their climb
Through violence into exquisite disciplines
Of which, as it now appeared, they all expired.
Soon she would fetch another and start over,
Easy in the presence of her lover.

Laboratory Poem. 8. *kymograph:* device to record wavelike motions or pulsations on a piece of paper fastened to a revolving drum.

W. S. Merwin (b. 1927)

For the Anniversary of My Death 1967

Every year without knowing it I have passed the day
When the last fires will wave to me
And the silence will set out
Tireless traveller
Like the beam of a lightless star

Then I will no longer
Find myself in life as in a strange garment
Surprised at the earth
And the love of one woman
And the shamelessness of men
As today writing after three days of rain
Hearing the wren sing and the falling cease
And bowing not knowing to what

Compare:

"For the Anniversary of My Death" with "Twenty-four years" by Dylan Thomas (page 380).

John Milton (1608–1674)

When I consider how my light is spent (1655?)

When I consider how my light is spent,
   Ere half my days in this dark world and wide,
   And that one talent which is death to hide
Lodged with me useless, though my soul more bent
To serve therewith my Maker, and present
   My true account, lest He returning chide;
   "Doth God exact day-labor, light denied?"
I fondly° ask. But Patience, to prevent *foolishly*
That murmur, soon replies, "God doth not need
   Either man's work or His own gifts. Who best
   Bear His mild yoke, they serve Him best. His state
Is kingly: thousands at His bidding speed,
   And post o'er land and ocean without rest;
   They also serve who only stand and wait."

When I consider how my light is spent. 1. *my light is spent:* Milton had become blind. 3. *that one talent:* For Christ's parable of the talents (measures of money), see Matthew 25:14–30.

Marianne Moore (1887–1972)

The Mind is an Enchanting Thing 1944

is an enchanted thing
      like the glaze on a
katydid-wing
            subdivided by sun
            till the nettings are legion.
Like Gieseking playing Scarlatti;

like the apteryx-awl
      as a beak, or the
kiwi's rain-shawl
            of haired feathers, the mind
            feeling its way as though blind,
walks along with its eyes on the ground.

It has memory's ear
      that can hear without
having to hear.
            Like the gyroscope's fall,
            truly unequivocal
because trued by regnant certainty,

it is a power of
      strong enchantment. It
is like the dove-

neck animated by
sun; it is memory's eye;
it's conscientious inconsistency.

It tears off the veil; tears
the temptation, the
mist the heart wears,
from its eyes,—if the heart
has a face; it takes apart
dejection. It's fire in the dove-neck's

iridescence; in the
inconsistencies
of Scarlatti.
Unconfusion submits
its confusion to proof; it's
not a Herod's oath that cannot change.

THE MIND IS AN ENCHANTING THING. 6. *Gieseking . . . Scarlatti:* Walter Gieseking (1895–1956), German pianist, was a celebrated performer of the difficult sonatas of Italian composer Domenico Scarlatti (1685–1757). 7. *apteryx-awl:* awl-shaped beak of the apteryx, one of the kiwi family. (An awl is a pointed tool for piercing wood or leather.) 36. *Herod's oath:* King Herod's order condemning to death all infants in Bethlehem (Matthew 2:1–16). In one medieval English version of the Herod story, a pageant play, the king causes the death of his own child by refusing to withdraw his command.

Howard Nemerov (b. 1920)

STORM WINDOWS 1958

People are putting up storm windows now,
Or were, this morning, until the heavy rain
Drove them indoors. So, coming home at noon,
I saw storm windows lying on the ground,
Frame-full of rain; through the water and glass
I saw the crushed grass, how it seemed to stream
Away in lines like seaweed on the tide
Or blades of wheat leaning under the wind.
The ripple and splash of rain on the blurred glass
Seemed that it briefly said, as I walked by,
Something I should have liked to say to you,
Something . . . the dry grass bent under the pane
Brimful of bouncing water . . . something of
A swaying clarity which blindly echoes
This lonely afternoon of memories
And missed desires, while the wintry rain
(Unspeakable, the distance in the mind!)
Runs on the standing windows and away.

John Frederick Nims (b. 1914)

Love Poem

1947

My clumsiest dear, whose hands shipwreck vases,
At whose quick touch all glasses chip and ring,
Whose palms are bulls in china, burs in linen,
And have no cunning with any soft thing

Except all ill-at-ease fidgeting people:
The refugee uncertain at the door
You make at home; deftly you steady
The drunk clambering on his undulant floor.

Unpredictable dear, the taxi drivers' terror,
Shrinking from far headlights pale as a dime
Yet leaping before red apoplectic streetcars—
Misfit in any space. And never on time.

A wrench in clocks and the solar system. Only
With words and people and love you move at ease.
In traffic of wit expertly manoeuvre
And keep us, all devotion, at your knees.

Forgetting your coffee spreading on our flannel,
Your lipstick grinning on our coat,
So gayly in love's unbreakable heaven
Our souls on glory of spilt bourbon float.

Be with me, darling, early and late. Smash glasses—
I will study wry music for your sake.
For should your hands drop white and empty
All the toys of the world would break.

Compare:

"Love Poem" with "Love Song: I and Thou" by Alan Dugan (page 702).

Sylvia Plath (1932–1963)

Daddy

1965

You do not do, you do not do
Any more, black shoe
In which I have lived like a foot
For thirty years, poor and white,
Barely daring to breathe or Achoo.

Daddy, I have had to kill you.
You died before I had time—

Marble-heavy, a bag full of God,
Ghastly statue with one grey toe
Big as a Frisco seal

And a head in the freakish Atlantic
Where it pours bean green over blue
In the waters off beautiful Nauset.
I used to pray to recover you.
Ach, du.

In the German tongue, in the Polish town
Scraped flat by the roller
Of wars, wars, wars.
But the name of the town is common.
My Polack friend

Says there are a dozen or two.
So I never could tell where you
Put your foot, your root,
I never could talk to you.
The tongue stuck in my jaw.

It stuck in a barb wire snare.
Ich, ich, ich, ich,
I could hardly speak.
I thought every German was you.
And the language obscene

An engine, an engine
Chuffing me off like a Jew.
A Jew to Dachau, Auschwitz, Belsen.
I began to talk like a Jew.
I think I may well be a Jew.

The snows of the Tyrol, the clear beer of Vienna
Are not very pure or true.
With my gypsy ancestress and my weird luck
And my Taroc pack and my Taroc pack
I may be a bit of a Jew.

I have always been scared of *you,*
With your Luftwaffe, your gobbledygoo.
And your neat moustache
And your Aryan eye, bright blue.
Panzer-man, panzer-man, O You—

Not God but a swastika
So black no sky could squeak through.
Every woman adores a Fascist,
The boot in the face, the brute
Brute heart of a brute like you.

You stand at the blackboard, daddy,
In the picture I have of you,

A cleft in your chin instead of your foot
But no less a devil for that, no not
Any less the black man who

Bit my pretty red heart in two.
I was ten when they buried you.
At twenty I tried to die
And get back, back, back at you.
I thought even the bones will do.

But they pulled me out of the sack,
And they stuck me together with glue.
And then I knew what to do.
I made a model of you,
A man in black with a Meinkampf look

And a love of the rack and the screw.
And I said I do, I do.
So daddy, I'm finally through.
The black telephone's off at the root,
The voices just can't worm through.

If I've killed one man, I've killed two—
The vampire who said he was you
And drank my blood for a year,
Seven years, if you want to know.
Daddy, you can lie back now.

There's a stake in your fat black heart
And the villagers never liked you.
They are dancing and stamping on you.
They always *knew* it was you.
Daddy, daddy, you bastard, I'm through.

DADDY. Introducing this poem in a reading, Sylvia Plath remarked:

The poem is spoken by a girl with an Electra complex. Her father died while she thought he was God. Her case is complicated by the fact that her father was also a Nazi and her mother very possibly part Jewish. In the daughter the two strains marry and paralyze each other—she has to act out the awful little allegory before she is free of it.

(Quoted by A. Alvarez, *Beyond All This Fiddle,* New York, 1971.) In some details "Daddy" is autobiography: the poet's father, Otto Plath, a German, had come to the United States from Grabow, Poland. He had died following amputation of a gangrened foot and leg, when Sylvia was eight years old. Politically, Otto Plath was a Republican, not a Nazi; but was apparently a somewhat domineering head of the household. (See the recollections of the poet's mother, Aurelia Schober Plath, in her edition of *Letters Home* by Sylvia Plath, New York, 1975.) 15. *Ach, du:* Oh, you. 27. *Ich, ich, ich, ich:* I, I, I, I. 51. *blackboard:* Otto Plath had been a professor of biology at Boston University. 65. *Meinkampf:* Adolf Hitler entitled his autobiography *Mein Kampf* ("My Struggle").

COMPARE:

"Daddy" with "American Primitive" by William Jay Smith (page 766).

Sylvia Plath (1932–1963)

MORNING SONG 1965

Love set you going like a fat gold watch.
The midwife slapped your footsoles, and your bald cry
Took its place among the elements.

Our voices echo, magnifying your arrival. New statue.
In a drafty museum, your nakedness
Shadows our safety. We stand round blankly as walls.

I'm no more your mother
Than the cloud that distils a mirror to reflect its own slow
Effacement at the wind's hand.

All night your moth-breath
Flickers among the flat pink roses. I wake to listen:
A far sea moves in my ear.

One cry, and I stumble from bed, cow-heavy and floral
In my Victorian nightgown.
Your mouth opens clean as a cat's. The window square

Whitens and swallows its dull stars. And now you try
Your handful of notes;
The clear vowels rise like balloons.

COMPARE:

"Morning Song" with "Preface to a Twenty Volume Suicide Note" by Amiri Baraka (page 290) and "My Son, My Executioner" by Donald Hall (page 235).

Ezra Pound (1885–1972)

THE RIVER-MERCHANT'S WIFE: A LETTER 1915

While my hair was still cut straight across my forehead
I played about the front gate, pulling flowers.
You came by on bamboo stilts, playing horse,
You walked about my seat, playing with blue plums.
And we went on living in the village of Chokan:
Two small people, without dislike or suspicion.
At fourteen I married My Lord you.
I never laughed, being bashful.
Lowering my head, I looked at the wall.
Called to, a thousand times, I never looked back.

At fifteen I stopped scowling,
I desired my dust to be mingled with yours
Forever and forever and forever.
Why should I climb the lookout?

At sixteen you departed,
You went into far Ku-to-yen, by the river of swirling eddies,
And you have been gone five months.
The monkeys make sorrowful noise overhead.

You dragged your feet when you went out.
By the gate now, the moss is grown, the different mosses,
Too deep to clear them away!
The leaves fall early this autumn, in wind.
The paired butterflies are already yellow with August
Over the grass in the West garden;
They hurt me. I grow older.
If you are coming down through the narrows of the river Kiang,
Please let me know beforehand,
And I will come out to meet you
        As far as Cho-fu-sa.

THE RIVER-MERCHANT'S WIFE: A LETTER. A free translation from the Chinese poet Li Po (eighth century).

Ezra Pound (1885–1972)

THE SEAFARER 1912

From the Anglo-Saxon

May I for my own self song's truth reckon,
Journey's jargon, how I in harsh days
Hardship endured oft.
Bitter breast-cares have I abided,
Known on my keel many a care's hold,
And dire sea-surge, and there I oft spent
Narrow nightwatch nigh the ship's head
While she tossed close to cliffs. Coldly afflicted,
My feet were by frost benumbed.
Chill its chains are; chafing sighs
Hew my heart round and hunger begot
Mere-weary mood. Lest man know not
That he on dry land loveliest liveth,
List how I, care-wretched, on ice-cold sea,
Weathered the winter, wretched outcast
Deprived of my kinsmen;
Hung with hard ice-flakes, where hail-scur flew,
There I heard naught save the harsh sea
And ice-cold wave, at whiles the swan cries,
Did for my games the gannet's clamour,
Sea-fowls' loudness was for me laughter,
The mews' singing all my mead-drink.
Storms, on the stone-cliffs beaten, fell on the stern

In icy feathers; full oft the eagle screamed
With spray on his pinion.
Not any protector
May make merry man faring needy.
This he little believes, who aye in winsome life
Abides 'mid burghers some heavy business,
Wealthy and wine-flushed, how I weary oft
Must bide above brine.
Neareth nightshade, snoweth from north,
Frost froze the land, hail fell on earth then,
Corn of the coldest. Nathless° there knocketh now *nevertheless*
The heart's thought that I on high streams
The salt-wavy tumult traverse alone.
Moaneth alway my mind's lust
That I fare forth, that I afar hence
Seek out a foreign fastness.
For this there's no mood-lofty man over earth's midst,
Not though he be given his good, but will have in his youth greed;
Nor his deed to the daring, nor his king to the faithful
But shall have his sorrow for sea-fare
Whatever his lord will.
He hath not heart for harping, nor in ring-having
Nor winsomeness to wife, nor world's delight
Nor any whit else save the wave's slash,
Yet longing comes upon him to fare forth on the water.
Bosque° taketh blossom, cometh beauty of berries, *grove or thicket*
Fields to fairness, land fares brisker,
All this admonisheth man eager of mood,
The heart turns to travel so that he then thinks
On flood-ways to be far departing.
Cuckoo calleth with gloomy crying,
He singeth summerward, bodeth sorrow,
The bitter heart's blood. Burgher knows not—
He the prosperous man—what some perform
Where wandering them widest draweth.
So that but now my heart burst from my breastlock,
My mood 'mid the mere-flood,
Over the whale's acre, would wander wide.
On earth's shelter cometh oft to me,
Eager and ready, the crying lone-flyer,
Whets for the whale-path the heart irresistibly,
O'er tracks of ocean; seeing that anyhow
My lord deems to me this dead life
On loan and on land, I believe not
That any earth-weal eternal standeth
Save there be somewhat calamitous
That, ere a man's tide go, turn it to twain.
Disease or oldness or sword-hate
Beats out the breath from doom-gripped body.
And for this, every earl whatever, for those speaking after—

Laud of the living, boasteth some last word,
That he will work ere he pass onward,
Frame on the fair earth 'gainst foes his malice,
Daring ado, . . .
So that all men shall honour him after
And his laud beyond them remain 'mid the English,
Aye, for ever, a lasting life's-blast,
Delight 'mid the doughty.
                                        Days little durable,
And all arrogance of earthen riches,
There come now no kings nor Cæsars
Nor gold-giving lords like those gone.
Howe'er in mirth most magnified,
Whoe'er lived in life most lordliest,
Drear all this excellence, delights undurable!
Waneth the watch, but the world holdeth.
Tomb hideth trouble. The blade is layed low.
Earthly glory ageth and seareth.
No man at all going the earth's gait,
But age fares against him, his face paleth,
Grey-haired he groaneth, knows gone companions,
Lordly men, are to earth o'ergiven,
Nor may he then the flesh-cover, whose life ceaseth,
Nor eat the sweet nor feel the sorry,
Nor stir hand nor think in mid heart,
And though he strew the grave with gold,
His born brothers, their buried bodies
Be an unlikely treasure hoard.

THE SEAFARER. A free translation of an Anglo-Saxon (or Old English) poem written before 1000 A.D. Pound's version affords us a sense of the rhythm and sound of Old English verse, at the expense of literal accuracy. In line 1, for instance, Pound gives us *reckon* for *wrecan* ("to make"); in line 7, *narrow nightwatch* for *nearo nihtwaco* ("on a hard, demanding watch by night"); in line 12, *mere-weary mood* for *merewerges mod* ("soul wearied by the sea"). He accurately renders several **kennings,** or poetic synonyms conventional in Old English verse (*whale-path* for sea, *flesh-cover* for body), and he coins others (*hail-scur, earth-weal*). For the meter of an Old English alliterative line, see page 126.

COMPARE:

"The Seafarer" with the ballad of "Sir Patrick Spence" (page 281) and "Ulysses" by Alfred, Lord Tennyson (page 377).

Dudley Randall (b. 1914)

BALLAD OF BIRMINGHAM 1966

(On the Bombing of a Church in
Birmingham, Alabama, 1963)

"Mother dear, may I go downtown
Instead of out to play,

And march the streets of Birmingham
In a Freedom March today?"

"No, baby, no, you may not go,
For the dogs are fierce and wild,
And clubs and hoses, guns and jail
Aren't good for a little child."

"But, mother, I won't be alone.
Other children will go with me,
And march the streets of Birmingham
To make our country free."

"No, baby, no, you may not go,
For I fear those guns will fire.
But you may go to church instead
And sing in the children's choir."

She has combed and brushed her night-dark hair,
And bathed rose petal sweet,
And drawn white gloves on her small brown hands,
And white shoes on her feet.

The mother smiled to know her child
Was in the sacred place,
But that smile was the last smile
To come upon her face.

For when she heard the explosion,
Her eyes grew wet and wild.
She raced through the streets of Birmingham
Calling for her child.

She clawed through bits of glass and brick,
Then lifted out a shoe.
"O here's the shoe my baby wore,
But, baby, where are you?"

COMPARE:

"Ballad of Birmingham" with "Song for a Dark Girl" by Langston Hughes (page 332). Compare it as a ballad with "Edward" (page 280) or "The Cruel Mother" (page 105).

John Crowe Ransom (1888–1974)

JANET WAKING 1927

Beautifully Janet slept
Till it was deeply morning. She woke then
And thought about her dainty-feathered hen,
To see how it had kept.

One kiss she gave her mother,
Only a small one gave she to her daddy
Who would have kissed each curl of his shining baby;
No kiss at all for her brother.

"Old Chucky, Old Chucky!" she cried,
Running on little pink feet upon the grass
To Chucky's house, and listening. But alas,
Her Chucky had died.

It was a transmogrifying° bee *change-working*
Came droning down on Chucky's old bald head
And sat and put the poison. It scarcely bled,
But how exceedingly

And purply did the knot
Swell with the venom and communicate
Its rigor! Now the poor comb stood up straight
But Chucky did not.

So there was Janet
Kneeling on the wet grass, crying her brown hen
(Translated far beyond the daughters of men)
To rise and walk upon it.

And weeping fast as she had breath
Janet implored us, "Wake her from her sleep!"
And would not be instructed in how deep
Was the forgetful kingdom of death.

COMPARE:

"Janet Waking" with "Spring and Fall" by Gerard Manley Hopkins (page 328).

Henry Reed (b. 1914)

NAMING OF PARTS 1946

Today we have naming of parts. Yesterday,
We had daily cleaning. And tomorrow morning,
We shall have what to do after firing. But today,
Today we have naming of parts. Japonica
Glistens like coral in all of the neighboring gardens,
        And today we have naming of parts.

This is the lower sling swivel. And this
Is the upper sling swivel, whose use you will see,
When you are given your slings. And this is the piling swivel,
Which in your case you have not got. The branches
Hold in the gardens their silent, eloquent gestures,
        Which in our case we have not got.

This is the safety-catch, which is always released
With an easy flick of the thumb. And please do not let me
See anyone using his finger. You can do it quite easy
If you have any strength in your thumb. The blossoms
Are fragile and motionless, never letting anyone see
Any of them using their finger.

And this you can see is the bolt. The purpose of this
Is to open the breech, as you see. We can slide it
Rapidly backwards and forwards: we call this
Easing the spring. And rapidly backwards and forwards
The early bees are assaulting and fumbling the flowers:
They call it easing the Spring.

They call it easing the Spring: it is perfectly easy
If you have any strength in your thumb: like the bolt,
And the breech, and the cocking-piece, and the point of balance,
Which in our case we have not got; and the almond-blossom
Silent in all of the gardens and the bees going backwards and forwards,
For today we have naming of parts.

COMPARE:

"Naming of Parts" with "The Fury of Aerial Bombardment" by Richard Eberhart (page 55).

Adrienne Rich (b. 1929)

AUNT JENNIFER'S TIGERS 1951

Aunt Jennifer's tigers prance across a screen,
Bright topaz denizens of a world of green.
They do not fear the men beneath the tree;
They pace in sleek chivalric certainty.

Aunt Jennifer's fingers fluttering through her wool
Find even the ivory needle hard to pull.
The massive weight of Uncle's wedding band
Sits heavily upon Aunt Jennifer's hand.

When Aunt is dead, her terrified hands will lie
Still ringed with ordeals she was mastered by.
The tigers in the panel that she made
Will go on prancing, proud and unafraid.

Adrienne Rich (b. 1929)

DIVING INTO THE WRECK 1973

First having read the book of myths,
and loaded the camera,

and checked the edge of the knife-blade,
I put on
the body-armor of black rubber
the absurd flippers
the grave and awkward mask.
I am having to do this
not like Cousteau with his
assiduous team
aboard the sun-flooded schooner
but here alone.

There is a ladder.
The ladder is always there
hanging innocently
close to the side of the schooner.
We know what it is for,
we who have used it.
Otherwise
it's a piece of maritime floss
some sundry equipment.

I go down.
Rung after rung and still
the oxygen immerses me
the blue light
the clear atoms
of our human air.
I go down.
My flippers cripple me,
I crawl like an insect down the ladder
and there is no one
to tell me when the ocean
will begin.

First the air is blue and then
it is bluer and then green and then
black I am blacking out and yet
my mask is powerful
it pumps my blood with power
the sea is another story
the sea is not a question of power
I have to learn alone
to turn my body without force
in the deep element.

And now: it is easy to forget
what I came for
among so many who have always
lived here
swaying their crenellated fans
between the reefs

and besides
you breathe differently down here.

I came to explore the wreck.
The words are purposes.
The words are maps.
I came to see the damage that was done
and the treasures that prevail.
I stroke the beam of my lamp
slowly along the flank
of something more permanent
than fish or weed

the thing I came for:
the wreck and not the story of the wreck
the thing itself and not the myth
the drowned face always staring
toward the sun
the evidence of damage
worn by salt and sway into this threadbare beauty
the ribs of the disaster
curving their assertion
among the tentative haunters.

This is the place.
And I am here, the mermaid whose dark hair
streams black, the merman in his armored body
We circle silently
about the wreck
we dive into the hold.
I am she: I am he

whose drowned face sleeps with open eyes
whose breasts still bear the stress
whose silver, copper, vermeil cargo lies
obscurely inside barrels
half-wedged and left to rot
we are the half-destroyed instruments
that once held to a course
the water-eaten log
the fouled compass

We are, I am, you are
by cowardice or courage
the one who find our way
back to this scene
carrying a knife, a camera
a book of myths
in which
our names do not appear.

Edwin Arlington Robinson (1869–1935)

MR. FLOOD'S PARTY 1921

Old Eben Flood, climbing alone one night
Over the hill between the town below
And the forsaken upland hermitage
That held as much as he should ever know
On earth again of home, paused warily.
The road was his with not a native near;
And Eben, having leisure, said aloud,
For no man else in Tilbury Town to hear:

"Well, Mr. Flood, we have the harvest moon
Again, and we may not have many more;
The bird is on the wing, the poet says,
And you and I have said it here before.
Drink to the bird." He raised up to the light
The jug that he had gone so far to fill,
And answered huskily: "Well, Mr. Flood,
Since you propose it, I believe I will."

Alone, as if enduring to the end
A valiant armor of scarred hopes outworn,
He stood there in the middle of the road
Like Roland's ghost winding° a silent horn. *blowing*
Below him, in the town among the trees,
Where friends of other days had honored him,
A phantom salutation of the dead
Rang thinly till old Eben's eyes were dim.

Then, as a mother lays her sleeping child
Down tenderly, fearing it may awake,
He set the jug down slowly at his feet
With trembling care, knowing that most things break;
And only when assured that on firm earth
It stood, as the uncertain lives of men
Assuredly did not, he paced away,
And with his hand extended paused again:

"Well, Mr. Flood, we have not met like this
In a long time; and many a change has come
To both of us, I fear, since last it was
We had a drop together. Welcome home!"
Convivially returning with himself,
Again he raised the jug up to the light;
And with an acquiescent quaver said:
"Well, Mr. Flood, if you insist, I might.

"Only a very little, Mr. Flood—
For auld lang syne. No more, sir; that will do."
So, for the time, apparently it did,

And Eben evidently thought so too;
For soon amid the silver loneliness
Of night he lifted up his voice and sang,
Secure, with only two moons listening,
Until the whole harmonious landscape rang—

"For auld lang syne." The weary throat gave out,
The last word wavered; and the song being done,
He raised again the jug regretfully
And shook his head, and was again alone.
There was not much that was ahead of him,
And there was nothing in the town below—
Where strangers would have shut the many doors
That many friends had opened long ago.

MR. FLOOD'S PARTY. 11. *the poet:* Omar Khayyám, Persian poet, a praiser of wine, whose *Rubáiyát,* translated by Edward FitzGerald, included the lines:

> Come, fill the Cup, and in the fire of Spring
> Your Winter-garment of Repentance fling:
> The Bird of Time has but a little way
> To flutter and the Bird is on the Wing.

20. *Roland's ghost . . . horn:* In the battle of Roncesvalles (eighth century), Roland fought to his death, refusing to sound his horn for help until all hope was gone.

Theodore Roethke (1908–1963)

ELEGY FOR JANE — 1953

My Student, Thrown by a Horse

I remember the neckcurls, limp and damp as tendrils;
And her quick look, a sidelong pickerel smile;
And how, once startled into talk, the light syllables leaped for her,
And she balanced in the delight of her thought,
A wren, happy, tail into the wind,
Her song trembling the twigs and small branches.
The shade sang with her;
The leaves, their whispers turned to kissing;
And the mold sang in the bleached valleys under the rose.

Oh, when she was sad, she cast herself down into such a pure depth,
Even a father could not find her:
Scraping her cheek against straw;
Stirring the clearest water.

My sparrow, you are not here,
Waiting like a fern, making a spiny shadow.
The sides of wet stones cannot console me,
Nor the moss, wound with the last light.

If only I could nudge you from this sleep,
My maimed darling, my skittery pigeon.
Over this damp grave I speak the words of my love:
I, with no rights in this matter,
Neither father nor lover.

Theodore Roethke (1908–1963)

THE WAKING

1953

I wake to sleep, and take my waking slow.
I feel my fate in what I cannot fear.
I learn by going where I have to go.

We think by feeling. What is there to know?
I hear my being dance from ear to ear.
I wake to sleep, and take my waking slow.

Of those so close beside me, which are you?
God bless the Ground! I shall walk softly there,
And learn by going where I have to go.

Light takes the Tree; but who can tell us how?
The lowly worm climbs up a winding stair;
I wake to sleep, and take my waking slow.

Great Nature has another thing to do
To you and me; so take the lively air,
And, lovely, learn by going where to go.

This shaking keeps me steady. I should know.
What falls away is always. And is near.
I wake to sleep, and take my waking slow.
I learn by going where I have to go.

COMPARE:

"The Waking" with "Do not go gentle into that good night" by Dylan Thomas (page 175).

Gibbons Ruark (b. 1941)

SAYING GOODBYE TO MY DAUGHTERS

1978

Though the room is the same room I am always in,
In the colloquy the voice grows less a stranger,
More nearly an old friend, nearly my grandfather
Telling me yes, you are allowed to go away.
Slowly the whole room fills with the dusk of summer.

It is as if we were stretching on the sun porch
For a long evening, talking of the tall marsh birds
That settle down for winter in the bayshore pools.
In the light the room has never known, a white bird
Flaps and flaps so harmlessly against the window
I release the latch and let it float to the lawn
Where the young girls calm their wings down into their arms
In gestures so casual and lovely they might
Be brushing the snowdust from their sleeves and shoulders.

COMPARE:

"Saying goodbye to my daughters" with "At the San Francisco Airport" by Yvor Winters (page 389).

Anne Sexton (1928–1975)

FOR MY LOVER, RETURNING TO HIS WIFE 1969

She is all there.
She was melted carefully down for you
and cast up from your childhood,
cast up from your one hundred favorite aggies.

She has always been there, my darling.
She is, in fact, exquisite.
Fireworks in the dull middle of February
and as real as a cast-iron pot.

Let's face it, I have been momentary.
A luxury. A bright red sloop in the harbor.
My hair rising like smoke from the car window.
Littleneck clams out of season.

She is more than that. She is your have to have,
has grown you your practical your tropical growth.
This is not an experiment. She is all harmony.
She sees to oars and oarlocks for the dinghy,

has placed wild flowers at the window at breakfast,
sat by the potter's wheel at midday,
set forth three children under the moon,
three cherubs drawn by Michelangelo,

done this with her legs spread out
in the terrible months in the chapel.
If you glance up, the children are there
like delicate balloons, resting on the ceiling.

She has also carried each one down the hall
after supper, their heads privately bent,
two legs protesting, person to person,
her face flushed with a song and their little sleep.

I give you back your heart.
I give you permission—

for the fuse inside her, throbbing
angrily in the dirt, for the bitch in her
and the burying of her wound—
for the burying of her small red wound alive—

for the pale flickering flare under her ribs,
for the drunken sailor who waits in her left pulse,
for the mother's knee, for the stockings,
for the garter belt, for the call—

the curious call
when you will burrow in arms and breasts
and tug at the orange ribbon in her hair
and answer the call, the curious call.

She is so naked and singular.
She is the sum of yourself and your dream.
Climb her like a monument, step after step.
She is solid.

As for me, I am a watercolor.
I wash off.

William Shakespeare (1564–1616)

That time of year thou mayst in me behold 1609

That time of year thou mayst in me behold
When yellow leaves, or none, or few, do hang
Upon those boughs which shake against the cold,
Bare ruined choirs where late the sweet birds sang.
In me thou see'st the twilight of such day
As after sunset fadeth in the west,
Which by-and-by black night doth take away,
Death's second self that seals up all in rest.
In me thou see'st the glowing of such fire
That on the ashes of his youth doth lie,
As the deathbed whereon it must expire,
Consumed with that which it was nourished by.
  This thou perceiv'st, which makes thy love more strong,
  To love that well which thou must leave ere long.

William Shakespeare (1564–1616)

WHEN, IN DISGRACE WITH FORTUNE AND MEN'S EYES 1609

When, in disgrace with Fortune and men's eyes,
I all alone beweep my outcast state,
And trouble deaf heaven with my bootless° cries, *futile*
And look upon myself and curse my fate,
Wishing me like to one more rich in hope,
Featured like him, like him with friends possessed,
Desiring this man's art, and that man's scope,
With what I most enjoy contented least,
Yet in these thoughts myself almost despising,
Haply° I think on thee, and then my state, *luckily*
Like to the lark at break of day arising
From sullen earth, sings hymns at heaven's gate;
  For thy sweet love rememb'red such wealth brings
  That then I scorn to change my state with kings.

William Shakespeare (1564–1616)

WHEN DAISIES PIED AND VIOLETS BLUE 1598

When daisies pied and violets blue
  And lady-smocks all silver-white
And cuckoo-buds° of yellow hue *buttercups*
  Do paint the meadows with delight,
The cuckoo then, on every tree,
Mocks married men; for thus sings he,
        "Cuckoo,
Cuckoo, cuckoo!"—O word of fear,
Unpleasing to a married ear!

When shepherds pipe on oaten straws,
  And merry larks are ploughmen's clocks,
When turtles tread°, and rooks, and daws, *turtledoves mate*
  And maidens bleach their summer smocks,
The cuckoo then, on every tree,
Mocks married men; for thus sings he,
        "Cuckoo,
Cuckoo, cuckoo!"—O word of fear,
Unpleasing to a married ear!

WHEN DAISIES PIED. This song and "When icicles hang by the wall" conclude the play *Love's Labor's Lost*. 2. *lady-smocks:* also named cuckoo-flowers. 8. *O word of fear:* because it sounds like the sound *cuckold*.

William Shakespeare (1564–1616)

When icicles hang by the wall — 1598

When icicles hang by the wall,
And Dick the shepherd blows his nail,
And Tom bears logs into the hall,
And milk comes frozen home in pail,
When blood is nipped and ways° be foul, *roads*
Then nightly sings the staring owl:
"Tu-whit, to-who!"
A merry note,
While greasy Joan doth keel° the pot. *cool (as by skimming or stirring)*

When all aloud the wind doth blow,
And coughing drowns the parson's saw°, *old saw, platitude*
And birds sit brooding in the snow,
And Marian's nose looks red and raw,
When roasted crabs° hiss in the bowl, *crab apples*
Then nightly sings the staring owl:
"Tu-whit, to-who!"
A merry note,
While greasy Joan doth keel the pot.

Karl Shapiro (b. 1913)

The Dirty Word — 1947

The dirty word hops in the cage of the mind like the Pondicherry vulture, stomping with its heavy left claw on the sweet meat of the brain and tearing it with its vicious beak, ripping and chopping the flesh. Terrified, the small boy bears the big bird of the dirty word into the house, and grunting, puffing, carries it up the stairs to his own room in the skull. Bits of black feather cling to his clothes and his hair as he locks the staring creature in the dark closet.

All day the small boy returns to the closet to examine and feed the bird, to caress and kick the bird, that now snaps and flaps its wings savagely whenever the door is opened. How the boy trembles and delights at the sight of the white excrement of the bird! How the bird leaps and rushes against the walls of the skull, trying to escape from the zoo of the vocabulary! How wildly snaps the sweet meat of the brain in its rage.

And the bird outlives the man, being freed at the man's death-funeral by a word from the rabbi.

(But I one morning went upstairs and opened the door and entered the closet and found in the cage of my mind the great bird dead. Softly I wept it and softly removed it and softly buried the body of the bird in the hollyhock garden of the house I lived in twenty years before. And out of the worn black feathers of the wing have I made these pens to write these elegies, for I have outlived the bird, and I have murdered it in my early manhood.)

Sir Philip Sidney (1554–1586)

Now that of Absence, the Most Irksome Night 1591

Now that of absence, the most irksome night,
  With darkest shade doth overcome my day,
  Since Stella's eyes, wont° to give me my day, *accustomed*
Leaving my hemisphere, leave me in night,
Each day seems long, and longs for long-stayed night;
  The night, as tedious, woos th' approach of day;
  Tired with the dusty toils of busy day,
Languished with horrors of the silent night,
Suffering the evils both of the day and night,
  While no night is more dark than is my day,
Nor no day hath less quiet than my night;
  With such bad mixture of my night and day,
That living thus in blackest winter night,
  I feel the flames of hottest summer day.

Charles Simic (b. 1938)

Butcher Shop 1971

Sometimes walking late at night
I stop before a closed butcher shop.
There is a single light in the store
Like the light in which the convict digs his tunnel.

An apron hangs on the hook:
The blood on it smeared into a map
Of the great continents of blood,
The great rivers and oceans of blood.

There are knives that glitter like altars
In a dark church
Where they bring the cripple and the imbecile
To be healed.

There's a wooden block where bones are broken,
Scraped clean—a river dried to its bed
Where I am fed,
Where deep in the night I hear a voice.

Christopher Smart (1722–1771)

For I will consider my Cat Jeoffry (1759–1763)

For I will consider my Cat Jeoffry.
For he is the servant of the Living God, duly and daily serving him.
For at the first glance of the glory of God in the East he worships in his way.
For is this done by wreathing his body seven times round with elegant quickness.
For then he leaps up to catch the musk°, which is the blessing of God upon his prayer. *catnip*
For he rolls upon prank to work it in.
For having done duty and received blessing he begins to consider himself.
For this he performs in ten degrees.
For first he looks upon his fore-paws to see if they are clean.
For secondly he kicks up behind to clear away there.
For thirdly he works it upon stretch° with the fore-paws extended. *he works his muscles, stretching*
For fourthly he sharpens his paws by wood.
For fifthly he washes himself.
For sixthly he rolls upon wash.
For seventhly he fleas himself, that he may not be interrupted upon the beat°. *his patrol*
For eighthly he rubs himself against a post.
For ninthly he looks up for his instructions.
For tenthly he goes in quest of food.
For having considered God and himself he will consider his neighbor.
For if he meets another cat he will kiss her in kindness.
For when he takes his prey he plays with it to give it a chance.
For one mouse in seven escapes by his dallying.
For when his day's work is done his business more properly begins.
For he keeps the Lord's watch in the night against the Adversary.
For he counteracts the powers of darkness by his electrical skin and glaring eyes.
For he counteracts the Devil, who is death, by brisking about the life.
For in his morning orisons he loves the sun and the sun loves him.
For he is of the tribe of Tiger.
For the Cherub Cat is a term of the Angel Tiger.
For he has the subtlety and hissing of a serpent, which in goodness he suppresses.
For he will not do destruction if he is well-fed, neither will he spit without provocation.
For he purrs in thankfulness when God tells him he's a good Cat.
For he is an instrument for the children to learn benevolence upon.
For every house is incomplete without him, and a blessing is lacking in the spirit.
For the Lord commanded Moses concerning the cats at the departure of the Children of Israel from Egypt.
For every family had one cat at least in the bag.

For the English cats are the best in Europe.
For he is the cleanest in the use of his fore-paws of any quadruped.
For the dexterity of his defense is an instance of the love of God to him exceedingly.
For he is the quickest to his mark of any creature.
For he is tenacious of his point.
For he is a mixture of gravity and waggery.
For he knows that God is his Savior.
For there is nothing sweeter than his peace when at rest.
For there is nothing brisker than his life when in motion.
For he is of the Lord's poor, and so indeed is he called by benevolence perpetually—Poor Jeoffry! poor Jeoffry! the rat has bit thy throat.
For I bless the name of the Lord Jesus that Jeoffry is better.
For the divine spirit comes about his body to sustain it in complete cat.
For his tongue is exceeding pure so that it has in purity what it wants in music.
For he is docile and can learn certain things.
For he can sit up with gravity which is patience upon approbation.
For he can fetch and carry, which is patience in employment.
For he can jump over a stick which is patience upon proof positive.
For he can spraggle upon waggle at the word of command.
For he can jump from an eminence into his master's bosom.
For he can catch the cork and toss it again.
For he is hated by the hypocrite and miser.
For the former is afraid of detection.
For the latter refuses the charge.
For he camels his back to bear the first notion of business.
For he is good to think on, if a man would express himself neatly.
For he made a great figure in Egypt for his signal services.
For he killed the Icneumon-rat, very pernicious by land.
For his ears are so acute that they sting again.
For from this proceeds the passing quickness of his attention.
For by stroking of him I have found out electricity.
For I perceived God's light about him both wax and fire.
For the electrical fire is the spiritual substance which God sends from heaven to sustain the bodies both of man and beast.
For God has blessed him in the variety of his movements.
For, though he cannot fly, he is an excellent clamberer.
For his motions upon the face of the earth are more than any other quadruped.
For he can tread to all the measures upon the music.
For he can swim for life.
For he can creep.

FOR I WILL CONSIDER MY CAT JEOFFRY. This is a self-contained extract from Smart's long poem *Jubilate Agno* ("Rejoice in the Lamb"), written during his confinement for insanity. 35. *For the Lord commanded Moses concerning the cats:* No such command is mentioned in Scripture. 54. *spraggle upon waggle:* W. F. Stead, in his edition of Smart's poem, suggests that this means Jeoffry will sprawl when his master waggles a finger or a stick. 59. *the charge:* perhaps the cost of feeding a cat.

William Jay Smith (b. 1918)

American Primitive

1953

Look at him there in his stovepipe hat,
His high-top shoes, and his handsome collar;
Only my Daddy could look like that,
And I love my Daddy like he loves his Dollar.

The screen door bangs, and it sounds so funny—
There he is in a shower of gold;
His pockets are stuffed with folding money,
His lips are blue, and his hands feel cold.

He hangs in the hall by his black cravat,
The ladies faint, and the children holler:
Only my Daddy could look like that,
And I love my Daddy like he loves his Dollar.

Compare:
"American Primitive" with "Daddy" by Sylvia Plath (page 348).

W. D. Snodgrass (b. 1926)

The Operation

1959

From stainless steel basins of water
They brought warm cloths and they washed me,
From spun aluminum bowls, cold Zephiran sponges, fuming;
Gripped in the dead yellow glove, a bright straight razor
Inched on my stomach, down my groin,
Paring the brown hair off. They left me
White as a child, not frightened. I was not
Ashamed. They clothed me, then,
In the thin, loose, light, white garments,
The delicate sandals of poor Pierrot,
A schoolgirl first offering her sacrament.

I was drifting, inexorably, on toward sleep.
In skullcaps, masked, in blue-green gowns, attendants
Towed my cart, afloat in its white cloths,
The body with its tributary poisons borne
Down corridors of the diseased, thronging:
The scrofulous faces, contagious grim boys,
The huddled families, weeping, a staring woman
Arched to her gnarled stick,—a child was somewhere
Screaming, screaming—then, blind silence, the elevator rising
To the arena, humming, vast with lights; blank hero,
Shackled and spellbound, to enact my deed.

Into flowers, into women, I have awakened.
Too weak to think of strength, I have thought all day,
Or dozed among standing friends. I lie in night, now,
A small mound under linen like the drifted snow.
Only by nurses visited, in radiance, saying, Rest.
Opposite, ranked office windows glare; headlamps, below,
Trace out our highways; their cargoes under dark tarpaulins,
Trucks climb, thundering, and sirens may
Wail for the fugitive. It is very still. In my brandy bowl
Of sweet peas at the window, the crystal world
Is inverted, slow and gay.

THE OPERATION. 3. *Zephiran:* like Zephirus, Greek personification of the west wind: gentle, cool, and soothing. Also the name of an antiseptic, so named to indicate that it does not sting. 10. *Pierrot:* traditional clown in French pantomime, white-faced, wearing loose pantaloons.

Gary Soto (b. 1952)

DAYBREAK 1977

In this moment when the light starts up
In the east and rubs
The horizon until it catches fire,

We enter the fields to hoe,
Row after row, among the small flags of onion,
Waving off the dragonflies
That ladder the air.

And tears the onions raise
Do not begin in your eyes but in ours,
In the salt blown
From one blister into another;

They begin in knowing
You will never waken to bear
The hour timed to a heart beat,
The wind pressing us closer to the ground.

When the season ends,
And the onions are unplugged from their sleep,
We won't forget what you failed to see,
And nothing will heal
Under the rain's broken fingers.

DAYBREAK. This poem is one of a sequence, "The Elements of San Joaquin," recording the poet's experience as a worker in the fields of California's San Joaquin Valley.

William Stafford (b. 1914)

At the Klamath Berry Festival 1966

The war chief danced the old way—
the eagle wing he held before his mouth—
and when he turned the boom-boom
stopped. He took two steps. A sociologist
was there; the Scout troop danced.
I envied him the places where he had not been.

The boom began again. Outside he heard
the stick game, and the Blackfoot gamblers
arguing at poker under lanterns.
Still-moccasined and bashful, holding
the eagle wing before his mouth,
listening and listening, he danced after others stopped.

He took two steps, the boom caught up,
the mountains rose, the still deep river
slid but never broke its quiet.
I looked back when I left:
he took two steps, he took two steps,
past the sociologist.

At the Klamath Berry Festival. The Klamath Indians have a reservation at the base of the Cascade Range in southern Oregon.

Gerald Stern (b. 1925)

Behaving Like a Jew 1977

When I got there the dead opossum looked like
an enormous baby sleeping on the road.
It took me only a few seconds—just
seeing him there—with the hole in his back
and the wind blowing through his hair
to get back again into my animal sorrow.
I am sick of the country, the bloodstained
bumpers, the stiff hairs sticking out of the grilles,
the slimy highways, the heavy birds
refusing to move;
I am sick of the spirit of Lindbergh over everything,
that joy in death, that philosophical
understanding of carnage, that
concentration on the species.
—I am going to be unappeased at the opossum's death.

I am going to behave like a Jew
and touch his face, and stare into his eyes,
and pull him off the road.
I am not going to stand in a wet ditch
with the Toyotas and the Chevies passing over me
at sixty miles an hour
and praise the beauty and the balance
and lose myself in the immortal lifestream
when my hands are still a little shaky
from his stiffness and his bulk
and my eyes are still weak and misty
from his round belly and his curved fingers
and his black whiskers and his little dancing feet.

COMPARE:

"Behaving Like a Jew" with "Thoughts on Capital Punishment" by Rod McKuen and "Traveling Through the Dark" by William Stafford pages 257–258)

Wallace Stevens (1879–1955)

PETER QUINCE AT THE CLAVIER 1923

I

Just as my fingers on these keys
Make music, so the selfsame sounds
On my spirit make a music, too.

Music is feeling, then, not sound;
And thus it is that what I feel,
Here in this room, desiring you,

Thinking of your blue-shadowed silk,
Is music. It is like the strain
Waked in the elders by Susanna.

Of a green evening, clear and warm,
She bathed in her still garden, while
The red-eyed elders watching, felt

The basses of their beings throb
In witching chords, and their thin blood
Pulse pizzicati of Hosanna.

II

In the green water, clear and warm,
Susanna lay.
She searched
The touch of springs,

And found
Concealed imaginings.
She sighed,
For so much melody.

Upon the bank, she stood
In the cool
Of spent emotions.
She felt, among the leaves,
The dew
Of old devotions.

She walked upon the grass,
Still quavering.
The winds were like her maids,
On timid feet,
Fetching her woven scarves,
Yet wavering.

A breath upon her hand
Muted the night.
She turned—
A cymbal crashed,
And roaring horns.

III

Soon, with a noise like tambourines,
Came her attendant Byzantines.

They wondered why Susanna cried
Against the elders by her side;

And as they whispered, the refrain
Was like a willow swept by rain.

Anon, their lamps' uplifted flame
Revealed Susanna and her shame.

And then, the simpering Byzantines
Fled, with a noise like tambourines.

IV

Beauty is momentary in the mind—
The fitful tracing of a portal;
But in the flesh it is immortal.

The body dies; the body's beauty lives.
So evenings die, in their green going,
A wave, interminably flowing.
So gardens die, their meek breath scenting
The cowl of winter, done repenting.
So maidens die, to the auroral
Celebration of a maiden's choral.

Susanna's music touched the bawdy strings
Of those white elders; but, escaping,
Left only Death's ironic scraping.
Now, in its immortality, it plays
On the clear viol of her memory,
And makes a constant sacrament of praise.

PETER QUINCE AT THE CLAVIER. In Shakespeare's *Midsummer Night's Dream,* Peter Quince is a clownish carpenter who stages a mock-tragic play. In The Book of Susanna in the Apocrypha, two lustful elders who covet Susanna, a virtuous married woman, hide in her garden, spy on her as she bathes, then threaten to make false accusations against her unless she submits to them. When she refuses, they cry out, and her servants come running. All ends well when the prophet Daniel cross-examines the elders and proves them liars. 15. *pizzicati:* thin notes made by plucking a stringed instrument. 42. *Byzantines:* Susanna's maidservants.

Mark Strand (b. 1934)

KEEPING THINGS WHOLE 1964

In a field
I am the absence
of field.
This is
always the case.
Wherever I am
I am what is missing.

When I walk
I part the air
and always
the air moves in
to fill the spaces
where my body's been.

We all have reasons
for moving.
I move
to keep things whole.

May Swenson (b. 1919)

QUESTION 1954

Body my house
my horse my hound
what will I do
when you are fallen

Where will I sleep
How will I ride
What will I hunt

Where can I go
without my mount
all eager and quick
How will I know
in thicket ahead
is danger or treasure
when Body my good
bright dog is dead

How will it be
to lie in the sky
without roof or door
and wind for an eye

With cloud for shift
how will I hide?

Jonathan Swift (1667–1745)

A Description of the Morning 1711

Now hardly here and there an hackney-coach°, *horse-drawn cab*
Appearing, showed the ruddy morn's approach.
Now Betty from her master's bed had flown
And softly stole to discompose her own.
The slipshod 'prentice from his master's door
Had pared the dirt, and sprinkled round the floor.
Now Moll had whirled her mop with dextrous airs,
Prepared to scrub the entry and the stairs.
The youth with broomy stumps began to trace
The kennel°-edge, where wheels had worn the place. *gutter*
The small-coal man was heard with cadence deep
Till drowned in shriller notes of chimneysweep,
Duns° at his lordship's gate began to meet, *bill-collectors*
And Brickdust Moll had screamed through half the street.
The turnkey° now his flock returning sees, *jailkeeper*
Duly let out a-nights to steal for fees;
The watchful bailiffs° take their silent stands; *constables*
And schoolboys lag with satchels in their hands.

A Description of the Morning. 9. *youth with broomy stumps:* a young man sweeping the gutter's edge with worn-out brooms, looking for old nails fallen from wagonwheels, which were valuable. 14. *Brickdust Moll:* woman selling brickdust to be used for scouring.

Alfred, Lord Tennyson (1809–1892)

Dark house, by which once more I stand 1850

Dark house, by which once more I stand
  Here in the long unlovely street,
  Doors, where my heart was used to beat
So quickly, waiting for a hand,

A hand that can be clasped no more—
  Behold me, for I cannot sleep,
  And like a guilty thing I creep
At earliest morning to the door.

He is not here; but far away
  The noise of life begins again,
  And ghastly through the drizzling rain
On the bald street breaks the blank day.

Dark house. This poem is one part of the series *In Memoriam,* an elegy for Tennyson's friend Arthur Henry Hallam.

Alfred, Lord Tennyson (1809–1892)

Ulysses (1833)

It little profits that an idle king,
By this still hearth, among these barren crags,
Matched with an agèd wife, I mete and dole
Unequal laws unto a savage race
That hoard, and sleep, and feed, and know not me.
I cannot rest from travel; I will drink
Life to the lees. All times I have enjoyed
Greatly, have suffered greatly, both with those
That loved me, and alone; on shore, and when
Through scudding drifts the rainy Hyades
Vexed the dim sea. I am become a name;
For always roaming with a hungry heart
Much have I seen and known—cities of men
And manners, climates, councils, governments,
Myself not least, but honored of them all—
And drunk delight of battle with my peers,
Far on the ringing plains of windy Troy.
I am a part of all that I have met;
Yet all experience is an arch wherethrough
Gleams that untraveled world whose margin fades
Forever and forever when I move.
How dull it is to pause, to make an end,
To rust unburnished, not to shine in use!
As though to breathe were life! Life piled on life

Were all too little, and of one to me
Little remains; but every hour is saved
From that eternal silence, something more,
A bringer of new things; and vile it were
For some three suns to store and hoard myself,
And this grey spirit yearning in desire
To follow knowledge like a sinking star,
Beyond the utmost bound of human thought.
  This is my son, mine own Telemachus,
To whom I leave the scepter and the isle—
Well-loved of me, discerning to fulfill
This labor, by slow prudence to make mild
A rugged people, and through soft degrees
Subdue them to the useful and the good.
Most blameless is he, centered in the sphere
Of common duties, decent not to fail
In offices of tenderness, and pay
Meet adoration to my household gods,
When I am gone. He works his work, I mine.
  There lies the port; the vessel puffs her sail;
There gloom the dark, broad seas. My mariners,
Souls that have toiled, and wrought, and thought with me—
That ever with a frolic welcome took
The thunder and the sunshine, and opposed
Free hearts, free foreheads—you and I are old;
Old age hath yet his honor and his toil.
Death closes all; but something ere the end,
Some work of noble note, may yet be done,
Not unbecoming men that strove with Gods.
The lights begin to twinkle from the rocks;
The long day wanes; the low moon climbs; the deep
Moans round with many voices. Come, my friends,
'Tis not too late to seek a newer world.
Push off, and sitting well in order smite
The sounding furrows; for my purpose holds
To sail beyond the sunset, and the baths
Of all the western stars, until I die.
It may be that the gulfs will wash us down;
It may be we shall touch the Happy Isles,
And see the great Achilles, whom we knew.
Though much is taken, much abides; and though
We are not now that strength which in old days
Moved earth and heaven, that which we are, we are—
One equal temper of heroic hearts,
Made weak by time and fate, but strong in will
To strive, to seek, to find, and not to yield.

ULYSSES. 10. *Hyades:* daughters of Atlas, who were transformed into a group of stars. Their rising with the sun was thought to be a sign of rain. 63. *Happy Isles:* Elysium, a paradise believed to be attainable by sailing west.

COMPARE:
"Ulysses" with "The Seafarer" by Ezra Pound (page 352).

Dylan Thomas (1914–1953)

FERN HILL

1946

Now as I was young and easy under the apple boughs
About the lilting house and happy as the grass was green,
The night above the dingle° starry,
Time let me hail and climb
Golden in the heydays of his eyes,
And honored among wagons I was prince of the apple towns
And once below a time I lordly had the trees and leaves
Trail with daisies and barley
Down the rivers of the windfall light.

wooded valley

And as I was green and carefree, famous among the barns
About the happy yard and singing as the farm was home,
In the sun that is young once only,
Time let me play and be
Golden in the mercy of his means,
And green and golden I was huntsman and herdsman, the calves
Sang to my horn, the foxes on the hills barked clear and cold,
And the sabbath rang slowly
In the pebbles of the holy streams.

All the sun long it was running, it was lovely, the hay
Fields high as the house, the tunes from the chimneys, it was air
And playing, lovely and watery
And fire green as grass.
And nightly under the simple stars
As I rode to sleep the owls were bearing the farm away,
All the moon long I heard, blessed among stables, the nightjars
Flying with the ricks, and the horses
Flashing into the dark.

And then to awake, and the farm, like a wanderer white
With the dew, come back, the cock on his shoulder: it was all
Shining, it was Adam and maiden,
The sky gathered again
And the sun grew round that very day.
So it must have been after the birth of the simple light
In the first, spinning place, the spellbound horses walking warm
Out of the whinnying green stable
On to the fields of praise.

And honored among foxes and pheasants by the gay house
Under the new made clouds and happy as the heart was long,

In the sun born over and over,
I ran my heedless ways,
My wishes raced through the house high hay
And nothing I cared, at my sky blue trades, that time allows
In all his tuneful turning so few and such morning songs
Before the children green and golden
Follow him out of grace,

Nothing I cared, in the lamb white days, that time would take me
Up to the swallow thronged loft by the shadow of my hand,
In the moon that is always rising,
Nor that riding to sleep
I should hear him fly with the high fields
And wake to the farm forever fled from the childless land.
Oh as I was young and easy in the mercy of his means,
Time held me green and dying
Though I sang in my chains like the sea.

Dylan Thomas (1914–1953)

Twenty-four years 1939

Twenty-four years remind the tears of my eyes.
(Bury the dead for fear that they walk to the grave in labor.)
In the groin of the natural doorway I crouched like a tailor
Sewing a shroud for a journey
By the light of the meat-eating sun.
Dressed to die, the sensual strut begun,
With my red veins full of money,
In the final direction of the elementary town
I advance for as long as forever is.

Twenty-four years. "This very short poem is for my birthday just arriving," wrote Thomas, copying out the poem on a postcard to his friend Vernon Watkins three days before his twenty-fourth birthday (October 27, 1938).

Compare:

"Twenty-four years" with "For the Anniversary of My Death" by W. S. Merwin (page 345).

David Wagoner (b. 1926)

Staying Alive 1966

Staying alive in the woods is a matter of calming down
At first and deciding whether to wait for rescue,
Trusting to others,
Or simply to start walking and walking in one direction
Till you come out—or something happens to stop you.

By far the safer choice
Is to settle down where you are, and try to make a living
Off the land, camping near water, away from shadows.
Eat no white berries:
Spit out all bitterness. Shooting at anything
Means hiking further and further every day
To hunt survivors;
It may be best to learn what you have to learn without a gun,
Not killing but watching birds and animals go
In and out of shelter
At will. Following their example, build for a whole season:
Facing across the wind in your lean-to,
You may feel wilder,
But nothing, not even you, will have to stay in hiding.
If you have no matches, a stick and a fire-bow
Will keep you warmer,
Or the crystal of your watch, filled with water, held up to the sun
Will do the same in time. In case of snow
Drifting toward winter,
Don't try to stay awake through the night, afraid of freezing—
The bottom of your mind knows all about zero;
It will turn you over
And shake you till you waken. If you have trouble sleeping
Even in the best of weather, jumping to follow
With eyes strained to their corners
The unidentifiable noises of the night and feeling
Bears and packs of wolves nuzzling your elbow,
Remember the trappers
Who treated them indifferently and were left alone.
If you hurt yourself, no one will comfort you
Or take your temperature,
So stumbling, wading, and climbing are as dangerous as flying.
But if you decide, at last, you must break through
In spite of all danger,
Think of yourself by time and not by distance, counting
Wherever you're going by how long it takes you;
No other measure
Will bring you safe to nightfall. Follow no streams: they run
Under the ground or fall into wilder country.
Remember the stars
And moss when your mind runs into circles. If it should rain
Or the fog should roll the horizon in around you,
Hold still for hours
Or days if you must, or weeks, for seeing is believing
In the wilderness. And if you find a pathway,
Wheel-rut, or fence-wire,
Retrace it left or right: someone knew where he was going
Once upon a time, and you can follow
Hopefully, somewhere,
Just in case. There may even come, on some uncanny evening,

A time when you're warm and dry, well fed, not thirsty,
Uninjured, without fear,
When nothing, either good or bad, is happening.
This is called staying alive. It's temporary.
What occurs after
Is doubtful. You must always be ready for something to come bursting
Through the far edge of a clearing, running toward you,
Grinning from ear to ear
And hoarse with welcome. Or something crossing and hovering
Overhead, as light as air, like a break in the sky,
Wondering what you are.
Here you are face to face with the problem of recognition.
Having no time to make smoke, too much to say,
You should have a mirror
With a tiny hole in the back for better aiming, for reflecting
Whatever disaster you can think of, to show
The way you suffer.
These body signals have universal meaning: If you are lying
Flat on your back with arms outstretched behind you,
You say you require
Emergency treatment; if you are standing erect and holding
Arms horizontal, you mean you are not ready;
If you hold them over
Your head, you want to be picked up. Three of anything
Is a sign of distress. Afterward, if you see
No ropes, no ladders,
No maps or messages falling, no searchlights or trails blazing,
Then, chances are, you should be prepared to burrow
Deep for a deep winter.

Derek Walcott (b. 1930)

Sea Canes 1976

Half my friends are dead.
I will make you new ones, said earth.
No, give me them back, as they were, instead,
with faults and all, I cried.

Tonight I can snatch their talk
from the faint surf's drone
through the canes, but I cannot walk

on the moonlit leaves of ocean
down that white road alone,
or float with the dreaming motion

of owls leaving earth's load.
O earth, the number of friends you keep
exceeds those left to be loved.

The sea-canes by the cliff flash green and silver;
they were the seraph lances of my faith,
but out of what is lost grows something stronger

that has the rational radiance of stone,
enduring moonlight, further than despair,
strong as the wind, that through dividing canes

brings those we love before us, as they were,
with faults and all, not nobler, just there.

Edmund Waller (1606–1687)

Go, Lovely Rose 1645

Go, lovely rose,
Tell her that wastes her time and me
That now she knows,
When I resemble° her to thee, *compare*
How sweet and fair she seems to be.

Tell her that's young
And shuns to have her graces spied,
That hadst thou sprung
In deserts where no men abide,
Thou must have uncommended died.

Small is the worth
Of beauty from the light retired:
Bid her come forth,
Suffer herself to be desired,
And not blush so to be admired.

Then die, that she
The common fate of all things rare
May read in thee,
How small a part of time they share
That are so wondrous sweet and fair.

Compare:

"Go, Lovely Rose" with "To the Virgins, to Make Much of Time" by Robert Herrick (page 327) and "To His Coy Mistress" by Andrew Marvell (page 8).

Robert Penn Warren (b. 1905)

Brotherhood in Pain 1976

Fix your eyes on any chance object. For instance,
That leaf, prematurely crimson, of the swamp maple

That dawdles down gold air to the velvet-black water
Of the moribund beaver-pond. Or the hunk

Of dead chewing gum in the gutter with the mark of a molar
Yet distinct on it, like the most delicate Hellenistic chisel-work.

Or a black sock you took off last night and by mistake
Left lying, to be found in the morning, on the bathroom tiles.

Or pick up a single stone from the brookside, inspect it
Most carefully, then throw it back in. You will never

See it again. By the next spring flood, it may have been hurled
A mile downstream. Fix your gaze on any of these objects,

Or if you think me disingenuous in my suggestions,
Whirl around three times like a child, or a dervish, with eyes shut,

Then fix on the first thing seen when they open.
In any case, you will suddenly observe an object in the obscene moment of birth.

It does not know its own name. The matrix from which it is torn
Bleeds profusely. It has not yet begun to breathe. Its experience

Is too terrible to recount. Only when it has completely forgotten
Everything, will it smile shyly, and try to love you,

For somehow it knows that you are lonely, too.
It pityingly knows that you are more lonely than it is, for

You exist only in the delirious illusion of language.

Tom Wayman (b. 1945)

WAYMAN IN LOVE 1973

At last Wayman gets the girl into bed.
He is locked in one of those embraces
so passionate his left arm is asleep
when suddenly he is bumped in the back.
"Excuse me," a voice mutters, thick with German.
Wayman and the girl sit up astounded
as a furry gentleman in boots and a frock coat
climbs in under the covers.

"My name is Doktor Marx," the intruder announces
settling his neck comfortably on the pillow.
"I'm here to consider for you the cost of a kiss."
He pulls out a notepad. "Let's see now,
we have the price of the mattress, the room must be rented,
your time off work, groceries for two,
medical fees in case of accidents. . . ."

"Look," Wayman says,
"couldn't we do this later?"
The philosopher sighs, and continues: "You are affected too, Miss.
If you are not working, you are going to resent
your dependent position. This will influence
I assure you, your most intimate moments. . . ."

"Doctor, please," Wayman says. "All we want
is to be left alone."
But another beard, more nattily dressed,
is also getting into the bed.
There is a shifting and heaving of bodies
as everyone wriggles out room for themselves.
"I want you to meet a friend from Vienna,"
Marx says. "This is Doktor Freud."

The newcomer straightens his glasses,
peers at Wayman and the girl.
"I can see," he begins,
"that you two have problems. . . ."

Walt Whitman (1819–1892)

I Saw in Louisiana a Live-Oak Growing 1867

I saw in Louisiana a live-oak growing,
All alone stood it and the moss hung down from the branches,
Without any companion it grew there uttering joyous leaves of dark green,
And its look, rude, unbending, lusty, made me think of myself,
But I wonder'd how it could utter joyous leaves standing alone there without its friend near, for I knew I could not,
And I broke off a twig with a certain number of leaves upon it, and twined around it a little moss,
And brought it away, and I have placed it in sight in my room,
It is not needed to remind me as of my own dear friends,
(For I believe lately I think of little else than of them,)
Yet it remains to me a curious token, it makes me think of manly love;
For all that, and though the live-oak glistens there in Louisiana solitary in a wide flat space,
Uttering joyous leaves all its life without a friend a lover near,
I know very well I could not.

Walt Whitman (1819–1892)

When I Heard the Learn'd Astronomer 1865

When I heard the learn'd astronomer,
When the proofs, the figures, were ranged in columns before me,

When I was shown the charts and diagrams, to add, divide, and measure them
When I sitting heard the astronomer where he lectured with much applause in the lecture-room,
How soon unaccountable I became tired and sick,
Till rising and gliding out I wander'd off by myself,
In the mystical moist night-air, and from time to time,
Look'd up in perfect silence at the stars.

COMPARE:

"I Saw in Louisiana a Live-Oak Growing" and "When I Heard the Learn'd Astronomer" with "A Supermarket in California" by Allen Ginsberg (page 320).

Richard Wilbur (b. 1921)

PLAYBOY 1969

High on his stockroom ladder like a dunce
The stock-boy sits, and studies like a sage
The subject matter of one glossy page,
As lost in curves as Archimedes once.

Sometimes, without a glance, he feeds himself.
The left hand, like a mother-bird in flight,
Brings him a sandwich for a sidelong bite,
And then returns it to a dusty shelf.

What so engrosses him? The wild décor
Of this pink-papered alcove into which
A naked girl has stumbled, with its rich
Welter of pelts and pillows on the floor,

Amidst which, kneeling in a supple pose,
She lifts a goblet in her farther hand,
As if about to toast a flower-stand
Above which hovers an exploding rose

Fired from a long-necked crystal vase that rests
Upon a tasseled and vermilion cloth
One taste of which would shrivel up a moth?
Or is he pondering her perfect breasts?

Nothing escapes him of her body's grace
Or of her floodlit skin, so sleek and warm
And yet so strangely like a uniform,
But what now grips his fancy is her face,

And how the cunning picture holds her still
At just that smiling instant when her soul,
Grown sweetly faint, and swept beyond control,
Consents to his inexorable will.

PLAYBOY. 4. *Archimedes:* Greek mathematician and inventor (287?–212 B.C.), slain by a Roman soldier while, lost in thought, he drew geometric figures in the sand. When the soldier approached, Archimedes is said to have cried, "Don't mess up my circles!"

Oscar Wilde (1856–1900)

THE HARLOT'S HOUSE 1881

We caught the tread of dancing feet,
We loitered down the moonlit street,
And stopped beneath the harlot's house.

Inside, above the din and fray,
We heard the loud musicians play
The "Treues Liebes Herz" of Strauss.

Like strange mechanical grotesques,
Making fantastic arabesques,
The shadows raced across the blind.

We watched the ghostly dancers spin
To sound of horn and violin,
Like black leaves wheeling in the wind.

Like wire-pulled automatons,
Slim silhouetted skeletons
Went sidling through the slow quadrille.

They took each other by the hand,
And danced a stately saraband;
Their laughter echoed thin and shrill.

Sometimes a clockwork puppet pressed
A phantom lover to her breast,
Sometimes they seemed to try to sing.

Sometimes a horrible marionette
Came out, and smoked its cigarette
Upon the steps like a live thing.

Then, turning to my love, I said,
'The dead are dancing with the dead,
The dust is whirling with the dust."

But she—she heard the violin,
And left my side, and entered in:
Love passed into the house of lust.

Then suddenly the tune went false,
The dancers wearied of the waltz,
The shadows ceased to wheel and whirl.

And down the long and silent street,
The dawn, with silver-sandaled feet,
Crept like a frightened girl.

THE HARLOT'S HOUSE. 6. *"Treues Liebes Herz"*: "Dear Faithful Heart," a waltz.

COMPARE:
"The Harlot's House" with "Playboy" by Richard Wilbur (page 386).

William Carlos Williams (1883–1963)

SPRING AND ALL 1923

By the road to the contagious hospital
under the surge of the blue
mottled clouds driven from the
northeast—a cold wind. Beyond, the
waste of broad, muddy fields
brown with dried weeds, standing and fallen

patches of standing water
the scattering of tall trees

All along the road the reddish
purplish, forked, upstanding, twiggy
stuff of bushes and small trees
with dead, brown leaves under them
leafless vines—

Lifeless in appearance, sluggish
dazed spring approaches—

They enter the new world naked,
cold, uncertain of all
save that they enter. All about them
the cold, familiar wind—

Now the grass, tomorrow
the stiff curl of wildcarrot leaf
One by one objects are defined—
It quickens: clarity, outline of leaf

But now the stark dignity of
entrance—Still, the profound change
has come upon them: rooted, they
grip down and begin to awaken

COMPARE:
"Spring and All" with "in Just-" by E. E. Cummings (page 192) and "Root Cellar" by Theodore Roethke (page 72).

William Carlos Williams (1883–1963)

To Waken an Old Lady — 1921

Old age is
a flight of small
cheeping birds
skimming
bare trees
above a snow glaze.
Gaining and failing
they are buffeted
by a dark wind—
But what?
On harsh weedstalks
the flock has rested,
the snow
is covered with broken
seedhusks
and the wind tempered
by a shrill
piping of plenty.

Compare:

"To Waken an Old Lady" with "Castoff Skin" by Ruth Whitman (page 89).

Yvor Winters (1900–1968)

At the San Francisco Airport — 1952

To My Daughter, 1954

This is the terminal: the light
Gives perfect vision, false and hard;
The metal glitters, deep and bright.
Great planes are waiting in the yard—
They are already in the night.

And you are here beside me, small,
Contained and fragile, and intent
On things that I but half recall—
Yet going whither you are bent.
I am the past, and that is all.

But you and I in part are one:
The frightened brain, the nervous will,
The knowledge of what must be done,
The passion to acquire the skill
To face that which you dare not shun.

The rain of matter upon sense
Destroys me momently. The score:
There comes what will come. The expense
Is what one thought, and something more—
One's being and intelligence.

This is the terminal, the break.
Beyond this point, on lines of air,
You take the way that you must take;
And I remain in light and stare—
In light, and nothing else, awake.

COMPARE:

"At the San Francisco Airport" with "Saying goodbye to my daughters" by Gibbons Ruark (page 362).

William Wordsworth (1770–1850)

COMPOSED UPON WESTMINSTER BRIDGE 1807

Earth has not anything to show more fair:
Dull would he be of soul who could pass by
A sight so touching in its majesty:
This City now doth, like a garment, wear
The beauty of the morning; silent, bare,
Ships, towers, domes, theatres, and temples lie
Open unto the fields, and to the sky;
All bright and glittering in the smokeless air.
Never did sun more beautifully steep
In his first splendor, valley, rock, or hill;
Ne'er saw I, never felt, a calm so deep!
The river glideth at his own sweet will:
Dear God! the very houses seem asleep;
And all that mighty heart is lying still!

William Wordsworth (1770–1850)

STEPPING WESTWARD 1807

While my Fellow-traveler and I were walking by the side of Lock° Ketterine, one fine evening after sunset, in our road to a hut where, in the course of our tour, we had been hospitably entertained some weeks before, we met, in one of the loneliest parts of that solitary region, two well-dressed women, one of whom said to us, by way of greeting, "What, are you stepping westward?"

Lake

"What, are you stepping westward?"—"Yea."
—'Twould be a *wildish* destiny,
If we, who thus together roam
In a strange land, and far from home,

Were in this place the guests of Chance;
Yet who would stop, or fear to advance,
Though home or shelter he had none,
With such a sky to lead him on?

The dewy ground was dark and cold;
Behind, all gloomy to behold;
And stepping westward seemed to be
A kind of *heavenly* destiny:
I liked the greeting; 'twas a sound
Of something without place or bound
And seemed to give me spiritual right
To travel through that region bright.

The voice was soft, and she who spake
Was walking by her native lake;
The salutation had to me
The very sound of courtesy:
Its power was felt; and while my eye
Was fixed upon the glowing sky,
The echo of the voice enwrought
A human sweetness with the thought
Of traveling through the world that lay
Before me in my endless way.

STEPPING WESTWARD. Wordsworth's "Fellow-traveler" was his sister Dorothy, with whom in 1803 he made a tour of the Highlands of Scotland.

James Wright (1927–1980)

A BLESSING 1961

Just off the highway to Rochester, Minnesota,
Twilight bounds softly forth on the grass.
And the eyes of those two Indian ponies
Darken with kindness.
They have come gladly out of the willows
To welcome my friend and me.
We step over the barbed wire into the pasture
Where they have been grazing all day, alone.
They ripple tensely, they can hardly contain their happiness
That we have come.
They bow shyly as wet swans. They love each other.
There is no loneliness like theirs.
At home once more,
They begin munching the young tufts of spring in the darkness.
I would like to hold the slenderer one in my arms,
For she has walked over to me
And nuzzled my left hand.
She is black and white,

Her mane falls wild on her forehead,
And the light breeze moves me to caress her long ear
That is delicate as the skin over a girl's wrist.
Suddenly I realize
That if I stepped out of my body I would break
Into blossom.

James Wright (1927–1980)

Autumn Begins in Martins Ferry, Ohio — 1963

In the Shreve High football stadium,
I think of Polacks nursing long beers in Tiltonsville,
And gray faces of Negroes in the blast furnace at Benwood,
And the ruptured night watchman of Wheeling Steel,
Dreaming of heroes.

All the proud fathers are ashamed to go home.
Their women cluck like starved pullets,
Dying for love.

Therefore,
Their sons grow suicidally beautiful
At the beginning of October,
And gallop terribly against each other's bodies.

Sir Thomas Wyatt (1503?–1542)

They flee from me that sometime did me sekë — (about 1535)

They flee from me that sometime did me sekë
  With naked fotë° stalking in my chamber. — *foot*
I have seen them gentle, tame and mekë
  That now are wild, and do not remember
  That sometime they put themself in danger
To take bread at my hand; and now they range
Busily seeking with a continual change.

Thankèd be fortune, it hath been otherwise
  Twenty times better; but once in speciàll,
In thin array, after a pleasant guise,
  When her loose gown from her shoulders did fall,
  And she me caught in her armës long and small,
Therëwith all sweetly did me kiss,
And softly said, *Dear heart, how like you this?*

It was no dremë: I lay broadë waking.
  But all is turned thorough° my gentleness — *through*
Into a strangë fashion of forsaking;

And I have leave to go of her goodness,
And she also to use newfangleness°. *to seek novelty*
But since that I so kindëly am served
I would fain knowë what she hath deserved.

THEY FLEE FROM ME THAT SOMETIME DID ME SEKË. Some latter-day critics have called Sir Thomas Wyatt a careless poet because some of his lines appear faltering and metrically inconsistent; others have thought he knew what he was doing. It is uncertain whether the final *e*'s in English spelling were still pronounced in Wyatt's day as they were in Chaucer's, but if they were, perhaps Wyatt has been unjustly blamed. In this text, spellings have been modernized except in words where the final *e* would make a difference in rhythm. To sense how it matters, try reading the poem aloud leaving out the *e*'s and then putting them in wherever indicated. Sound them like the *a* in *sofa*. 20. *kindëly:* according to my kind (or hers); that is, as befits the nature of man (or woman). Perhaps there is also irony here, and the word means "unkindly."

William Butler Yeats (1865–1939)

CRAZY JANE TALKS WITH THE BISHOP 1933

I met the Bishop on the road
And much said he and I.
"Those breasts are flat and fallen now,
Those veins must soon be dry;
Live in a heavenly mansion,
Not in some foul sty."

"Fair and foul are near of kin,
And fair needs foul," I cried.
"My friends are gone, but that's a truth
Nor° grave nor bed denied, *neither*
Learned in bodily lowliness
And in the heart's pride.

"A woman can be proud and stiff
When on love intent;
But Love has pitched his mansion in
The place of excrement;
For nothing can be sole or whole
That has not been rent."

William Butler Yeats (1865–1939)

FOR ANNE GREGORY 1933

"Never shall a young man,
Thrown into despair
By those great honey-colored
Ramparts at your ear,
Love you for yourself alone
And not your yellow hair."

"But I can get a hair-dye
And set such color there,
Brown, or black, or carrot,
That young men in despair
May love me for myself alone
And not my yellow hair."

"I heard an old religious man
But yesternight declare
That he had found a text to prove
That only God, my dear,
Could love you for yourself alone
And not your yellow hair."

William Butler Yeats (1865–1939)

The Lake Isle of Innisfree

1892

I will arise and go now, and go to Innisfree,
And a small cabin build there, of clay and wattles made:
Nine bean-rows will I have there, a hive for the honey-bee,
And live alone in the bee-loud glade.

And I shall have some peace there, for peace comes dropping slow,
Dropping from the veils of the morning to where the cricket sings;
There midnight's all a glimmer, and noon a purple glow,
And evening full of the linnet's wings.

I will arise and go now, for always night and day
I hear lake water lapping with low sounds by the shore;
While I stand on the roadway, or on the pavements grey,
I hear it in the deep heart's core.

The Lake Isle of Innisfree. Yeats refers to an island in Lough (Lake) Gill, in County Sligo in the west of Ireland. 2. *wattles:* frameworks of interwoven sticks or branches, used to make walls and roofs.

Compare:

"The Lake Isle of Innisfree" with Yeats's "Sailing to Byzantium" (page 260).

William Butler Yeats (1865–1939)

Lapis Lazuli

1938

For Harry Clifton

I have heard that hysterical women say
They are sick of the palette and fiddle-bow,

Of poets that are always gay,
For everybody knows or else should know
That if nothing drastic is done
Aeroplane and Zeppelin will come out,
Pitch like King Billy bomb-balls in
Until the town lie beaten flat.

All perform their tragic play,
There struts Hamlet, there is Lear,
That's Ophelia, that Cordelia;
Yet they, should the last scene be there,
The great stage curtain about to drop,
If worthy their prominent part in the play,
Do not break up their lines to weep.
They know that Hamlet and Lear are gay;
Gaiety transfiguring all that dread.
All men have aimed at, found and lost;
Black out; Heaven blazing into the head:
Tragedy wrought to its uttermost.
Though Hamlet rambles and Lear rages,
And all the drop-scenes drop at once
Upon a hundred thousand stages,
It cannot grow by an inch or an ounce.

On their own feet they came, or on shipboard,
Camel-back, horse-back, ass-back, mule-back,
Old civilizations put to the sword.
Then they and their wisdom went to rack:
No handiwork of Callimachus,
Who handled marble as if it were bronze,
Made draperies that seemed to rise
When sea-wind swept the corner, stands;
His long lamp-chimney shaped like the stem
Of a slender palm, stood but a day;
All things fall and are built again,
And those that build them again are gay.

Two Chinamen, behind them a third,
Are carved in lapis lazuli,
Over them flies a long-legged bird,
A symbol of longevity;
The third, doubtless a serving-man,
Carries a musical instrument.
Every discoloration of the stone,
Every accidental crack or dent,
Seems a water-course or an avalanche,
Or lofty slope where it still snows
Though doubtless plum or cherry-branch
Sweetens the little half-way house
Those Chinamen climb towards, and I
Delight to imagine them seated there;

There, on the mountain and the sky,
On all the tragic scene they stare.
One asks for mournful melodies;
Accomplished fingers begin to play.
Their eyes mid many wrinkles, their eyes,
Their ancient, glittering eyes, are gay.

LAPIS LAZULI. Lapis lazuli is a deep blue semiprecious stone. A friend had given Yeats the carving made from it, which he describes in lines 37-56. 7. *King Billy:* William of Orange, king of England who used cannon against the Irish in the Battle of the Boyne, 1690. Yeats also may have in mind Kaiser Wilhelm II of Germany, who sent zeppelins to bomb London in World War I. 29. *Callimachus:* Athenian sculptor, fifth century B.C.

COMPARE:

"Lapis Lazuli" with "Ode on a Grecian Urn" by John Keats (page 335) and "Anecdote of the Jar" by Wallace Stevens (page 213).

William Butler Yeats (1865–1939)

THE MAGI 1914

Now as at all times I can see in the mind's eye,
In their stiff, painted clothes, the pale unsatisfied ones
Appear and disappear in the blue depth of the sky
With all their ancient faces like rain-beaten stones,
And all their helms of silver hovering side by side,
And all their eyes still fixed, hoping to find once more,
Being by Calvary's turbulence unsatisfied,
The uncontrollable mystery on the bestial floor.

COMPARE:

"The Magi" with "Journey of the Magi" by T. S. Eliot (page 309).

Anthology: Criticism

The critical power is of lower rank than the creative. True, but in assenting to this proposition, one or two things are to be kept in mind. It is undeniable that the exercise of a creative power, that a free creative activity, is the true function of man; it is proved to be so by man's finding in it his true happiness. But it is undeniable, also, that men may have the sense of exercising this free creative activity in other ways than in producing great works of literature or art; if it were not so, all but a very few men would be shut out from the true happiness of all men; they may have it in well-doing, they may have it in learning, they may have it even in criticising.

—Matthew Arnold, "The Function of Criticism"

Anthology: Criticism

"A poem is a pheasant," said Wallace Stevens. Studying poetry, you may find it useful at times to have before you the exact words of a critic who has described that elusive, easily startled bird. Here then are twenty critical insights. Some are unfamiliar; others are among the best-known, most stimulating remarks about poetry ever made. Included are a few remarks by poets, such as Robert Frost's to his friend about the "sound of sense," which Frost called "the most important thing I know." May they widen your own thinking about poetry and perhaps give you something tough to argue with. Some are controversial. Socrates' case against poets, for instance, remains a fresh and lively opinion still debatable even after twenty-three-hundred-odd years. Nor do these critics chime in perfect harmony. You may hear a certain jangling in their views.

After each passage, its source is indicated. Should one of these ideas capture your interest, why settle for the excerpt given here?

Plato (427?–347? B.C.)

INSPIRATION[1] (ABOUT 390 B.C.)

Ion: The world agrees with me in thinking that I do speak better and have more to say about Homer than any other man. But I do not speak equally well about others—tell me the reason for this.

Socrates: I perceive, Ion; and I will proceed to explain to you what I imagine to be the reason for this. The gift which you possess of speaking excellently about Homer is not an art, but, as I was just saying, an inspiration; there is a divinity moving you, like that contained in the stone which Euripides calls a magnet, but which is commonly known as the stone of Heraclea. This stone not only attracts iron rings, but also imparts to them a similar power of attracting other rings; and sometimes you may see a number of pieces of iron and rings suspended from one another so as to form quite a long chain: and all of them derive their power of suspension from the original stone. In like manner the Muse first of all inspires men herself; and from these inspired persons a chain of other persons is suspended, who take the inspiration. For all good poets, epic as well as lyric, compose their beautiful poems not by art, but because they are inspired and possessed. And as the Corybantian revellers when they dance are not in their right mind, so the lyric poets are not in their right mind when they are composing their beautiful strains: but when falling under the power of music and meter they are inspired and possessed; like Bacchic maidens who draw milk and honey from the rivers when they are under the influence of Dionysus but not when they are in their right mind. And the soul of the lyric poet does the same, as they themselves say; for they tell us that they bring songs from honeyed fountains, culling them out of the gardens and dells of the Muses; they, like the bees, winging their way from

[1] Translated by Benjamin Jowett.

flower to flower. And this is true. For the poet is a light and winged and holy thing, and there is no invention in him until he has been inspired and is out of his senses, and the mind is no longer in him: when he has not attained to this state, he is powerless and is unable to utter his oracles. Many are the noble words in which poets speak concerning the actions of men; but like yourself when speaking about Homer, they do not speak of them by any rules of art: they are simply inspired to utter that to which the Muse impels them, and that only; and when inspired, one of them will make dithyrambs, another hymns of praise, another choral strains, another epic or iambic verses—and he who is good at one is not good at any other kind of verse: for not by art does the poet sing, but by power divine. Had he learned by rules of art, he would have known how to speak not of one theme only, but of all; and therefore God takes away the minds of poets, and uses them as his ministers, as he also uses diviners and holy prophets, in order that we who hear them may know them to be speaking not of themselves who utter these priceless words in a state of unconsciousness, but that God himself is the speaker, and that through them he is conversing with us. And Tynnichus the Chalcidian affords a striking instance of what I am saying: he wrote nothing that any one would care to remember but the famous paean which is in every one's mouth, one of the finest poems ever written, simply an invention of the Muses, as he himself says. For in this way the God would seem to indicate to us and not allow us to doubt that these beautiful poems are not human, or the work of man, but divine and the work of God; and that the poets are only the interpreters of the Gods by whom they are severally possessed. Was not this the lesson which the God intended to teach when by the mouth of the worst of poets he sang the best of songs? Am I not right, Ion?

Ion

INSPIRATION. Plato records a dialogue between his master, the philosopher Socrates (469 B.C.–399 B.C.) and Ion, a young man of Athens. *Corybantian revellers:* The Corybants, priests or attendants of the nature goddess Cybele, deity of the ancient peoples of Asia Minor, were given to orgiastic rites and frenzied dances. *Bacchic maidens:* attendants of the god of wine and fertility, called Dionysus by the Greeks, Bacchus by the Romans. *Muses:* In Greek mythology, nine sister goddesses who presided over poetry and song, the arts and sciences.

Plato (427?–347? B.C.)

SOCRATES BANISHES POETS FROM HIS IDEAL STATE[2]

(ABOUT 373 B.C.)

Socrates: Hear and judge: The best of us, I conceive, when we listen to a passage of Homer, or one of the tragedians, in which he represents some pitiful hero who is drawling out his sorrows in a long oration, or weeping, and smiting his breast—the best of us, you know, delight in giving way to sympathy, and are in raptures at the excellence of the poet who stirs our feelings most.

Glaucon: Yes, of course I know.

[2] Translated by Benjamin Jowett.

Socrates: But when any sorrow of our own happens to us, then you may observe that we pride ourselves on the opposite quality—we would fain be quiet and patient; this is the manly part, and the other which delighted us in the recitation is now deemed to be the part of a woman.

Glaucon: Very true.

Socrates: Now can we be right in praising and admiring another who is doing that which any one of us would abominate and be ashamed of in his own person?

Glaucon: No, that is certainly not reasonable.

Socrates: Nay, quite reasonable from one point of view.

Glaucon: What point of view?

Socrates: If you consider that when in misfortune we feel a natural hunger and desire to relieve our sorrow by weeping and lamentation, and that this feeling which is kept under control in our own calamities is satisfied and delighted by the poets;—the better nature in each of us, not having been sufficiently trained by reason or habit, allows the sympathetic element to break loose because the sorrow is another's; and the spectator fancies that there can be no disgrace to himself in praising and pitying any one who comes telling him what a good man he is, and making a fuss about his troubles; he thinks that the pleasure is a gain, and why should he be supercilious and lose this and the poem too? Few persons ever reflect, as I should imagine, that from the evil of other men something of evil is communicated to themselves. And so the feeling of sorrow which has gathered strength at the sight of the misfortunes of others is with difficulty repressed in our own.

Glaucon: How very true!

Socrates: And does not the same hold also of the ridiculous? There are jests which you would be ashamed to make yourself, and yet on the comic stage, or indeed in private, when you hear them, you are greatly amused by them, and are not at all disgusted at their unseemliness;—the case of pity is repeated;—there is a principle in human nature which is disposed to raise a laugh, and this which you once restrained by reason, because you were afraid of being thought a buffoon, is now let out again; and having stimulated the risible faculty at the theater, you are betrayed unconsciously to yourself into playing the comic poet at home.

Glaucon: Quite true.

Socrates: And the same may be said of lust and anger and all the other affections, of desire and pain and pleasure, which are held to be inseparable from every action—in all of them poetry feeds and waters the passions instead of drying them up; she lets them rule, although they ought to be controlled, if mankind are ever to increase in happiness and virtue.

Glaucon: I cannot deny it.

Socrates: Therefore, Glaucon, whenever you meet with any of the eulogists of Homer declaring that he has been the educator of Hellas, and that he is profitable for education and for the ordering of human things, and that you should take him up again and again and get to know him and regulate your whole life according to him, we may love and honor those who say these things—they are excellent people, as far as their lights extend; and we are ready to acknowledge that Homer is the greatest of poets and first of tragedy writers; but we must remain firm in our conviction that hymns to the gods and praises of famous men are the only poetry which ought to be admitted into our State. For if you go beyond this and allow the honeyed muse to enter, either in epic or lyric verse, not law and the reason of mankind, which by common consent have ever been deemed best, but pleasure and pain will be the rulers in our State.

Glaucon: That is most true.

Socrates: And now since we have reverted to the subject of poetry, let this our defense serve to show the reasonableness of our former judgment in sending away out of our State an art having the tendencies which we have described; for reason constrained us. But that she may not impute to us any harshness or want of politeness, let us tell her that there is an ancient quarrel between philosophy and poetry; of which there are many proofs, such as the saying of 'the yelping hound howling at her lord,' or of one 'mighty in the vain talk of fools,' and 'the mob of sages circumventing Zeus,' and the 'subtle thinkers who are beggars after all'; and there are innumerable other signs of ancient enmity between them. Notwithstanding this, let us assure our sweet friend and the sister arts of imitation, that if she will only prove her title to exist in a well-ordered State we shall be delighted to receive her—we are very conscious of her charms; but we may not on that account betray the truth.

The Republic, X

Aristotle (384–322 B.C.)

TWO CAUSES OF POETRY[3] (ABOUT 330 B.C.)

Poetry in general seems to have sprung from two causes, each of them lying deep in our nature. First, the instinct of imitation is implanted in man from childhood, one difference between him and other animals being that he is the most imitative of living creatures; and through imitation he learns his earliest lessons; and no less universal is the pleasure felt in things imitated. We have evidence of this in the facts of experience. Objects which in themselves we view with pain, we delight to contemplate when reproduced with minute fidelity: such as the forms of the most ignoble animals and of dead bodies. The cause of this again is, that to learn gives the liveliest pleasure, not only to philosophers but to men in general; whose capacity, however, of learning is more limited. Thus the reason why men enjoy seeing a likeness is, that in contemplating it they find themselves learning or inferring, and saying perhaps, "Ah, that is he." For if you happen not to have seen the original, the pleasure will be due not to the imitation as such, but to the execution, the coloring, or some such other cause.

Imitation, then, is one instinct of our nature. Next, there is the instinct for "harmony" and rhythm, meters being manifestly sections of rhythm. Persons, therefore, starting with this natural gift developed by degrees their special aptitudes, till their rude improvisations gave birth to Poetry.

Poetics, IV

[3] Translated by S. H. Butcher.

Sir Philip Sidney (1554–1586)

NATURE AND THE POET 1595

There is no art delivered unto mankind that hath not the works of nature for [its] principal object, without which they could not consist, and on which they so depend as they become actors and players, as it were, of what nature will have set forth. So doth the astronomer look upon the stars, and, by that he seeth, set down what order nature hath taken therein. . . . The physician weigheth the nature of man's body, and the nature of things helpful or hurtful unto it. And the metaphysician, though it be in the second and abstract notions, and therefore be counted supernatural, yet doth he, indeed, build upon the depth of nature.

Only the poet, disdaining to be tied to any such subjection, lifted up with the vigor of his own invention, doth grow, in effect, into another nature, in making things either better than nature bringeth forth, or, quite anew, forms such as never were in nature, as the heroes, demi-gods, cyclops, chimeras, furies, and such like; so as he goeth hand in hand with nature, not enclosed within the narrow warrant of her gifts, but freely ranging within the zodiac of his own wit. Nature never set forth the earth in so rich tapestry as divers poets have done; neither with pleasant rivers, fruitful trees, sweet-smelling flowers, nor whatsoever else may make the too-much-loved earth more lovely; her world is brazen, the poets only deliver a golden.

The Defense of Poetry

Samuel Johnson (1709–1784)

'THE BUSINESS OF A POET' 1759

The business of a poet is to examine, not the individual, but the species; to remark general properties and large appearances; he does not number the streaks of the tulip, or describe the different shades in the verdure of the forest. He is to exhibit in his portraits of nature such prominent and striking features as recall the original to every mind, and must neglect the minuter discriminations, which one may have remarked and another have neglected, for those characteristics which are alike obvious to vigilance and carelessness.

But the knowledge of nature is only half the task of a poet; he must be acquainted likewise with all the modes of life. His character requires that he estimate the happiness and misery of every condition, observe the power of all the passions in all their combinations, and trace the changes of the human mind as they are modified by various institutions and accidental influences of climate or custom, from the sprightliness of infancy to the despondency of decrepitude. He must divest himself of the prejudices of his age or country; he must consider right and wrong in their abstracted and variable state; he must disregard present laws and opinions, and rise to general and transcendental truths, which will always be the same.

The History of Rasselas,
Prince of Abyssinia

William Wordsworth (1770–1850)

'EMOTION RECOLLECTED IN TRANQUILLITY' 1800

I have said that poetry is the spontaneous overflow of powerful feelings: it takes its origin from emotion recollected in tranquillity: the emotion is contemplated till, by a species of reaction, the tranquillity gradually disappears, and an emotion, kindred to that which was before the subject of contemplation, is gradually produced, and does itself actually exist in the mind. In this mood successful composition generally begins, and in a mood similar to this it is carried on; but the emotion, of whatever kind, and in whatever degree, from various causes, is qualified by various pleasures, so that in describing any passions whatsoever, which are voluntarily described, the mind will, upon the whole, be in a state of enjoyment. If Nature be thus cautious to preserve in a state of enjoyment a being so employed, the Poet ought to profit by the lesson held forth to him, and ought especially to take care, that, whatever passions he communicates to his Reader, those passions, if his Reader's mind be sound and vigorous, should always be accompanied with an overbalance of pleasure. Now the music of harmonious metrical language, the sense of difficulty overcome, and the blind association of pleasure which has been previously received from works of rhyme or meter of the same or similar construction, an indistinct perception perpetually renewed of language closely resembling that of real life, and yet, in the circumstance of meter, differing from it so widely—all these imperceptibly make up a complex feeling of delight, which is of the most important use in tempering the painful feeling always found intermingled with powerful descriptions of the deeper passions. This effect is always produced in pathetic and impassioned poetry; while, in lighter compositions, the ease and gracefulness with which the Poet manages his numbers are themselves confessedly a principal source of the gratification of the Reader. All that it is *necessary* to say, however, upon this subject, may be effected by affirming, what few persons will deny, that, of two descriptions, either of passions, manners, or characters, each of them equally well executed, the one in prose and the other in verse, the verse will be read a hundred times where the prose is read once.

Preface to *Lyrical Ballads*,
second edition

'EMOTION RECOLLECTED IN TRANQUILLITY.' For information on Wordsworth's methods of composition in his poem "I Wandered Lonely as a Cloud," see pages 18–19.

Samuel Taylor Coleridge (1772–1834)

'THAT SYNTHETIC AND MAGICAL POWER' 1817

What is poetry?—is so nearly the same question with, what is a poet?—that the answer to the one is involved in the solution of the other. For it is a distinction resulting from the poetic genius itself, which sustains and modifies the images, thoughts, and emotions of the poet's own mind.

The poet, described in ideal perfection, brings the whole soul of man into activity, with the subordination of its faculties to each other according to their relative worth and dignity. He diffuses a tone and spirit of unity, that blends, and (as it were) *fuses*, each into each, by that synthetic and magical power, to which I would exclusively appropriate the name of Imagination. This power, first put in action by the will and understanding, and retained under their irremissive, though gentle and unnoticed, control, *laxis effertur habenis,* reveals itself in the balance or reconcilement of opposite or discordant qualities; of sameness, with difference; of the general with the concrete; the idea with the image; the individual with the representative; the sense of novelty and freshness with old and familiar objects; a more than usual state of emotion with more than usual order; judgment ever awake and steady self-possession, with enthusiasm and feeling profound and vehement; and while it blends and harmonizes the natural and the artificial, still subordinates art to nature; the manner to the matter; and our admiration of the poet to our sympathy with the poetry.

Biographia Literaria: or, Biographical Sketches of My Literary Life and Opinions, Chapter XIV

'THAT SYNTHETIC AND MAGICAL POWER.' The Latin phrase *laxis effertur habenis* means "is driven with reins relaxed."

Samuel Taylor Coleridge (1772–1834)

THE 'OBSCURITY' OF MILTON (1818?)

The reader of Milton must always be on his duty: he is surrounded with sense; it rises in every line; every word is to the purpose. There are no lazy intervals; all has been considered, and demands and merits observation. If this be called obscurity, let it be remembered that it is such obscurity as is a compliment to the reader; not that vicious obscurity which proceeds from a muddled head.

Lectures on Shakespeare and Milton

Percy Bysshe Shelley (1792–1822)

'UNACKNOWLEDGED LEGISLATORS' (1821)

The most unfailing herald, companion, and follower of the awakening of a great people to work a beneficial change in opinion or institution, is poetry. At such periods there is an accumulation of the power of communicating and receiving intense and impassioned conceptions respecting man and nature. The persons in whom this power resides, may often, as far as regards many portions of their nature, have little apparent correspondence with that spirit of good of which they are the ministers. But even whilst they deny and abjure, they are yet compelled to serve, the power which is seated on the throne of their own soul. It is impossible to read the compositions of the most celebrated writers of the present day without being startled with the electric life which burns within their words. They measure the circumference and sound the depths of human nature with a comprehensive and all-penetrating spirit, and they are themselves perhaps the most sincerely astonished at its manifestations; for it is less their spirit than the spirit of the age. Poets are the hierophants of an unapprehended inspiration; the mirrors of the gigantic shadows which futurity casts upon the present; the words which express what they understand not; the trumpets which sing to battle, and feel not what they inspire; the influence which is moved not, but moves. Poets are the unacknowledged legislators of the world.

A Defense of Poetry

Ralph Waldo Emerson (1803–1882)

'Meter-making argument' — 1844

I took part in a conversation the other day concerning a recent writer of lyrics, a man of subtle mind, whose head appeared to be a music-box of delicate tunes and rhythms, and whose skill and command of language we could not sufficiently praise. But when the question arose whether he was not only a lyrist but a poet, we were obliged to confess that he is plainly a contemporary, not an eternal man. He does not stand out of our low limitations, like a Chimborazo under the line, running up from a torrid base through all the climates of the globe, with belts of the herbage of every latitude on its high and mottled sides; but this genius is the landscape-garden of a modern house adorned with fountains and statues, with well-bred men and women standing and sitting in the walks and terraces. We hear, through all the varied music, the ground-tone of conventional life. Our poets are men of talents who sing, and not the children of music. The argument is secondary, the finish of the verses is primary.

For it is not meters, but a meter-making argument that makes a poem,—a thought so passionate and alive that like the spirit of a plant or an animal it has an architecture of its own, and adorns nature with a new thing. The thought and the form are equal in the order of time, but in the order of genesis the thought is prior to the form. The poet has a new thought; he has a whole new experience to unfold; he will tell us how it was with him, and all men will be the richer in his fortune. For the experience of each new age requires a new confession, and the world seems always waiting for its poet.

The Poet

'Meter-making argument.' *Chimborazo under the line:* mountain in Ecuador, south of the Equator.

Edgar Allan Poe (1809–1849)

'A long poem does not exist' — 1848

I hold that a long poem does not exist. I maintain that the phrase, "a long poem," is simply a flat contradiction in terms.

I need scarcely observe that a poem deserves its title only inasmuch as it excites, by elevating the soul. The value of the poem is in the ratio of its elevative excitement. But all excitements are, through a psychal necessity, transient. That degree of excitement which would entitle a poem to be so called at all cannot be sustained throughout a composition of any great length. After the lapse of half an hour, at the very utmost, it flags—fails—a revulsion ensues—and then the poem is in effect, and in fact, no longer such.

The Poetic Principle

Robert Frost (1874–1963)

'THE SOUND OF SENSE' (1913)

I alone of English writers have consciously set myself to make music out of what I may call the sound of sense. Now it is possible to have sense without the sound of sense (as in much prose that is supposed to pass muster but makes very dull reading) and the sound of sense without sense (as in Alice in Wonderland which makes anything but dull reading). The best place to get the abstract sound of sense is from voices behind a door that cuts off the words. Ask yourself how these sentences would sound without the words in which they are embodied:

You mean to tell me you can't read?
I said no such thing.
Well read then.
You're not my teacher.

• • •

He says it's too late.
Oh, say!
Damn an Ingersoll watch anyway.

• • •

One-two-three—go!
No good! Come back——come back.
Haslam go down there and make those kids get out of the track.

• • •

Those sounds are summoned by the [audial] imagination and they must be positive, strong, and definitely and unmistakably indicated by the context. The reader must be at no loss to give his voice the posture proper to the sentence. The simple declarative sentence used in making a plain statement is one sound. But Lord love ye it mustn't be worked to death. It is against the law of nature that whole poems should be written in it. If they are written they won't be read. The sound of sense, then. You get that. It is the abstract vitality of our speech. It is pure sound—pure form. One who concerns himself with it more than the subject is an artist. But remember we are still talking merely of the raw material of poetry. An ear and an appetite for these sounds of sense is the first qualification of a writer, be it of prose or verse. But if one is to be a poet he must learn to get cadences by skillfully breaking the sounds of sense with all their irregularity of accent across the regular beat of the meter. Verse in which there is nothing but the beat of the meter furnished by the accents of the polysyllabic words we call doggerel. Verse is not that. Neither is it the sound of sense alone.

It is a resultant from those two. There are only two or three meters that are worth anything. We depend for variety on the infinite play of accents in the sound of sense. The high possibility of emotional expression all lets in this mingling of sense-sound and word-accent. A curious thing. And all this has its bearing on your prose, me boy. Never if you can help it write down a sentence in which the voice will not know how to posture *specially*.

Letter to John T. Bartlett, from *Selected Letters of Robert Frost,* edited by Lawrence Thompson (New York: Holt, Rinehart and Winston, 1964)

Wallace Stevens (1879–1955)

PROVERBS 1957

The poet makes silk dresses out of worms.

After one has abandoned a belief in God, poetry is that essence which takes its place as life's redemption.

All poetry is experimental poetry.

One reads poetry with one's nerves.

A poet looks at the world as a man looks at a woman.

Aristotle is a skeleton.

Thought tends to collect in pools.

Poetry must resist the intelligence almost successfully.

One cannot spend one's time in being modern when there are so many more important things to be.

Adagia, *Opus Posthumous*

William Carlos Williams (1883–1963)

'THE RHYTHM PERSISTS' (1913?)

No action, no creative action is complete but a period from a greater action going in rhythmic course. . . . Imagination creates an image, point by point, piece by piece, segment by segment—into a whole, living. But each part as it plays into its neighbor, each segment into its neighbor segment and every part into every other, causing the whole—exists naturally in rhythm, and as there are waves there are tides and as there are ridges in the sand there are bars after bars. . . .

I do not believe in *vers libre*, this contradiction in terms. Either the motion continues or it does not continue, either there is rhythm or no rhythm. *Vers libre* is prose. In the hands of Whitman it was a good tool, a kind of synthetic chisel—the best he had. In his bag of chunks even lie some of the pieces of rhythmic life of which we must build. This is honor enough. *Vers libre* is finished—Whitman did all that was necessary with it. Verse has nothing to gain here and all to lose. . . . .

Each piece of work, rhythmic in whole, is then in essence an assembly of tides, waves, ripples—in short, of greater and lesser rhythmic particles regularly repeated or destroyed.

Essay "Speech Rhythm" quoted by Mike Weaver,
William Carlos Williams, The American Background
(New York: Cambridge University Press, 1971)

William Carlos Williams (1883–1963)

THE CRAB AND THE BOX 1952

Forcing twentieth-century America into a sonnet—gosh, how I hate sonnets—is like putting a crab into a square box. You've got to cut his legs off to make him fit. When you get through, you don't have a crab any more.

Statement to Dorothy Tooker,
Interviews with William Carlos Williams,
edited by Linda Welshimer Wagner
(New York: New Directions, 1976)

Ezra Pound (1885–1972)

POETRY AND MUSIC 1934

The great lyric age lasted while Campion made his own music, while Lawes set Waller's verses, while verses, if not actually sung or set to music, were at least made with the intention of going to music.

Music rots when it gets *too far* from the dance. Poetry atrophies when it gets too far from music.

ABC of Reading

T. S. Eliot (1888–1965)

EMOTION AND PERSONALITY 1920

It is not in his personal emotions, the emotions provoked by particular events in his life, that the poet is in any way remarkable or interesting. His particular emotions may be simple, or crude, or flat. The emotion in his poetry will be a very complex thing, but not with the complexity of the emotions of people who have very complex or unusual emotions in life. One error, in fact, of eccentricity in poetry is to seek for new human emotions to express; and in this search for novelty in the wrong place it discovers the perverse. The business of the poet is not to find new emotions, but to use the ordinary ones and, in working them up into poetry, to express feelings which are not in actual emotions at all. And emotions which he has never experienced will serve his turn as well as those familiar to him. Consequently, we must believe that "emotion recollected in tranquillity" is an inexact formula. For it is neither emotion, nor recollection, nor, without distortion of meaning, tranquillity. It is a concentration, and a new thing resulting from the concentration, of a very great number of experiences which to the practical and active person would not seem to be experiences at all; it is a concentration which does not happen consciously or of deliberation. These experiences are not "recollected," and they finally unite in an atmosphere which is "tranquil" only in that it is a passive attending upon the event. Of course this is not quite the whole story. There is a great deal, in the writing of poetry, which must be conscious and deliberate. In fact, the bad poet is usually unconscious where he ought to be conscious, and conscious where he ought to be unconscious. Both errors tend to make him "personal." Poetry is not a turning loose of emotion, but an escape from emotion; it is not the expression of personality, but an escape from personality. But, of course, only those who have personality and emotions know what it means to want to escape from these things.

Tradition and the Individual Talent

Yvor Winters (1900–1968)

'The fallacy of expressive form' 1939

I cannot grasp the contemporary notion that the traditional virtues of style are incompatible with a poetry of modern subject matter; it appears to rest on the fallacy of expressive form, the notion that the form of the poem should express the matter. This fallacy results in the writing of chaotic poetry about the traffic; of loose poetry about our sprawling nation; of semi-conscious poetry about our semi-conscious states. But the matter of poetry is and always has been chaotic; it is raw nature. To let the form of the poem succumb to its matter is and always will be the destruction of poetry and may be the destruction of intelligence.

Before Disaster

Randall Jarrell (1914–1965)

On the charge that modern poetry is obscure 1953

That the poet, the modern poet, is, understandably enough, for all sorts of good reasons, more obscure than even he has any imaginable right to be—this is one of those great elementary (or, as people say nowadays, *elemental*) attitudes about which it is hard to write anything that is not sensible and gloomily commonplace; one might as well talk on faith and works, on heredity and environment, or on that old question: why give the poor bath-tubs when they only use them to put coal in? Anyone knows enough to reply to this question: "They don't; and, even if they did, *that's* not the reason you don't want to help pay for the tubs." Similarly, when someone says, "I don't read modern poetry because it's all stuff that nobody on earth can understand," I know enough to be able to answer, though not aloud: "It isn't; and, even if it were, *that's* not the reason you don't read it." . . . And people who have inherited the custom of not reading poets justify it by referring to the obscurity of the poems they have never read—since most people decide that poets are obscure very much as legislators decide that books are pornographic: by glancing at a few fragments someone has strung together to disgust them. When a person says accusingly that he can't understand Eliot, his tone implies that most of his happiest hours are spent at the fireside among worn copies of the *Agamemnon, Phèdre,* and the Symbolic Books of William Blake; and it is melancholy to find, as one commonly will, that for months at a time he can be found pushing eagerly through the pages of *Gone with the Wind* or *Forever Amber.*

The Obscurity of the Poet,
Poetry and the Age

On the charge that modern poetry is obscure. *Forever Amber:* novel by Kathleen Winsor, a best-seller in its day (1945). Much of its action takes place in bed.

Barbara Herrnstein Smith (b. 1932)

Closure and anti-closure 1968

"Openness," the "anti-teleological," the positive value placed on the unfinished look or sound—anti-closure, in other words, is evidently a sign of the times in contemporary art; and whether one refers it specifically to a revolution in philosophy or in art history, one suspects that it is ultimately related to even more general developments and crises. . . . We know too much and are skeptical of all that we know, feel, and say. All traditions are equally viable partly because all are equally suspect. Where conviction is seen as self-delusion and all last words are lies, the only resolution may be in the affirmation of irresolution, and conclusiveness may be seen as not only less honest but *less stable* than inconclusiveness. . . .

The song of uncertainty in modern poetry expresses the temper (or distemper) of our times thematically; it also reflects in its very structure. The relation between structure and closure is of considerable importance here, for "anti-closure" in all the arts is a matter not only of how the works terminate but how and whether they are organized throughout. The "openness" and "unfinished" look and sound of *avant-garde* poetry and music is not a quality of their endings only, but affects the audience's entire experience of such works. . . . Whereas the weak closure of much modern poetry can be understood partly as the result of the prevalence of formal and thematic structures that offer minimal resources for closure, the reverse is also likely: the prevalence of free verse, for example, probably reflects, in part, the impulse to anti-closure, the reaction against poems that "click like a box." . . .

But if the anti-teleology of the modern poet is not so thoroughgoing as that of the painter or composer, it may be due more to the conservatism of the material of his art than to the conservatism of the poet himself. While he may share the general impulse to "radical empiricism," he is confined by the fact that if his empiricism is too radical, his art loses both its identity and, more important, the sources of its characteristic effects. For the material of poetry is not words, but *language*—a system of conventions previously determined and continuously mediated by usage in a community—and if the poem divorces itself utterly from the structure of discourse, it ceases to be poetry and ceases to affect us as such. Although traditional *formal* structures may yield to deliberate dissolution, the design of a poem is never wholly formal and a considerable degree of organization is built into it by virtue of its fundamental relation to the structure of discourse. Consequently, to the extent that anti-closure is a matter of anti-structure, the poet cannot go all the way.

Poetic Closure:
A Study of How Poems End

Supplement

Writing about Literature

That masterly poet and critic T. S. Eliot once declared that, in approaching a work of literature to write about it, the only method he knew was to be very intelligent. Eliot wasn't boasting about his I.Q.; he was suggesting that to a critic of literature, a keen sensibility is more valuable than a carefully worked out method, any day. Although none of us may be another Eliot, all of us have some powers of reasoning and perception. And when we come to a story, a poem, or a play, we can do little other than to trust whatever powers we have, like one who enters a shadowy room, clutching a decent candle.

After all, in the study of literature, common sense (as poet Gerard Manley Hopkins said) is never out of place. For most of a class hour, a renowned English professor once rhapsodized about the arrangement of the contents of W. H. Auden's *Collected Poems.* Auden, he claimed, was a master of thematic continuity, who had brilliantly placed the poems in the best possible order, in which (to the ingenious mind) they complemented each other. Near the end of the hour, his theories were punctured – with a great inaudible pop – when a student timidly raising a hand pointed out that Auden had arranged the poems in the book not according to theme but in alphabetical order according to the first word of each poem. The professor's jaw dropped: "Why didn't you say that sooner?" The student was apologetic: "I – I was afraid I'd sound too *ordinary.*"

Emerson makes a similar point in his essay "The American Scholar": "Meek young men grow up in libraries, believing it their duty to accept the views which Cicero, which Locke, which Bacon have given; forgetful that Cicero, Locke, and Bacon were only young men in libraries when they wrote these books." Don't be afraid to state a conviction, though it seems obvious. Does it matter that you may be repeating something that, once upon a time or even just the other day, has been said before? There are excellent old ideas as well as new.

SOME APPROACHES TO LITERATURE

Though T. S. Eliot may be right in preferring intelligence to method, there are certain familiar approaches to stories, poems, and plays which most critical essays tend to follow. Underlying each of these four approaches is a certain way of regarding the nature of a work of literature.

1. *The Work by Itself.* This view assumes a story, poem, or play to be an individual entity, existing on its page, that we can read and understand in its own right, without necessarily studying the life of its author, or the age in which it was written, or its possible effect on its readers. This is the approach of most papers written in response to college assignments; to study just the work (and not its backgrounds or its influence) does not require the student to spend prolonged time doing research in a library. The three common ways of writing a paper discussed earlier in this book — explication, analysis, and comparison and contrast — are concerned mainly with the work of literature in itself.

2. *The Work as Imitation of Life.* Aristotle called the art of writing a tragedy *mimesis:* the imitation or re-creation of an action that is serious and complete in itself. From this classic theory in the *Poetics* comes the view that a work of literature in some way imitates the world or the civilization in which it was produced. We can say, for instance, that Ibsen's play *A Doll House* places before our eyes actors whose life-like speeches and movements represent members of an upper-middle-class society in provincial Norway in the late nineteenth century and that the play reflects their beliefs and attitudes. Not only the subject and theme of a work imitate life in this view: John Ciardi has remarked that the heroic couplet, dominant stanza form in poetry read by educated people in eighteenth-century England, reflects, in its exact form and its use of antitheses, the rhythms of the minuet — another contemporary form, fashionable also among the well-to-do: "now on this hand, now on that." The writer concerned with literature as imitation usually studies the world that the literary work imitates. He or she goes into the ideas underlying the writer's society, showing how the themes, assumptions, and conventions of the writer's work arose out of that time and that place. Obviously, this takes more research than one can do for a weekly paper; it is usually the approach taken for a book or a dissertation, or perhaps an honors thesis or a term paper. (The other two approaches we will mention also take research.) Reasonably short studies of the relation between the work and its world are, however, sometimes possible: "World War II as Seen in Henry Reed's 'Naming of Parts' "; "Faulkner's 'Barn Burning': A Mirror of Mississippi?"

3. *The Work as Expression.* In this view, a work of literature expresses the feelings of the person who wrote it; therefore, to study it, one studies the author's life. Typical paper topics: "*A Glass Menagerie* and the Early Life of Tennessee Williams"; "Sylvia Plath's Lost Father and Her View of Him in 'Daddy.' " To write any truly deep-reaching biographical criticism takes research, clearly, but one could write a term paper on topics such as these by reading a single biography.

Biographical criticism fell into temporary disrepute around 1920, when T. S. Eliot questioned the assumption that a poem has to be a personal statement of the poet's thoughts and emotions.[1] Eliot and other critics did much to clear the air of speculation that the "Ode on a Grecian Urn" may have been shaped by what Keats had had for breakfast. Evidently, in any search for what went on in an author's mind, and for the influence of life upon work, absolute certainty is unattainable. Besides, such an approach can be grossly reductive — holding, for example, that Shakespeare was sad when he wrote his tragedies and especially happy when he wrote *A Midsummer Night's Dream.* Still, there are works that gain in meaning from even a slight knowledge of the author's biography. In reading *Moby-Dick,* it helps to know that Herman Melville served aboard a whaling vessel.

4. *The Work as Influence.* From this perspective, a literary work is a force that affects people. It stirs certain responses in them, rouses their emotions, perhaps argues for ideas that change their minds. The artist, said Tolstoi in a famous pronouncement *(What Is Art?),* "hands on to others those feelings he himself has felt, that they too may be moved, and experience them." Part of the function of art, Tolstoi continued, is to enlighten and to lead its audience into an acceptance of better moral attitudes (religious faith, or a sense of social justice). The critic who takes this approach is generally concerned with the ideas that a literary work imparts and the reception of those ideas by a particular audience: "Did *Uncle Tom's Cabin* Cause the Civil War?"; "The Early Reception of Allen Ginsberg's *Howl*"; "Ed Bullins's Plays and Their Newly Proud Black Audience." As you can see, this whole approach is closely related to viewing a literary work as an imitation of life. Still another way of discussing a work's influence is to trace its impact upon other writers: "Robert Frost's Debt to Emily Dickinson"; "*Moby-Dick* and William Faulkner's *The Bear:* Two Threatened Wildernesses."

FINDING A TOPIC

Offered a choice of literary works to write about, you probably will do best if, instead of choosing what you think will impress your instructor, you choose what appeals to you. And how to find out what appeals? Whether you plan to write a short paper that requires no research beyond the story or poem or play itself, or a long term paper that will take you to the library, the first stage of your project is reading — and note taking. To concentrate your attention, one time-honored method is to read with a pencil, marking (if the book is yours) passages that stand out in importance, jotting brief notes in a margin (*"Key symbol — this foreshadows the ending"; "Dramatic irony"; "IDIOT!!!"*; or other possibly useful remarks). In a long story or poem or play, some students

[1] See Eliot's essay "Tradition and the Individual Talent," in *Selected Essays* (New York: Harcourt Brace, 1932).

asterisk certain passages that cry for comparison: for instance, all the places in which they find the same theme or symbol. Later, at a glance, they can review the highlights of a work and, when writing a paper about it, quickly refer to evidence. This method shoots holes in a book's resale value, but many find the sacrifice worthwhile. Patient souls who dislike butchering a book prefer to take notes on looseleaf notebook paper, holding one sheet beside a page in the book and giving it the book's page-number. Later, in writing a paper, they can place book page and companion note page together again. This method has the advantage of affording a lot of room for note taking; it is a good one for short poems closely packed with complexities.

But by far the most popular method of taking notes (besides writing on the pages of books) is to write on index cards — the 3 x 5 kind, for brief notes and titles; 5 x 8 cards for longer notes. Write on one side only; notes on the back of the card usually get overlooked later. Cards are easy to shuffle and, in organizing your material, to deal. To save work, instead of copying out on a card the title and author of a book you're taking a note from, just keep a numbered list of the books you're using. Then, when making a note, you need write only the book's identifying number on the card in order to identify your source. (Later, when writing footnotes, you can translate the number into title, author, and other information.)

Now that coin-operated photocopy machines are to be found in many libraries, you no longer need to spend hours copying by hand whole poems and longer passages. If accuracy is essential (surely it is) and if a poem or passage is long enough to be worth the investment of a dime, you can lay photocopied material into place in your paper with transparent tape or rubber cement. The latest copyright law permits students and scholars to reproduce books and periodicals in this fashion; it does not, however, permit making a dozen or more copies for public sale.

Certain literary works, because they offer intriguing difficulties, have attracted professional critics by the score. On library shelves, great phalanxes of critical books now stand at the side of James Joyce's complex novels *Ulysses* and *Finnegans Wake*, and T. S. Eliot's allusive poem *The Waste Land*. The student who undertakes to study such works seriously is well advised to profit from the critics' labors. Chances are, too, that even in discussing a relatively uncomplicated work you will want to seek the aid of the finest critics. If you quote them, quote them exactly, in quotation marks, and give them credit. When employed in any but the most superlative student paper, a brilliant phrase (or even a not so brilliant sentence) from a renowned critic is likely to stand out like a golf ball in a gartersnake's midriff, and most English instructors are likely to recognize it. If you rip off the critic's words, then go ahead and steal the whole essay, for good critics tend to write in seamless unities. Then, when apprehended, you can exclaim — like the student whose term paper was found to be the work of a well-known scholar — "I've been robbed! That paper cost me twenty dollars!" But of course the worst rip-off is the one the student inflicted on himself, having got nothing for his money out of a college course but a little practice in touch-typing.

Taking notes on your readings, you will want to jot down the title of every book you might refer to in your paper, and the page number of any passage you might wish to quote. Even if you summarize a critic's idea in your own words, rather than quote, you have to give credit to your source. Nothing is cheaper to give than proper credit. Certainly it's easier to take notes while you read than to have to run back to the library during the final typing.

Choose a topic appropriate to the assigned length of your paper. How do you know the probable length of your discussion until you write it? When in doubt, you are better off to define your topic narrowly. Your paper will be stronger if you go deeper into your subject than if you choose some gigantic subject and then find yourself able to touch on it only superficially. A thorough explication of a short story is hardly possible in a paper of 250 words. There are, in truth, four-line poems whose surface 250 words might only begin to scratch. A profound topic ("The Character of Shakespeare's Hamlet") might overflow a book; but a topic more narrowly defined ("Hamlet's Views of Acting"; "Hamlet's Puns") might result in a more nearly manageable term paper. You can narrow and focus a large topic while you work your way into it. A general interest in "Hemingway's Heroes," for instance, might lead you, in the process of reading, taking notes, and thinking further, to the narrower topic, "Jake Barnes: Spokesman for Hemingway's Views of War."

Many student writers find it helpful, in defining a topic, to state an emerging idea for a paper in a provisional **thesis sentence:** a summing-up of the one main idea or argument that the paper will embody. (A thesis sentence is for your own use; you don't have to implant it in your paper unless your instructor asks for it.) Complete with subject and verb, a good statement of a thesis is not just a disembodied subject; it comes with both subject and verb. ("The Downfall of Oedipus Rex" is not yet a complete idea for a paper; "What Caused the Downfall of Oedipus Rex" is.) A thesis sentence helps you see for yourself what the author you are studying is *saying about* a subject. Not a full thesis, and not a sentence, "The Isolation of City-dwellers in Edward Albee's *A Zoo Story*" might be a decent title for a paper. But it isn't a useful thesis because it doesn't indicate what one might say about that isolation (nor what Albee is saying about it). While it may be obvious that isolation isn't desirable, a clear and workable thesis sentence might be, "In *A Zoo Story* Albee demonstrates that city-dwellers' isolation from one another prompts one city dweller to action"; the paper might well go on to demonstrate just what that action is.

ORGANIZING YOUR THINKING

Topic in hand, perhaps in the form of a thesis sentence on paper, you now begin to sort your miscellaneous thoughts and impressions. To outline or not to outline? Unless your topic, by its very nature, suggests some obvious way to organize your paper ("An Explication of a Wordsworth Sonnet" might mean simply working through the poem line by line), then some kind of outline is practically indispensable. In high school or other prehistoric times, you perhaps learned how to construct a beautiful outline, laid out with Roman numerals, capital letters, Arabic numerals, and small letters. It was a thing of beauty and symmetry, and possibly even had something to do with paper writing. But if now you are skeptical of the value of outlining, reflect: not every outline needs to be detailed and elaborate. Some students, of course, find it helpful to outline in detail — particularly if they are planning a long term paper involving several literary works, comparing and contrasting several aspects of them. For a 500-word analysis of a short story's figures of speech, however, all you might need is a simple list of points to make, scribbled down in the order in which you will make them. This order is probably not, of course, the order in which the points first occurred to you. Thoughts, when they first come to mind, tend to be a confused rabble.

While granting the need for order in a piece of writing, the present writer confesses that he is a reluctant outliner. His tendency (or curse) is to want to keep whatever random thoughts occur to him; to polish his prose right then and there; and finally to try to juggle his disconnected paragraphs into something like logical order. The usual result is that he has large blocks of illogical thought left over. This process is wasteful, and if you can learn to live with an outline, then you belong to the legion of the blessed, and will never know the pain of scrapping pages that cost you hours. On the other hand, you will never know the joy of meandering — of bursting into words and setting them down however wildly, to see what you truly want to say. There is value in such wasteful and self-indulgent writing — but not if a deadline is imminent.

An outline is not meant to stand as an achievement in itself. It should—as Ezra Pound said literary criticism ought to do—consume itself and disappear. Here, for instance, is a once-valuable outline not worth keeping—a very informal one that enabled a student to organize the paper comparing "Design" by Robert Frost with "Wing-Spread" by Abbie Huston Evans that appears on page 436. Before he wrote, the student simply jotted down the points he had in mind. Looking over this "mess of garbage" (as he then regarded it), he could see that, among his scattered thoughts, two topics predominated. One was about figures of speech and about connotations, and these ideas he decided to join under the heading LANGUAGE. His other emerging idea had to do with the two poets' quite different themes. Having perceived that his thoughts weren't totally jumbled, he then proceeded to go through his list, numbering with the same numbers any ideas that seemed to go together, and so arranging them in the order he wanted to follow. His outline then looked like this:

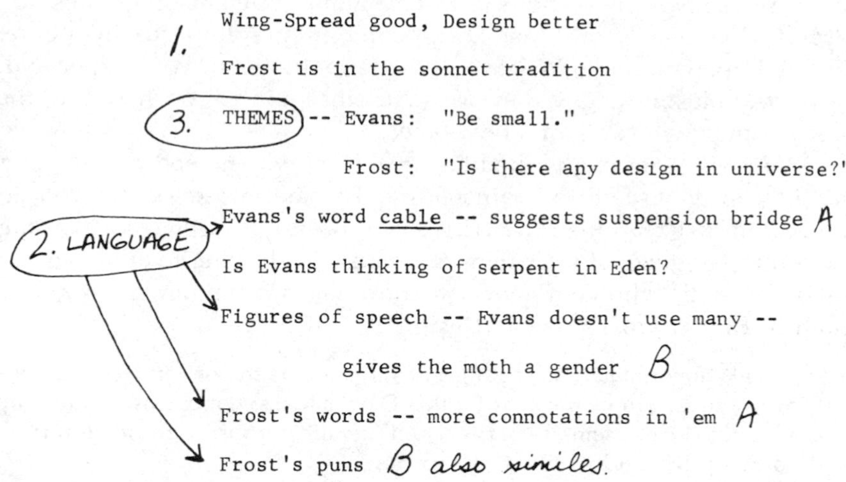
1. Wing-Spread good, Design better

Frost is in the sonnet tradition

3. THEMES -- Evans: "Be small."

Frost: "Is there any design in universe?"

2. LANGUAGE

Evans's word <u>cable</u> -- suggests suspension bridge A

Is Evans thinking of serpent in Eden?

Figures of speech -- Evans doesn't use many --

gives the moth a gender B

Frost's words -- more connotations in 'em A

Frost's puns B also similes.

Labeling with "A" the two points about words full of connotations, and with "B" the two points about figures of speech, the student indicated to himself that these points were to be taken up together. He found, as you can see in the finished essay, two ideas that didn't seem to relate to his purpose. These were the points about Frost's being in the sonnet tradition and about Evans's possible interest in the Garden of Eden serpent. Reluctantly but wisely, he decided to leave them out. These ideas might have led him to make interesting comments on the individual poems, but would not have got him to *compare* the poems, as the assignment asked. Having made this rough outline, he felt encouraged to return to the two poems; and, on rereading them, noticed some further points, which now fell readily into his plan. One of these points was that Frost's poem also contains similes. He added it to his outline and so remembered it.

WRITING A DRAFT

Seated at last, or striking some other businesslike stance,[2] you prepare to write, only to find yourself besieged with petty distractions. All of a sudden you remember a friend you had promised to call, some dry-cleaning you were supposed to pick up, a neglected Coke (in another

[2] R. H. Super of the University of Michigan wrote a definitive biography of Walter Savage Landor while standing up, typing on a machine atop a filing cabinet.

room) growing warmer and flatter by the minute. If your paper is to be written, you have one course of action: to collar these thoughts and for the moment banish them.

Other small problems are merely mechanical: for instance, what to call the author whose work you now confront. Decide at the outset. Most critics favor the author's last name alone: "Dickinson implies . . ." ("Miss Dickinson" or "Ms. Dickinson" may sound fussily polite; "Emily," too chummy.) Will you include footnotes in your paper and, if so, do you know how they work? (Some pointers on handling the pesky things will come in a few pages.)

You will want to give credit to any critics who helped you out, and properly to do so is to be painstaking. To paraphrase a critic, you do more than just rearrange the critic's words and phrases; you translate them into language of your own. Say you wish to refer to an insight of Randall Jarrell, who comments on the images of spider, flower, and moth in Robert Frost's poem "Design":

> Notice how the *heal-all,* because of its name, is the one flower in all the world picked to be the altar for this Devil's Mass; notice how holding up the moth brings something ritual and hieratic, a ghostly, ghastly formality to this priest and its sacrifical victim. . . .

It would be incorrect to say, without any quotation marks:

> Frost picks the heal-all as the one flower in all the world to be the altar for this Devil's Mass. There is a ghostly, ghastly formality to the spider holding up the moth, like a priest holding a sacrificial victim.

That rewording, although not exactly in Jarrell's language, manages to steal his memorable phrases without giving him credit. Nor is it sufficient just to list Jarrell's essay in a bibliography at the end of your paper. If you do, you are still a crook; you merely point to the scene of your crime. What is needed, clearly, is to think through Jarrell's words to the point he is making; and if you want to keep any of his striking phrases (and why not?), put them in quotation marks:

> As Randall Jarrell points out, Frost portrays the spider as a kind of priest in a Mass, or Black Mass, elevating the moth like an object for sacrifice, with "a ghostly, ghastly formality."

To be scrupulous in your acknowledgment, you could even put a footnote after the phrase in quotation marks, citing the book and the page.

But unless your instructor expects you to write such a formal, footnoted paper, the passage as it now stands would make sufficiently clear your source, and your obligation.

One more word of Dutch-uncle warning. This book has offered you a vocabulary with which to discuss literature: a flurry of terms such as *irony, symbol,* and *image,* printed in **bold face** when first introduced. In your writing, perhaps, you may decide to enlist a few of them. And yet, critical terminology—especially if unfamiliar—can tempt a beginning critic to sling it about. Nothing can be less sophisticated, or more misleading, than a technical term grandly misapplied: "The *myth-symbolism* of this *rime scheme* leaves one aghast." Far better to choose plain words you're already at ease with. Your instructor, no doubt, has met many a critical term and is not likely to be impressed by the mere sight of another one. Knowingly selected and placed, a critical term can help sharpen a thought and make it easier to handle. Clearly it is less cumbersome to refer to the *tone* of a story than to have to say, "the way the author makes you feel that she feels about what she is talking about." But the paper-writer who declares, "The tone of this poem is full of ironic imagery," fries words to a hash—mixed up and indigestible.

REVISING

Is it possible to write with perfect clarity on first try, to drop ideas with a single shot at them? Doubtless there are writers who can do so. Jack Kerouac, a believer in spontaneous prose, used to write entire novels on uncut ribbons of teletype paper, which custom saved him the interruption of stopping at the bottom of each page; and he declared that he rarely felt the need to change a word. His specialty, though, was fiction of ecstasy and hallucination, not essays in explication, or comparison and contrast. D. H. Lawrence also liked to let first drafts stand. If on finishing a story he felt dissatisfied, he sometimes declined to tinker with it but would write the whole thing over from scratch, hoping to do better. This habit accounts for the existence of at least three versions of his novel *Lady Chatterley's Lover.* For most of us, however, good writing is largely a matter of revising — of going back over our first thoughts word by word.

Still, to achieve good writing you have to have the courage to be wild. Aware that no reader need see your rough drafts, you can treat them mercilessly — scissor them apart, rearrange their pieces, reassemble them into a stronger order, using staples or tape or glue. The art of revising calls for a textbook in itself, but here are a few simple rules:

1. When you write your first draft, leave generous space between lines, and enormous margins. You may find later thoughts to add; make room.

2. As you reread your early draft, try to strike out any superfluous words or phrases. Eliminate whole paragraphs if they don't advance your main argument. Watch out, though, for any gaping holes that result. Often, when you eliminate a sizeable passage, you'll need to add a transition to lead your reader on to the next idea.

3. Try reading your first draft aloud. Awkward sound effects may be detected: "An excellent excuse for exercise"; "Doom blooms in the second line . . ."

4. Short, skimpy paragraphs may indicate points that deserve more thought. Can you supply them with any more evidence, more explanation or illustration?

5. A classic method of revision is to lay your manuscript aside for a while, forget about it, and then, after a long interval (the Roman poet Horace recommended nine years), go back to it for a fresh look. If you lack that much time, take a nap, or a walk, or at least a yawn and a stretch before taking yet another look.

If you type your papers, by the way, it is a great help to be a reasonably expert typist — one who uses something other than the Christopher Columbus method (to discover a key and land on it). Then you can revise while you retype. All to what end? "Each clear sentence," according to Robert Russell, "is that much ground stripped clean of the undergrowth of one's own confusion. Sometimes it's thrilling to feel you have written even a single paragraph that makes sense."[3]

THE FORM OF YOUR FINISHED PAPER

Now that you have smoothed your rough draft as fleck-free as you can, your instructor may have specific advice for the form of your finished paper. If none is forthcoming, it is only reasonable

1. to choose standard letter-size (8½ x 11) paper;
2. to give your name at the top of your title page;
3. to leave an inch or more of margin on all four sides of each page, and a few inches of blank paper or an additional sheet after your conclusion, so that your instructor can offer comment;
4. to doublespace, or (if you handwrite) to use paper with widely spaced lines.

And what of titles of works discussed: when to put them in quotation marks, when to underline them? One rule of thumb is that titles of works shorter than book length rate quotation marks (poems, short stories, articles); while titles of books (including book-length poems: *The Odyssey*), plays, and periodicals take underlining. (In a manuscript to be set in type, an underline is a signal to the printer to use *italics*.)

[3] *To Catch an Angel* (New York: Vanguard, 1962), p. 301.

A word about footnotes, if you're using them. A footnote number comes (following any punctuation) after the last word of a quotation or other item of information whose source you wish to credit. So that the number will stand out, roll your typewriter carriage up a click, thus lifting the number slightly above the usual level of your prose. At the bottom of your page, put the footnote itself; like this, for a book:

> [8]Sylvan Barnet, A Short Guide to Writing About Literature, 4th ed. (Boston: Little, Brown, 1979), page 102.

Or like this, for a magazine article:

> [9]Paul Ramsey, "The Biding Place: Reflections on Hart Crane," Parnassus: Poetry in Review 5 (Fall/Winter 1976), 187-199.

In that last footnote, the number *5* is the volume number; *187–199* are the pages in it spanned by the article. Of course, you might wish instead to refer to a specific page. Should you return, later in your paper, for another quotation from Ramsey's article, you need not repeat all its information. Just make it

> [10]Ramsey, p. 192.

(If your paper quoted two articles by Paul Ramsey, you would have to provide full information for the second article on *its* first mention; and then in further footnote references to either article, would mention its title so that the reader could tell the two apart.)

Footnotes enable your readers to go to the same place you did and read the same material. Most readers, of course, will not take the trouble to do so; but at least you give them a chance, and the process of footnoting keeps you as writer looking carefully at your sources, and so it helps you, as well.

Your readers should not have to interrupt their reading of your essay to glance down at a footnote simply to find out whom you are quoting. It is poor form to write:

> Dylan Thomas's poem "Fern Hill" is a memory of the poet's childhood: of his Aunt Ann Jones's farm, where he spent his holidays. "Time, which has an art to throw dust on all things, broods over the poem."[1] The farm, indeed, is a lost paradise -- a personal garden of Eden.
>
> ---
>
> [1]William York Tindall, A Reader's Guide to Dylan Thomas (New York: Noonday Press, 1962), p. 268.

That is annoying, because the reader has to stop reading and look at the footnote to find out who made that resonant statement about Time brooding over the poem. A better way:

"Time," as William York Tindall has observed, "which has an art to throw dust on all things, broods over the poem."[1]

---

[1] A Reader's Guide to Dylan Thomas (New York: Noonday Press, 1962), p. 268.

What to do now but hand in your paper? "And good riddance," you may feel, after such an expenditure of thinking, time, and energy. But a good paper is not only worth submitting, it is worth keeping. If you return to it, after a while, you may find to your surprise that it will preserve and even renew what you have learned.

Writing about a Poem

Assignment: a paper about a poem. You can approach it as a grim duty, of course: any activity can so be regarded. For Don Juan, in Spanish legend, even the act of love became a chore. But the act of writing, like the act of love, is much easier if your feelings take part in it. Write about anything you dislike and don't understand, and you not only set yourself the labors of Hercules, but you guarantee your reader discouragingly hard labor, too.

To write about a poem informatively, you need first of all to experience it. It helps to live with the poem for as long as possible: there is little point in trying to encompass the poem in a ten-minute tour of inspection on the night before the paper falls due. However challenging, writing about poetry has immediate rewards, and to mention just one, the poem you spend time with and write about is going to mean much more to you than poems skimmed quickly ever do.

Most of the problems you will meet in writing about a poem will be the same ones you meet in writing about a play or a story: finding a topic, organizing your thoughts, writing, revising. For general advice on writing papers about any kind of literature, see the Appendix at the back of this book. There are, however, a few ways in which a poem requires a different approach. This chapter will deal briefly with some of them, and it will offer a few illustrations of papers that students have written. These papers may not be works of inimitable genius, but they are pretty good papers, the likes of which most students can write with a modest investment of time and care.

Briefer than most stories and most plays, lyric poems *look* easier to write about. They call, however, for your keenest attention. You may find that, before you can discuss a short poem, you will have to read it slowly and painstakingly, with your mind (like your pencil) sharp and ready. Unlike a play or a short story, a lyric poem tends to have very little plot, and perhaps you will find little to say about what happens in it. In order to understand a poem, you'll need to notice elements other than narrative: the connotations or suggestions of its words, surely, and the rhythm of phrases and lines. The subtleties of language, almost apart from story, are so essential to a poem (and so elusive) that Robert

Frost was moved to say, "Poetry is what gets lost in translation." Once in a while, of course, you'll read a story whose prose abounds in sounds, rhythms, figures of speech, imagery, and other elements you expect of poetry. Certain novels of Herman Melville and William Faulkner contain paragraphs that, if extracted, seem in themselves prose-poems—so lively are they in their word-play, so rich in metaphor. But such writing is exceptional, and the main business of most fiction is to get a story told. To take an extreme case of a fiction writer who didn't want his prose to sound poetic, Georges Simenon, best known for his mystery novels, said that whenever he noticed in his manuscript any word or phrase that called attention to itself, he struck it out. That method of writing would never do for a poet, who revels in words and phrases that fix themselves in memory. It is safe to say that, in order to write well about a poem, you have to read it carefully enough to remember at least part of it word for word.

Let's consider three commonly useful approaches to writing about poetry.

EXPLICATION

In an **explication** (literally, "an unfolding") of a poem, a writer explains the entire poem in detail, unraveling any particular complexities to be found in it. This method is a valuable one in approaching a lyric poem, especially if the poem is rich in complexities (or in suggestions worth rendering explicit). Most poems that you'll ever be asked to explicate are short enough to discuss thoroughly within a limited time; fully to explicate a long and involved work, such as John Milton's epic *Paradise Lost,* might require a lifetime. (To explicate a short passage of Milton's long poem would be a more usual course assignment.)

All the details or suggestions in a poem that a sensitive and intelligent reader might consider, the writer of an explication considers and tries to unfold. These might include allusions, the denotations or connotations of words, the possible meanings of symbols, the effects of certain sounds and rhythms and formal elements (rime schemes, for instance), the sense of any statements that contain irony, and other particulars. Not intent on ripping a poem to pieces, the author of a useful explication instead tries to show how each part contributes to the whole.

An explication is easy to organize. You can start with the first line of the poem and keep working straight on through. An explication should not be confused with a paraphrase. A paraphrase simply puts the words of the poem into other words; it is a sort of translation, useful in getting at the plain prose sense and therefore especially helpful in clarifying a poem's main theme. Perhaps in writing an explication you will wish to do some paraphrasing; but an explication (unlike a paraphrase) does not simply restate: it explains a poem, in great detail.

Here, for example, is a famous poem by Robert Frost, followed by a student's concise explication. (The assignment was to explain whatever in "Design" seemed most essential, in not more than 750 words.)

Robert Frost (1874–1963)

DESIGN 1936

I found a dimpled spider, fat and white,
On a white heal-all, holding up a moth
Like a white piece of rigid satin cloth—
Assorted characters of death and blight
Mixed ready to begin the morning right,
Like the ingredients of a witches' broth—
A snow-drop spider, a flower like a froth,
And dead wings carried like a paper kite.

What had that flower to do with being white,
The wayside blue and innocent heal-all?
What brought the kindred spider to that height,
Then steered the white moth thither in the night?
What but design of darkness to appall?—
If design govern in a thing so small.

An Unfolding of Robert Frost's "Design"

Starting with the title, "Design," any reader of this poem will find it full of meaning. As *Webster's New World Dictionary* defines *design*, the word can denote among other things a plan, or "purpose; intention; aim." Some arguments for the existence of God (I remember from Sunday School) are based on the "argument from design": that because the world shows a systematic order, there must be a Designer who made it. But the word *design* can also mean "a secret or sinister scheme" -- such as we attribute to a "designing person." As we shall see, Frost's poem incorporates all of these meanings. His poem raises the question of whether there is a Designer, or an evil Designer, or no Designer at all.

Like many other sonnets, the poem is divided into two parts. The first eight lines draw a picture centering on the spider, who at first seems almost jolly. It is _dimpled_ and _fat_ like a baby, or Santa Claus. It stands on a wild flower whose name, _heal-all_, seems an irony: a heal-all is supposed to cure any disease, but it certainly has no power to restore life to the dead moth. (Later, in line ten, we learn that the heal-all used to be blue. Presumably it has died and become bleached-looking.) In this second line we discover, too, that the spider has hold of another creature. Right away we might feel sorry for the moth, were it not for the simile applied to it in line three: "Like a white piece of rigid satin cloth." Suddenly the moth becomes not a creature but a piece of fabric -- lifeless and dead -- and yet _satin_ has connotations also beautiful. For me satin, used in rich ceremonial costumes such as coronation gowns and brides' dresses, has a formality and luxury about it. Besides, there is great accuracy in the word: the smooth and slightly plush surface of satin is like the powder-smooth surface of moths' wings. But this "cloth," rigid and white, could be the lining to Dracula's coffin. Like the spider, with its snow-drop-shaped body, the moth reminds us both of beauty and of grim death. Spider, flower, and moth are indeed "assorted characters."

In the fifth line an invisible hand enters. The characters are "mixed" like ingredients in an evil potion. Some force doing the mixing is behind the scene. The characters in themselves are innocent enough, but when brought together and concocted, their whiteness and look of _rigor mortis_ are overwhelming. There is something diabolical in the spider's feast. The "morning right" echoes the word _rite_, a ritual -- in this case apparently a Black Mass or a Witches' Sabbath. The simile in line seven ("a flower like a froth") is more ambiguous and harder to describe. A froth is white, foamy, and delicate -- something found on a brook in the woods or on a beach after a wave recedes. However, in the natural world, froth also can be ugly: the foam on a dead dog's mouth. The dualism in nature -- its beauty and its horror -- is there in that one simile.

So far, the poem has portrayed a small, frozen scene, with the dimpled killer holding its victim as innocently as a boy holds a kite. Already, Frost has hinted that Nature may be, as Radcliffe Squires suggests, "nothing but an ash-white plain without love or faith or hope, where ignorant appetites cross by chance."[1] Now, in the last six lines of the sonnet, Frost comes out and directly states his theme. What else could bring these deathly pale, stiff things together "but design of darkness to appall?" The question is clearly rhetorical, meant to be answered, "Why, nothing but that, of course!" I take the next-to-last line to mean, "What except a design so dark and sinister that we're appalled by it." "Appall," by the way, is the second pun in the poem: it sounds like _a pall_ or shroud. _Steered_ carries the suggestion of a steering-wheel or rudder that some pilot had to control. Like the word _brought_, it implies that some Captain charted the paths of spider, heal-all, and moth, so that they arrived together.

Having suggested that the universe is in the hands of that sinister Captain (Fate? the Devil?), Frost adds a final note of doubt. The Bible tells us that "His eye is on the sparrow," but at the moment the poet doesn't seem sure. Maybe, he hints, when things in the universe drop below a certain size, they pass completely out of the Designer's notice. When creatures are that little, maybe He doesn't bother to govern them, but just lets them run wild. And possibly the same ~~idiotic~~ mindless chance is all that governs human lives. Maybe we're not even "sinners in the hands of an angry God,"[2] but ~~amazingly~~ are nothing but little dice being slung. And that -- because it is even more senseless -- is the worst suspicion of all.

1 _The Major Themes of Robert Frost_ (Ann Arbor, Mich.: University of Michigan Press, 1963), p. 87.

[2]Title of an early American sermon by Jonathan Edwards.

This excellent paper, while finding something worth unfolding in every line in Frost's poem, does so without seeming mechanical. Notice that, although the student proceeds through the poem from the title to the last line, she takes up points when necessary, in any sequence. In paragraph one, the writer looks ahead to the end of the poem and briefly states its main theme. (She does so in order to relate this theme to the poem's title.) In the second paragraph, she deals with the poem's *later* image of the heal-all, relating it to the first image. Along the way, she comments on the form of the poem ("Like many other sonnets"), on its similes and puns, its denotations and connotations.

Incidentally, this paper demonstrates good use of manuscript form. Each word in a quotation is reproduced faithfully. The student is within her rights to give Frost's *steered* a capital letter when beginning her own sentence with it. The critic she quotes (Radcliffe Squires) is identified in the essay and his book is given a footnote. Another footnote proves useful to give Jonathan Edwards credit for a memorable phrase. This paper demonstrates, too, how to make final corrections without retyping. In the last paragraph, notice how the student legibly added a word and neatly changed another word by crossing it out and writing a substitute above it. In her next-to-last sentence, the writer clearly transposes two letters with a handy mark (∩∪), deletes a word, and strikes out a superfluous letter.

It might seem that to work through a poem line by line is a lockstep task; and yet there can be high excitement in it. Randall Jarrell once wrote an explication of "Design" in which he managed to convey such excitement. In the following passage taken from it, see if you can sense the writer's joy in his work. (Don't, incidentally, feel obliged to compare the quality of your own insights with Jarrell's, nor the quality of your own prose. Be fair to yourself: unlike most students, Jarrell had the advantage of being an excellent poet and a gifted critic; besides, he had read and pondered Frost for years before he wrote his essay, and as a teacher he probably had taught "Design" many times.)

> Frost's details are so diabolically good that it seems criminal to leave some unremarked; but notice how *dimpled, fat,* and *white* (all but one; all but one) come from our regular description of any baby; notice how the *heal-all,* because of its name, is the one flower in all the world picked to be the altar for this Devil's Mass; notice how *holding up* the moth brings something ritual and hieratic, a ghostly, ghastly formality, to this priest and its sacrificial victim; notice how terrible to the fingers, how full of the stilling rigor of death, that *white piece of rigid satin cloth* is. And *assorted characters of death and blight* is, like so many things in this poem, sharply ambiguous: *a mixed bunch of actors* or *diverse representative signs.* The tone of the phrase *assorted characters of death and blight* is beautifully developed in the ironic Breakfast-Club-calisthenics, Radio-Kitchen heartiness of *mixed ready to begin the morning right* (which assures us, so unreassuringly, that this isn't any sort of Strindberg *Spook Sonata,* but hard fact), and con-

> cludes in the *ingredients* of the witches' broth, giving the soup a sort of cuddly shimmer that the cauldron in *Macbeth* never had; the *broth*, even, is brought to life—we realize that witches' broth *is* broth, to be supped with a long spoon.[1]

Evidently, Jarrell's cultural interests are broad: ranging from August Strindberg's ground-breaking modern classic down to the Breakfast Club (a once-popular radio program that cheerfully exhorted its listeners to march around their tables). And yet breadth of knowledge, however much it deepens and enriches Jarrell's writing, isn't all that he brings to the reading of poetry. For him, an explication isn't a dull plod, but a voyage of discovery. His prose—full of figures of speech (*diabolically good, cuddly shimmer*)—conveys the apparent delight he takes in showing off his findings. Such a joy, of course, can't be acquired deliberately. But it can grow, the more you read and study poetry.

ANALYSIS

An **analysis** of a poem, like a news commentator's analysis of a crisis in the Middle East or a chemist's analysis of an unknown fluid, separates its subject into elements, as a means to understand that subject—to see what composes it. Usually, the writer of such an essay singles out one of those elements for attention: "Imagery of Light and Darkness in Frost's 'Design' "; "The Character of Satan in *Paradise Lost*."

Like explication, analysis can be particularly useful in dealing with a short poem. Unlike explication (which inches through a poem line by line), analysis often suits a long poem too, because it allows the writer to discuss just one manageable element in the poem. A good analysis casts intense light upon a poem from one direction. If you care enough about a poem, and about some perspective on it—its theme, say, or its symbolism, or its singability—writing an analysis can enlighten and give pleasure.

In this book you probably have met a few brief analyses: the discussion of connotations in John Masefield's "Cargoes" (page 60), for instance, or the examination of symbols in T. S. Eliot's "The *Boston Evening Transcript*" (page 205). In fact, most of the discussions in this book are analytic. Temporarily, we have separated the whole art of poetry into elements such as tone, irony, literal meaning, suggestions, imagery, figures of speech, sound, rhythm, and so on. No element of a poem, of course, exists apart from all the other elements. Still, by taking a closer look at particular elements, one at a time, we see them more clearly and more easily study them.

[1] From *Poetry and the Age* (New York: Alfred A. Knopf, 1953).

Long analyses of metrical feet, rime schemes, and indentations tend to make ponderous reading: such formal and technical elements are perhaps the hardest to discuss engagingly. And yet formal analysis (at least a little of it) can be interesting and illuminating: it can measure the very pulsebeat of lines. If you do care about the technical side of poetry, then write about it, by all means. You will probably find it helpful to learn the terms for the various meters, stanzas, fixed forms, and other devices, so that you can summon them to your aid with confidence. Here is a short formal analysis of "Design" by a student who evidently cares for technicalities yet who manages not to be a bore in talking about them. Concentrating on the sonnet form of Frost's poem, the student actually casts light upon the poem in its entirety.

The Design of "Design"

For "Design," the sonnet form has at least two advantages. First, as in most strict Italian sonnets, the argument of the poem falls into two parts. In the octave Frost draws his pale still-life of spider, flower, and moth; then in the sestet he contemplates the meaning of it. The sestet deals with a more general idea: the possible existence of a vindictive deity who causes the spider to catch the moth, and no doubt also causes other suffering. Frost weaves his own little web. The unwary reader is led into the poem by its opening story, and pretty soon is struggling with more than he expected. Even the rime scheme, by the way, has something to do with the poem's meaning. The word *white* ends the first line of the sestet. The same sound is echoed in the rimes that follow. All in all, half the lines in the poem end in an "ite." It seems as if Frost places great weight on the whiteness of his little scene, for the riming words both introduce the term *white* and keep reminding us of it.

A sonnet has a familiar design, and that is its second big advantage to this particular poem. In a way, writing "Design" as a sonnet almost seems a foxy joke. (I can just imagine Frost chuckling to himself, wondering if anyone will get it.) A sonnet, being a classical form, is an orderly world with certain laws in it. There is ready-made irony in its containing a meditation on whether there is any order in the universe at large. Obviously there's design in back of the poem, but is there any design to insect life, or human life? Whether or not the poet can answer this question (and it seems he can't), at least he discovers an order while writing the poem. Actually, that is just what Frost said a poet achieves: "a momentary stay against confusion."[1]

Although design clearly governs in this poem -- in "this thing so small" -- the design isn't entirely predictable. The poem starts out as an Italian sonnet, with just two riming sounds; then (unlike an Italian sonnet) it keeps the "ite" rimes going. It ends in a couplet, like a Shakespearean sonnet. From these unexpected departures from the pattern of the Italian sonnet announced in the opening lines, I get the impression that Frost's poem is somewhat like the larger universe. It looks perfectly orderly, until you notice the small details in it.

[1]"The Figure a Poem Makes," preface to Complete Poems of Robert Frost (New York: Holt, Rinehart and Winston, 1949), p. vi.

COMPARISON AND CONTRAST

To write a **comparison** of two poems, you place them side by side and point out their likenesses; to write a **contrast**, you point out their differences. If you wish, you can combine the two methods in the same paper. For example, even though you may emphasize similarities you may also call attention to differences, or vice versa.

Such a paper makes most sense if you pair two poems that have much in common. It would be possible to compare Eliza Cook's sentimentalized elegy "The Old Arm Chair" with John Milton's profound "Lycidas," but comparison would be difficult, perhaps futile. Though both poems are in English, the two seem hopelessly remote from each other in diction, in tone, in complexity, and in worth.

Having found, however, a couple of poems that throw light on each other, you then go on in your paper to show further, unsuspected resemblances—not just the ones that are obvious ("'Design' and 'Wing-Spread' are both about bugs"). The interesting resemblances are ones that take thinking to discover. Similarly, you may want to show noteworthy differences—besides those your reader will see without any help.

In comparing two poems, you may be tempted to discuss one of them and be done with it, then spend the latter half of your paper discussing the other. This simple way of organizing an essay can be dangerous if it leads you to keep the two poems in total isolation from each other. The whole idea of such an assignment, of course, is to get you to do some comparing. There is nothing wrong in discussing all of poem A first, then discussing poem B—*if* in discussing B you keep looking back at A. Another procedure is to keep comparing the two poems all the way through your paper—dealing first, let's say, with their themes; then with their metaphors; and finally, with their respective merits.

More often than not, a comparison is an analysis: a study of a theme common to two poems, for instance; or of two poets' similar fondness for the myth of Eden. But you also can evaluate poems by comparing and contrasting them: placing them side by side in order to decide which poet deserves the brighter laurels. Here, for example, is a paper that considers "Design" and "Wing-Spread," a poem of Abbie Huston Evans (first printed in 1938, two years later than Frost's poem). By comparing and contrasting the two poems for (1) their language and (2) their themes, this student shows us reasons for his evaluation.

"Wing-Spread" Does a Dip

The midge spins out to safety
Through the spider's rope;
But the moth, less lucky,
Has to grope.

Mired in glue-like cable
See him foundered swing
By the gap he opened
With his wing,

Dusty web enlacing
All that blue and beryl.
In a netted universe
Wing-spread is peril.

-- Abbie Huston Evans

"Wing-Spread," quoted above, is a good poem, but it is not in the same class with "Design." Both poets show us a murderous spider and an unlucky moth, but there are two reasons for Robert Frost's superiority. One is his more suggestive use of language, the other is his more memorable theme.

Let's start with language. "Design" is full of words and phrases rich in suggestions. "Wing-Spread," by comparison, contains few. To take just one example, Frost's "dimpled spider, fat and white" is certainly a more suggestive description. Actually, Evans doesn't describe her spider; she just says, "the spider's rope." (I have to hand Evans the palm for showing us the spider and moth in action. In Frost's view, they are dead and petrified -- but I guess that is the impression he is after.) In "Design," the spider's dimples show that it is like a chubby little kid, who further turns out to be a kite-flier. This seems an odd, almost freaky way to look at a spider. I find it more refreshing than Evans's view (although I like her word *cable*, suggesting that the spider's web is a kind of suspension bridge). Frost's word-choice -- his harping on *white* -- paints a more striking scene than Evans's slightly vague "All that blue and beryl." Except for her personification of the moth in her second stanza, Evans doesn't go in for any figures of speech, and even that one isn't a clear personification -- she simply gives the moth a sex by referring to it as "him." Frost's striking metaphors, similes, and even puns (*right*, *appall*) show him, as usual, to be a master of figures of speech. He calls the moth's wings "satin cloth" and "a paper kite"; Evans just refers in line 8 to a moth's wing. As far as the language of the two poems goes, you might as well compare a vase ~~full of~~ brimming with flowers and a single flower stuck in a vase. (That is a poor metaphor, since Frost's poem contains only one flower, but I hope you will know what I mean.)

In fairness to Evans, I would say that she picks a pretty good solitary flower. And her poem has powerful sounds: short lines with the riming words coming at us again and again very frequently. In theme, however, "Wing-Spread" seems much more narrow than "Design." The first time I read Evans's poem all I felt was: Ho hum, the moth too was wide and got stuck. The second time I read it, I figured that she is saying something with a universal application. This message comes out in line 11, in "a netted universe." That is the most interesting phrase in her poem, one that you can think about. *Netted* makes me imagine the universe as being full of nets rigged by someone who is fishing for us. Maybe, like Frost, Evans sees an evil plan operating. She does not, though, investigate it. She says that the midge escapes because it is tiny. On the other hand, things with wide wing-spreads get stuck. Her theme as I read it is, "Be small and inconspicuous if you want to survive," or maybe, "Isn't it too bad that in this world the big beautiful types crack up and die, while the miserable little puny punks keep sailing?" Now, that is a valuable idea. I have often thought that very same thing myself. But Frost's closing note ("If design govern in a thing so small") is really devastating, because it raises a huge uncertainty. "Wing-Spread" leaves us with not much besides a moth stuck in a web, and a moral. In both language and theme, "Design" climbs to a higher altitude.

HOW TO QUOTE A POEM

Preparing to discuss a short poem, it is a good idea to emulate the student who wrote on "Wing-Spread" and to quote the whole text of the poem at the beginning of your paper, with its lines numbered. Then you can refer to it with ease, and your instructor, without having to juggle a book, can follow you.

Quoted to illustrate some point, memorable lines can add interest to your paper, and good commentators on poetry tend to be apt quoters, helping their readers to experience a word, a phrase, a line, or a passage that otherwise might be neglected. However, to quote from poetry is slightly more awkward than to quote from prose. There are lines to think about—important and meaningful units whose shape you will need to preserve. If you are quoting more than a couple of lines, it is good policy to arrange your quotation just as its lines occur in the poem, white space and all:

```
At the outset, the poet tells us of his discovery of

                 a dimpled spider, fat and white,
          On a white heal-all, holding up a moth
          Like a white piece of rigid satin cloth --

and implies that the small killer is both childlike and sinister.
```

But if you are quoting less than two lines of verse, it would seem wasteful of paper to write:

```
The color white preoccupies Frost.  The spider is

                                 fat and white,
          On a white heal-all

and even the victim moth is pale, too.
```

In such a case, it saves space to transform Frost's line arrangement into prose:

```
The color white preoccupies Frost.  The spider is "fat and white, /

On a white heal-all" -- and even the victim moth is pale, too.
```

Here, a diagonal (/) indicates the writer's respect for where the poet's lines begin and end. Some writers prefer to note line-breaks without diagonals, just by keeping the initial capital letter of a line (if there is any): "fat and white, On a white heal-all. . . ." Incidentally, the ellipsis (. . .) in that last remark indicates that words are omitted from the end of Frost's sentence; the fourth dot is a period. Some writers—meticulous souls—also stick in an ellipsis at the *beginning* of a quotation, if they're leaving out words from the beginning of a sentence in the original:

The color white preoccupies Frost in his description of the spider " . . .fat and white, / On a white heal-all. . . ."

Surely there's no need for an initial ellipsis, though, if you begin quoting at the beginning of a sentence. No need for a final ellipsis, either, if your quotation goes right to the end of a sentence in the original. If it is obvious that only a phrase is being quoted, no need for an ellipsis in any case:

The speaker says he "found a dimpled spider" and he goes on to portray it as a kite-flying boy.

If you leave out whole lines, indicate the omission by an ellipsis all by itself on a line:

```
The midge spins out to safety
Through the spider's rope;
          . . .
In a netted universe
Wing-spread is peril.
```

BEFORE YOU BEGIN

Ready at last to write, you will have spent considerable time in reading, thinking, and feeling. After having chosen your topic, you probably will have taken a further look at the poem or poems you have picked, letting further thoughts and feelings come to you. The quality of your paper will depend, above all, upon the quality of your readiness to write.

Exploring a poem, a sensitive writer handles it with care and affection as though it were a living animal, and, done with it, leaves it still alive. The unfeeling writer, on the other hand, disassembles the poem in a dull, mechanical way, like someone with a blunt ax filling an order for one horse-skeleton. Again, to write well is a matter of engaging your feelings. Writing to a deadline, on an assigned topic, you easily can sink into a drab, workaday style, especially if you regard the poet as some uninspired builder of chicken-coops who hammers themes and images into place, and then slaps the whole thing with a coat of words. Certain expressions, if you lean on them habitually, may tempt you to think of the poet in that way. Here, for instance, is a discussion—by a plodding writer—of Robert Frost's poem.

The symbols Frost <u>uses</u> in "Design" are very successful. Frost makes the spider <u>stand for</u> Nature. He <u>wants</u> us to see Nature as blind and cruel. He also <u>employs</u> good sounds. He <u>uses</u> a lot of <u>i</u>'s because he is <u>trying to</u> make you think of falling rain.

(Underscored words are worth questioning.) What's wrong with that comment? While understandable, the words *uses* and *employs* seem to lead the writer to see Frost only as a conscious tool-manipulator. To be sure, Frost in a sense "uses" symbols, but did he grab hold of them and lay them into his poem? For all we know, perhaps the symbols arrived quite unbidden, and used the poet. To write a good poem, Frost maintained, a poet himself has to be surprised. (How, by the way, can we hope to know what a poet *wants* to do? And there isn't much point in saying that the poet is *trying to* do something. He has already done it, if he has written a good poem.) At least, it is likely that Frost didn't plan to fulfill a certain quota of *i*-sounds. Writing his poem, not by following a blueprint but probably by bringing it slowly to the surface of his mind (like Elizabeth Bishop's hooked fish), Frost no doubt had enough to do without trying to engineer the reactions of his possible audience. Like all true symbols, Frost's spider doesn't *stand for* anything. The writer would be closer to the truth to say that the spider *suggests* or *reminds us* of Nature, or of certain forces in the natural world. (Symbols just hint, they don't indicate.)

After the student discussed the paper in a conference, he rewrote the first two sentences like this:

> The symbols in Frost's "Design" are highly effective. The spider, for instance, suggests the blindness and cruelty of Nature. Frost's word-sounds, too, are part of the meaning of his poem, for the <u>i</u>'s remind the reader of falling rain.

Not every reader of "Design" will hear rain falling, but the student's revision probably comes closer to describing the experience of the poem most of us know.

In writing about poetry, an occasional note of self-doubt can be useful: now and then a *perhaps* or a *possibly*, an *it seems* or a modest *I suppose*. Such expressions may seem timid shilly-shallying, but at least they keep the writer from thinking, "I know all there is to know about this poem."

Facing the showdown with your empty sheaf of paper, however, you can't worry forever about your critical vocabulary. To do so is to risk the fate of the centipede in a bit of comic verse, who was running along efficiently until someone asked, "Pray, which leg comes after which?," whereupon "He lay distracted in a ditch / Considering how to run." It is a safe bet that your instructor is human. Your main task as a writer is to communicate to another human being your sensitive reading of a poem.

TOPICS FOR WRITING

Topics for Brief Papers (250–500 words)

1. Write a concise *explication* of a short poem of your choice, or one suggested by your instructor. In a paper this brief, probably you won't have room to explain everything in the poem; explain what you think most needs explaining. (An illustration of one such explication appears on page 429.)
2. Write an *analysis* of a short poem, first deciding which one of its elements to deal with. (An illustration of such an analysis appears on page 434.) For examples, here are a few specific topics:

   "Language of the Street: What It Contributes to Dylan's 'Subterranean Homesick Blues' "

   "Kinds of Irony in Hardy's 'The Workbox' "

   "The Attitude of the Speaker in Marvell's 'To His Coy Mistress' "

   "Folk Ballad Traits in Randall's 'Ballad of Birmingham' "

   "An Extended Metaphor in Rich's 'Diving into the Wreck.' " (Explain the one main comparison that the poem makes and show how the whole poem makes it. Other likely possibilities for a paper on extended metaphor: Dickinson's "Because I could not stop for Death," Nemerov's "Storm Windows," Frost's "The Silken Tent.")

   "What the Skunks Mean in Lowell's 'Skunk Hour' "

   "The Rhythms of Plath's 'Daddy' "

   (To locate any of these poems, see the Index of Authors, Titles, and Quotations at the back of this book.)
3. Select a poem in which the main speaker is a character who for any reason interests you. You might consider, for instance, Betjeman's "In Westminster Abbey," Browning's "My Last Duchess" or "Soliloquy of the Spanish Cloister," Eliot's "Love Song of J. Alfred Prufrock," Frost's "Witch of Coös," or Jarrell's "Woman at the Washington Zoo." Then write a brief profile of this character, drawing only on what the poem tells you (or reveals). What is the character's approximate age? Situation in life? Attitude toward self? Attitude toward others? General personality? Do you find this character admirable?
4. Although each of these poems tells a story, what happens in the poem isn't necessarily obvious: Cummings's "anyone lived in a pretty how town," Eliot's "Love Song of J. Alfred Prufrock," Lawrence's "A Youth Mowing," Stafford's "At the Klamath Berry Festival," Winter's "At the San Francisco Airport," James Wright's "A Blessing." Choose one of these poems and in a paragraph sum up what you think happens in it. Then in a second paragraph ask yourself: what, *besides* the element of story, did you consider in order to understand the poem?
5. Think of someone you know (or someone you can imagine) whose attitude toward poetry in general is dislike. Suggest a particular poem for that person to read—a poem that you personally like—and, addressing your skeptical reader, point out whatever you find to enjoy in it, that you think the skeptic just might enjoy too.

6. Keeping in mind what Coleridge and Jarrell have to say about "obscurity" in poetry (see their statements in Anthology II), write a brief defense of some poem you like against the possible charge that it is obscure.

Topics for More Extensive Papers (600–1,000 words)

1. Write an explication of a poem short enough for you to work through line by line — for instance, Emily Dickinson's "My Life had stood–a loaded Gun" or MacLeish's "The End of the World." As if offering your reading experience to a friend who hadn't read the poem before, try to point out all the leading difficulties you encountered, and set forth in detail your understanding of any lines that contain such difficulties.
2. Write an explication of a longer poem — for instance, Eliot's "Love Song of J. Alfred Prufrock," Frost's "Witch of Coös," Hardy's "Convergence of the Twain," Rich's "Diving into the Wreck," or Wagoner's "Staying Alive." Although you will not be able to go through every line of the poem, explain what you think most needs explaining.
3. In this book, you will find from six to eleven poems by each of these poets: Blake, Dickinson, Donne, Frost, Hardy, Housman, Keats, Roethke, Shakespeare, Stevens, Whitman, William Carlos Williams, Wordsworth, and Yeats; and multiple selections for many more. (See Index of Authors, Titles, and Quotations.) After you have read a few specimens of the work of a poet who interests you, write an analysis of *more than one* of the poet's poems. To do this, you will need to select just one characteristic theme (or other element) to deal with — something typical of the poet's work, not found only in a single poem. Here are a few specific topics for such an analysis:

   "What Angers William Blake? A Look at Three Poems of Protest"

   "How Emily Dickinson's Lyrics Resemble Hymns"

   "The Humor of Robert Frost"

   "John Keats's Sensuous Imagery"

   "The Vocabulary of Music in Poems of Wallace Stevens"

   "Non-free Verse: Patterns of Sound in Three Poems of William Carlos Williams"

   "Yeats as a Poet of Love"

4. Compare and contrast two poems in order to evaluate them: which is more satisfying and effective poetry? To make a meaningful comparison, be sure to choose two poems that genuinely have much in common: perhaps a similar theme or subject. (For an illustration of such a paper, see the one given in this chapter. For suggestions of poems to compare, see the Anthology.)
5. Evaluate by the method of comparison two different versions of a poem: early and late drafts, perhaps, or two translations from another language. For parallel versions to work on, see Chapter Fourteen, "Alternatives."
6. If the previous topic appeals to you, consider this. In 1912, twenty-four years before he printed "Design," Robert Frost sent a correspondent this early version:

   In White

   A dented spider like a snow drop white
   On a white Heal-all, holding up a moth

Like a white piece of lifeless satin cloth—
Saw ever curious eye so strange a sight?—
Portent in little, assorted death and blight
Like ingredients of a witches' broth?—
The beady spider, the flower like a froth,
And the moth carried like a paper kite.

What had that flower to do with being white,
The blue prunella every child's delight.
What brought the kindred spider to that height?
(Make we no thesis of the miller's plight.)
What but design of darkness and of night?
Design, design! Do I use the word aright?

Compare "In White" with "Design." In what respects is the finished poem superior?

Topics for Long Papers (1,500 words or More)

1. Write a line-by-line explication of a poem rich in matters to explain, or a longer poem that offers ample difficulty. While relatively short, Donne's "Valediction: Forbidding Mourning" or Hopkins's "The Windhover" are poems that will take a good bit of time to explicate; but even a short, apparently simple poem such as Frost's "Stopping by Woods on a Snowy Evening" can provide more than enough to explicate thoughtfully in a longer paper.
2. Write an analysis of the work of one poet (as suggested above, in the third topic for more extensive papers) in which you go beyond this book to read an entire collection of that poet's work.
3. Write an analysis of a certain theme (or other element) that you find in the work of two or more poets. It is probable that in your conclusion you will want to set the poets' work side by side, comparing or contrasting it, and perhaps making some evaluation. Sample topics:

   "Langston Hughes, Etheridge Knight, and Dudley Randall as Prophets of Social Change."

   "What It Is to Be a Woman: The Special Knowledge of Sylvia Plath, Anne Sexton, Adrienne Rich, and Ruth Pitter"

   "Language of Science in Some Poems of Eberhart, Merrill, and Ammons"

   "Frost and His Parodists"

4. Taking from Anthology II a passage of criticism, see what light it will cast on a poem that interests you. For example, you might test Gray's "Elegy" by Poe's dictum that there is no such thing as a long poem. (Does the "Elegy" flag in intensity?) Or try reading several poems of Robert Frost, looking for the "sound of sense" (which Frost explains in his letter to John Bartlett).

Writing a Poem

HOW DOES A POEM BEGIN?

After you have read much poetry and (as Keats said) "traveled in the realms of gold," it is natural to want to write a poem. And why shouldn't you? Whether or not you aspire ever to publish your work, the attempt itself offers profound satisfactions; and it offers, too, a way to become a finer reader of poetry. To learn how to carry a football may not equip you to play for the Oilers, but it may help you appreciate the timing and skill of an Earl Campbell. In a roughly similar way, you may find yourself better able to perceive the artistry of an excellent sonnet from having written a sonnet of your own—even a merely acceptable one.

Poems, like new comets, tend to arrive mysteriously. Sometimes they go burning right past a serious, hard-working poet only to dawn, as though by accident, upon a madman, an idler, or a child. This may be why no one has ever devised a formula for synthesizing memorable poems. "A good poet," said Randall Jarrell, "is someone who manages, in a lifetime of standing out in thunderstorms, to be struck by lightning five or six times." In this view, poetic inspiration, like grace, is something beyond human control. Still, most of the best lightning bolts tend to strike those poets who keep waiting patiently, writing and rewriting and discarding, keeping their lightning rods lifted as they work. As Louis Pasteur said—speaking of scientists—"Chance favors the prepared mind."

Teachers of creative writing do not promise to create poets. All they can try to create is an atmosphere in which good poems may be written, given a hearing, and perhaps rendered stronger and more concise. As a member of a class or writing workshop, you have certain advantages. At least, you have companions in your struggles and chagrins. You may even find a sympathetic audience.

Even though the writing of poetry cannot be taught with great efficiency, some knowledge useful to poets can be imparted. What does a poet need to know? Half-jokingly, W. H. Auden once proposed a College for Bards with this curriculum:

> 1. In addition to English, at least one ancient language, probably Greek or Hebrew, and two modern languages would be required.
> 2. Thousands of lines of poetry in these languages would be learned by heart.
> 3. The library would contain no books of literary criticism, and the only critical exercise required of students would be the writing of parodies.
> 4. Courses in prosody, rhetoric, and comparative philology would be required of all students, and every student would have to select three courses out of courses in mathematics, natural history, geology, meteorology, archeology, mythology, liturgics, and cooking.
> 5. Every student would be required to look after a domestic animal and cultivate a garden plot.[1]

Auden, though he pokes fun at the notion of systematically training poets, makes constructive suggestions. He would have the aspiring poet study languages and something besides literature, and store up some poetry in memory. William Butler Yeats, too, thought that poets learn mainly by reading the work of other poets. There can be no "singing school" except the study of great poems—monuments, Yeats calls them, of the human soul's magnificence. (See "Sailing to Byzantium," page 260.)

Begin by reading. Don't limit yourself to poems assigned for college credit. Until you explore poetry more widely and roam around in it, how will you know what kind you most care to write? Pick up current poetry magazines, read your contemporaries. Browse in anthologies: recent paperbacks, surveys of older literature. Browse in bookshops. Lift some dust from library stacks. Read methodically or read by whim. Whatever poetry you come to love may nourish a poem you will write.

As you read, make your own personal, selective anthology. Don't let in a poem of Tennyson just because your instructor thinks it is great stuff, let it in only because you cherish it. Instead of just banging out Xerox copies of the poems you admire, you would do well to copy them by hand into a book with blank pages, or to type them on looseleaf notebook paper. By doing so, you'll pay close attention to them, and you'll grow accustomed to seeing excellent poetry (no matter whose) flow from your fingertips. If you would please the ghost of W. H. Auden, you'll say aloud the poems from your personal anthology until you can say them by heart. The suggestion that you memorize poetry may strike you as boring, but its benefits may be surprising. You just might transfer some poetry from your head down to your viscera and into

[1] "The Poet and the City" in *The Dyer's Hand* (New York: Random House, 1962).

your bones. Then, the music of words, especially their rhythms, will become part of you. Your own work may well prove richer for knowing poetry on a deeper level than that of the mind and eye.

It would save time, of course, not to read anything, but simply to look into your heart and write. And yet, because poetry is (among other things) an art of choosing words and arranging them, the usual result of just looking into one's heart and writing is a lot of words hastily chosen and stodgily arranged. "But," the novice might protest, "why should I read Keats and Yeats and the Beats? I don't want to be influenced by all those old birds – I want to be myself!" Excellent poets, though they may be bundles of influences, are still themselves. In truth, when you are starting out, you can learn a great deal by deliberately imitating the work of any excellent poets you deeply love. Spenser studied Chaucer; Keats studied Spenser; Tennyson and Stevens studied Keats. (Auden said he began by imitating Thomas Hardy, because Hardy's work looked imitable.) If you borrow any mannerisms from your models, they will probably disappear as soon as you gain in confidence. Although the novice poet is sometimes urged, "Discover your own voice!" such advice can lead to a painful self-consciousness. Your own voice is probably the last thing to concern yourself about. Certainly it would be a mistake to settle on any one particular voice or style before you have practiced singing in many registers. Imitate whomever you choose, and see what you can do best. Try a Levertovian lyric or a Miltonic meditation. Let out a Whitmanic yawp. Express what you feel in the strongest words you can find, and your voice will take care of itself. It will be your own, in the end, though Donne or Emily Dickinson went into the training of it.

From your reading, you will probably notice that long-lasting poems – those that remain in print after a century or more – tend to express powerful feelings. "In poetry," as Ezra Pound observed, "only emotion endures." Certainly, to name only one instance, the ballad of "Edward" remains vital after hundreds of years, still brimming with sorrow and hate. Asked by a student, "What shall I write about?" Karl Shapiro replied, "Praise something – anything!" – and that is good advice. Although it is possible to write a memorable poem out of piddling, nugatory feelings (or a poem about being unable to feel anything, like Eliot's "The *Boston Evening Transcript*"), a poem written out of love, or loathing, is more likely to radiate energy. (One of John Donne's most energetic poems begins with the impassioned outburst, "For God's sake hold your tongue, and let me love.")

Very often, beginning to write a poem is a process of discovering, and opening, some deep resource of feeling. You have to search within yourself; no map can lead you to such a discovery. Whatever quickens your imagination is your resource. It may be a dream or a nightmare. It may be the memory of some moving experience. At times, your resource may lie in some unexpected place. You might want to write—as Whitman, Keats, and Elizabeth Bishop did—a deeply felt poem about a spider, a piece of ancient pottery, or a filling station.

This is not to say that you can mechanically cram your past life into your poetry-mill and grind it into poems. Although poems may rise from your experience, sometimes in becoming a poem the experience will "suffer a sea change / Into something rich and strange" (like the drowned man's bones in the song in Shakespeare's *Tempest*). You have to leave room for your imagination freely to operate, to transform the raw matter of experience however it will. You will probably limit and constrict your poetry if you regard it as a diary to be kept—as a complete and faithful transcript of what happens to you. Your imagination may yearn to improve upon the literal truth for the sake of the truth of art. Inevitably, a successful poem (even one that sticks to the facts) will be more than journalism. It will be, as Robert Frost memorably described it, "a performance in words."

If it takes feelings to write a memorable poem, yet in poetry the hardest thing to do is to talk about those feelings directly. Readers grow weary of poets who bleat, "Woe is me! I'm so lonely! How miserably sterile I feel!" But probably no reader has ever failed to sympathize with the poet who begins, "Western wind, when wilt thou blow, / The small rain down can rain?" Such a poem does not *discuss* the poet's feelings. It utters them, and it points to objects in the world that invite the reader to feel similarly. Notice that in a modern example, Philip Dow's "Drunk Last Night With Friends, I Go To Work Anyway" (page 212), the speaker omits any description of his inner condition. Instead of expounding on the horrors of a hangover, he reports what the boss said, and what he finds out in the weed patch. Rather than telling us what we should feel, the poet gives us occasion to feel a complex blend of helplessness, misery, and happiness.

Drink or drugs, by the way, seem of little aid to poets in search of inspiration. The trouble with trying to write while stoned (according to one contemporary) is that poetry may seem too far below you to be worth noticing. Coleridge's visionary "Kubla Khan," though possibly inspired by an opium dream, was written by daylight, after the poet for years had stored his mind with descriptions of exotic landscapes in accounts of travel and exploration. In this regard, the poet Robert Wallace has made an excellent suggestion: "Get high on what you write." Some poets try to prod the unconscious by natural means. Donald Hall has testified to the advantages of rising before dawn and writing poetry when thoughts seem fruitful, being close to dream. (However, some writers who try Hall's method find themselves staring sleepily at blank paper.)

Novice poets sometimes begin a poem in a language clouded not with dream, but with gaseous abstraction:

Indifferent cosmos!
O ye cryptic force!
Don't you notice our pitiful human
Agonies and sufferings?
Are we mere tools of careless, crushing Fate?

Far better for a poet to open his eyes and begin with whatever small object he sees:

I found a dimpled spider, fat and white,
On a white heal-all, holding up a moth . . .

Unlike the novice's complaint about the indifference of the universe, Robert Frost's lines on a similar theme are many times more inviting—more striking, more definite.

Poetry, then, tends to inhere not in abstract editorial stands, but in particulars. William Carlos Williams's brief poem about eating the plums in the ice box (page 34) may not be great, but it is human, and hard to forget. Sources for poems may lurk in front of your eyes. The advice of W. Somerset Maugham to budding novelists may be useful to poets, too: Keep a notebook of any memorable details you observe, and any revealing bits of conversation you overhear. Jot them down for the sole purpose of gaining skill in noticing and recording them. Feel no duty to incorporate this material into anything you write. Perhaps none of it will ever be of any use to you.

All right, then, how is your poem to begin? Some poets begin with something to say, then strive for the best way of saying it. Others start with nothing much in mind. In the grip of strong but perhaps woolly and indefinite feelings, they play around with words until they discover to their surprise that they have said something. Evidently, a poem can arise from any adequate provocation. T. S. Eliot, speaking of the habits of poets in general, but probably referring to his own, said that at times a rhythm will begin to course through a poet's mind even before there are words to embody it. Some poets begin from a memorable image; Ezra Pound said he began writing "In a Station of the Metro" from being haunted by a glimpse of a woman's face. Following still another procedure, Dylan Thomas and many other poets have taken some promising line or phrase that swam to mind, and without knowing where it might lead, have trustingly gone on with it. Clearly, what matters isn't whether you begin with an idea or an emotion, a rhythm or an image, a phrase or a line. What matters is that, somehow, you begin.

Plunge in and blunder about. Why be afraid of a blank sheet of paper? You're writing only a first draft. No one is judging you. True poets, as they start to write a poem, don't worry whether a reader will find it admirable. They are too busy finding the words for an idea (or emotion, or rhythm) before it can get away. If you begin to write in a state of high excitement, by all means keep going until you simmer down. Let the words flow. Are some of them not the right ones? Have you misspelled something? No matter, you can make repairs later. Go on with your task and, whatever you do, don't stop to congratulate yourself on your splendid workmanship, or to contemplate the poetic process. The point may be expressed in this "Ars Poetica," or poem about how poetry is written:

> The goose that laid the golden egg
> Died looking up its crotch
> To find out how its sphincter worked.
> Would you lay well? Don't watch.

Later on, of course, you will want to examine your first draft critically; but for now, write as though you were divinely inspired and sustained. When you revise and try to amend your faults, you can view yourself as the lowest sinner. When you write a first draft, you are (with any luck) bringing something out of obscure depths, raising it to the surface. It may mean more than you consciously know. If you are going ahead blindly—that is, if you have begun to write without any burning idea in mind—let the poem choose its own direction. See where it wants to go. Be reluctant to bark orders to it.

A quite different method of composition, which some poets find fruitful, is to compose a poem entirely in the mind, revolving it around and around, saying it over to oneself and trying to perfect it before setting it down on paper. The result tends to have a certain seamless consistency. This method, though, will probably work only for poets who write short poems in rime and meter—devices that help to hold a poem in the mind—or for those with excellent memories.

In a first draft, it is usually a good idea to write everything out in great detail, even at the risk of driveling. If, when you revise, you discover that changes are necessary, it is generally easier to delete than to amplify. A common reason for failure—for the poem that nobody knows what to make of, or feels any positive reaction toward—is mistakenly to assume that the reader is as thoroughly grounded in the facts behind the poem as the poet is. Sometimes, however, a reader will fail to grasp a poem because some vital bit of knowledge still lies within the poet's mind, folded like a green bud. In your first draft, spell out the background of the poem. Define its setting, flesh out out any people in it. Show us how they relate to one another, and why they behave the way they do. Perhaps you will only set down a lot of unnecessary explanation, but when you revise, you will then have all the matter arrayed before you, and you can easily see what to cut, or to retain.

Special challenges face anyone who writes a poem in meter and rime. Most students who attempt a traditionally formal poem, such as a ballad or a sonnet, quickly discover that to write skillfully in meter and rime is difficult. Thwarted by the requirements of strict form, they feel hindered from saying things. "This straitjacket isn't for me," they hastily conclude, adding that, anyhow, contemporary poets don't use such moldy-fig devices. It is true that most don't. Formally, poetry these days is wide open—or, some would say, the quest for form in poetry has moved away from meter and rime and has proceeded in other directions. Auden, although an oldfangled formalist himself, said he could understand why. Many poets, he believed, now distrust meter and rime because such forms imply repetition and discipline—" all that is most boring and lifeless in modern life: road drills, time-clock punching, bureaucratic regulations."[2]

There are still poets, however, for whom meter and rime do not denote lockstep routine, but rather, meaningful music. Continuing to work mainly in traditional form, Helen Adam, Anthony Hecht, Geoffrey Hill, Philip Larkin, W. D. Snodgrass, Richard Wilbur, and others are not merely affirming their loyalty to an outworn fashion. In their work, meter and rime help to impress a poem powerfully upon the reader's inner ear. As Stanley Kunitz, not arguing for a return to meter and rime but observing the current state of poetry, has shrewdly remarked, the flight from these traditional elements "has made poetry easier to write, but harder to remember."

Writing a poem in rime is like walking blindfolded down a dark road with your hand in the hand of an inexorable guide. With the conscious, lighted portion of your mind, you may want to express some idea. But a line that ends in *year* must be followed by another ending in *atmosphere, beer, bier, bombardier, cashier, deer, friction-gear, frontier,* or some other word that probably would not have occurred if the rime scheme had not suggested it. As Rolfe Humphries once pointed out, rime sometimes "makes you think of better things than you would all by yourself." Far from being a coldly rational process of filling a form with wordage, to write a riming poem is to pit yourself against (or to enter into a playful relationship with) some of the wildest and most chaotic forces of the unconscious.

Learn to write a decent poem in rimed stanzas, and you will have at your fingertips certain skills useful in writing poems of any kind. You will know, for instance, how to condense a thought to its gist, from having wrestled with metrical lines that allow you only so many syllables. In revising and finishing your poem, you will become an old hand at replacing stumbling words and phrases with rhythmic ones, at choosing words for their sounds as well as their senses. But this won't be

[2] "The Virgin and the Dynamo," *The Dyer's Hand.*

easy. Although the iambic rhythm is native to English, learning to speak in it with ease and grace is almost like learning a foreign language. Alexander Pope's observation remains accurate:

> True ease in writing comes from art, not chance,
> As those move easiest who have learned to dance.

With practice, the day will come when a rime or a metrical line will spring to your lips almost thoughtlessly. And then, even if you decide to write poetry in *open* forms, you will do so from choice, not from inability to do otherwise. At the moment, it is commonly assumed that open form is intrinsically superior to closed form in poetry; but in truth, the form of an excellent poem, whether open or closed, is whatever the poem requires. The poet's task is to discover it.

Whatever your formal preference, it is probably a mistake to try to plan out the direction of your poetic career, and then grimly oblige yourself to go in it. Better to write a hundred poems and place them in a row, and see where they have taken you. Your life will shape what you write, and the words you write in. Richard Hugo, speaking hyperbolically, has argued that the study of poetry writing fulfills a unique function: "Creative writing is the last class you can go where your life as an individual is important."[3] Professors of mathematics, natural history, and geology might well argue that individual lives matter in their disciplines, too; but Hugo is surely right in at least one regard. Writing a poem calls for a kind of knowledge that only a poet can provide.

By the way, if a poem doesn't come to you all in one sitting, don't despair. Forget about it for a while. It may need more time to gather its forces. Many poets carefully save their fragments: lines and passages that arrive easily, but which do not immediately want to go anywhere. In dry seasons, when inspiration is scarce, they can look back over their notebooks, and sometimes a fragment will spring to life at last, and grow into an entire poem. Try this and see if you have any luck with it. For many, being a poet is like being a beggar: like standing with outstretched bowl by the side of a road, hoping for charity. Thankful poets keep whatever a passing Muse may throw, whether it is a Brasher doubloon or only a bent bottlecap.

ON BLOTTING OUT LINES

Your first draft is done, and the excitement of writing it has cooled. Your next step is to take a step back from it.

A hard but necessary part of being a poet is to try to see your work through a reader's eyes. How to reread it with detachment? The advice of the Roman poet Horace—to put aside a poem for nine years—may

[3] Quoted by Harriet Heyman, "Eleven American Poets," *Life*, April 1981.

seem too discouraging. At least, you can put your poem aside for a week, or even overnight. You may then take a more nearly objective look at it. To help distance yourself from it, try reading it aloud—at least to yourself. Friends may be asked for their criticism, but it is a rare friend who is also a competent critic of poetry. Probably it is best to try to cultivate your own faculties for tough and demanding self-criticism.

Told that his friend Shakespeare in writing his plays never blotted out a line, Ben Jonson wished he had blotted a thousand. (Scholars, by the way, think that even Shakespeare blotted many lines.[4]) Although there is a school of thought that holds for total spontaneity in writing, and for leaving words just the way they land on a page, most poets probably feel that second thoughts, too, can be spontaneous, and often more memorable. If you regard your first draft as holy writ, and refuse to make any changes in it, you may be preserving a work of genius, but more probably you will be passing up your chance to write a good poem. Poets usually don't mind revision; in fact, they find the task fascinating. "What happiness!" exclaimed Yeats, in a letter to a friend, on facing months of demanding rewriting. (It was Yeats, incidentally, who pointed out that, no less than the original act of writing a poem, the act of revision may be inspired.) A contemporary poet, James Dickey, says he writes a poem over and over in many ways. "After I've tried every possible way I can think of," he explains, "I finally get maybe not absolutely the right poem, but the poem that is less wrong than the others."[5]

Is there not a danger that much revision will drain the life out of a poem—or cause it to become ornate and needlessly complicated? Perhaps; but more often, the poem that seems beautifully simple, as if casually dropped from the lips, is the result of hard work; while the poem that the poet didn't retouch makes difficult reading. As you can tell from the two versions Yeats made of his "Old Pensioner," the one written a half-century later, far from lacking in life, seems the more youthful and spontaneous. (For these and other illustrations of poets' revisions, see pages 231–236.)

Working on your second draft, you have the leisure to look up spellings and to verify information. For the poet who is stuck for a rime, a riming dictionary will suggest some likely—and some outlandish—possibilities. When in such a fix, you will probably do better to proceed down the alphabet (*air, bear, bare, care, dare . . .*) and discover a rime among common words you know already. Rimes will strike your reader as reached-for and strange if you enlist them from far beyond your vocabulary.

[4] In Shakespeare's plays, at least a few passages exist in what seem to be both earlier and revised versions, thanks to the printer who, apparently by mistake, included both. A celebrated instance of such a passage occurs in *Romeo and Juliet* II, ii, 187–190.

[5] *Self-Interviews*, edited by Barbara and James Reiss (New York: Doubleday, 1970), p. 64.

Some poets make a typewritten first draft, then revise in longhand. When additions, deletions, and substitutions accumulate and the page becomes too crosshatched to decipher, they type a fresh version (keeping the old version just in case they botch the revision and want to go back to the original and start over). Some poets—Richard Wilbur is one—prefer to keep working on a single poem till it is done; others simultaneously revise many poems, going around and making fresh moves like a chess master playing all comers.

In your first draft, when you were trying to include everything essential, you could allow yourself a multitude of words. But in revising and striving for concision, you have to select what is essential and decide what to leave out. Ask yourself whether every line—every word—deserves the room it occupies. Does it *do* anything? To decide, imagine your poem without the word or line. Begin your inspection with your opening lines. Are they valuable, or do they only delay the reader's entry into something more essential? What if, instead, the poem began with some line that now comes later? Opening lines, of course, don't have to be sensational, but there is much to be said for a beginning that stops the reader in his tracks and hangs on to him:

> You do not do, you do not do
> Any more, black shoe
> In which I have lived like a foot . . .

(To quote Sylvia Plath's brilliant opening to "Daddy.") Samuel Johnson, that down-to-earth critic, insisted that a writer's first duty is to excite the reader of his work "to *read it through*," and to that purpose, it helps to be interesting. Don't be afraid to be obvious. Go ahead and say, if necessary, "I started Early–Took my Dog–/And visited the Sea," or whatever will begin a story, or clearly set forth a situation. Excellent poems may be clear and yet be profound—like bodies of water.

Here are some other questions to ask yourself while you revise:

1. Does this poem express what I feel? Does it claim to feel more than I do—that is, is it sentimental? Or does it hang back, afraid to declare itself? (If it does, see if you can persuade the feelings out into the open.) The advice of W. D. Snodgrass is worth remembering:

> Our only hope as artists is to continually ask ourselves, "Am I writing what I *really* think? Not what is acceptable; not what my favorite intellectual would think in this situation; not what I wish I felt. Only what I cannot help thinking."[6]

2. Somewhere in its first half-dozen lines, does the poem offer the reader any temptation to go on reading? If so, something will have been begun: perhaps a story, dramatic situation, metaphor, or intriguing perplexity. To recognize it, you will need to put yourself into the reader's seat. One veteran teacher of poetry-writing, John Ciardi, places

[6] "Finding a Poem," *In Radical Pursuit* (New York: Harper & Row, 1974), p. 32.

great weight on engaging a reader early. Ciardi sometimes pencils a line underneath the line in the poem at which, out of boredom or disgust, he quits reading.

3. Is there anything in my poem that doesn't make sense to me? (*Careful! Such a difficulty may not be a fault!*) Does the difficulty come in stating something I feel to be valuable, or is it just an unsuccessful attempt to say something unimportant or needlessly explanatory? If it is the latter, away with it.

Here is some further advice, from Ezra Pound:

> Use no superfluous word, no adjective which does not reveal something.
>
> Don't use such an expression as 'dim lands *of peace*'. It dulls the image. It mixes an abstraction with the concrete. It comes from the writer's not realizing that the natural object is always the *adequate* symbol.
>
> Go in fear of abstractions. Do not retell in mediocre verse what has already been done in good prose. Don't think any intelligent person is going to be deceived when you try to shirk all the difficulties of the unspeakably difficult art of good prose by chopping your composition into line lengths. . . .
>
> Don't be 'viewy'—leave that to the writers of pretty little philosophic essays. Don't be descriptive; remember that the painter can describe a landscape much better than you can, and that he has to know a deal more about it.
>
> When Shakespeare talks of the 'Dawn in russet mantle clad' he presents something which the painter does not present. There is in this line of his nothing that one can call description; he presents. . . .
>
> If you are using a symmetrical form, don't put in what you want to say and then fill up the remaining vacuums with slush.[7]

In Pound's view, a poet ought to pay attention to vivid detail, and usually that is good advice. But like all general advice to poets, it is not to be followed absolutely. Some details may point us nowhere. They distract us from what matters, and they will need to be cut. Edwin Arlington Robinson probably wouldn't have improved "Mr. Flood's Party" by naming the brand of liquor Eben Flood preferred, nor by describing the picture on its label.

Evidently, the details to render vividly are the ones that mean the most. Unless you agree with Edgar Allan Poe that a short intense poem is the only true poem (see page 406), revision isn't a matter of polishing an entire poem to a level of high intensity. Long poems, said T. S. Eliot in "The Music of Poetry," naturally contain prosaic passages as well as intensely "poetic" ones. See the advice of Yeats (page 233) on the need for deliberately putting in a bit of dullness now and again.

Of all the skills a poet has, one of the most valuable is to know where to end lines. If your poem happens to be written in meter and

[7] Excerpts from "A Retrospect," *Literary Essays of Ezra Pound*, edited by T. S. Eliot (New York: New Directions, 1954), pp. 4–6.

rime, where to end lines is clearly suggested for you: lines end on riming words, or they end when their metrical expectation has been fulfilled. (An iambic pentameter line stops on its tenth syllable, give or take a syllable or two.) But in "free verse" or formally open poetry, you do not have any guidance other than your mind and eye and ear. To place your line breaks effectively calls for much care during revision, and at all times, a certain sensibility. Because the ending of a line compels the reader to make a slight pause—at least a moment for his eyes to relocate at the beginning of the next line—the placement of these pauses is a great resource to you. If most of your lines end on strong words (such as verbs and nouns), the effect is different from that of slicing your lines after weak words (such as articles—*a, the*—or prepositions).

Robert Creeley (b. 1916)

THE LOVER 1957

What should the young
man say, because he is buying
Modess? Should he

blush or not. Or
turn coyly, his head, to
one side, as if in

the exactitude of his emotion he
were not offended? Were
proud? Of what? To buy

a thing like that.

In this quiet, humorous poem reflecting on the young man's embarrassment, phrases tend to be sliced apart, requiring the reader to go on to the following line to complete each unit of sense. The effect of these line breaks is jerky, hesitant, wavering. Suppose that Creeley had arranged the poem instead:

> What should the young man say
> Because he is buying Modess?
> Should he blush or not?
> Or coyly turn his head to one side
> As if in the exactitude of his emotion
> He were not offended?
> Were proud? Of what?
> To buy a thing like that.

Here, units of sense are kept intact. Lines end on strong terms. The result isn't bad, but Creeley's placement of his line breaks is much better—for this particular poem, because he makes the lines, like the young man, wear an air of uncertainty. Some poets make it a habit to break *every* phrase in two, regardless of what they are saying. The result is a style as predictable as that of a limerick. (For more about line breaks, see the discussion of open form, pages 176–180.)

Notice that in the arbitrarily rewritten version of "The Lover" the lines are locked more tightly shut by a traditional device that Creeley shuns: starting each line with a capital letter. At some moment, after you have written many poems, you may care to decide your policy on such matters. Early in life, William Carlos Williams decided that he thought it pretentious to begin each line with a capital. Favoring lower-case letters, he went on all his life writing in what he believed to be a more flowing, less clearly end-stopped line, closer to ordinary speech and prose. Such avoidance of convention, of course, is in general neither right nor wrong; and your choice depends on the effect you are after. Although capital letters seemed pretentious to Williams, any evident attempt to defy convention calls attention to itself. Say "i think, therefore i am," and you aren't necessarily being modest. The effect is as though you were to print the letter *I* in red. E. E. Cummings, who favored the small letter *i*, was, according to many who knew him, an egotist.

When should you declare your poem done? Never, according to the French poet Paul Valéry, who said that a poem is never finished, only abandoned in despair. Other poets feel a definite sense of completion—as did Yeats, to whom a poem came shut with a click. But if you hear no such click, just stop when you see no more verbiage to prune, no more weak words to tighten. Abandon the poem, but don't despair. Maybe you will find another possible improvement in it—some day.

If by now a title for your poem hasn't occurred to you, you may want to consider one. Some poets, to be sure, dispense with any title—as was the usual practice of Cummings and Emily Dickinson. To a reader, however, a title may sometimes be valuable. If a poem is difficult, its title can show the reader how to take hold of it. An explicit title can supply needed background, tell us who is speaking, indicate tone, or explain a dramatic situation. By calling his poem "Soliloquy of the Spanish Cloister," Robert Browning indicates that we listen in on the thoughts of a single character, a monk in a religious order. Even a flatly indicative title ("Stopping by a Market in Pismo Beach to Buy Wine for a Wedding Present") may be more helpful to a reader than a merely decorative title ("Subterfuge with Sea-green Raisins").

REACHING AN AUDIENCE

Few contemporary poets seem to follow the custom of Emily Dickinson and store their poems in the family attic. Most poets want to share their work with the world, and some, as soon as they have written a first poem, rush to send it to a magazine. Hopes of instant acclaim, of course, often meet with disappointment. "Don't imagine," Ezra Pound warned, "that you can please the expert before you have spent at least as much effort on the art of verse as the average piano teacher spends on the art of music." Nevertheless, if you master your art, it is reasonable to expect that sooner or later people will listen to it.

In a writing class, you already have an audience: your fellow students, your instructor. Still, some beginning poets feel reluctant to display their work even to friendly eyes. They have an uncomfortable sense, at first, that they are being asked to parade their inmost emotions in public, while at the same time they risk being ridiculed for their weak artistry. That is why a writing class needs to agree that the poems its members share are to be regarded as works of the imagination, not as personal diaries. As for the risk of ridicule, nobody expects the beginner to be T. S. Eliot. Probably you will find your fellow students reading your poems as considerately and sympathetically as (they trust) you'll read theirs. As for your instructor, don't worry. He or she has seen worse poems.

If you *enjoy* reading your poems aloud, live audiences may be yours for the asking. Does your campus have a coffeehouse or other room in which to hold readings? Audience responses, while sometimes misleading, can encourage you. Be aware, however, that audiences like to laugh together, and often prefer funny, outrageous, immediately understandable poems to more difficult, subtle ones that require more than a single hearing. If any of your fellow student poets are interested, it may be even more valuable to form a small group for mutual criticism and support. In some informal setting (preferably with a *quiet* jukebox), you can exchange copies of your poems, and not only practice reading them aloud, but also have them read in manuscript.

Some novice poets crave early publication, and some who hurry into print are later sorry. However, should the day arrive when, tired of staring at a tall stack of beautiful finished poems, you just have to break into print, why not begin near home? Submit poems to your campus literary magazine, if there is any. If there isn't, can you see about starting one? Another alternative is to bring out your own magazine of limited circulation, with the aid of a mimeograph or a copier. Eventually, you may decide that your work belongs in magazines of wider readership—but first, make sure it is ready. Unlike your fellow students and your instructor, who know you personally and are likely to sympathize with your creative labors, the editor of a national magazine, to whom you are only a licked stamp, cares for nothing but what you can show on cold white paper. While a writing class may deal patiently with a faulted poem, taking time to rummage it for meaning, the glance of an overworked editor will be more cursory. A bungled opening, a cliché, a line of bombast or sentiment, and back goes the manuscript with a rejection slip. Not that this threat should discourage you. Just realize that, in trying to print your poems, you'll be venturing forth into a crowded marketplace.

At the moment, American poetry seems in the throes of an inflation: Karl Shapiro, somewhat grimly, has called it a "poetry glut." For a number of reasons (including, no doubt, the popularity of creative writing programs), thousands of people today are trying to throng into print. Perhaps, in a world of social-security numbers sorted out into zip-code areas, they feel nameless, and so hope to make a lasting name —however small—from writing poetry. Whatever the explanation, in the latest *Directory of American Poets and Fiction Writers,* 3,536 published poets are listed—an incomplete listing at that.[8] Although the ranks of poets are thick, recent years have seen a dwindling in the number of paying markets for a poem. Few magazines currently sold on newsstands regularly print poetry: *The Atlantic, The New Yorker*—the list expires. Most publishers of trade books, harried by rising costs, have pared books of poetry from their lists in favor of better sellers.

Still, poets need not consign their work to their attics. Lately, in noncommercial publishing, there has been a tremendous explosion of energy. As the latest *International Directory of Little Magazines and Small Presses* will indicate,[9] literary publishers now number in the thousands. **Little magazines,** periodicals edited and published as labors of love, exist not to turn a profit but to turn up new writing. That they succeed in this aim has been apparent since early in our century, when little magazines introduced the work of practically every modern American poet now celebrated—not to mention fiction writers such as Faulkner, Hemingway, and Eudora Welty. A few such magazines, thick and printed handsomely, appear on more or less regular schedules. The majority, less expensively produced, usually lag behind their declared frequencies. Most little magazines, if well established, reach an audience of perhaps 500 to 5,000.[10]

Read a magazine before sending it your work; if need be, write off (and pay) for a sample copy. There is no sense in offering, say, a pastoral elegy in heroic couplets to the radically experimental *Hanging Loose,* or a pornographic punk rock song to *The American Scholar.* Decent respect for editors requires that along with your poems you enclose a stamped,

[8] 1980–81 edition (New York: Poets & Writers, Inc., 1980).

[9] Edited by Len Fulton and Ellen Ferber, and published annually by Dustbooks, Box 100, Paradise, CA 95969. It may be in the reference department of your library.

[10] Among the heftier and more faithfully appearing little magazines are *Antaeus, Canto, Hudson Review, Paris Review,* and *Ploughshares;* also those reviews subsidized by universities (*Georgia Review, Massachusetts Review, Sewanee Review,* and others). *Poetry,* which printed the early poems of Eliot, Frost, Marianne Moore, and Stevens, still issues monthly from Chicago, as essential as ever. The influential *American Poetry Review,* a bimonthly in tabloid newspaper format, claims the largest circulation of any little magazine: according to one report, more than 20,000.

self-addressed envelope; send original copies, not carbons or Xeroxes; and submit a poem to one magazine at a time. Whole collections of poems may be offered to small presses, but usually it is necessary to publish in magazines first.

Delmore Schwartz once made a brilliant observation: a poet is wise to write as much and to publish as little as possible. Which of your poems deserve to be printed? Usually they will stand up and declare themselves. Should you have grave doubts about a poem, keep it for further revision. Print it in haste and readers, too, will have grave doubts about it.

With so many noncommercial publishers, it is a safe bet that any halfway competent poet who persists in licking stamps will break into print sooner or later. Yet the difficulty for poets today is not merely to be printed, but to be read. Ours seems a time of many more good voices than good listeners. It is, besides, an age of disagreement and diversity. Ask any published poet what he thinks of poetry, and he will probably tell you that most poetry now being printed, other than his own, is bad or mediocre. But ask any six poets (selected at random) what other poets among their contemporaries they admire, and you will receive six lists of names with little duplication. To add to the confusion about what is excellent (or, some might say, to add to the merriment), most literary critics, as if discouraged by the vastness of the task of keeping up with contemporary poetry, have folded their practices. (To be sure, a very few brave and overworked critics of contemporary poetry are still operating.) Some poets feel that, since criticism isn't a help to them anyhow, who needs it? Still, without critics, who used to be poets' most devoted readers, it is more difficult for excellence to be recognized. Whatever is to be made of the current poetic scene, two truths seem evident. It is hard for a new poet today to gain an audience and a reputation. And yet, in the last few years, despite all odds, several excellent new poets have succeeded in doing so.

If you are a dedicated poet, and your work truly deserves your dedication, you'll keep faith that you will eventually find your audience. You'll listen to the voice of your Muse, not to the siren warblings of the marketplace. (In John Ciardi's view, it is hardly possible to prostitute your talent for poetry, anyway, there being so few paying customers.) You will become a more severe critic of your own work than your fellow students or your instructor. Although when you send out your poems to the handsome magazines you'll have to elbow through a crowd, and if you ever apply for a writing grant you will encounter steep competition, you can be sure that, among contenders for immortality, there can no more be any rivalry than there is among gold prospectors. That is, when poets strike paydirt and achieve renown, it is usually because they have stalwart backs, eyes for a gleam, and likely claims, not because they know someone at the assay office.

Apparently, poets are not paid in bullion. In fact, nowhere in the English-speaking world at the moment is the writing of poems a full-time paying occupation. Most poets survive by other honest trades (such as teaching), receiving nothing or almost nothing for their poems, making a spare dollar from an occasional reading. Still, most derive an ample compensation. No one has better summed up the payment of being a poet than John Keats, in a letter to a friend: "I should write for the mere yearning and fondness I have for the beautiful, even if my night's labors should be burnt every morning and no eye shine upon them." For any poet so intently dedicated, writing a poem is today—as it always has been—its own considerable, immediate reward.

EXPERIMENTS: *Writing Poetry*

Doing finger exercises is generally less fruitful to a poet than trying to write poems. Here are a few suggestions that might result in poems, if they arouse any responses in you.

1. Try to recall, and recapture in a poem, some experience that deeply moved you. The experience does not have to be anything world-shaking or traumatic; it might be as small as a memory from early childhood, a chance meeting with someone, a visit to a beach, the realization that some ordinary object is beautiful.
2. Try writing a poem in a voice *remote* from your own—speaking, say, as a character in history or fiction or film; an ordinary citizen in a different place or time; a child; an octogenarian. (For one famous illustration of a poet's speaking through a mask or persona, see Robert Browning's "Soliloquy of the Spanish Cloister," page 295. Presumably Browning set himself a problem: What would a hate-filled, envious monk think and mutter about a devout brother? Then, having imagined such a character, the poet found the character some artful and appropriate words.)
3. Attempt a poem in which you convey the joy of performing some simple, familiar, routine act: running, driving a car, peeling an orange, stroking a cat, changing a baby—or whatever you like to do.
4. Here is an experiment suggested by Ezra Pound: Write words to a well-known tune "in such a way that the words will not be distorted when one sings them."
5. Find, in a current magazine, a poem that strikes you as silly, pretentious, or simple-minded. Write a take-off on it.
6. Taking the same weak poem, try to revise it, freely cutting it or adding to it. See if you can make of it something worth reading.
7. The aim of the following experiment is to lead you to wrestle with arbitrary difficulties. Observe some limitation that may seem to you pointless, but which might set up a certain tension within your poem—provide a bottle (to echo Richard Wilbur) for your genie to try to burst out of. For instance, write a poem entirely in simple declarative subject-plus-verb sentences. Write a poem that is all one metaphor (like, for example, Emily Dickinson's "Because I could not stop for Death" or Whitman's "A Noiseless Patient Spider." Write a poem in blank verse (the form of Tennyson's "Ulysses" or Frost's "Mending Wall"). Or, as Theodore Roethke was fond of asking his students to do, write a poem without adjectives.

8. Write a poem in praise of someone you admire, allowing yourself no general terms (*beautiful, wonderful,* etc.); try to describe the person in language so specific that a reader, too, will find your subject admirable.
9. Write a curse in verse: a damnation of someone or something you can't abide.
10. From an opening line (or lines) supplied by your instructor, try to develop a poem. Then compare the result with poems developed by others from the same beginning.
11. In verse (whether rimed or opened), write a letter to a friend. For neoclassical examples, see the works of Swift and Pope (the latter's "Epistle to Dr. Arbuthnot" and other epistles in particular); for less formal contemporary examples, see Richard Hugo's collection *31 Letters and 13 Dreams* (New York: Norton, 1977) – mostly verse-letters to fellow poets.
12. Write a poem in the form of a dialogue between two people. (Frost's "The Witch of Coös" may help illustrate such an exchange of speeches, although in it two characters are speaking to a third.)
13. Intently observe something for twenty or thirty minutes, then write a poem full of images through which your reader, too, can apprehend it. An excellent object for scrutiny would be any small living thing that will stand still long enough: an animal, bird, tropical fish, insect, or plant.
14. In a bookstore or library, select a book of poems that appeal to you. Take it home and read it thoroughly. If you have chosen well, the book may quicken your feelings and encourage you, too, to devote yourself to words. See if you can write a poem suggested or inspired by it – not necessarily an imitation.

Acknowledgments *(continued)*

Roy Campbell. "On Some South African Novelists" from *Adamastor* by Roy Campbell. Reprinted by permission of Curtis Brown Ltd. on behalf of the Estate of Roy Campbell.

Bliss Carman. Lines from "A Vagabond Song" from *Bliss Carman's Poems.* Reprinted by permission of Dodd, Mead & Company and McClelland & Stewart Ltd.

Geoffrey Chaucer. Lines from Part I. "Merciles Beaute" from *The Works of Geoffrey Chaucer,* Second Edition, edited by F. N. Robinson (1957). Reprinted by permission of Houghton Mifflin Company.

G. K. Chesterton. "The Donkey" from *The Wild Knight and Other Poems* by G. K. Chesterton. Reprinted by permission of J. M. Dent & Sons Ltd. Publishers, Miss D. Collins and the author.

John Ciardi. "By a Bush in Half Twilight" by John Ciardi. First appeared in *Poultry,* No. 1, 1980. Reprinted by permission of the poet.

Sarah N. Cleghorn. "The Golf Links Lie So Near the Mill" from *Portraits and Protests* by Sarah N. Cleghorn. All rights reserved. Reprinted by permission of Holt, Rinehart and Winston, Publishers.

Leonard Cohen. "All There Is To Know about Adolph Eichmann" from *Selected Poems 1956–1968* by Leonard Cohen. Copyright © 1964 by Leonard Cohen. Reprinted by permission of Viking Penguin Inc.

Cid Corman. "The Tortoise" from *Words for Each Other* by Cid Corman. First appeared in *In Good Time* by Cid Corman. Reprinted by permission of Andre Deutsch Limited.

Frances Cornford. "The Watch" from *Collected Poems* by Frances Cornford (Cresset Press). Reprinted by permission of Barrie and Jenkins Ltd.

Hart Crane. "My Grandmother's Love Letters" is reprinted from *The Complete Poems and Selected Letters and Prose of Hart Crane,* edited by Brom Weber, with the permission of Liveright Publishing Corporation. Copyright 1933, © 1958, 1966 by Liveright Publishing Corporation.

Robert Creeley. "Oh No" and "The Lover" by Robert Creeley from *For Love: Poems 1950–1960.* Copyright © 1962 by Robert Creeley (New York: Charles Scribner's Sons, 1962). Reprinted with the permission of Charles Scribner's Sons.

Countee Cullen. "For a Lady I Know" from *On These I Stand* by Countee Cullen. Copyright 1925 by Harper & Row, Publishers, Inc., renewed 1953 by Ida M. Cullen. Reprinted by permission of Harper & Row, Publishers, Inc.

E.E. Cummings. From *Complete Poems 1913–1962:* "anyone lived in a pretty how town" (copyright 1940 by E.E. Cummings, copyright © 1968 by Marion Morehouse Cummings); "Buffalo Bill's," and "in Just-" (both copyright 1923, 1951 by E. E. Cummings); "a politician is an arse upon" (copyright 1944 by E. E. Cummings); and "r-p-o-p-h-e-s-s-a-g-r" (copyright 1935 by E.E. Cummings, copyright © 1963 by Marion Morehouse Cummings). Reprinted by permission of Harcourt Brace Jovanovich Inc.

J. V. Cunningham. "Friend, on this scaffold . . .," "Motto for a Sundial," "You serve the best wines . . .," and "This Humanist whom . . ." from *The Exclusions of a Rhyme* by J. V. Cunningham. Copyright © 1971 by J. V. Cunningham. Reprinted with the permission of The Ohio University Press, Athens.

Peter Davison. "The Last Word" (Part IV of "Four Love Poems") from *Pretending to Be Asleep* by Peter Davison. Copyright © 1970 by Peter Davison. Reprinted by permission of Atheneum Publishers.

Emily Dickinson. "Because I could not stop for Death," "I heard a Fly buzz–when I died," "I like to see it lap the Miles," "I started Early – Took my Dog." "The Lightning is a yellow Fork." "The Soul selects her own Society," "Victory comes late." "It dropped so low–in my Regard." "Safe in their Alabaster Chambers," "A Dying Tiger–moaned for Drink," "My Life had stood–a Loaded Gun," and lines from "Hope is the thing with feathers" reprinted by permission of the publishers and Trustees of Amherst College from *The Poems of Emily Dickinson,* edited by Thomas H. Johnson, Cambridge, Mass., The Belknap Press of Harvard University Press, Copyright 1951, © 1955, 1979 by the President and Fellows of Harvard College. Twenty-two lines from "My Life had stood–a Loaded Gun," copyright 1929 by Martha Dickinson Bianchi; copyright © renewed 1957 by Mary L. Hampson. By permission of Little, Brown and Company in association with the Atlantic Monthly Press.

Emanuel diPasquale. "Rain," reprinted by permission of the poet.

Reinhard Döhl. Reprinted by permission of the poet.

Philip Dow. "Drunk Last Night with Friends, I Go to Work Anyway" from *Paying Back the Sea* (1979) by Philip Dow. Reprinted by permission of Carnegie-Mellon University Press.

Alan Dugan. "Love Song: I and Thou" from *Poems* by Alan Dugan. Copyright © 1961 by Alan Dugan. First published by Yale University Press. Reprinted by permission.

Bob Dylan. *Subterranean Homesick Blues* by Bob Dylan. © 1965 Warner Bros. Inc. All rights reserved. Used by permission.

Richard Eberhart. "The Fury of Aerial Bombardment" from *Collected Poems 1930–1976* by Richard Eberhart. Copyright © 1976 by Richard Eberhart. Reprinted by permission of Oxford University Press and Chatto & Windus Ltd.

T. S. Eliot "Journey of the Magi," "Virginia" (from "Landscapes"), "The Love Song of J. Alfred Prufrock," and "The *Boston Evening Transcript*" from *Collected Poems 1909–1962* by T. S. Eliot. Copyright 1936 by Harcourt Brace Jovanovich, Inc., copyright © 1963, 1964 by T. S. Eliot. Excerpt from "Tradition and the Individual Talent" from *Selected Essays,* New Edition, published by Harcourt Brace Jovanovich. Reprinted by permission of Harcourt Brace Jovanovich, Inc. and Faber and Faber Limited.

James Emanuel. "The Negro" Copyright © 1968 by James Emanuel. Reprinted by permission of Broadside Press.

Abbie Huston Evans. "Wing Spread" Reprinted from *Collected Poems* by Abbie Huston Evans by permission of the University of Pittsburgh Press. © 1950 by Abbie Huston Evans.

Donald Finkel. "Hands" from *A Joyful Noise* by Donald Finkel. Copyright © 1965, 1966 by Donald Finkel. "Gesture" from *The Garbage Wars* by Donald Finkel. Copyright © 1969, 1970 by Donald Finkel. Reprinted by permission of Atheneum Publishers.

Carolyn Forché. Lines from "Dulcimer Maker" from *Gathering the Tribes* by Carolyn Forché. Copyright © 1976 by Carolyn Forché. Reprinted by permission of Yale University Press.

Robert Francis. "Catch" from *The Orb Weaver* by Robert Francis. Copyright © 1950 by Robert Francis. Reprinted by permission of Wesleyan University Press.

Robert Frost. "Desert Places," "Stopping by Woods on a Snowy Evening," "Never Again Would Birds' Song Be the Same," "Design," "The Secret Sits," "Fire and Ice," "Mending Wall," "The Witch of Coös," and "The Silken Tent" from *The Poetry of Robert Frost,* edited by Edward Connery Lathem. Copyright 1923, 1930, 1939, © 1969 by Holt, Rinehart and Winston. Copyright 1936, 1942, 1951, © 1958 by Robert Frost. Copyright © 1964, 1967, 1970 by Lesley Frost Ballantine. "In White" from *The Dimensions of Robert Frost* by Reginald L. Cook. Copyright © 1958 by Reginald L. Cook. Excerpt from letter No. 53 from *Selected Letters of Robert Frost,* edited by Lawrance Thompson. Copyright © 1964 by Lawrance Thompson and Holt, Rinehart and Winston. Reprinted by permission of Holt, Rinehart and Winston, Publishers.

Tess Gallagher. "Under Stars" (copyright 1978 Tess Gallagher) is from *Under Stars* by Tess Gallagher, published by Graywolf Press. Reprinted by permission.

Gary Gildner. "First Practice" reprinted from *First Practice* by Gary Gildner by permission of the University of Pittsburgh Press. © 1969 by Gary Gildner.

Allen Ginsberg. "A Supermarket in California" from *Howl and Other Poems* by Allen Ginsberg. Copyright © 1956, 1959 by Allen Ginsberg. Reprinted by permission of City Lights Books.

Paul Goodman. Lines from "Hokku" from *Collected Poems* by Paul Goodman, edited by Taylor Stoehr. Copyright © 1973 by The Estate of Paul Goodman. Reprinted by permission of Random House, Inc.

Robert Graves. "Down, Wanton, Down" and "Love Without Hope" from *Collected Poems* by Robert Graves. Copyright 1939, © 1955, 1958, 1961, 1965 by Robert Graves. Reprinted by permission of Robert Graves.

Ronald Gross. "Yield" from *Pop Poems* by Ronald Gross. Copyright © 1967 by Ronald Gross. Reprinted by permission of Simon & Schuster, A Division of Gulf & Western Corporation.

Bruce Guernsey. "Louis B. Russell," first published in *Xanadu*, V. 1, No. 1, Summer, 1975. Copyright by Long Island Poetry Collective, Inc. Reprinted by permission of Long Island Poetry Collective, Inc., and the poet.

Arthur Guiterman. "On the Vanity of Earthly Greatness" from *Gaily the Troubador* by Arthur Guiterman. Copyright 1936 by E. P. Dutton & Co., Inc.; renewed 1954 by Mrs. Vida Lindo Guiterman. Reprinted by permission of Louise M. Sclove.

Woody Guthrie. "Plane Wreck at Los Gatos (Deportee)." Copyright © 1961 and 1963 by Ludlow Music, Inc., New York, N.Y. Used by permission.

H. D. (Hilda Doolittle). "Heat" from *Selected Poems* by Hilda Doolittle. Copyright © 1957 by Norman Holmes Pearson. Reprinted by permission of New Directions Publishing Corporation.

Donald Hall. "The Town of Hill" from *The Town of Hill* by Donald Hall. Copyright © 1975 by Donald Hall. Reprinted by permission of David R. Godine, Publisher, Inc. "My Son, My Executioner" from *The Alligator Bride: Poems New and Selected*, copyright 1954 by Donald Hall. First appeared in *The New Yorker* as "First Child." Reprinted by permission.

William Harmon. "Bureaucratic Limerick" and the first selection from "Ms. D.'s College Diary—Aetat. 150" ("The Soul selects her own sorority. . .") by William Harmon. Copyright © 1981 by William Harmon. Reprinted by permission of the poet.

Seamus Heaney. "Sunlight" (the first poem from "Mossbawn: Two Poems in Dedication for Mary Heaney") from *North* by Seamus Heaney. Reprinted by permission of Faber and Faber Limited.

Anthony Hecht. "The Vow" from *The Hard Hours* by Anthony Hecht. Copyright 1954, © 1957, 1967 by Anthony E. Hecht. Appeared originally in the Hudson Review. Reprinted by permission of Atheneum Publishers.

Geoffrey Hill. "Merlin" from *Somewhere Is Such a Kingdom: Poems: 1952–1971* by Geoffrey Hill. Copyright © 1975 by Geoffrey Hill. Reprinted by permission of Houghton Mifflin Company and Andre Deutsch Ltd.

John Hollander. "Swan and Shadow" from John Hollander, *Types of Shape*. Copyright © 1969 by John Hollander (New York: Atheneum, 1969). Reprinted by permission of Atheneum Publishers.

A. D. Hope. "The Brides" from *Collected Poems 1930–1965* by A. D. Hope. Copyright © 1960, 1962 by A. D. Hope. Reprinted by permission of Viking Penguin Inc.

A. E. Housman. "Loveliest of trees, the cherry now," "Terence, this is stupid stuff," "To an Athlete Dying Young," "When I was One-and-Twenty," "With rue my heart is laden" from "A Shropshire Lad"—Authorized Edition—from *The Collected Poems of A. E. Housman*. Copyright 1939, 1940, © 1965 by Holt, Rinehart and Winston. Copyright © 1967, 1968 by Robert E. Symons. "Eight O'Clock" from *The Collected Poems of A. E. Housman*. Copyright 1922 by Holt, Rinehart and Winston. Copyright 1950 by Barclay's Bank Ltd. Reprinted by permission of Holt, Rinehart and Winston, Publishers; The Society of Authors as literary representative of the Estate of A. E. Housman, and Jonathan Cape Ltd., publishers of A. E. Housman's *Collected Poems*.

Langston Hughes. "Dream Deferred" from *The Panther and the Lash: Poems of Our Times* by Langston Hughes. Copyright 1951 by Langston Hughes. "Song for a Dark Girl" from *Selected Poems by Langston Hughes* by Langston Hughes. Copyright 1927 by Alfred A. Knopf, Inc. and renewed 1955 by Langston Hughes. Reprinted by permission of Alfred A. Knopf, Inc.

Richard Hugo. "In Your Young Dream" is reprinted from *13 Letters and 13 Dreams*. Poems by Richard Hugo, with the permission of W. W. Norton & Company Inc. Copyright © 1977 by W. W. Norton & Company, Inc.

T. E. Hulme. "Image" from *The Life and Opinions of T. E. Hulme* by Alun R. Jones. Copyright © 1960 by Alun R. Jones. Reprinted with the permission of Beacon Press.

David Ignatow. "Get the Gasworks" from *Figures of the Human* by David Ignatow. Copyright © 1948 by David Ignatow. Reprinted by permission of Wesleyan University Press.

Randall Jarrell. From *The Complete Poems* by Randall Jarrell: "The Death of the Ball Turret Gunner" (Copyright 1945, renewed © 1973 by Mary von Schrader Jarrell) and "A Sick Child" (Copyright 1949 by Randall Jarrell, renewed © 1976 by Mary von Schrader Jarrell). Reprinted by permission of Farrar, Straus & Giroux, Inc. "The Woman at the Washington Zoo" from *The Woman at the Washington Zoo* by Randall Jarrell. Copyright © 1960 by Randall Jarrell. Reprinted by permission of Atheneum Publishers. Two excerpts from *Poetry and the Age* by Randall Jarrell. Copyright 1952, 1953 by Randall Jarrell. Reprinted by permission of Mrs. Mary von Schrader Jarrell.

Elizabeth Jennings. "Delay" from *Collected Poems* by Elizabeth Jennings, 1953, © 1967 by Elizabeth Jennings. Reprinted by permission of David Higham Associates Limited.

Greg Keeler. Eight lines from "There Ain't No Such Thing as a Montana Cowboy." Reprinted by permission of the poet.

Jane Kenyon. "The Suitor" from *From Room to Room*, © 1978 by Jane Kenyon. Reprinted courtesy of Alice James Books, 138 Mt. Auburn St., Cambridge, Mass., 02138.

James C. Kilgore. "The White Man Pressed the Locks" from *Poets on the Platform*. Copyright © 1970 by James C. Kilgore. Reprinted by permission of the poet.

Hugh Kingsmill. "What, still alive at twenty-two" from *The Best of Hugh Kingsmill*. Reprinted by permission of Victor Gollancz Ltd.

Galway Kinnell. "Blackberry Eating" from *Mortal Acts, Mortal Words* by Galway Kinnell. Copyright © 1980 by Galway Kinnell. Reprinted by permission of Houghton Mifflin Company.

Etheridge Knight. "For Black Poets Who Think of Suicide" from *Poems From Prison* by Etheridge Knight. Copyright © 1968 by Etheridge Knight. Reprinted by permission of Broadside Press.

William Knott. "Poem" from *The Naomi Poems: Corpse and Beans* by Saint Geraud. Copyright © 1968 by William Knott. Used by permission of Follett Publishing Company.

Kenneth Koch. "Mending Sump" from *The New American Poetry*, ed. by Donald M. Allen. Copyright © 1960 by Kenneth Koch. Reprinted by permission of International Creative Management.

Ted Kooser. "Beer Bottle" from *Sure Signs: New and Selected Poems* by Ted Kooser; © 1980 by Ted Kooser. Reprinted by permission of the University of Pittsburgh Press.

Richard Kostelanetz. "Disintegration" from *Visual Language* (Assembling Press, 1970). Reprinted by permission of the poet.

Maxine Kumin. "Woodchucks" from *Up Country* by Maxine Kumin. Copyright © 1971 by Maxine Kumin. Originally appeared in *The Boston Review of the Arts*. Reprinted by permission of Curtis Brown, Ltd.

Philip Larkin. "Vers de Societé" from *High Windows* by Philip Larkin. Copyright © 1974 by Philip Larkin. Reprinted by permission of Farrar, Straus & Giroux and Faber and Faber Ltd.

D. H. Lawrence. From *The Complete Poems of D. H. Lawrence*, edited by Vivian de Sola and F. Warren Roberts: "A Youth Mowing" and "Piano" (Copyright © 1964, 1971 by Angelo Ravagli and C. M. Weekley, Executors of the Estate of Frieda Lawrence Ravagli), "Bavarian Gentians" (Copyright 1933 by Frieda Lawrence. All rights reserved.) Reprinted by permission of The Viking Press.

Irving Layton. "The Bull Calf" from *A Red Carpet for the Sun* by Irving Layton. Reprinted by permission of the Canadian Publishers, McClelland and Stewart Limited, Toronto.

John Lennon and Paul McCartney. "Eleanor Rigby" Copyright © 1966 Northern Songs Limited. All rights for the U.S.A., Mexico and the Philippines controlled by Maclen Music, Inc. Used by permission. All rights reserved.

Denise Levertov. "Sunday Afternoon" and "Six Variations, iii" from *The Jacob's Ladder* by Denise Levertov. Copyright © 1958, 1969 by Denise Levertov Goodman. "Leaving Forever" from *O Taste and See* by Denise Levertov. Copyright © 1963 by Denise Levertov. "Six Variations, iii" and "Leaving Forever" were first published in *Poetry*. Reprinted by permission of New Directions Publishing Corporation.

Philip Levine. "To a Child Trapped in a Barber Shop" from *Not This Pig* by Philip Levine. Copyright © 1966 by Philip Levine. Reprinted by permission of Wesleyan University Press.

Janet Lewis. "Girl Help" from *Poems 1924–1944* by Janet Lewis. Copyright © 1950 by Janet Lewis. Reprinted with the permission of The Ohio University Press, Athens.

J. A. Lindon. "My Garden," reprinted by permission of Hazel J. Lindon.

Myra Cohn Livingston. "Driving" from *The Malibu and Other Poems* by Myra Cohn Livingston (A Margaret K. McElderry Book). Copyright © 1972 by Myra Cohn Livingston. Reprinted by permission of Atheneum Publishers.

Federico García Lorca, "La Guitarra" (translated by Keith Waldrop) from *Obras Completas*. Copyright © Aguilar S. A. de Ediciones 1954. All Rights Reserved. Reprinted by permission of New Directions Publishing Corporation.

Robert Lowell. "At the Altar" from *Lord Weary's Castle* by Robert Lowell. Copyright 1946 by Robert Lowell. Reprinted by permission of Harcourt Brace Jovanovich, Inc. "Meditation" from *Imitations* by Robert Lowell. Copyright © 1958, 1959, 1960, 1961 by Robert Lowell. Reprinted by permission of Farrar, Straus & Giroux, Inc. "Skunk Hour" from *Life Studies* by Robert Lowell. Copyright © 1956, 1959 by Robert Lowell. Reprinted by permission of Farrar, Straus & Giroux.

Hugh MacDiarmid. "Weesht, Weesht" from *Collected Poems* by Hugh MacDiarmid. Copyright 1948, © 1962 by Christopher Murray Grieve. Reprinted by permission of Macmillan Publishing Co., Inc.

Archibald Macleish. "Ars Poetica" and "The End of the World" from *New and Collected Poems 1917–1976* by Archibald MacLeish. Copyright © 1976 by Archibald MacLeish. Reprinted by permission of Houghton Mifflin Company.

John Masefield. "Cargoes" from *Poems* by John Masefield. Copyright 1912 by Macmillan Publishing Co., Inc.; renewed 1940 by John Masefield. Reprinted by permission of Macmillan Publishing Co., Inc.

Rod McKuen. "Thoughts on Capital Punishment" from *Stanyan Street and Other Sorrows* by Rod McKuen. Copyright 1954, © 1960, 1961, 1962, 1963, 1964, 1965, 1966 by Rod McKuen. Reprinted by permission of Random House, Inc.

James Merrill. "Laboratory Poem" from *The Country of a Thousand Years of Peace* by James Merrill. Copyright © 1958, 1970 by James Merrill. This poem originally appeared in *Poetry*. Reprinted by permission of Atheneum Publishers.

W. S. Merwin. "For the Anniversary of My Death" from *The Lice* by W. S. Merwin. Copyright © 1967 by W. S. Merwin. Appeared originally in the *Southern Review*. "Song of a Man Chipping an Arrowhead" from *Writings to an Unfinished Accompaniment* by W. S. Merwin. Copyright © 1972, 1973 by W. S. Merwin. Reprinted by Atheneum Publishers.

Josephine Miles. "Reason" from *Poems 1930–1960* by Josephine Miles. Copyright © 1960 by Indiana University Press. Reprinted by permission of the publisher, Indiana University Press.

Edna St. Vincent Millay. "Counting-out Rhyme" from *Collected Poems* by Edna St. Vincent Millay, published by Harper & Row. Copyright 1928, © 1955 by Edna St. Vincent Millay and Norma Millay Ellis. Reprinted by permission of Norma Millay Ellis.

A. A. Milne. Excerpt from "Disobedience" from *When We Were Very Young* by A. A. Milne. Copyright 1924 by E. P. Dutton & Co., Inc.; renewed 1952 by A. A. Milne. Reprinted by permission of the publisher, E. P. Dutton and The Canadian Publishers, McClelland and Stewart Limited, Toronto.

Marianne Moore. "The Mind is an Enchanting Thing" from *Collected Poems* by Marianne Moore. Copyright 1944, © 1972 by Marianne Moore. Reprinted by permission of Macmillan Publishing Co., Inc.

Edwin Morgan. "Siesta of a Hungarian Snake" from *The Second Life* by Edwin Morgan. Copyright © 1968 by Edwin Morgan and Edinburgh University Press. Reprinted by permission of Edinburgh University Press.

Howard Moss. "Shall I Compare Thee to a Summer's Day?" from *A Swim Off the Rocks* by Howard Moss. Copyright © 1976. This poem appeared originally in *Commentary*. Reprinted by permission of Atheneum Publishers.

Ogden Nash. "Very Like a Whale" from *Verses From 1929 On* by Ogden Nash. Copyright 1934 by The Curtis Publishing Company. First appeared in *The Saturday Evening Post*. Reprinted by permission of Little, Brown and Company.

Willie Nelson. "Heaven and Hell" from the album *Phases and Stages* by Willie Nelson. Copyright © 1974 by Willie Nelson Music, Inc.

Howard Nemerov. "Storm Windows" from *The Collected Poems of Howard Nemverov* (1977). Reprinted by permission of the poet.

John Frederick Nims. "Love Poem" from *The Iron Pastoral* by John Nims. Copyright 1947 by John Frederick Nims. "Contemplation" from *Of Flesh and Bone*. Copyright © 1967 by Rutgers University Press. Reprinted by permission of the poet.

Alden Nowlan. "The Loneliness of the Long Distance Runner" from *Bread, Wine and Salt* by Alden Nowlan. Copyright © 1967 by Clarke, Irwin & Co. Ltd. Used by permission.

Charles Olson. "La Chute," copyright by Charles Olson. Reprinted by permission of the Estate of Charles Olson.

Guy Owen. "The White Stallion" from *The White Stallion* by Guy Owen (John F. Blair, Publisher, 1969). Reprinted by permission of the poet and the publisher.

Wilfred Owen. "Dulce et Decorum Est" from *The Collected Poems of Wilfred Owen*. Copyright 1946, © 1963 by Chatto and Windus Ltd. Reprinted by permission of New Directions Publishing Corporation, the Owen Estate, and Chatto and Windus Ltd.

Dorothy Parker. "Resume" from *The Portable Dorothy Parker*. Copyright 1926, 1954 by Dorothy Parker. Reprinted by permission of the Viking Press.

Linda Pastan. "Ethics" is reprinted from *Waiting For My Life*, Poems by Linda Pastan, with the permission of the author and W. W. Norton & Company, Inc. Copyright © 1981 by Linda Pastan. This poem first appeared in *Poetry* in December 1979.

Ruth Pitter. "But for Lust" from *Collected Poems* by Ruth Pitter.

Sylvia Plath. "Daddy" (Copyright © 1963 by Ted Hughes) and "Morning Song" (Copyright © 1961 by Ted Hughes) from *Ariel* by Sylvia Plath. Published by Harper & Row, Publishers and Faber and Faber, London. Copyright Ted Hughes, 1965. "Metaphors" from *Crossing the Water* by Sylvia Plath. Copyright © 1960 by Ted Hughes. Published by Harper & Row, Publishers and Faber and Faber, London. Copyright Ted Hughes, 1971. Reprinted by permission of Harper & Row, Publishers, and Olwyn Hughes, representing the estate of Sylvia Plath.

Cole Porter. Lines from "You're the Top" by Cole Porter. Copyright © 1934 (renewed) Warner Bros. Inc. All Rights Reserved. Used by permission.

Ezra Pound. "The Seafarer," "In a Station of the Metro," and "The River Merchant's Wife" from *Personate* by Ezra Pound. Copyright 1926 by Ezra Pound. Excerpt from "A Retrospect" from *Literary Essays* of Ezra Pound. Copyright 1935 by Ezra Pound. Excerpt from *ABC of Reading*. Copyright 1934 by Ezra Pound. All reprinted by permission of New Directions Publishing Corporation. First six lines from "III Hiang Niao" reprinted by permission of the publishers from Ezra Pound, *Shih-Ching: The Classic Anthology Defined by Confucius*; Cambridge, Mass., Harvard University Press. Copyright © 1954 by the President and Fellows of Harvard College.

Dudley Randall. "Ballad of Birmingham" from *Poem Counterpoem* by Margaret Danner and Dudley Randall. Copyright © 1966 by Dudley Randall. Reprinted by permission of the poet.

John Crowe Ransom. "Janet Waking" from *Selected Poems*, Third Edition, Revised and Enlarged by John Crowe Ransom. Copyright 1927 by Alfred A. Knopf, Inc. and renewed 1955 by John Crowe Ransom. Reprinted by permission of Alfred A. Knopf, Inc.

Henry Reed. "Naming of Parts" from *A Map of Verona* by Henry Reed (1946). Reprinted by permission of Jonathan Cape Ltd.

Kenneth Rexroth. "A dawn in a tree of birds . . ." from *New Poems* by Kenneth Rexroth. Copyright © 1974 by Kenneth Rexroth. Reprinted by permission of New Directions Publishing Corporation.

Adrienne Rich. "Diving into the Wreck" and "Aunt Jennifer's Tigers" from *Poems, Selected and New, 1950–1974* by Adrienne Rich. Copyright © 1975, 1973, 1971, 1969, 1966 by W. W. Norton & Company, Inc. Copyright © 1967, 1963, 1962, 1961, 1960, 1959, 1958, 1957, 1956, 1955, 1954, 1953, 1952, 1951 by Adrienne Rich. Reprinted with the permission of W. W. Norton & Company, Inc.

Edwin Arlington Robinson. "Richard Cory" from *The Children of the Night* by Edwin Arlington Robinson. Copyright under the Berne Convention. (New York: Charles Scribner's Sons, 1897). Reprinted with the permission of Charles Scribner's Sons. "Mr. Flood's Party" from *Collected Poems* by Edwin Arlington Robinson. Copyright 1921 by Edwin Arlington Robinson, renewed 1949 by Ruth Nivison. Reprinted with the permission of Macmillan Publishing Co., Inc.

Theodore Roethke. From *The Collected Poems of Theodore Roethke:* "I Knew a Woman" (Copyright 1954 by Theodore Roethke), "The Waking" (Copyright 1953 by Theodore Roethke), "My Papa's Waltz" (Copyright 1942 by Hearst Magazine, Inc.), "Root Cellar" (Copyright 1943 by Modern Poetry Association, Inc.), and "Night Crow" (Copyright 1944 by Saturday Review Association, Inc.). All poems reprinted by permission of Doubleday & Company, Inc.

Raymond Roseliep. Two haiku—"the old woman holds . . ." and "campfire extinguished" from *Listen to the Light: Haiku* by Raymond Roseliep. Copyright 1980 by Raymond Roseliep (Alembic Press, Ithaca, New York). Reprinted by permission of the poet.

Gibbons Ruark. "Saying goodbye to my daughters" from *Reeds* by Gibbons Ruark. Reprinted by permission of Texas Tech University Press.

Carl Sandburg. "Fog" from *Chicago Poems* by Carl Sandburg. Copyright 1916 by Holt, Rinehart and Winston, Inc., 1944 by Carl Sandburg. Reprinted by permission of Harcourt Brace Jovanovich, Inc.

Aram Saroyan. Lines from "crickets" from *Works* by Aram Saroyan. Copyright © 1966 by Aram Saroyan. Reprinted by permission of the poet.

Anne Sexton. "For My Lover, Returning to His Wife" and lines from "Eighteen Days Without You" from *Love Poems* by Anne Sexton. Copyright © 1967, 1968, 1969 by Anne Sexton. Reprinted by permission of Houghton Mifflin Company.

Karl Shapiro. "The Dirty Word" from *Selected Poems* by Karl Shapiro. Copyright 1947 by Karl Shapiro. Reprinted by permission of Random House, Inc.

Charles Simic. "The Butcher Shop" from *Dismantling the Silence* by Charles Simic. Copyright © 1971 by Charles Simic. Reprinted by permission of the publisher, George Braziller. Inc.

Paul Simon. "Richard Cory" from the album, *Sounds of Silence.* © 1966 by Paul Simon. Used by permission.

L. E. Sissman. Lines from "In and Out: A Home Away from Home" from *Dying: An Introduction* by L. E. Sissman. Copyright © 1967 by L. E. Sissman. Reprinted by permission of Little, Brown and Company in association with The Atlantic Monthly Press.

Knute Skinner. "The Cold Irish Earth" from *A Close Sky Over Killas-Puglonane* (The Dolmen Press, 1968). Reprinted by permission of the poet and the publisher.

Desmond Skirrow. "Ode on a Grecian Urn Summarized." First appeared in *The New Statesman*, July 30, 1960. Reprinted by permission of the Statesman and Nation Publishing Company Limited.

Barbara Herrnstein Smith. Excerpt from *Poetic Disclosure: A Study of How Poems End* by Barbara Herrnstein Smith. Copyright © 1968 by The University of Chicago Press. All rights reserved. Reprinted by permission of The University of Chicago Press.

Stevie Smith. "I Remember" from *Selected Poems* by Stevie Smith. Copyright © 1962, 1964 by Stevie Smith. Reprinted by permission of New Directions Publishing Corporation.

William Jay Smith. "American Primitive" from *The Traveler's Tree* by William Jay Smith. Copyright © 1980 by William Jay Smith. Reprinted by permission of Persea Books, Inc.

W. D. Snodgrass. "The Operation" from *Heart's Needle* by W. D. Snodgrass. Copyright © 1959 by W. D. Snodgrass. Reprinted by permission of Alfred A. Knopf, Inc.

Gary Snyder. "Hitch Haiku" from *The Back Country* by Gary Snyder. Copyright © 1968 by Gary Snyder. Reprinted by permission of New Directions Publishing Corporation. "Mid-August at Sourdough Mountain Lookout" from *Riprap* by Gary Snyder (Kyoto: Origin Press, 1959). Reprinted by permission of the poet.

Gary Soto. "Daybreak" from *The Elements of San Joaquin.* © 1977 by Gary Soto. Reprinted by permission of the University of Pittsburgh Press.

Richard Snyder. "A Mongoloid Child Handling Shells on the Beach" from *A Keeping in Touch* by Richard Snyder (The Ashland Poetry Press, 1971). Reprinted by permission.

Barry Spacks. "Teaching the Penguins to Fly" from *Teaching the Penguins to Fly* by Barry Spacks. Copyright © 1975 by David R. Godine. Reprinted by permission of David R. Godine, Publishers, Inc.

William Stafford. "Traveling through the Dark" (Copyright © 1960 by William Stafford) and "At the Klamath Berry Festival" (Copyright © 1961 by William Stafford) from *Stories That Could Be True* by William Stafford. Reprinted by permission of Harper & Row, Publishers, Inc.

George Starbuck. "Verses to Exhaust My Stock of Four-Letter Words" from *Desperate Measures* by George Starbuck. Copyright © 1978 by David R. Godine. Reprinted by permission of David R. Godine, Publisher, Inc. "Margaret Are You Drug" from "Translations of the English" in *White Paper: Poems* by George Starbuck. Copyright © 1965 by George Starbuck. This poem first appeared in the *Atlantic*. Reprinted by permission of Little, Brown and Company in association with the Atlantic Monthly Press.

Timothy Steele. "Here lies Sir Tact" from *Uncertainties and Rest* by Timothy Steele. Copyright © 1979. Reprinted by permission of Louisiana State University Press.

James Stephens. From *The Collected Poems of James Stephens:* "The Wind" (Copyright 1915 by Macmillan Publishing Co., Inc., renewed 1943 by James Stephens) and "A Glass of Beer" (Copyright 1918 by Macmillan Publishing Co., Inc., renewed 1946 by James Stephens). Reprinted by permission of Macmillan Publishing Co., Inc., Mrs. Iris Wise, Macmillan London & Basingstoke, and the Macmillan Company of Canada Limited.

Gerald Stern. "Behaving Like a Jew" from *Lucky Life* by Gerald Stern. Copyright © 1977 by Gerald Stern. Reprinted by permission of Houghton Mifflin Company.

Wallace Stevens. From *The Collected Poems of Wallace Stevens:* "The Emperor of Ice Cream," "Disillusionment of Ten O'Clock," "Peter Quince at the Clavier," "Thirteen Ways of Looking at a Blackbird," "Anecdote of the Jar," and lines from "Sunday Morning" and "Bantams in Pine-Woods" (Copyright 1923 renewed 1951 by Wallace Stevens); "Metamorphosis" (Copyright 1942 by Wallace Stevens) and "Study of Two Pears" (Copyright 1942 by Wallace Stevens, renewed © 1970 by Holly Stevens). Nine proverbs from "Adagia" from *Opus Posthumous* by Wallace Stevens, edited by Samuel French Morse. Copyright © 1957 by Elsie Stevens and Holly Stevens. Reprinted by permission of Alfred A. Knopf, Inc.

Michael B. Stillman. "In Memoriam John Coltrane" from *Memories of Grace Street* by Michael B. Stillman. Reprinted from *Occident* (Berkeley, Fall, 1972). Reprinted by permission of the poet.

Mark Strand. "Keeping Things Whole" from *Selected Poems* by Mark Strand. Copyright © 1964, 1980 by Mark Strand (New York: Atheneum, 1980). Reprinted with the permission of Atheneum Publishers.

May Swenson. "Question" from *New and Selected Things Taking Place* by May Swenson. Copyright © 1954 by May Swenson. Reprinted by permission of Little, Brown and Company in association with the Atlantic Monthly Press.

Henry Taylor. "Riding a One-Eyed Horse" from *An Afternoon of Pocket Billiards* by Henry Taylor. Copyright © 1975 by Henry Taylor. Salt Lake City: University of Utah Press Poetry Series, 1975. Reprinted by permission of the University of Utah Press.

Cornelius J. Ter Maat. "Etienne de Silouette," reprinted by permission of the poet.

Dylan Thomas. "Twenty-four years," "Fern Hill," and "Do not go gentle into that good night" from *The Poems of Dylan Thomas.* Copyright 1952 by Dylan Thomas; copyright 1939, 1946 by New Directions Publishing Corporation. Line from *Under Milkwood* by Dylan Thomas. Copyright 1954 by New Directions Publishing Corporation. All rights reserved. Reprinted by permission of New Directions Publishing Corporation and David Higham Associates Limited.

Jean Toomer. "Reapers" from *Cane* by Jean Toomer. Copyright 1923 by Boni and Liveright. Copyright renewed 1951 by Jean Toomer. Reprinted with the permission of Liveright Publishing Corporation.

John Updike. "Winter Ocean" from *Telphone Poles and Other Poems* by John Updike. Copyright © 1960 by John Updike. Reprinted by permission of Alfred A. Knopf, Inc.

Constance Urdang. "The Miracle-Factory" from *The Lone Woman and Others* by Constance Urdang. Copyright © 1980 by Constance Urdang. Reprinted by permission of the University of Pittsburgh Press.

Nicholas Virgilio. "Into the blinding sun . . ." first appeared in *American Haiku Magazine*, Plattesville, Wisconsin, 1964, Vol. II, no. 1. Reprinted by permission of the poet.

David Wagoner. "Staying Alive" from *Collected Poems 1956–1976* by David Wagoner. Copyright © 1976 by Indiana University Press. Reprinted by permission of the publisher, Indiana University Press.

Derek Walcott. "Sea Canes" from *Sea Grapes* by Derek Walcott. Copyright © 1971, 1973, 1974, 1975, 1976 by Derek Walcott. Reprinted by permission of Farrar, Straus and Giroux, Inc., Jonathan Cape Limited, and the poet.

Keith Waldrop. "On Measure" from *Windmill Near Calvary* by Keith Waldrop. Copyright © 1968 by the University of Michigan Press. All rights reserved. Reprinted by permission of the poet.

Rosmarie Waldrop. "The Relaxed Abalone" from *The Relaxed Abalone: Or What-You-May-Find* by Rosmarie Waldrop (Burning Deck, 1970). Reprinted by permission of the publisher.

Wang Wei. "Bird Singing Stream," translated by Wai-lim Yip. Reprinted by permission of Wai-lim Yip.

Robert Penn Warren. "Brotherhood in Pain" from *Selected Poems 1923–1975* by Robert Penn Warren. Copyright © 1972 by Robert Penn Warren. Reprinted by permission of Random House, Inc.

E. B. White. "A Classic Waits for Me" from *The Second Tree From the Corner* by E. B. White. Copyright 1944 by E. B. White. Originally appeared in *The New Yorker*. Reprinted by permission of Harper & Row, Publishers, Inc.

Tom Wayman. "Wayman in Love" from *Introducing Tom Wayman: Selected Poems 1973–1980*. Copyright ©1980 by Tom Wayman. Reprinted by permission of the Ontario Review Press.

Ruth Whitman. "Castoff Skin" from *The Passion of Lizzie Borden*. Copyright © 1973 by Ruth Whitman. Reprinted by permission of October House.

Richard Wilbur. "In the Elegy Season" and "A Simile for her Smile" from *Ceremony and Other Poems* by Richard Wilbur. Copyright 1948, 1949, 1950 by Richard Wilbur. "In the Elegy Season" first appeared in *The New Yorker*. Line from "Junk" from *Advice to a Prophet and Other Poems*. Copyright © 1961 by Richard Wilbur. "Sleepless at Crown Point" from *The Mind Reader* by Richard Wilbur. Copyright © 1976 by Richard Wilbur. "Playboy" from *Walking to Sleep*. Copyright © 1968 by Richard Wilbur. Reprinted by permission of Harcourt Brace Jovanovich, Inc.

Miller Williams. "On the Symobolic Consideration of Hands and the Significance of Death" from *Halfway From Hoxie: New and Selected Poems* by Miller Williams. Copyright © 1964, 1968, 1971, 1973 by Miller Williams. Reprinted by permission of the publisher, E. P. Dutton.

William Carlos Williams. "The Great Figure," "Spring and All," "Poem," "This is Just to Say," "The Red Wheelbarrow," "To Waken an Old Lady" "The Descent of Winter" and lines from "The Waitress" from *Collected Earlier Poems* by William Carlos Williams. Copyright 1938 by New Directions Publishing Corporation. "The Dance" from *Collected Later Poems* of William Carlos Williams. Copyright 1954 by William Carlos Williams. Two prose quotations from *Interviews With William Carlos Williams:* "Speaking Straight Ahead," edited by Linda Wagner. Copyright © 1966 by the Estate of William Carlos Williams. Reprinted by permission of New Directions Publishing Corporation.

Yvor Winters. "At the San Francisco Airport" from *Collected Poems* by Yvor Winters. Copyright 1952, © 1960 by Yvor Winters. Reprinted with the permission of the Ohio University Press, Athens.

James Wright. "Autumn Begins in Martins Ferry, Ohio" and "A Blessing" from *Collected Poems* by James Wright. Copyright © 1961, 1962 by James Wright. "A Blessing" first appeared in *Poetry*. Reprinted by permission of Wesleyan University Press. "Saying Dante Aloud" from *Moments of the Italian Summer*. Copyright © 1976 by James Wright. Reprinted by permission of the Dryad Press.

Richard Wright. One Stanza from "Haikus" in *Richard Wright Reader*, edited by Ellen Wright and Michel Fabre. Copyright © 1978 by Ellen Wright and Michel Fabre. Reprinted by permission of Harper & Row, Publishers, Inc.

William Butler Yeats. From *The Collected Poems of W. B. Yeats*: "The Lake Isle of Innisfree," "Who Goes with Fergus," "The Lamentation of the Old Pensioner" (Copyright 1906 by Macmillan Publishing Co., Inc.; renewed 1934 by William Butler Yeats); "The Magi," (Copyright 1916 by Macmillan Publishing Co., Inc.; renewed 1944 by Bertha Georgie Yeats); "Sailing to Byzantium," "Leda and the Swan," and lines from "Among School Children" (Copyright 1928 by Macmillan Publishing Co., Inc.; renewed © 1956 by Bertha Georgie Yeats); "Crazy Jane Talks with the Bishop" and lines from "For Anne Gregory" (Copyright 1933 by Macmillan Publishing Co., Inc.; renewed © 1961 by Bertha Georgie Yeats); "Lapis Lazuli" (Copyright 1940 by Georgie Yeats, renewed © 1968 by Bertha Georgie Yeats, Michael Butler Yeats and Anne Yeats); lines from "A Prayer for Old Age" (Copyright 1934 by Macmillan Publishing Co., Inc.; renewed © 1962 by Bertha Georgie Yeats); "The Second Coming" (Copyright 1924 by Macmillan Publishing Co., Inc.; renewed 1952 by Bertha Georgie Yeats). From *The Variorium Edition of the Poems of W. B. Yeats;* edited by Peter Allt and Russell K. Alspach: "The Old Pensioner." Copyright © 1957 by Macmillan Publishing Co., Inc. Reprinted by permission of Macmillan Publishing Co., Inc., M.B Yeats, Anne Yeats, and Macmillan London Limited.

Paul Zimmer. "The Day Zimmer Lost Religion" from *The Zimmer Poems* by Paul Zimmer. Copyright © 1976 by Paul Zimmer. Reprinted by permission of the Dryad Press.

Anonymous. Lines From "Carnation Milk is the best in the land . . ." quoted in *Confessions of an Advertising Man* by David Ogilvy. Copyright © 1963 by David Ogilvy (New York: Atheneum, 1969). Reprinted with the permission of Atheneum Publishers.

INDEX OF FIRST LINES

INDEX OF AUTHORS AND TITLES

(Each page number immediately following a poet's name indicates a line or passage from a poem quoted in the text.)

To the Student

As publishers, we realize that one way to improve education is to improve textbooks. We also realize that you, the student, largely determine the success or failure of textbooks. Although the instructor assigns them, the student buys and uses them. If enough of you don't like a book and make your feelings known, the chances are your instructor will not assign it again.

Usually only instructors are asked about the quality of a text; their opinion alone is considered as revisions are planned or as new books are developed. Now, we would like to ask you about X. J. Kennedy's *An Introduction to Poetry, 5th Edition:* how you liked or disliked it; why it was interesting or dull; if it taught you anything. Please fill in this form and return it to us at: Little, Brown and Co., College English, 34 Beacon Street, Boston, Mass. 02106.

School: ______________________________

Instructor's name: ______________________________

Title of course: ______________________________

1. Did you find this book too easy? __________ too difficult? __________

   about right? __________

2. Which chapters did you find the most interesting? __________

   ____

3. Which chapters did you find least interesting? __________

   ____

4. Which poems did you like most? __________

   ____

5. Were there any poems you particularly disliked? __________

   ____

6. Which statement comes closest to expressing your feelings about reading and studying literature? (Please check one, or supply your own statement.)

   ______ Love to read literature. It's my favorite subject.

   ______ Usually enjoy reading most literature.

   ______ Can take it or leave it.

_______ Usually find little of interest in most literature.

_______ Literature just is not for me.

Other: ____

7. Did you find this book helped you to enjoy poetry any more than you did?

____

8. Were the supplements "Writing about Literature," "Writing about a Poem," and "Writing a Poem" very useful? _______ somewhat useful? _______ of no help? _______

9. In the sections about writing papers, do you prefer to see examples of writing by students? _______ or by professional critics? _______

10. Do you intend to keep this book for your personal library? Yes _______ No _______

11. Any other comments or suggestions: ____

____

____

____

12. May we quote you in our efforts to promote this book? Yes _______ No _______

Date: ____

Signature (optional): ____

Address (optional): ____